Fodor's
SAN DIEGO

FODOR'S SAN DIEGO

Writers: Seth Combs, Claire Deeks van der Lee, Maren Dougherty, Amanda Knoles, Bobbi Zane

Editor: Caroline Trefler

Production Editor: Carolyn Roth
Maps & Illustrations: David Lindroth, Mark Stroud (Moon Street Cartography), *cartographers;* Rebecca Baer, *map editor;* William Wu, *information graphics*
Design: Fabrizio La Rocca, *creative director;* Tina Malaney, Chie Ushio, Jessica Ramirez, *designers;* Melanie Marin, *associate director of photography;* Jennifer Romains, *photo research*
Cover Photos: Front cover (Beluga whale, San Diego SeaWorld): Reinhard Dirscherl/age fotostock. Back cover (from left to right): Joelle Gould/iStockphoto; Michael DeLeon/iStockphoto; Yi Fan/iStockphoto. Spine: Sebastien Burel/Shutterstock.
Production Manager: Angela L. McLean

SPECIAL SALES

This book is available at special discounts for bulk purchases for sales promotions or premiums. Special editions, including personalized covers, excerpts of existing books, and corporate imprints, can be created in large quantities for special needs. For more information, write to Special Markets/Premium Sales, 1745 Broadway, MD 3-1, New York, NY 10019, or e-mail specialmarkets@randomhouse.com.

AN IMPORTANT TIP & AN INVITATION

Although all prices, opening times, and other details in this book are based on information supplied to us at press time, changes occur all the time in the travel world, and Fodor's cannot accept responsibility for facts that become outdated or for inadvertent errors or omissions. So **always confirm information when it matters,** especially if you're making a detour to visit a specific place. Your experiences—positive and negative— matter to us. If we have missed or misstated something, **please write to us.** Share your opinion instantly through our online feedback center at fodors.com/contact-us.

PRINTED IN CHINA

10 9 8 7 6 5 4 3 2 1

CONTENTS

MAPS

ABOUT THIS GUIDE

Fodor's Ratings

Everything in this guide is worth doing—we don't cover what isn't—but exceptional sights, hotels, and restaurants are recognized with additional accolades. **Fodor's Choice**★ indicates our top recommendations; ★ highlights places we deem highly recommended; and **Best Bets** call attention to notable hotels and restaurants in various categories. Care to nominate a new place? Visit Fodors.com/contact-us.

Trip Costs

We list prices wherever possible to help you budget well. Hotel and restaurant price categories from **$** to **$$$$** are noted alongside each recommendation. For hotels, we include the lowest cost of a standard double room in high season. For restaurants, we cite the average price of a main course at dinner or, if dinner isn't served, at lunch. For attractions, we always list adult admission fees; discounts are usually available for children, students, and senior citizens.

Hotels

Our local writers vet every hotel to recommend the best overnights in each price category, from budget to expensive. Unless otherwise specified, you can expect private bath, phone, and TV in your room. For expanded hotel reviews, facilities, and deals visit Fodors.com.

Ratings

★	Fodor's Choice
★	Highly recommended
☾	Family-friendly

Listings

✉	Address
✉	Branch address
☎	Telephone
🖷	Fax
⊕	Website
✉	E-mail
🎟	Admission fee
☉	Open/closed times
Ⓜ	Subway
⊕	Directions or Map coordinates

Hotels & Restaurants

🏨	Hotel
⤵	Number of rooms
⑩	Meal plans
✕	Restaurant
⌨	Reservations
👔	Dress code
⊟	No credit cards
$	Price

Other

⇨	See also
☞	Take note
🏌	Golf facilities

Restaurants

Unless we state otherwise, restaurants are open for lunch and dinner daily. We mention dress code only when there's a specific requirement and reservations only when they're essential or not accepted. To make restaurant reservations, visit Fodors.com.

Credit Cards

The hotels and restaurants in this guide typically accept credit cards. If not, we'll say so.

Experience
San Diego

SAN DIEGO TODAY

Although most visitors know little about San Diego beyond its fun-in-the-sun reputation, locals are talking about much more than the surf forecast and their tan lines. Like much of the country, the recent years saw financial woes taking their toll on local infrastructure and services, while residents struggled with plummeting home values and rising unemployment. But San Diegans aren't known as a dour bunch, and they've managed to keep the forecast sunny. The buzz around San Diego's science and biotech industry continues to grow, and several large companies, including Qualcomm, PETCO, and Bridgepoint Education, continue to call San Diego home base. San Diego has been busy shedding its image as LA's less sophisticated neighbor, and coming into an urban identity of its own. Across the region, residents are embracing new trends in the local art, shopping, dining, and cultural scenes.

Today's San Diego:

. . . is eating well. Once considered somewhat of a culinary wasteland, the San Diego dining scene is enjoying a renaissance. All over town, new and exciting restaurants are popping up, celebrating both the local bounty and the region's diversity. Healthy and fresh California Modern cuisine remains a feature on many menus, while neighboring Baja Mexico has given rise to the new trend of BajaMed, a fusion of Mexican and Mediterranean styles. San Diego's sizable Asian population has introduced everything from dim sum carts to Mongolian hot pot, while local sushi chefs take advantage of San Diego's reputation for some of the finest sea urchin in the world. The locavore trend has become somewhat of an obsession for San Diegans, and many restaurants are happy to highlight how and where they source their ingredients.

. . . is toasting the town. San Diego continues to gain recognition as one of the most exciting beer towns in the nation. Craft brewers creating a buzz include AleSmith, Ballast Point, and Lost Abbey, just to name a few, and Stone Brewing Company, creator of the notorious Arrogant Bastard Ale, has several locations. All this enthusiasm for San Diego's suds has given rise to a beer tourism industry, from bus tours of local brewers, to large beer-themed events such as the popular San Diego Beer Week. There's even an app to help you find the perfect

WHAT WE'RE TALKING ABOUT

After more than a decade of discussion, the San Diego Public Market is set to open in its permanent space sometime during 2013. Seeing the rising demand for local and artisan foods, co-founders Catt White and Dale Steele felt San Diego was ready for a permanent market along the lines of the Ferry Building in San Francisco, or Pike Place in Seattle. The project's original fundraising campaign through Kickstarter raised well above the anticipated goals, and a twice-weekly temporary market began in the fall of 2012. If this momentum continues, the project could become a huge local and tourist attraction.

Construction on Phase 1 of the North Embarcadero Visionary Plan is well underway. The project promises to transform the landscape of San Diego's waterfront and better connect the Embarcadero with downtown.

pint: inspired by the local brewing scene, a San Diego couple created the TapHunter website and mobile application that helps beer lovers find what's on tap, and where.

. . . is building for the future, and conserving its past. A drive around San Diego reveals a huge range of architecture, from hip to historic to downright hideous. Urban planning from half a century ago, such as the decision to run Interstate 5 right through Little Italy and Downtown, is hard to undo but other efforts to conserve the city's architectural integrity have been more successful. Downtown's Gaslamp Quarter is the most famous conservation area, but the residential neighborhoods of Uptown, Kensington, and South Park delight early-20th-century architecture buffs with streets full of historically designated homes. New projects making waves in San Diego today include the revitalization of the Embarcadero, and the highly contentious Plaza de Panama Project to reroute vehicular traffic and create underground parking in Balboa Park. The latter is currently mired in public battles and lawsuits pitting one of the city's leading conservation groups, Save Our Heritage Organization,

against one of the city's leading philanthropists, Qualcomm co-founder Irwin Jacobs, who is bankrolling the project. The legal battles may be resolved and construction may get underway during the lifetime of this book, but the project will likely remain a sensitive issue for years to come.

. . . is getting outside. San Diego's near-perfect climate and gorgeous natural landscape make it hard to find an excuse not to get outside and exercise. In fact, San Diego is home to one of the most active populations in the country. Year-round opportunities to surf, sail, bike, or hike offer something for everyone. On weekends and throughout the summer, beaches and parks teem with locals enjoying the great weather and fresh air. Gas barbecues, bouncy houses, and huge shade tents take the concept of the picnic to a whole new level. So when visitors hailing from harsher climates wonder if San Diegans appreciate how good they have it, the answer is a resounding yes.

Public art installations, green spaces, shade pavilions, and ample room to stroll should help transform the Embarcadero into one of the world's great urban waterfronts.

The buzz surrounding the San Diego winemaking community is growing louder. The recent

easing of requirements for boutique wineries gave a major boost to the local winemaking community, including several small wine producers around the town of Ramona in North San Diego country. In addition, wine production facilities known as urban wineries are cropping up

in towns around the county. Until now, San Diego's primary wine region, Temecula, was actually over the border in neighboring Riverside County. Before long, locals and visitors alike may be exploring a San Diego wine country that is actually located in San Diego county itself.

WHAT'S WHERE

1 Downtown. Downtown used to be a real downer, a mix of bland office towers and seedy sidewalks after sundown. Preservationists and entrepreneurs saved the day, starting with Horton Plaza, a six-block shopping and dining complex. Now, the streets are lined with nightclubs, boutiques, and restaurants, from the glam Gaslamp Quarter (a former red-light district) to the edgier East Village (where Padres fans get their baseball fix at PETCO Park). Also nearby are Seaport Village, the Embarcadero, and Little Italy.

2 Balboa Park. In the center of the city, this 1,200-acre patch of greenery is home to world-class museums and performing arts, stunning Spanish colonial revival architecture, and the famed San Diego Zoo. Paths wind around gardens, fountains, and groves of shady trees. It's a sort of Central Park of the west—a leafy getaway for locals, and a must for tourists. Bankers Hill, just west of the park, is a gentrifying neighborhood with hip dining options.

3 Old Town. Before there was a sprawling city, there was an Old Town, where you'll find remnants of San Diego's—and California's—first permanent European settlement. The former pueblo is now a pedestrian-friendly state historic park, with original and reconstructed buildings and sites, along with a tourist bazaar of souvenir shops, art galleries, and Mexican eateries with margaritas and mariachi aplenty.

4 Uptown. Uptown is a catchall for a cluster of trendy neighborhoods near downtown and north of Balboa Park. Hillcrest is the heart of the city's gay and lesbian community, while in North Park, a hip and edgy set keeps boutiques, galleries, eateries, and bars hopping. The cool crowd has also converged on University Heights, with its eclectic mix of dining and nightlife. Mission Hills is a lovely historic neighborhood between Old Town and Hillcrest, while Mission Valley, northeast of Uptown, is mostly known for office towers, shopping malls, and Qualcomm Stadium.

5 Mission Bay and the Beaches. Home to SeaWorld, Mission Bay also boasts a 4,600-acre aquatic park perfect for boating, jet skiing, swimming, and fishing, plus activities like biking, basketball, and kite flying. It's neighbored by bustling Mission Beach and Pacific Beach, where streets are lined with surf shops, ice-cream stands, and beach bars.

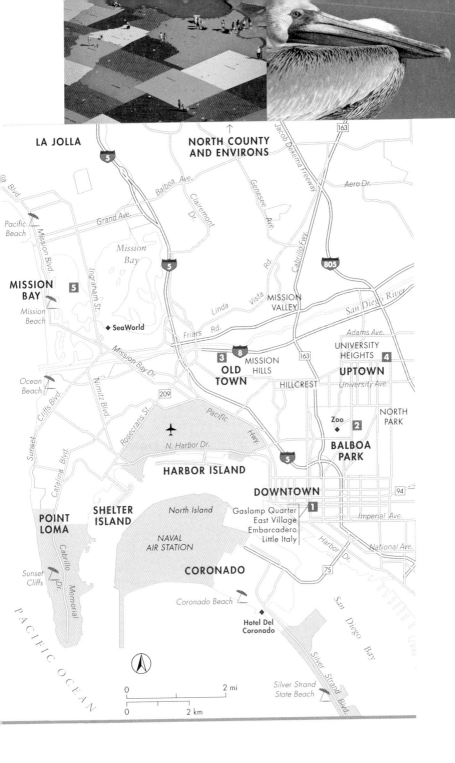

WHAT'S WHERE

6 La Jolla. La Jolla lands lavish praise for its picturesque cliffs and beaches, not to mention a bevy of the finest hotels, restaurants, art galleries, and shopping. From Windansea's locals-only surf scene to cocktails at a grand hotel where the Hollywood elite once retreated, there's something for everyone.

7 Point Loma. Point Loma curves crescentlike along the bay. Its main drags are cluttered with fast-food joints and budget motels, but farther back, grand old houses give way to ocean views. At the southern tip of the peninsula, the majestic Cabrillo Monument commemorates the landing of explorer Juan Rodríguez Cabrillo at San Diego Bay in 1542; the 360-degree vista sometimes includes glimpses of migrating gray whales. Farther north, make time for tide pools at Ocean Beach's Sunset Cliffs.

8 Harbor and Shelter Islands. Harbor Island is a man-made strip of land in the bay across from the airport, while to the west, Shelter Island is known for its yacht-building and sport fishing industries. Both have a handful of hotels and restaurants, plus unsurpassed views of the downtown skyline in one direction and Coronado in the other.

9 Coronado. Historic Coronado, an islandlike peninsula across from the San Diego waterfront, came of age as a Victorian resort community. Its seaside centerpiece is the fabled (and gabled) Hotel Del Coronado, a favorite haunt of celebs, A-listers, and—well—ghosts, if you believe local lore. The upscale area, also home to a naval base, offers plenty of shopping, dining, and pleasant stretches of sand. Drive across the bridge or take the ferry to reach it.

10 North County and Environs. Getting outside of San Diego proper is a must for beach towns like Del Mar and family attractions like LEGOLAND and the San Diego Zoo Safari Park. There are a growing number of wineries to visit in Temecula, while the Anzo-Borrego Desert offers a variety of exploring opportunities.

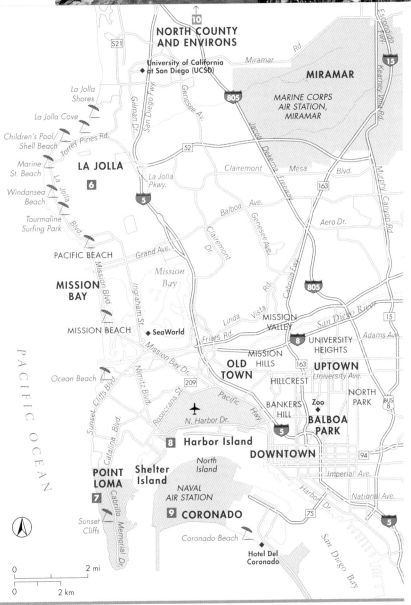

S21

◆ University of California
at San Diego (UCSD)

Miramar Rd.

MIRAMAR

805

**MARINE CORPS
AIR STATION,
MIRAMAR**

La Jolla
Shores

La Jolla Cove

Children's Pool/
Shell Beach

Marine
St. Beach

LA JOLLA

6

Gilman Dr.

Genesee Ave.

San Diego Fwy.

Torrey Pines Rd.

52

La Jolla
Pkwy.

Clairemont

Mesa

Blvd.

163

Jacob Dekema Freeway

Kearny Villa Rd.

Murphy Canyon Rd.

Escondido Fwy.

15

Windansea
Beach

Tourmaline
Surfing Park

PACIFIC BEACH

Grand Ave.

Balboa

Ave.

Genesee Ave.

Aero Dr.

La Jolla Blvd.

5

**MISSION
BAY**

Mission Blvd.

Ingraham St.

*Mission
Bay*

Clairemont

Dr.

Cabrillo Fwy.

805

MISSION BEACH

◆ SeaWorld

Mission Bay Dr.

Friars Rd.

Linda

Vista

Rd.

**MISSION
VALLEY**

San Diego River

8

15

**UNIVERSITY
HEIGHTS**

Adams Ave.

PACIFIC OCEAN

Ocean Beach

Sunset Cliffs Blvd.

Nimitz Blvd.

Rosecrans St.

209

Pacific

Hwy.

N. Harbor Dr.

MISSION HILLS

**OLD
TOWN**

163

HILLCREST

**BANKERS
HILL**

UPTOWN

University Ave.

Zoo
◆

**NORTH
PARK**

BUS
8

8 **Harbor Island**

Catalina Blvd.

**POINT
LOMA**

7

Sunset
Cliffs

Cabrillo Memorial Dr.

**Shelter
Island**

North
Island

**NAVAL
AIR STATION**

9 **CORONADO**

Coronado Beach

Hotel Del
Coronado

**BALBOA
PARK**

5

DOWNTOWN

94

Imperial Ave.

Harbor Dr.

National Ave.

75

San Diego Bay

5

0 ——— 2 mi

0 ——— 2 km

SAN DIEGO PLANNER

When to Go

San Diego's weather is so ideal that most locals shrug off the high cost of living and relatively lower wages as a "sunshine tax." Along the coast, average temperatures range from the mid-60s to the high 70s, with clear skies and low humidity. Annual rainfall is minimal, less than 10 inches per year.

The peak season for sun seekers is July through October. In July and August, the mercury spikes and everyone spills outside. Beaches are a popular daytime destination, as is Balboa Park, thanks to its shady groves and air-conditioned museums. Summer's nightlife scene thrives with the usual bars and clubs, plus outdoor concerts, theater, and movie screenings. Early fall is a pleasant time to visit, as many tourists have already left town and the temperature is nearly perfect. From mid-December to mid-March, whale-watchers can glimpse migrating gray whales frolicking in the Pacific. In spring and early summer, a marine layer hugs the coastline for much or all of the day (locals call it "June Gloom"), which can be dreary and disappointing for those who were expecting to bask in Southern California sunshine. However, wildflowers also blanket the mountainsides and desert in early spring.

Getting Around

Car Travel: To fully explore sprawling San Diego—especially with kids in tow—consider renting a car. Nearly everything of interest can be found off I–5 or I–163, and the county's freeways are wide and easy to use. Traffic isn't a major issue if you avoid rush hour. Parking in urban areas is typically metered, Monday through Saturday, 8 to 6, unless otherwise marked. You may park for free outside those hours, and on Sunday and holidays.
■ TIP→ Yellow commercial loading zones are fair game for parking after 6. During special downtown events, such as Padres games, you'll likely have to settle for one of the many paid parking structures—they cost around $20 close to the action. Parking at beaches is free for the most part, though tough to come by on sunny days unless you stake out a spot early.

Foot Travel: Walking is the way to go once you've reached a destination area. Balboa Park and the zoo are walkers' paradises, and all of downtown is pedestrian friendly.

Public Transportation: Visit ⊕ www.sdcommute.com, which lists routes and timetables for the Metropolitan Transit System and North County Transit District.

The "Trip Planner" section is a terrific resource.

Local/urban bus fare is $2.25 one-way, but you can pick up an unlimited day pass for $5 (exact change only; pay when you board). A one-way ride on the city's iconic red trolleys is $2.50; get your ticket at any trolley vending machine.

Taxi Travel: Cabs are a fine choice for trips to and from the airport and short jaunts around town. The approximate rates are: $2.80 for the first 1/10 mile, $3 each additional mile, and $24 per hour of waiting time. You can find taxicab stands at the airport, hotels, major attractions, and shopping centers. Downtown, your best bet is to flag one down, New York City–style.

Pedicab Travel: These pedal-powered chariots are a great way to get around downtown. Just be sure to agree on a price before you start moving, or you could get taken for the wrong kind of ride. Many pedicab drivers offer up their own unique commentary on the sights, though take what they say with a grain of salt—fibbing is part of the fun.

What to Wear

You won't find a more casual big city. Flip-flops are the favored footwear, shorts and beachy skirts comprise the summer uniform, and designer jeans qualify as dressing up. Despite the city's easygoing vibe, San Diegans value labels—just look at Fashion Valley's lineup of high-end outposts like Jimmy Choo and Louis Vuitton. Dining out warrants a little research; some eateries barely toe the "no shirt, no shoes" rule, while others require more elegant attire.

Safety

San Diego has some sketchy areas, although tourists typically encounter few problems. Downtown can get a little rowdy at night, especially toward 2 am, when bars boot drunken patrons out on the sidewalks. The city also has a large homeless population, who often camp out on shadowy side streets not far from East Village. Most are harmless, aside from the occasional panhandling, but it's safest to stick to well-lighted, busy areas. Certain pockets of Balboa Park are frequented by drug dealers and prostitutes after hours; if you're attending a nighttime theater or art event, park nearby or use the valet.

Where to www

Browse these online options for more about what's on.

⊕ www.fodors.com, check out the forums on our site for answers to your travel questions and tips.

⊕ www.sandiego.org for the San Diego visitor bureau.

⊕ www.sandiegoreader.com posts tons of event listings, from big concerts to little community to-dos.

⊕ www.utsandiego.com is where the scaled-down *San Diego Union-Tribune* posts all its daily newspaper and original online content, including a searchable entertainment section.

⊕ www.sdcitybeat.com for the online version of the alternative weekly *San Diego CityBeat,* a guide to the city's edgier side, from regional politics to the hottest local bands.

⊕ www.urbanistguide.com is the ultimate how-to for hip urban explorers, including curated calendar picks, Q&As with local scene makers, and an interactive map feature.

Festivals

Pencil in these festivals when you're in town.

Winter: Drawing 100,000 visitors the first Friday and Saturday of December, **Balboa Park December Nights** offers festive carolers, food, music, and dance. The **San Diego Bay Parade of Lights,** also in December, lights up the harbor with boats decked out for the holidays.

January's **Farmers Insurance Open** is the Holy Grail for golf fans; the celeb-heavy tourney has been held at the scenic Torrey Pines Golf Course for decades. In February, the **Mardi Gras** block party in the Gaslamp Quarter invites revelers to let the good times roll.

Spring: Adams Avenue Roots Unplugged gives music fans a weekend of free acoustic music, while Little Italy's annual **Art-Walk** showcases local art talent on tent-lined streets.

Summer: The **San Diego County Fair,** the Old Globe's **Summer Shakespeare Festival,** the city's huge **LGBT Pride Festival,** racing season at the **Del Mar Fairgrounds,** and outdoor classical concerts at the **Embarcadero** all take place in summer.

Fall: Music fans eagerly wait for the **Adams Avenue Street Fair,** a weekend of concerts and a carnival.

SAN DIEGO TOP ATTRACTIONS

Balboa Park

(A) Oasis is hardly hyperbole when it comes to describing this 1,200-acre cultural heart of San Diego. Take a peaceful stroll or plan a full day of perusing Balboa Park's many museums, theater spaces, gardens, trails, and playing fields. And don't forget the park's famous San Diego Zoo.

Beaches

San Diego boasts 70 miles of coastline, with beaches for everybody, from pail-and-shovel-toting toddlers to hard-bodied adventurous types—even nudists have their own sheltered spot at Black's Beach. Coronado is a family favorite, twenty-somethings soak up sun at Pacific Beach, and surfers swear by various stretches of shore. Life's a beach, here, literally.

Cabrillo National Monument

(B) On the southern tip of the Point Loma peninsula, this landmark commemorates the 1542 landing of explorer Juan Rodríguez Cabrillo in San Diego Bay. Unparalleled harbor and skyline views, a military history museum, tidal pools, and an old lighthouse are among the offerings. In winter, lucky visitors may even catch sight of migrating gray whales along the coast.

Carlsbad Flower Fields

(C) Fifty acres of flowers, mostly ranunculus, bloom in Technicolor hues every March on a hillside perched above the Pacific Ocean. Timing is everything, but if you visit in spring, don't miss this showy display of stunning natural beauty.

La Jolla

(D) First things first: It's pronounced La Hoya. And it's one of the prettiest places in California, a wealthy enclave with a small-town feel and world-class scenic coastline. Visit the Children's Pool, populated by sun-bathing seals, or watch locals ride waves at Windansea Beach. Then again, you could just shop and nosh the day away.

LEGOLAND California

(E) A whole universe of LEGO fun awaits the pint-size set and their chaperones in Carlsbad, including more than 60 rides and attractions. Especially cool is Miniland USA, scaled-down cities built entirely from LEGO bricks, as well as Dino Island and the Egyptian-theme Dune Raiders, a 30-foot racing slide.

San Diego Zoo

(F) One word: pandas. The San Diego Zoo has several of the roly-poly crowd pleasers. And yes, they're that cute. But the conservation-minded zoo offers much more, from Polar Bear Plunge, the arctic creature's recently revamped habitat, to oh-so-close encounters of lions, tigers, and bears. Explore the huge, hilly attraction by foot, or take advantage of the guided bus tours, aerial tram, and seated shows. Also a roaring good time: Escondido's Safari Park.

SeaWorld

(G) Awe-inspiring orcas and other cute sea critters perform splashy tricks at stage shows, but there's plenty else for families to enjoy, from the Journey of Atlantis water ride to feeding chum to bottlenose dolphins at Rocky Point Preserve. And don't miss SeaWorld's Penguin Encounter, one of two places in the world where emperor penguins are kept in captivity.

Torrey Pines State Natural Reserve

(H) The nation's rarest pine tree calls this area home, as do the last salt marshes and waterfowl refuges in Southern California. Hikers can wind their way down windswept trails that stretch from the high coastal bluffs to sandy Torrey Pines State Beach below. Panoramic views abound.

TOP EXPERIENCES

Did we mention the beach?

If stretching out on the sand with a sun-screen-stained paperback sounds like a snooze, there's always swimming, snorkeling, surfing, diving, and deep-sea fishing. And that's just in the water. On the sand, serve and spike in a friendly beach volleyball pickup or pal around with your pooch at a leash-free dog beach. The truly adventurous should sign up for Over-the-Line, a massive beach softball tourney that takes place every July—the title refers as much to blood alcohol levels as the rules of the game.

Sail away

So you don't own a historic tall ship. Who says you can't experience the thrill of sailing the seas in high style? Several times a year, the **San Diego Maritime Museum** offers public adventure sails aboard the *Star of India,* the *Californian,* and the HMS *Surprise.* And, on very rare occasions, the ships even stage cannon battle reenactments in the San Diego Bay. *Master and Commander* wannabes, consider it your shot at combat glory.

Culture vulture

San Diego's artistic scene gets short shrift compared to the city's outdoorsy offerings, which is a shame. Truly top-notch theater dominates the dance cards of local culturati, like **La Jolla Playhouse,** which routinely hosts Broadway-bound shows before they head east. **The Old Globe**—the oldest professional theater in the state—stages everything from Shakespeare to the avant-garde at its cluster of spaces, including the state-of-the-art Conrad Prebys Theatre Center. Both locations (downtown and La Jolla) of the **Museum of Contemporary Art San Diego** showcase thought-provoking exhibitions, from regionally focused to international retrospectives, while niche galleries throughout the county cater to the visually curious. And no matter what the season, visitors will find something fetching from area performing-arts staples such as the **San Diego Symphony Orchestra, San Diego Opera,** and **San Diego Ballet.**

Bogey bliss

Whether you're timid at the tee or an aspiring golf pro, San Diego's wide-ranging golf options will wow you. Never mind the fact that water restrictions have left some greens a little less, er, green. Golfing in San Diego is an experience par none, no matter what your price range and ability. If you can swing the fees, splurge at Carlsbad's **Park Hyatt Resort Aviara** or at the **Rancho Bernardo Resort & Spa.** La Jolla's **Torrey Pines Golf Course,** home to the 2008 U.S. Open and every Buick Invitational (now the Farmers Insurance Open) since 1968, is one of the finest 18-hole public courses in the country, and a more affordable outing. Just be sure to book tee times well in advance.

Sky high

Sometimes, soaring above the earth is the best way to get a sense of its mind-blowing scale—to wit, the colorful hot-air balloons that dot the horizon at sunrise and sunset. Tiny and toylike from the ground, they offer big bird's-eye views to those who take flight. The annual **Temecula Balloon & Wine festival,** typically in June, is a favorite among fliers. If standing beneath an open flame makes you a basket case, perhaps tandem paragliding will put you in your proper airborne place. At the Torrey Pines Gliderport, an instructor handles the hard work. All you have to do is shout in glee as the winged glider climbs and dips above cliff-bordered beaches.

Charge it

When your Visa bill reads like a vacation diary, you know you're a serious shopaholic. Jimmy Choo, Hermès, and Louis Vuitton? That was just an afternoon at **Fashion Valley!** San Diego has options to suit every style of shopper. For unique, edgy scores, scour boutiques in neighborhoods like **Hillcrest, Little Italy,** and **North Park.** Sleek storefronts in **La Jolla** and other well-heeled areas carry all variety of luxury goods, while downtown's **Westfield Horton Plaza** stocks standard mall fare. For souvenirs—seashells and such—try **Seaport Village,** or browse festive Mexican arts and crafts at Old Town's **Fiesta de Reyes.**

Hang loose, dude

Only a grom (a newbie) would say "hang loose," but "dude" is definitely a prominent part of the local surfer's vocabulary (as in, duuuuude). If you have the courage to wriggle into a wetsuit and waddle into knee-deep white water with a big foam board, you might just catch a wave—or at least stand up for a few seconds. Learning to surf is hard work, so your best bet is to take lessons, either private instruction or group-based. Try La Jolla's **Surf Diva Surf School,** geared primarily toward ladies, or Carlsbad's **San Diego Surfing Academy** in North County.

Sample the fish tacos

The humble fish taco is a local foodie favorite. Beer-battered and fried or lightly grilled, topped with salsa or white sauce and cabbage, tacos around town appeal to every palate. Sample the different styles from simple storefront restaurants and mobile taco trucks, and be prepared for a heated discussion. The only thing most San Diegans agree on is that fish tacos taste even better with a cold beer.

Spa-tacular

Money may not buy happiness, but it can definitely purchase a day of pampering at one of San Diego's many upscale spas. There's no limit to the luxuriating, from youth-restoring facials to aromatherapy massages that unkink months' worth of muscle aches. If cost is no concern, book an afternoon at Carlsbad's idyllic **La Costa Resort and Spa,** or at the historic **Hotel Del Coronado,** a beauty-boosting seaside retreat since the Victorian days.

Skip town

San Diego's allure extends well beyond its famous coastline. To the east, visitors will find forested mountains and an otherworldly desert landscape. The tiny town of **Julian,** in the Cuyamaca Mountains, charms with olden-day bed-and-breakfasts and ample slices of apple pie. In winter, weather allowing, visitors can even take horse-drawn sleigh rides. One of San Diego's most underrated natural attractions is the vast **Anza-Borrego Desert State Park,** 600,000 jaw-dropping acres of protected land crisscrossed with hiking trails. Rough it at a campground or hole up at a hotel. Spring, which blankets the valleys with desert wildflowers, is peak season. Just steer clear of summer, when temperatures skyrocket into the 100s.

GREAT ITINERARIES

ONE DAY IN SAN DIEGO

If you've only got 24 hours to spare, start at **Balboa Park**, the cultural heart of San Diego. Stick to El Prado, the main promenade, where you'll pass by peaceful gardens and soaring Spanish colonial revival architecture (Balboa Park's unforgettable look and feel date to the 1914 Panama–California Exposition). Unless you're a serious museum junkie, pick whichever of the park's many offerings most piques your interest—choices range from photography to folk art.

If you're with the family, don't even think of skipping the **San Diego Zoo.** You'll want to spend the better part of your day there, but make an early start of it so you can head for one of San Diego's **beaches** while there's still daylight. Kick back under the late afternoon sun and linger for sunset. Or wander around **Seaport Village** and the **Embarcadero** before grabbing a bite to eat in the **Gaslamp Quarter**, which pulses with nightlife until last call (around 1:40 am).

Alternate plan: Start your day at **SeaWorld** and wrap it up with an ocean-view dinner in **La Jolla.**

FOUR DAYS IN SAN DIEGO

Day 1

The one-day itinerary above also works for the first day of an extended visit. If you're staying in North County, though, you may want to bypass the zoo and head for the **San Diego Safari Park**, a vast preserve with huge open enclosures. Here, you'll see herds of African and Asian animals acting as they would in the wild. It's the closest thing in the States to an exotic safari. Not included in the general admission—but worth the extra

cost if it's in the budget—are the park's "special experiences": guided photo caravans, rolling Segway tours, mule rides, and the Flightline, which sends harnessed guests soaring down a zip-line cable high above earthbound animals.

Another North County option for families with little ones: **LEGOLAND** in Carlsbad. **Note:** the San Diego Zoo, the San Diego Safari Park, and LEGOLAND are all-day, wipe-those-kids-right-out kind of adventures.

Day 2

Your first day was a big one so you might want to ease into your second with a leisurely breakfast—and there are some great places to eat in the city—followed by a 90-minute tour aboard the **SEAL Amphibious Tour,** which departs from Seaport Village daily. The bus-boat hybrid explores picturesque San Diego neighborhoods before rolling right into the water for a cruise around the bay, all with fun-facts narration.

Back on land, you can devote an hour or so to **Seaport Village** itself, a 14-acre waterfront entertainment complex with around 50 shops and more than a dozen restaurants. Meant to look like a harbor in the 19th century, Seaport features 4 miles of cobblestone pathways bordered by lush landscaping and water features.

From there, stroll north to the **Embarcadero,** where you'll marvel at the **Maritime Museum's** historic vessels, including the *Star of India* (the world's oldest active sailing ship), *Berkeley, Californian, Medea,* and *Pilot.*

Explore San Diego's military might at the **USS Midway Museum,** aboard the permanently docked aircraft carrier with more than 60 exhibits and 25 restored aircraft.

Spend the rest of your afternoon and evening in **Coronado**, a quick jaunt by ferry or bridge, or walk a few blocks north to the **Gaslamp Quarter**, where the shopping and dining will keep you busy for hours.

Day 3

Set out early enough, and you might snag a parking spot near **La Jolla Cove**, where you can laugh at the sea lions lounging on the beach like lazy couch potatoes at the **Children's Pool**. Then head up one block to Prospect Street, where you'll find the vaunted **La Valencia** hotel (called the "Pink Lady" for its blush-hue exterior) and dozens of posh boutiques and galleries.

Head east to the **Museum of Contemporary Art San Diego**'s La Jolla location, which impresses as much with its ocean views as it does with its world-class collection of artwork. MCASD's Museum Café is a casual but elegant spot for a light lunch.

If you're with kids, skip the museum and head for **La Jolla Shores**, a good beach for swimming and making sand castles, followed by a visit to the **Birch Aquarium** and a fresh bite to eat at **El Pescador Fish Market** (⇨ *For this and other restaurant reviews, see Where to Eat*), an always-crowded lunchtime favorite.

Once you've refueled, head for **Torrey Pines State Natural Reserve.** Your reward for hiking down the cliffs to the state beach: there are breathtaking views in every direction.

If you're with small children, the trek might prove too challenging, but you can still take in the views from the top.

For dinner, swing north to **Del Mar**—during racing season, the evening scene is happening—or, for families, head down to **Ocean Beach** for a juicy burger at the surf-theme **Hodad's.**

Day 4

Start the day with a morning visit to **Cabrillo National Monument,** a national park with a number of activities. Learn about 16th-century explorer Juan Rodríguez Cabrillo, take a gentle 2-mile hike on the beautiful Bayside Trail, look around the Old Point Loma Lighthouse, and peer at tide pools, which teem with sea life (remember: look but don't touch).
■ **TIP**➔ Find out if low tide is in the morning or afternoon before planning your itinerary.

After Cabrillo, hop in your car and head to **Old Town**, where San Diego's early history comes to carefully reconstructed life. The Mexican food here isn't the city's best (leading contenders for that honor are Las Cuatro Milpas in Barrio Logan and Tacos El Gordo in Chula Vista, both too out-of-the-way for most tourists). It's true that the Old Town restaurants aren't even particularly authentic, but they're definitely bustling and kid-friendly, and frosty margaritas make an added incentive for grown-ups.

After that, spend a few hours exploring whatever cluster of neighborhoods appeals to you most. If you like casual coastal neighborhoods with a youthful vibe, head to **Pacific, Mission,** or **Ocean Beach**, or venture up to **North County** for an afternoon in Encinitas, which epitomizes the old California surf town.

If edgy and artsy are more your thing, check out the hip and ever-changing neighborhoods in **Uptown**, where you'll find super-cool shops, bars, and eateries.

TIPS

■ Sure, it's fun to dip those toes in the sand and saunter through one of the world's most incredible zoos. But don't overlook San Diego's somewhat under-rated performing arts scene. It's extremely easy to add a theater performance or a concert to any of the four days described above. Some of the city's top performance venues are in Balboa Park (Day 1), downtown (Day 2), and La Jolla (Day 3).

■ If you plan to tour more than a couple of museums in Balboa Park, buy the Passport to Balboa Park, which gets you into 14 attractions for just $49, or the Passport to Balboa Park Combo Pass, which also gets you into the zoo (it costs $83). You can buy these at the Balboa Park Visitor Center (☎ 619/239–0512 ⊕ www.balboapark.org).

■ Locals complain about public transportation as often as they complain about the price of fuel, but the Trolley and the Coaster are a hassle-free way to get to foot-friendly neighborhoods up and down the coast. Public transportation saves you the headache of traffic and parking, and includes free sightseeing along the way. You can head almost anywhere from the historic Santa Fe Depot downtown (don't miss the cutting-edge Museum of Contemporary Art next door to the station).

ALTERNATIVES

If you're an **adventure junkie,** you might want to ignore all of the above suggestions and just skip to the Fodor's Sports and the Outdoors listings. You can easily fill four days or more with every imaginable outdoor activity, from swimming, surfing, and sailing to hiking, golfing, paragliding, and stand-up paddling. San Diego is an athletic enthusiast's heaven—unless you're a skier, that is.

In **winter,** adjust the itineraries to include more indoor activities—the museums are fantastic—as well as a whale-watching boat tour.

In **summer,** check local listings for outdoor concerts, theater, and movie screenings, the perfect way to relax and enjoy a warm evening outdoors.

LIKE A LOCAL

Just because San Diego has tourist attractions at every turn doesn't mean you shouldn't stray from the beaten path and pretend you're a local for a day.

A pared-down pace

Balboa Park is the city's preferred playground. Visitors with detailed agendas (Museums? Check. Zoo? Check.) often miss out on the sweet spots that keep locals coming back time and again. Grab a map from the visitor center and explore the park's nooks and crannies. Or throw down a blanket on the lawn and laugh at the other tourists with their impossibly long to-do lists.

The hoppiest place on Earth

Cold beer seems to suit San Diego's chill personality, which may be why their craft-brewing scene has been lauded as one of the most cutting-edge in the world. You could easily spend an entire day visiting breweries, from the tiny **Alpine Beer Company**—to Escondido's venerable **Stone Brewing,** which started off as a pet project and now ships nationwide. If a full-fledged beer tour is out of the question, try a bold double IPA—a San Diego specialty—at **O'Brien's,** a Kearny Mesa pub that's low on personality but high on hops, or head to **30th Street** in North Park, which is lined with so many brew-pubs that it's been nicknamed the "Belgian Corridor" by in-the-know imbibers.

Fill your heart with art

MCASD Downtown's **Thursday Night Thing**—aka TNT—is a boisterous quarterly museum party that puts to rest all notions of an artless art scene.

Sunrise, sunset

Our beaches can't be beat, but battling the crazy summer crowds for a spot on the sand is far from relaxing. Take a brisk stroll just after dawn, and savor the views without distraction. Or, find a secluded spot on the cliffs for a sunset happy hour. Booze is banned at beaches, but a little creativity will have you toasting in no time (hint: wash and save a couple of paper coffee cups).

Break for breakfast

Even fitness freaks—and San Diegans are among the country's fittest—will agree that a slow-paced morning meal is a lovely start to the weekend, which explains the long lines at any place worth the wait.

The **Mission** has locations in Mission Beach (⊠ *3795 Mission Blvd.* ☎ 858/488–9060), North Park (⊠ *2801 University Ave.* ☎ 619/220–8992), and the East Village (⊠ *1250 J St.* ☎ 619/232–7662). The café food is simple and hearty, ranging from traditional fare (eggs, pancakes) to the Latino-inspired (the Papas Locas or "crazy potatoes" will burn a hole in your tongue).

Hash House A Go Go (⊠ *3628 5th Ave., Hillcrest* ☎ 619/298–4646) specializes in Southern-accented favorites, in large portions. There are a variety of the name-sake hashes and egg Benedicts, as well as fluffy pancakes and French toast. Weekends mean long lines, so try to visit during the week.

Kono's Surf Club Café (⊠ *704 Garnet Ave.* ☎ 858/483–1669) in Pacific Beach lures locals with an outdoor patio and ocean views, but the last thing you'll want to do after eating one of Kono's massive breakfast burritos is slip into a bikini. There's a reason for the expression "burrito belly"—but it's a small price to pay for brazenly overindulgent pleasure.

SAN DIEGO WITH KIDS

Beach fun

A pail and shovel can keep kids entertained for hours at the beach—**Coronado Beach** is especially family-friendly. Be liberal with the sunscreen, even if it's cloudy.

If you're visiting in summer, check out the **U.S. Open Sandcastle Competition** at Imperial Beach, which usually takes place in late July or early August. There is even a kids' competition.

Drop off the tweens and teens for a morning **surf lesson** and enjoy some guilt-free grown-up time. Or rent bikes for a casual family ride along the **Mission Bay boardwalk**. If that's not enough of an adventure, take your daring offspring on the **Giant Dipper**, an old wooden roller coaster at Mission Bay's **Belmont Park**, also home to a huge arcade.

Top attractions

LEGOLAND California is a full day of thrills for kids 12 and under, while the **San Diego Zoo, SeaWorld**, and **San Diego Safari Park** satisfy all age groups and every kind of kid, from the curious (plenty of educational angles) to the boisterous (room to run around and lots of animals to imitate). They even have family sleepover nights in summer.

Winter sightings

If you're visiting in winter, try a **whale-watching** tour. Even if you don't see any migrating gray whales, the boat ride is fun. La Jolla's **Birch Aquarium** has enough glowing and tentacled creatures to send imaginations plummeting leagues under the sea.

Museums geared to kids

An afternoon at the museum might elicit yawns until they spy all the neat stuff. Balboa Park's **San Diego Air and Space Museum** celebrates aviation and flight history with exhibitions that include actual planes, while **Reuben H. Fleet Science Center** inspires budding scientists with interactive exhibits and its IMAX dome theater. The **San Diego Model Railroad Museum** features miles and miles of model trains and track, including an incredibly detailed reproduction of the Tehachapi railroad circa 1952.

Downtown's **New Children's Museum** appeals to all age groups; too-cool teens can even retreat to the edgy Teen Studio. With installations geared just to them and dry and wet art-making areas (less mess for you), kids can channel all that excess vacation energy into something productive. While they color and craft, you can admire the museum's ultracontemporary, sustainable architecture.

Take me out to the ball game

Baseball buffs will have a blast at **PETCO Park**, where the San Diego Padres play all spring and summer. PETCO's Park at the Park, a grassy elevated area outside the stadium, offers stellar center-field views—plus all the action on a big-screen—with a sandy play space if your kids get bored after a few innings.

Treating your tots

Ocean Beach's yummy **Cupcakes Squared** (✉ *3772 Voltaire St.* ⊕ *cupcakessquared. com*) took first place in Martha Stewart's Southern California Cupcake Showdown. Also delish is Hillcrest's **Babycakes** (✉ *3766 5th Ave.* ⊕ *www.babycakessandiego. com*), a stylish spot nestled in an 1889 Craftsman near Balboa Park. Bonus: Babycakes serves beer and wine for weary moms and dads. If toys trump sweet treats, check out the classics at **Geppetto's** (⊕ *www.geppettostoys.com*), a family-run business with eight locations throughout San Diego, including Old Town, La Jolla and the Fashion Valley Mall.

FREE (AND ALMOST FREE) IN SAN DIEGO

San Diego may levy an unofficial "sunshine tax," but it makes up for it with plenty of free stuff. Aside from the beaches, backcountry trails, and verdant city parks—all as free as the steadfast sun and endless blue skies—a little careful planning can land you cost-free (or very cheap) fun for the whole family.

Free in Balboa Park

Balboa Park hosts its one-hour **Twilight in the Park** concert series from June to August, Tuesday through Thursday at 6:15 pm. Sit under the stars and take in everything from Dixieland Jazz to Latin salsa. Also at the park, check out the **Spreckels International Organ Festival** concerts Monday at 7:30 pm, from June to August, as well as 2 pm Sunday matinee concerts throughout the year. Balboa Park's **Screen on the Green**, an outdoor movie screening, runs throughout summer. The **Timken Museum of Art** in Balboa Park is free but a donation is suggested.

Free concerts

The Del Mar Fairgrounds' summertime **4 O'Clock Fridays** series features big-name local and national bands; it's technically free, though you still have to pay a few bucks for racetrack admission.

Also worth catching: Carlsbad's **TGIF Jazz in the Parks**, Friday at 6 pm; **Coronado Summer Concerts-in-the-Park**, Sunday at 6 pm, May–September; **La Jolla Concerts by the Sea**, Sunday at 2 pm, July and August; the **Del Mar Twilight Concert Series**, Tuesday at 7 pm, June–September; and Encinitas' **Sunday Summer Concerts by the Sea**, 3 pm, July and August.

The annual **Adams Avenue Unplugged** festival in spring and **Adams Avenue Street Festival** in September both hit pay dirt: blues, folk, country, jazz, indie, world, and more—all for free.

Tastings

Beer aficionados can take a 45-minute tour of the 55,000-square-foot **Stone Brewing Company**—groups fill up fast, maybe because of the free tastings at the end. At **Alpine Beer Company**, up to four tasters are just $1.50 each. Wine lovers might pack a lunch and head for **Orfila Vineyards & Winery**, where picnic tables dot the pastoral landscape—the wine's not free, but the views are. Or spend an entire afternoon in **Temecula Wine Country.** Tastings typically aren't free, but you can find twofer coupons and other discounts at ⊕ *www.temeculawines.org.*

October freebies

October is Kids Free Month at the **San Diego Zoo** and the **San Diego Safari Park;** all children under 11 get in free.

Free museums

Both locations of **MCASD** are always free for patrons under 25, and for everyone else the third Thursday of the month from 5 to 7 pm.

In February, you can pick up a free **Museum Month Pass** at Macy's that offers half-off admission to 40 museums for the entire month.

Many of San Diego's museums offer a once-a-month free Tuesday, on a rotating schedule (*See* ⊕ *www.balboapark.org for the schedule*) to San Diego city and county residents, active military, and their families; special exhibitions often require separate admission.

Discounts and deals

Try **Just My Ticket** (⊕ *www.justmyticket. com*) for deals on last-minute theater, concert, and sporting event tickets, as well as restaurant coupons.

A WALK THROUGH SAN DIEGO'S PAST

Downtown San Diego is a living tribute to history and revitalization. The Gaslamp Quarter followed up its boisterous boomtown years—the late 1800s, when Wyatt Earp ran gambling halls and sailors frequented brothels lining 4th and 5th avenues—with a long stint of seediness, emerging only recently as a glamorous place to live and play. Little Italy, once a bustling Italian fishing neighborhood, got a fresh start when the city took its cause to heart.

Where It All Started

Begin at the corner of 4th and Island. There you'll find the 150-year-old **William Heath Davis House**, a saltbox structure shipped around Cape Horn and assembled in the Gaslamp Quarter. Among its famous former residents: Alonzo Horton, the city's founder. Take a tour, keeping a lookout for the house's current resident: a lady ghost.

From there walk a block east to 5th Avenue and head north. Along the way, you'll see some of the 16½-block historic district's best-known Victorian-era commercial beauties, including the Italianate **Marston Building** (at F Street), the **Keating Building**, the **Spencer-Ogden Building**, and the **Old City Hall**. Architecture buffs should pick up a copy of *San Diego's Gaslamp Quarter*, a self-guided tour published by the Historical Society.

At E Street, head back over to 4th Avenue and you'll behold the **Balboa Theatre**, a striking Spanish Renaissance–style building that was constructed in 1923 and restored in 2007. Right next to it is **Westfield Horton Plaza** mall, which opened its doors in 1985. This multilevel mall played a huge role in downtown's revitalization, as entrepreneurs and preservationists realized the value of the Gaslamp Quarter. Pop across Broadway to check out the stately **U.S. Grant Hotel**, built in 1910 by the son of President Ulysses S. Grant.

Art Stop

Follow Broadway west to Kettner Boulevard, where the **Museum of Contemporary Art San Diego (MCASD)** makes a bold statement with its steel-and-glass lines. It's definitely worth a wander, as is MCASD's newest addition across the street, situated in the renovated baggage depot of the 1915 **Santa Fe Depot** (the station itself is also a stunner).

From Fishermen to Fashionistas

From there, head north on Kettner until you hit A Street, make a quick right, and then take a left on India Street. This is the heart of **Little Italy**, which at the turn of the 20th century was a bustling Italian fishing village. The area fell into disarray in the early 1970s due to a decline in the tuna industry and the construction of I–5, which destroyed 35% of the area. In 1996, a group of forward-thinking architects—commissioned by the city—created a cache of new residential, retail, and public areas that coexist beautifully with the neighborhood's historic charms. Now, it's a vibrant urban center with hip eateries, bars, and boutiques. You'll find remnants of retro Little Italy, from authentic cafés (check out **Pappalecco**, a popular gelateria) to boccie ball matches played by old-timers at **Amici Park**.

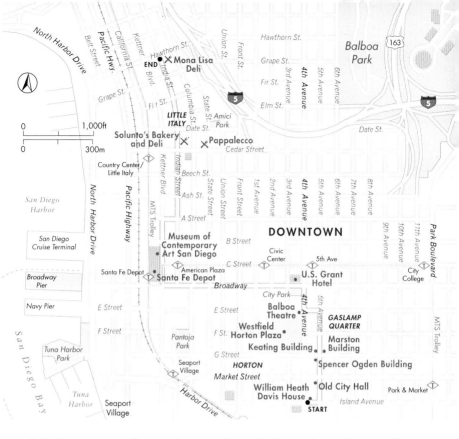

Highlights:	The restored gas lamps that give the Gaslamp its name; the juxtaposition of old and new architecture; Little Italy's sidewalk cafés.
Where to Start:	At the corner of 4th and Island avenues, at the William Heath Davis House. It's a short walk from most downtown hotels. If you drive, park in a paid lot or at nearby Horton Plaza, which offers three free hours with validation (get your ticket stamped at one of the validation machines).
Length:	About 3 miles and three to four hours round-trip with stops. Take the Orange Line trolley from Santa Fe Depot back if you're tired.
Where to Stop:	From Little Italy follow the same path back or head down Laurel Street to Harbor Drive and wander along the waterfront until you hit Broadway.
Best Time to Go:	Morning or early afternoon.
Worst Time to Go:	In the evening, when it's just too crowded.
Where to Refuel:	If your stomach is growling, Little Italy is waiting for you like an Italian mamma: mangia, mangia! Try Solunto's Bakery and Deli (⊠ 1643 India St.) or Mona Lisa (⊠ 2061 India St.).

FARMERS' MARKETS

Take advantage of San Diego's year-round gorgeous weather and visit a farmers' market or flea market during your stay. You'll have a chance to mingle with locals and pick up some bargains on things that are hard to find downtown or at the mall. Enjoy the festive atmosphere with live entertainment as you browse the tempting selection of fresh produce, gourmet foods, arts and crafts, fresh flowers, and more. Below are a few of our favorite markets. You can find more on ⊕ *www. sdfarmbureau.org.*

■ TIP➜ Before you head out, be sure you wear comfortable shoes and bring a tote bag to carry your purchases. Arrive early for the best selection, and assume that you'll have to pay with cash rather than plastic. A little haggling is expected, but be sure to do it politely, with a smile.

The **Hillcrest Farmers Market** is one of the city's best, held every Sunday from 9 am until 2 pm. There's farm-fresh produce, of course, but also handmade clothing and jewelry, and other types of handicrafts. Come browse and plan to stay for lunch: there are all sorts of vendors selling top-notch ready-to-eat food, from fresh made crepes to tamales and just about everything in between. Check their website for more information ⊕ *www. hillcrestfarmersmarket.com.*

Cedros Avenue Farmers Market. Located at the south end of the Cedros Design District, this upscale market offers organic veggies and herbs, regionally grown fruit, healthy juices, California wines, smoked salmon, to-die-for chocolates, freshly baked bread loaves, and all-natural dog treats. ⊠ *410 Cedros Ave., at corner of Cedros Ave. and Rosa St., Solana Beach* ☎ *858/755–0444* ⊕ *www.cedrosavenue. com* ☉ *Sun. 1–5.*

Coronado Farmers' Market. Located in the parking lot of Il Fornaio restaurant, this small market boasts a scenic bayside setting and more than a dozen vendors selling a variety of fresh produce and exotic flowers from local farms. Specialty foods include organic cheese, butter, and premium meats. ⊠ *Ferry Landing, 1st St. and B St., Coronado* ⊕ *www.sdfarmbureau. org* ☉ *Tues. 2:30–6.*

La Jolla Open Aire Market. Along with the usual fresh produce and flowers, this large market with a county fair atmosphere features paintings from local artists, handmade clothing and jewelry, and a tempting food court serving everything from crepes and tacos to gyros and roasted corn on the cob. ⊠ *La Jolla Elementary School playground, at corner of Girard St. and Genter St., 1111 Marine St., La Jolla* ☎ *858/454–1699* ⊕ *www.lajollamarket. com* ☉ *Sun. 9–1.*

Little Italy Mercato. This festive market is one of the largest and liveliest in San Diego. Shop for handcrafted gifts, cheese, nuts, Mexican candy, and olive oil to take home and enjoy a panino or Italian pastry as you stroll the aisles. ⊠ *Date St. (between India and Columbia Sts.), Little Italy* ⊕ *www.littleitalymercato.com* ☉ *Sat. 8–2.*

Ocean Beach Farmers' Market. Voted "Best Farmers Market in California" by *Sunset* magazine, this popular midweek event features live music, crafts, fresh produce, samples from local restaurants, and more. An adjacent parking lot offers handmade apparel and accessories, holistic products, and llama rides for kids. ⊠ *Newport Ave. between Cable St. and Bacon St., 4900 Newport Ave., Ocean Beach* ⊕ *www.sdfarmbureau.org* ☉ *Wed., summer 4–8, winter 4–7.*

Downtown

EAST VILLAGE, EMBARCADERO, GASLAMP QUARTER, AND LITTLE ITALY

WORD OF MOUTH

"Did you visit Seaport Village? It can be so beautiful on a sunny day. There are tons of casual restaurants to restaurants that overlook the bay. There are also tons of great attractions like the USS *Midway* (which you can tour) and the *Star of India*."

—kenem

GETTING ORIENTED

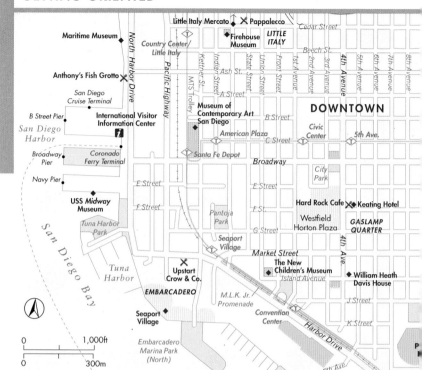

GETTING HERE

It's an easy drive into downtown, especially from the nearby airport. There are reasonably priced parking lots (about $10 per day) along Harbor Drive, Pacific Highway, and lower Broadway and Market Street. Most restaurants offer valet parking at night, but beware of fees of $15 and up.

If you tire of exploring downtown on foot, hop aboard a horse-drawn carriage, pedicab, San Diego Trolley, or a GoCar (three-wheel cars equipped with a GPS-guided audio tour).

TOP REASONS TO GO

Waterfront delights: Stroll along the Embarcadero, explore Seaport Village, or enjoy a harbor cruise.

Contemporary art for all ages: From the stunning galleries of the Museum of Contemporary Art to the clever incorporation of art and play at the New Children's Museum, downtown is the place for art.

Maritime history: Climb aboard and explore a wide array of vessels from sailing ships to submarines.

Delicious dining: Fresh seafood along the Embarcadero, authentic Italian cuisine in Little Italy, and the high-style restaurants of the Gaslamp make downtown San Diego a diner's delight.

Happening Gaslamp: It's hard to believe this hip neighborhood filled with street art, galleries, restaurants, and buzzing nightlife was once slated for the wrecking ball.

PLANNING YOUR TIME

Most downtown attractions are open daily, but the Museum of Contemporary Art and the New Children's Museum are closed Wednesday, and the Firehouse Museum is only open Thursday through Sunday. For guided tours of the Gaslamp Quarter Historic District, visit on Saturday. A boat trip on the harbor, or at least a hop over to Coronado on the ferry, is a must at any time of year. From December through March, when gray whales migrate between the Pacific Northwest and southern Baja, consider booking a whale-watching excursion from the Broadway Pier.

VISITOR INFORMATION

International Visitor Information Center. Temporarily located outside the cruise ship terminal while the Embarcadero is undergoing development, this is a great resource for information and discounts on hotels, restaurants, and attractions. ⊠ *1140 N. Harbor Dr., Embarcadero* ☎ *619/236-1212* ⊕ *www.sandiego.org* ⊘ *June–Sept., daily 9–5; Oct.–May, daily 9–4.*

QUICK BITES

Upstart Crow & Co. This combination bookstore and coffeehouse serves good cappuccino and espresso with pastries and cakes. ⊠ *835 W. Harbor Dr., #C, Seaport Village, Central Plaza, Embarcadero* ☎ *619/232-4855* ⊕ *www.upstartcrowtrading.com.*

Anthony's Fish Grotto. Choose a fried shellfish plate or any of the carefully grilled fish here before your bay cruise a few blocks north of Broadway Pier. Order a quick lunch at the Fishette counter just outside the main entrance, or head indoors for a more leisurely meal. ⊠ *1360 N. Harbor Dr., Embarcadero* ☎ *619/232-5103* ⊕ *www.gofishanthonys.com.*

You can get everything from cinnamon rolls to sushi at the food court on **Westfield Horton Plaza's top level.**

Pappalecco. Kids and adults alike will swoon over the addictive gelato at Pappalecco, near the Firehouse Museum. ⊠ *1602 State St., Little Italy* ☎ *619/238-4590* ⊕ *www.pappalecco.com.*

Sightseeing
★★★★★

Nightlife
★★★★★

Dining
★★★★★

Lodging
★★★★☆

Shopping
★★★★☆

Nearly written off in the 1970s, today downtown San Diego is a testament to conservation and urban renewal. Once derelict Victorian storefronts now house the hottest restaurants, and the *Star of India,* the world's oldest active sailing ship, almost lost to scrap, floats regally along the Embarcadero. Like many modern U.S. cities, downtown San Diego's story is as much about its rebirth as its history. Although many consider downtown to be the 16½-block Gaslamp Quarter, it's actually comprised of eight neighborhoods, including East Village, Little Italy, and Embarcadero.

GASLAMP QUARTER

Updated by
Claire Deeks
van der Lee

Considered the liveliest of the downtown neighborhoods, the Gaslamp Quarter's 4th and 5th avenues are peppered with trendy nightclubs, swanky lounge bars, chic restaurants, and boisterous sports pubs. The Gaslamp has the largest collection of commercial Victorian-style buildings in the country. Despite this, when the move for downtown redevelopment gained momentum in the 1970s, there was talk of bulldozing them and starting from scratch. In response, concerned history buffs, developers, architects, and artists formed the Gaslamp Quarter Council to clean up and preserve the quarter.

The majority of the quarter's landmark buildings are on 4th and 5th avenues, between Island Avenue and Broadway. If you don't have much time, stroll down 5th Avenue, where highlights include **Louis Bank of Commerce** (No. 835), **Old City Hall** (No. 664), **Nesmith-Greeley** (No. 825), and **Yuma** (No. 631) buildings. The Romanesque Revival **Keating Hotel** at 432 F Street was designed by the same firm that created the famous Hotel Del Coronado, the Victorian grande dame that presides over Coronado's beach. At the corner of 4th Avenue and F Street, peer into the **Hard Rock Cafe,** which occupies a restored turn-of-the-20th-century tavern with a 12-foot mahogany bar and a spectacular stained-glass domed ceiling.

The section of G Street between 6th and 9th avenues has become a haven for galleries; stop in one of them to pick up a map of the downtown arts district. The **Urban Art Trail** has added pizzazz to drab city thoroughfares by transforming such things as trash cans and traffic controller boxes into works of art. The Gaslamp is a lively place—during baseball season, the streets flood with Padres fans, and festivals, such as Mardi Gras in February, ShamROCK on St. Patrick's Day, and Monster Bash in October, keep the party atmosphere going throughout the year.

TOP ATTRACTIONS

Westfield Horton Plaza. This downtown shopping, dining, and entertainment mecca fronts Broadway and G Street from 1st to 4th avenues and covers more than six city blocks. Designed by Jon Jerde and completed in 1985, Westfield Horton Plaza is a collage of colorful tile work, banners waving in the air, and modern sculptures. The complex rises in uneven, staggered levels to five floors; great views of downtown from the harbor to Balboa Park and beyond can be had here.

Macy's and Nordstrom department stores anchor the plaza housing more than 100 clothing, sporting-goods, jewelry, book, and gift shops in all. Other attractions include the country's largest Sam Goody music store, a movie complex, restaurants, and the respected San Diego Repertory Theatre below ground level. In 2008 the **Balboa Theater**, contiguous with the shopping center, reopened its doors after a $26.5 million renovation. The historic 1920s theater seats 1,400 and offers live arts and cultural performances throughout the week.

The mall has a multilevel parking garage; even so, lines to find a space can be long. ■ TIP➡ Entering the parking structure on G Street rather than 4th Avenue generally means less traffic and more parking space. Parking validation is complimentary whether you spend a bundle or just window-shop. Validation machines throughout the center allow for three hours' free parking; after that it's $8 per hour (or $2 per 15-minute increment). If you use this notoriously confusing fruit-and-vegetable–themed garage, be sure to remember at which produce level you've left your car. If you're staying downtown, the Old Town Trolley Tour will drop you directly in front of Westfield Horton Plaza. ⊠ *324 Horton Plaza, Gaslamp Quarter* ☎ *619/238–1596* ⊕ *www.westfield.com/hortonplaza* ⊗ *Weekdays 10–9, Sat. 10–8, Sun. 11–6.*

WORTH NOTING

Gaslamp Museum at the William Heath Davis House. The oldest wooden house in San Diego houses the Gaslamp Quarter Historical Foundation, the district's curator. Before developer Alonzo Horton came to town, Davis, a prominent San Franciscan, had made an unsuccessful attempt to develop the waterfront area. In 1850 he had this prefab saltbox-style house, built in Maine, shipped around Cape Horn and assembled in San Diego (it originally stood at State and Market streets). Regularly scheduled two-hour walking tours of the historic district leave from the house on Saturday at 11 and cost $15. If you

Docked off the Navy pier, the USS *Midway* aircraft carrier was once home to 4,500 crew members.

can't time your visit with the weekly tour, a self-guided tour map is available for purchase for $2. ✉ *410 Island Ave., at 4th Ave., Gaslamp Quarter* ☎ *619/233–4692* ⊕ *www.gaslampquarter.org* 🖼 *$5* ☉ *Tues.– Sat. 10–5, Sun. noon–4.*

EMBARCADERO

The **Embarcadero** cuts a scenic swath along the harbor front and connects today's downtown San Diego to its maritime routes. The bustle of Embarcadero comes less these days from the activities of fishing folk than from the throngs of tourists, but this waterfront walkway, stretching from the Convention Center to the Maritime Museum, remains the nautical soul of the city. There are several seafood restaurants here, as well as sea vessels of every variety—cruise ships, ferries, tour boats, and Navy destroyers.

On the north end of the Embarcadero at Ash Street you'll find the **Maritime Museum.** South of it, the **B Street Pier** is used by ships from major cruise lines while tickets for harbor tours and whale-watching trips are sold at the foot of **Broadway Pier.** The terminal for the Coronado Ferry lies in between. Docked at the Navy Pier is the decommissioned **USS Midway.** At the foot of G Street, **Tuna Harbor** was once the hub of one of San Diego's earliest and most successful industries, commercial tuna fishing. The pleasant Tuna Harbor Park offers a great view of boating on the bay and across to any aircraft carriers docked at the North Island naval base. A few blocks south, **Embarcadero Marina Park North** is an 8-acre extension into the harbor from the center of **Seaport Village.** It's usually full of kite fliers, in-line skaters, and picnickers. Seasonal celebrations, including San Diego's Parade of Lights, the Port of San Diego Big Balloon Parade, the Sea and Air Parade, and the Big Bay July 4 Celebration, are held here and at the similar **Embarcadero Marina Park South.** The **San Diego Convention Center,** on Harbor Drive between 1st and 6th avenues, is a waterfront landmark designed by Canadian architect Arthur Erickson. The backdrop of blue sky and sea complements the building's nautical lines. The center often holds trade shows that are open to the public, and tours of the building are available.

WORD OF MOUTH

"The Embarcadero is good. Kids usually love the Star of India. You can go inside the actual ship. Nearby is the ship used to film the movie *Master & Commander.* There are several other boats/ships to tour as well. From the same area, you can catch the passenger ferry to Coronado. It's a fun and cheap way to actually go out in the bay."

—lcuy

A huge revitalization project, due to be completed in late 2013, is underway along the northern Embarcadero. The overhaul will create a wide esplanade with gardens, shaded pavilions, and public art installations along the water. There will also be a new information center building. While the end result promises to be beautiful, visitors should expect some minor construction inconveniences in the meantime.

TOP ATTRACTIONS

Maritime Museum.

Fodor's Choice ⇨ *See the highlighted listing in this chapter.*

Fodor's Choice ★ **Museum of Contemporary Art San Diego (MCASD).** At the Downtown branch of the city's contemporary art museum (the original is in La Jolla), explore the works of international and regional artists in a modern, urban space. The Jacobs Building—formerly the baggage building at the historic Santa Fe Depot—features large gallery spaces, high ceilings, and natural lighting, giving artists the flexibility to create large-scale installations. MCASD's collection includes many Pop Art, minimalist, and conceptual works from the 1950s to the present. The museum showcases both established and emerging artists in temporary exhibitions, and has permanent, site-specific commissions by Jenny Holzer and Richard Serra. ■**TIP➔** Admission, good for seven days, includes the Downtown and La Jolla locations. ⊠ *1100 and 1001 Kettner Blvd., Downtown* ☎ *858/454–3541* ⊕ *www.mcasd.org* ⬚ *$10; free 3rd Thurs. of month 5–7* ⊗ *Thurs.–Tues., 11–5; 3rd Thurs. until 7* ⊗ *Closed Wed.*

Fodor's Choice ★ **The New Children's Museum (NCM).** The NCM blends contemporary art with unstructured play to create an environment that appeals to children as well as adults. The 50,000-square-foot structure was constructed from recycled building materials, operates on solar energy, and is convection-cooled by an elevator shaft. It also features a nutritious and eco-conscious café. Interactive exhibits include designated areas for toddlers and teens, as well as plenty of activities for the entire family. Several art workshops are offered each day, as well as hands-on studios where visitors are encouraged to create their own art. The

MARITIME MUSEUM

✉ 1492 N. Harbor Dr., Embarcadero ☎ 619/234–9153
⊕ www.sdmaritime.org ⌨ $15 includes entry to all ships except Californian, $3 more for Pilot Boat Bay Cruise
⊙ Daily 9–8.

TIPS

■ Sail the Pacific on the Californian. Weekend sails, typically from noon to 4, cost $43 for adults; buy tickets online or at the museum on the day of sail. Arrive at least an hour early for a spot onboard.

■ Cruise San Diego Bay for only $3 plus museum admission on the 1914 Pilot boat. The 45-minute narrated tours are offered several times a day.

■ In partnership with the museum, the yacht America also offers sails on the bay, and whale-watching excursions in winter (times and prices vary).

■ Exploring the submarines requires climbing through several midsize hatches; wear flat shoes and pants.

■ Watch for the workshop on the Berkeley, where volunteers build model ships.

From sailing ships to submarines, the Maritime Museum is a must for anyone with an interest in nautical history. This collection of restored and replica ships gives a fascinating glimpse of San Diego during its heyday as a commercial seaport.

Highlights

The jewel of the collection, the *Star of India*, is often considered a symbol of the city. An iron windjammer built in 1863 and painstakingly restored, it made 21 trips around the world in the late 1800s, traveling the East Indian trade route, shuttling immigrants from England to New Zealand, and serving the Alaskan salmon trade.

The HMS *Surprise*, purchased in 2004, is a replica of an 18th-century British Royal Navy frigate and was used in the Academy Award–winning *Master and Commander: The Far Side of the World*.

The museum's headquarters are on the *Berkeley*, an 1898 steam-driven ferryboat, which served the Southern Pacific Railroad in San Francisco until 1958. Its ornate detailing carefully restored, the main deck is as a floating museum, with permanent exhibits on West Coast maritime history and rotating exhibits.

There are also two submarines: a *Soviet B-39* "Foxtrot" class submarine and the USS *Dolphin* research submarine. Take a peek at the harbor from a periscope, check out the engine control room, and wonder at the tight living quarters.

At Spanish Landing Park, about 2 miles to the west, the museum is constructing a full-scale working replica of the *San Salvador*, the first European ship to land on the western coast of the future United States. To view the work-in-progress (daily 10–3:30), get directions at the *Berkeley*. When complete, it will be on display at the main location.

studio projects change frequently and the entire museum changes exhibits every 18 to 24 months, so there is always something new to explore. The adjoining 1-acre park and playground is conveniently located across from the convention center trolley stop. ⊠ *200 W. Island Ave., Embarcadero* ☎ *619/233–8792* ⊕ *www.thinkplaycreate. org* ⊒ *$10; 2nd Sun. each month free 10–4* ⊙ *Mon., Tues., Fri., Sat. 10–4, Thurs. 10–6, Sun. noon–4.* ⊙ *Closed Wed. Sept.–June.*

ⓒ **Seaport Village.** You'll find some of the best views of the harbor at Seaport Village, three bustling shopping plazas designed to reflect the New England clapboard and Spanish Mission architectural styles of early California. On a prime stretch of waterfront the dining, shopping and entertainment complex connects the harbor with hotel towers and the convention center. Specialty shops offer everything from a kite store and swing emporium to a shop devoted to hot sauces. You can dine at snack bars and restaurants, many with harbor views. Seaport Village's shops are open daily 10 to 9; a few eateries open early for breakfast, and venues many have extended nighttime hours, especially in summer. Restaurant prices here are high and the food is only average, so your best bet is to go elsewhere for a meal.

Live music can be heard daily from noon to 4 at the main food court. Additional free concerts take place every Sunday from 1 to 4 at the East Plaza Gazebo. If you happen to visit San Diego in late November or early December, you might be lucky enough to catch Surfing Santa's Arrival and even have your picture taken with Santa on his wave. In April the Seaport Buskers Fest presents an array of costumed street performers. The **Seaport Village Carousel** (rides $2) has 54 animals, hand-carved and hand-painted by Charles Looff in 1895. ⊠ *849 W. Harbor Dr., Downtown* ☎ *619/235–4014 office and events hotline* ⊕ *www.seaportvillage.com.*

Fodor's Choice **USS Midway Museum.** After 47 years of worldwide service, the retired
★ USS *Midway* began a new tour of duty on the south side of the Navy pier in 2004. Launched in 1945, the 1,001-foot-long ship was the largest in the world for the first 10 years of its existence. The most visible landmark on the north Embarcadero, it now serves as a floating interactive museum—an appropriate addition to the town that is home to one-third of the Pacific fleet and the birthplace of naval aviation. A free audio tour guides you through the massive ship while offering insight from former sailors. As you clamber through passageways and up and down ladder wells, you'll get a feel for how the *Midway*'s 4,500 crew members lived and worked on this "city at sea."

Though the entire tour is impressive, you'll really be wowed when you step out onto the 4-acre flight deck—not only the best place to get an idea of the ship's scale, but also one of the most interesting vantage points for bay and city skyline views. An F-14 Tomcat jet fighter is just one of many vintage aircraft on display. Free guided tours of the bridge and primary flight control, known as "the Island," depart every 10 minutes from the flight deck. Many of the docents stationed throughout the ship served in the Navy, some even on the *Midway*, and they are eager to answer questions or share stories. The museum also offers multiple flight simulators for an additional fee, climb-aboard cockpits, and interactive exhibits focusing on naval aviation. There is a gift shop and a café with pleasant outdoor seating. This is a wildly popular stop, with most visits lasting several hours. ⚠ Despite efforts to provide accessibility throughout the ship, some areas can only be reached via fairly steep steps; a video tour of these areas is available on the hangar deck. ⊠ *910 N. Harbor Dr., Embarcadero* ☎ *619/544–9600* ⊕ *www. midway.org* 🖃 *$18* ⊙ *Mid-Aug.–June, daily 10–5; July–mid-Aug., daily 9–5; last admission 4 pm.*

WESTERN METAL SUPPLY

Initially scheduled for demolition to make room for PETCO Park, the historic Western Metal Supply Co. was instead incorporated into the ballpark and supports the left-field foul pole. Great care was taken to retain the historic nature of the building's exterior despite extensive interior renovations. Built in 1909, the four-story structure originally manufactured wagon wheels and war supplies, and today holds the Padres' Team Store, the Padres' Hall of Fame Bar and Grill, and rooftop seating.

EAST VILLAGE

The most ambitious of the downtown projects is **East Village,** not far from the Gaslamp Quarter, and encompassing 130 blocks between the railroad tracks up to J Street, and from 6th Avenue east to around 10th Street. Sparking the rebirth of this former warehouse district was the 2004 construction of the San Diego Padres' baseball stadium, **PETCO Park.** As the city's largest downtown neighborhood, East Village is continually broadening its boundaries with its urban design of redbrick cafés, spacious galleries, rooftop bars, sleek hotels, and warehouse restaurants.

WORTH NOTING

🔿 **PETCO Park.** Opened in 2004, PETCO Park is the state-of-the-art home to the San Diego Padres. The stadium features a 30- x 53-foot LED video board and more than 1,000 televisions, and is strategically designed to give fans a view of San Diego Bay, the skyline, and Balboa Park. Reflecting San Diego's beauty, the stadium is clad in sandstone from India to evoke the area's cliffs and beaches; the 42,000 seats are dark blue, reminiscent of the ocean, and the exposed steel is painted white to reflect the sails of harbor boats on the bay. The family-friendly lawnlike berm, "Park at the Park," is a popular and affordable place for fans to view the game. Behind-the-scenes guided tours of PETCO, including the press box and the dugout, are offered throughout the year. ⊠ *100 Park Blvd., East Village* ☎ *619/795–5011 tour hotline* ⊕ *www. sandiego.padres.mlb.com* 🖃 *$11 tour* ⊙ *Tours offered 7 days a week; times vary seasonally.*

Home of the San Diego Padres, PETCO Park offers behind-the-scenes tours.

LITTLE ITALY

Unlike many tourist-driven communities, the charming neighborhood of **Little Italy** is authentic to its roots, from the Italian-speaking residents to the imported delicacies. The main thoroughfare—from India Street to Kettner Boulevard—is filled with lively cafés, gelato shops, bakeries, and restaurants. Art lovers can browse gallery showrooms, while shoppers adore the Fir Street cottages. Home to many in San Diego's design community, Little Italy exudes a sense of urban cool. The neighborhood bustles each Saturday during the wildly popular Mercato farmer's market, and at special events throughout the year such as Artwalk in spring and FESTA! each fall. Yet the neighborhood is also marked by old-country charms: church bells ring on the half-hour, and Italians gather daily to play bocce in Amici Park. After an afternoon of gelati and espresso, you may just forget that you're in Southern California.

TOP ATTRACTIONS

★ **Little Italy Mercato.** Each Saturday tourists and residents alike flock to the Little Italy Mercato, one of the most popular farmers markets in San Diego. More than 150 vendors line Date Street selling everything from paintings and pottery, to flowers and farm fresh eggs. Come hungry, as several booths and food trucks serve prepared foods. Alternatively, the neighborhood's many cafés and restaurants are just steps away. The Mercato is a great opportunity to experience one of San Diego's most exciting urban neighborhoods. ⊠ *Date and India Sts., Little Italy* ⊕ *www.littleitalysd.com/mercato/* ⊗ *Sat. 8–2.*

WÓRTH NOTING

☺ **Firehouse Museum.** Firefighting artifacts of all sorts fill this converted fire station, which at one time also served as the repair shop for all of San Diego's firefighting equipment. Three large rooms contain everything from 19th-century horse- and hand-drawn fire engines to 20th-century motorized trucks, the latest dating from 1943. ⊠ *1572 Columbia St., Little Italy* ☎ *619/232–3473* ⊕ *www.sandiegofirehousemuseum.com* ✉ *$3* ☉ *Thurs. and Fri. 10–2, weekends 10–4.*

3

Balboa Park and San Diego Zoo

WORD OF MOUTH

"The beautiful Balboa Park has many attractions (Botanical Building,
Rose Garden) as well as a number of museums."

—Tomsd

GETTING ORIENTED

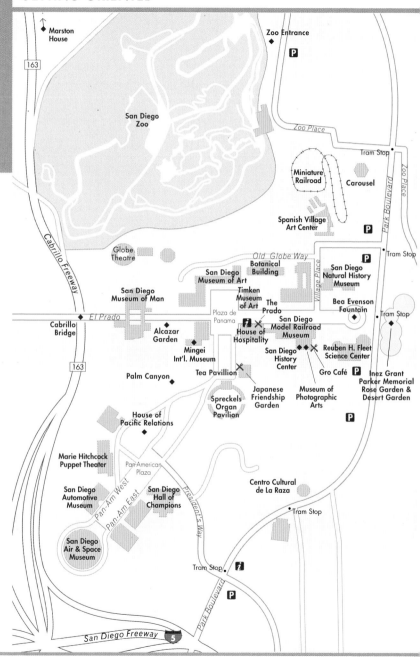

Marston House

163

San Diego Zoo

Zoo Entrance

Cabrillo Freeway

Zoo Place

Tram Stop

Miniature Railroad

Carousel

Park Boulevard

Zoo Place

Globe Theatre

Spanish Village Art Center

Old Globe Way

San Diego Museum of Art

Botanical Building

San Diego Natural History Museum

Tram Stop

San Diego Museum of Man

Timken Museum of Art

The Prado

Village Place

Bea Evenson Fountain

Tram Stop

Cabrillo Bridge

El Prado

Plaza de Panama

House of Hospitality

San Diego Model Railroad Museum

Alcazar Garden

Mingei Int'l. Museum

San Diego History Center

Reuben H. Fleet Science Center

Gro Café

Inez Grant Parker Memorial Rose Garden & Desert Garden

163

Palm Canyon

Tea Pavillion

Japanese Friendship Garden

Museum of Photographic Arts

Spreckels Organ Pavilion

House of Pacific Relations

Marie Hitchcock Puppet Theater

Pan-American Plaza

Pan-Am West

Pan-Am East

San Diego Automotive Museum

San Diego Hall of Champions

Centro Cultural de La Raza

President's Way

San Diego Air & Space Museum

Tram Stop

Park Boulevard

Tram Stop

San Diego Freeway

5

TOP REASONS TO GO

San Diego Zoo: San Diego's best-loved attraction, the world-renowned zoo, is set amidst spectacular scenery in the heart of Balboa Park.

Museums galore: Automobiles and spacecraft, international folk art and Baroque masters, dinosaur fossils and mummified humans—there is something for everyone at Balboa Park's many museums.

The great outdoors: Escape down a hiking trail, try your hand at a new sport, or just soak in the sunshine from your own stretch of grass. You may even forget you are in the middle of the city.

Gorgeous gardens: From the lush tropical feel of the Botanical Building to the refined design of the Rose Garden, Balboa Park's intricate gardens and landscaping are sure to delight.

Free cultural events: The park is full of freebies, from weekly concerts at the organ pavilion to annual events like Earth Day and December Nights.

QUICK BITES

Quick snacking opportunities abound throughout the park, from cafés tucked in among the museums and grounds, to hot dog, tamale, or ice-cream carts along the walkways and plazas. Good bets include the sushi, noodles, and, of course, tea at the **Tea Pavilion** outside the Japanese Friendship Garden, or soups, sandwiches, vegetarian and organic fare, and espresso drinks at the **Gro Café**, inside the Casa de Balboa.

The Prado. Enjoy inventive cuisine in a gracious setting inside the House of Hospitality. An extensive lunch and dinner menu is offered in the dining room; casual bites are served in the bar. ☎ 619/557–9441 ☉ No dinner Mon.

GETTING HERE

Located just north of downtown, Balboa Park is easily reached from both Interstate 5 and Highway 163. The most spectacular approach is from 6th Avenue over the Cabrillo Bridge. There are also several entrances off Park Boulevard.

Balboa Park is served by public buses, particularly the No. 3, 7, and 120 lines. Taxis can sometimes be found inside the park close to the visitor center, and more often, lined up outside the zoo.

While Balboa Park as a whole is massive, many of its star attractions are located quite close to each other. That being said, exploring the park can lead to a lot of walking, particularly if you throw in a trip to the zoo or take on one of the many hiking trails. The park's free tram service stops at several spots around the park, and can give tired feet a welcome rest at the end of a long day.

VISITOR INFORMATION

House of Hospitality. The visitor center located here is an excellent resource for planning your visit to the park. Check the website before you go or spend a few minutes there when you arrive. There's usually a special event happening on the weekend, from festivals to fun runs. ⊠ 1549 El Prado, Balboa Park ☎ 619/239–0512 ⊕ www. balboapark.org ☉ Daily 9:30–4:30 (until 5 pm in summer).

Sightseeing
★★★★★
Nightlife
★☆☆☆☆
Dining
★★★☆☆
Lodging
☆☆☆☆☆
Shopping
★★★☆☆

Overlooking downtown and the Pacific Ocean, 1,200-acre Balboa Park is the cultural heart of San Diego. Ranked as one of the world's best parks by the Project for Public Spaces, it's also where you can find most of the city's museums, art galleries, the Tony Award–winning Old Globe Theatre, and the world-famous San Diego Zoo. Often referred to as the "Smithsonian of the West" for its concentration of museums, Balboa Park is also a series of botanical gardens, performance spaces, and outdoor playrooms endeared in the hearts of residents and visitors alike.

Updated by
Claire Deeks
van der Lee

Thanks to the "Mother of Balboa Park," Kate Sessions, who suggested hiring a landscape architect in 1889, wild and cultivated gardens are an integral part of the park, featuring 350 species of trees. What Balboa Park would have looked like had she left it alone can be seen at Florida Canyon (between the main park and Morley Field, along Park Boulevard)—an arid landscape of sagebrush, cactus, and a few small trees.

In addition, the captivating architecture of Balboa's buildings, fountains, and courtyards gives the park an enchanted feel. Historic buildings dating from San Diego's 1915 Panama–California International Exposition are strung along the park's main east–west thoroughfare, El Prado, which leads from 6th Avenue eastward over the Cabrillo Bridge (formerly the Laurel Street Bridge), the park's official gateway. If you're a cinema fan, many of the buildings may be familiar—Orson Welles used exteriors of several Balboa Park buildings to represent the Xanadu estate of Charles Foster Kane in his 1941 classic, *Citizen Kane*. Prominent among them was the California Building, whose 200-foot tower, housing a 100-carillon bell that tolls the hour, is El Prado's tallest structure. Missing from the black-and-white film, however, was the magnificent blue of its tiled dome shining in the sun.

The parkland across the Cabrillo Bridge, at the west end of El Prado, is set aside for picnics and athletics. Rollerbladers zip along Balboa Drive, which leads to the highest spot in the park, Marston Point, overlooking downtown. At the green beside the bridge, ladies and gents in all-white outfits meet regularly on summer afternoons for lawn-bowling tournaments—a throwback to an earlier era.

East of Plaza de Panama, El Prado becomes a pedestrian mall and ends at a footbridge that crosses over Park Boulevard, the park's main north–south thoroughfare, to the perfectly tended Rose Garden, which has more than 2,000 rosebushes. In the adjacent Desert Garden, trails wind around cacti and succulents from around the world. Palm Canyon, north of the Spreckels Organ Pavilion, has more than 50 varieties of palms along a shady bridge. Pepper Grove, along Park Boulevard south of the museums, has lots of picnic tables as well as play equipment.

San Diegans spend years exploring this local jewel. And even though you'll just be scratching the surface, a visit here is worth peeling yourself away from the beaches for at least one day. To visit San Diego and overlook Balboa Park would be to miss out on the city's most cherished treasure.

BALBOA PARK PLANNER

BEST TIMES TO VISIT

San Diego's ideal climate and sophisticated horticultural planning make visiting Balboa Park a year-round delight. However, summer brings longer opening hours, additional concerts at the Spreckels Organ Pavilion, and the beloved Shakespeare Festival at the Old Globe's outdoor stage.

OPEN HOURS

Most of the park's museums and attractions are open from 10 or 11 am until 4 or 5 pm, with the zoo opening earlier. Some offer extended hours during the summer. Many of the park's museums are closed on Monday. Balboa Park is beautiful by night, with the buildings along El Prado gorgeously illuminated. The Prado restaurant and the Old Globe Theatre keep this portion of the park from feeling deserted after dark.

PLANNING YOUR TIME

It's impossible to cover all Balboa Park's museums and attractions in one day, so choose your focus before you head out. If you plan on visiting the San Diego Zoo, expect to spend at least half the day there, leaving no more than a couple of hours to explore Balboa's other attractions afterward. ⇨ *See the highlighted listing for more information about the San Diego Zoo.* Otherwise, check out these itineraries.

Two Hours: To help maximize your time, rent one of the 60-minute audio headsets that guide you on a tour of the park's history, architecture, and horticulture. Pick a garden of interest to explore or drop down into Palm Canyon. Spend the remainder of your time relaxing in front of the Botanical Building or around the Bea Evenson Fountain.

Half Day: Spend a little more time at the sights above, then select a museum to explore. Alternatively, catch a puppet show at the Marie Hitchcock Theater. Afterward, you might have time for a quick ride on the carousel or a browse around the studios of Spanish Village Art Center. Cap things off with lunch in the Sculpture Court Café.

Full Day: Consider purchasing a one-day discount pass from the visitor center if you want to tackle several museums. Depending on when you visit, enjoy a free concert at the Spreckels Organ Pavilion, a cultural dance at the House of Pacific Relations International Cottages, or join a guided walking tour. Active types can hit one of the more intensive hiking trails, while others can rest their feet at an IMAX or 3-D movie in the Fleet Center or Natural History Museum, respectively. In the evening, dine at the beautiful Prado restaurant, or catch a show at the Old Globe Theatre.

WHAT'S FREE WHEN

Many freebies can be found in Balboa Park, both on a weekly basis and at special times of the year. Free **Ranger Tours** depart from the visitor center Tuesday and Sunday at 11 am providing an overview of the history, architecture, and horticulture of the park. On Saturday at 10 am, volunteers offer a rotating selection of thematic **Offshoot Tours,** also free of charge and departing from the visitor center. If you prefer to explore on your own, head to the visitor center to pick up a free garden tour map.

The free concerts at the **Spreckels Organ Pavilion** take place Sunday afternoons at 2 pm year-round and on Monday evenings in summer. Also at the Speckels Organ Pavilion, the **Twilight in the Park Summer Concert Series** offers various performances Tuesday, Wednesday, and Thursday from 6:15 to 7:15.

The **Timken Museum of Art** is always free (a donation is suggested), as is admission to the **House of Pacific Relations International Cottages,** although the latter are only open on Sunday. You can explore the studios at the **Spanish Village Art Center** at no charge, although you just might be tempted to purchase a unique souvenir.

A fantastic deal for residents of San Diego County and active-duty military and their families is **Free Tuesdays in the Park,** a rotating schedule of free admission to most of Balboa Park's museums.

The **San Diego Zoo** is free for kids under 12 the whole month of October.

The **December Nights** festival on the first Friday and Saturday of that month includes free admission (and later hours) to most of the Balboa Park museums. The outdoor events during the festival make it something not to miss.

DISCOUNT: PASSPORT TO BALBOA

The visitor center offers a selection of Passport to Balboa discount passes that are worth considering if you plan on visiting several museums. The Passport ($49 adult, $27 children ages 3–12) offers one-time admission to 14 museums and attractions over the course of seven days. If you are also planning on visiting the zoo, the Zoo/Passport Combo might be a good choice ($73 adult/$47 child). A single-day pass includes entry to your choice of 5 out of the 14 options ($39 adult).

TIPS

■ Hop aboard the free trams that run every 10–20 minutes, 8:30 am–6 pm daily, with extended summer hours.

■ Wear comfortable shoes—you'll end up walking more than you might expect. Bring a sweater or light jacket for the evening drop in temperature.

■ Don't be afraid to wander off the main drag. Discovering a hidden space of your own is one of the highlights of a trip to Balboa.

■ Balboa Park is a good bet for the odd rainy day—the museums are nice and dry, and many of the park's buildings are connected by covered walkways.

■ Make reservations for the Prado restaurant; it's popular with both visitors and locals alike.

■ If you aren't receiving the discount, consider avoiding participating museums on Free Tuesdays, as they can become overcrowded.

■ Don't overlook the 6th Avenue side of the park, between the Marston House and the Cabrillo Bridge. There are several pathways and open fields that make for a quiet escape.

PARKING

Parking within Balboa Park, including at the zoo, is free. From the Cabrillo Bridge, the first parking area you come to is off El Prado to the right. Don't despair if there are no spaces here; you'll see more lots as you continue along El Prado. Alternatively, you can park at Inspiration Point on the east side of the park, off Presidents Way. Free trams run from Inspiration Point to the visitor center and museums. Valet parking is available outside the House of Hospitality on weekends and on weekday evenings, except Monday.

EXPLORING BALBOA PARK

BALBOA PARK WALK

While Balboa Park as a whole is huge, many of its top attractions are located within reasonable walking distance. A straight shot across the **Cabrillo Bridge**, through the **Plaza de Panama**, and on to the **Bea Evenson Fountain** will take you past several of the park's architectural gems, including the **California Building, House of Charm**, and **House of Hospitality.** Many of the parks museums are housed in the buildings lining the way. This route also encompasses the **Alcazar Garden** and **Botanical Building.** From the fountain, a quick jaunt across the pedestrian footbridge leads you into the **Desert Garden** and **the Inez Grant Parker Memorial Rose Garden.** Back at the fountain, your walking tour can continue by heading north toward the **San Diego Zoo.** This will take you past the **Spanish Village Art, Carousel,** and **Miniature Railroad** en route. Alternatively, double back to the Plaza de Panama and head south toward the **Spreckels Organ Pavilion.** Continuing on from here, a loop will take you past **Palm Canyon,** the **International Cottages,** the **Marie Hitchcock Puppet Theater,** several more museums, and the **Japanese Friendship Garden.**

20 Things We Love to Do in Balboa Park

1. Be awestruck with each stroll over Cabrillo Bridge

2. Visit the pandas at the San Diego Zoo

3. Enjoy a picnic on the lawns of the Botanical Building

4. Stop and smell the roses in one of the gorgeous gardens

5. Listen to a concert at the Spreckels Organ Pavilion

6. Get cultured under the stars at the Old Globe's Shakespeare Festival

7. Reach for the brass ring while riding the Carousel

8. Escape the city on a hiking trail

9. Browse the studios at Spanish Village Art Center

10. Enjoy the lights and decorations at December Nights

11. Feel the eerie stillness of the park when the fog rolls in

12. Catch a world-premiere musical, with preshow dining at the Prado

13. Go for a run, either solo or in one of the many races at the park

14. Observe a refined game of lawn bowls

15. Play a game of "Name That Tune" as you listen to the chime of the Carillon Bells

16. Find something new—a hidden courtyard, a remote trail—with each visit

17. Watch a movie under the stars at Screen on the Green

18. Play a round of golf, either Frisbee or the traditional variety

19. Eat new foods and watch cultural performances at the Pacific Relations Cottages

20. People-watch at the Bea Evenson Fountain

While the above routes provide a broad overview, there are several walking opportunities for those seeking more focused explorations of the park. Those wishing to experience the numerous gardens in depth will appreciate the excellent "Gardens of Balboa Park Self-Guided Walk," available free of charge at the visitor center. History and architecture buffs might consider buying a self-guided walking tour pamphlet from the visitor center, or taking the briefer audio tour. Opportunities for hiking abound, from a brief journey through **Palm Canyon** to more strenuous hikes through **Florida Canyon** or on the **Old Bridle Trail**. Stop in the visitor center for maps and guidance before setting out.

TOP ATTRACTIONS

★ **Alcazar Garden.** The gardens surrounding the Alcazar Castle in Seville, Spain, inspired the landscaping here; you'll feel like royalty resting on the benches by the exquisitely tiled fountains. The flower beds are ever-changing horticultural exhibits featuring more than 7,000 annuals for a nearly perpetual bloom. A replica of a garden created in 1935 by San Diego architect Richard Requa, the garden is open year-round offering a changing color palette. ✉ *1439 El Prado, Balboa Park* ⊕ *www.balboapark.org.*

The lily pond outside the Botanical Building is a beautiful spot to take a break.

Bea Evenson Fountain. A favorite of barefoot children, this fountain shoots cool jets of water upward of 50 feet. Built in 1972 between the Fleet Center and Natural History Museum, the fountain offers plenty of room to sit and watch the crowds go by. ⊠ *East end of El Prado, Balboa Park* ⊕ *www.balboapark.org.*

Fodor's Choice
★

Botanical Building. The graceful redwood-lath structure, built for the 1915 Panama–California International Exposition, now houses more than 2,000 types of tropical and subtropical plants plus changing seasonal flower displays. Ceiling-high tree ferns shade fragile orchids and feathery bamboo. There are benches beside miniature waterfalls for resting in the shade. The rectangular pond outside, filled with lotuses and water lilies that bloom in spring and fall, is popular with photographers. ⊠ *1549 El Prado, Balboa Park* ☎ *619/239–0512* ⊕ *www.balboapark.org* ⊡ *Free* ☉ *Fri.–Wed. 10–4* ☉ *Closed Thurs.*

Cabrillo Bridge. The park's official (and pedestrian-friendly) gateway soars 120 feet above a canyon floor. Crossing the 1,500-foot bridge into the park provides awe-inspiring views of the California Tower and El Prado beyond. This is a great spot for a photo capturing a classic image of the park. ⊠ *On El Prado, at 6th Ave. park entrance, Balboa Park* ⊕ *www.balboapark.org.*

☺
★

Carousel. Suspended an arm's length away on this antique merry-go-round is the brass ring that could earn you an extra free ride (it's one of the few carousels in the world that continue this bonus tradition). Hand-carved in 1910, the carousel features colorful murals, big-band music, and bobbing animals including zebras, giraffes, and dragons; real horsehair was used for the tails. ⊠ *1889 Zoo Pl., behind zoo*

Balboa's Best Bets

CLOSE UP

With so much on offer, Balboa Park truly has something for everyone. Here are some best bets based on area of interest.

ARTS AFICIONADOS
Globe Theatre (⇨ *Nightlife and the Arts*)

Museum of Photographic Arts

San Diego Art Institute

San Diego Museum of Art

Spanish Village Art Center

Spreckels Organ Pavilion

Timken Museum of Art

ARCHITECTURE BUFFS
Bea Evenson Fountain

Cabrillo Bridge

California Building and Tower

Casa de Balboa

House of Charm

House of Hospitality

Cultural Explorers

House of Pacific Relations

Mingei International Museum

HISTORY JUNKIES
San Diego Museum of Man

San Diego History Center

NATURE LOVERS
Alcazar Garden

Botanical Building

Inez Grant Parker Memorial Rose Garden

Japanese Friendship Garden

Palm Canyon

SCIENCE AND TECHNOLOGY GEEKS
Reuben H. Fleet Science Center

San Diego Air and Space Museum

San Diego Automotive Museum

KIDS OF ALL AGES
Carousel

Marie Hitchcock Puppet Theater

Miniature Railroad

San Diego Hall of Champions

San Diego Model Railroad Museum

San Diego Zoo

---

parking lot, Balboa Park ☎ 619/239–0512 ⬚ $2.50 ☽ *Mid-June–Labor Day, 11–5:30 daily; Labor Day–mid-June, 11–5:30 weekends and school holidays.*

Fodor's Choice **Inez Grant Parker Memorial Rose Garden and Desert Garden.** These neighboring gardens sit just across the Park Boulevard pedestrian bridge and offer gorgeous views over Florida Canyon. The formal rose garden contains 2,500 roses representing nearly 200 varieties; peak bloom is usually in April and May. The adjacent Desert Garden provides a striking contrast, with 2.5 acres of succulents and desert plants seeming to blend into the landscape of the canyon below. ⬚ *2525 Park Blvd., Balboa Park* ⬚ *www.balboapark.org.*

Japanese Friendship Garden. A koi pond with a cascading waterfall, a tea pavilion, and a large activity center are highlights of the park's authentic

Japanese garden, designed to inspire contemplation and evoke tranquillity. You can wander the various peaceful paths and meditate in the traditional stone and Zen garden. The development of an additional 9 acres is well underway and will include a traditional teahouse and a cherry orchard. ⊠ *2215 Pan American Rd., Balboa Park* ☎ *619/232–2721* ⊕ *www. niwa.org* ✉ *$4* ☺ *Summer weekdays 10–5, weekends 10–4; rest of yr Tues.–Sun. 10–4.*

SHOPPING SPREE

Balboa Park is an excellent place to shop for unique souvenirs and gifts. In addition to the wonderful artwork for sale in Spanish Village, several museums and the visitor center have excellent stores. Of particular note are the shops at the Reuben Fleet Science Center, the Mingei Museum, the Museum of Art, the United Nations Association and, of course, the zoo.

Mingei International Museum. All ages can enjoy the Mingei's colorful and creative exhibits of folk art, featuring toys, pottery, textiles, costumes, jewelry, and curios from around the globe. Traveling and permanent exhibits in the high-ceilinged, light-filled museum include everything from antique American carousel horses to the latest in Japanese ceramics. The name "Mingei" comes from the Japanese words *min*, meaning "all people," and *gei*, meaning "art." Thus the museum's name describes what you'll find under its roof: "art of all people." The gift shop carries artwork from cultures around the world, from Zulu baskets to Turkish ceramics to Mexican objects, plus special items related to major exhibitions. ⊠ *House of Charm, 1439 El Prado, Balboa Park* ☎ *619/239–0003* ⊕ *www.mingei. org* ✉ *$8* ☺ *Tues.–Sun. 10–4.*

Palm Canyon. Heading down into this lush canyon near the House of Charm provides an instant escape into another landscape. More than 450 palms are planted in 2 acres, with a small hiking trail emerging by the Balboa Park Club. ⊠ *South of House of Charm, Balboa Park.*

☺ ★ **Reuben H. Fleet Science Center.** The center's interactive exhibits are artfully educational. Older kids can get hands-on with inventive projects in the Tinkering Studio, while Kid City entertains the 5-and-under set. The IMAX Dome Theater, which screens exhilarating nature and science films, was the world's first, as is the Fleet's new "NanoSeam" (seamless) dome ceiling that doubles as a planetarium. The Nierman Challenger Learning Center—a realistic mock mission-control and futuristic space station—is a big hit. ⊠ *1875 El Prado, Balboa Park* ☎ *619/238–1233* ⊕ *www.rhfleet.org* ✉ *Gallery exhibits $12, gallery exhibits and 1 IMAX film $16, or 2 IMAX films $22* ☺ *Opens daily at 10; closing hrs vary from 5 to 9, so call ahead.*

☺ ★ **San Diego Air and Space Museum.** By day, the streamlined edifice looks like any other structure in the park; at night, outlined in blue neon, the round building appears—appropriately enough—to be a landed UFO. Every available inch of space in the rotunda is filled with exhibits about aviation and aerospace pioneers, including examples of enemy planes from the world wars. In all, there are more than 60 full-size aircraft on the floor and hanging from the rafters. In addition to exhibits from the

CLOSE UP

From Undeveloped Mesa to Urban Oasis

Looking at the intricate designs of Balboa Park today, it is hard to imagine its humble beginnings as empty scrubland on the outskirts of town.

1868: City leaders designate 1,400 acres of undeveloped land above Alonzo Horton's New Town (now San Diego's downtown) as a public park, known then as "City Park."

1892: Horticulturalist and entrepreneur Kate Sessions negotiates with the city to plant 100 trees within the park each year in return for the use of a 32-acre parcel of parkland to house her nursery business. In accordance with the deal, Sessions, the "Mother of Balboa Park," begins to transform the scrub-filled mesa into the landscaped oasis it is today.

1910: A local contest renames the park "Balboa Park" after Vasco Nuñez de Balboa, a European explorer who claims the first sighting of the Pacific Ocean.

1915–16: Balboa Park hosts the Panama–California Exhibition, in honor of the Panama Canal's successful completion. Several buildings are constructed for the expo, including the Spreckels Organ Pavilion, and the Houses of Charm and Hospitality. The Cabrillo Bridge and El Prado walkway are laid out, and the park takes on much of its current character.

1935–36: Balboa Park welcomes another major fair, the California Pacific International Exhibition, during the Great Depression. The House of Pacific Relations International Cottages as well as several buildings designed by lead architect Richard Requa are added to the park.

---

dawn of flight to the jet age, the museum displays a growing number of space-age exhibits, including the actual *Apollo 9* command module. To test your own skills, you can ride in a two-seat Max Flight simulator or try out the F-35 interactive simulator. Movies at the new 3D/4D theater are included with admission. ⊠ *2001 Pan American Plaza, Balboa Park* ☎ *619/234–8291* ⊕ *www.sandiegoairandspace.org* 🎫 *Museum $17.50 (more for special exhibitions), Max Flight Simulator $8 extra, restoration tour $5 extra* ☉ *Daily 10–4:30, until 5:30 Memorial Day–Labor Day.*

★ **San Diego Museum of Art.** Known primarily for its Spanish Baroque and Renaissance paintings, including works by El Greco, Goya, Rubens, and van Ruisdael, San Diego's most comprehensive art museum also has strong holdings of South Asian art, Indian miniatures, and contemporary California paintings. An outdoor Sculpture Court and Garden exhibits both traditional and modern pieces. The museum's exhibits tend to have broad appeal, and if traveling shows from other cities come to town, you can expect to see them here. Free docent tours are offered throughout the day. If you become hungry, head to the **Sculpture Court Café by Giuseppe,** which serves artisan pizzas, gourmet salads and sandwiches, and grilled burgers and steak. ⊠ *1450 El Prado, Balboa Park* ☎ *619/232–7931* ⊕ *www.sdmart.org* 🎫 *$12* ☉ *Mon., Tues., and Thurs.–Sat. 10–5, Sun. noon–5, Fri. until 9 Memorial Day–Labor Day*

🔄 **San Diego Museum of Man.** If the facade of this building—the landmark California Building—looks familiar, it's because filmmaker Orson

DID YOU KNOW?

You can visit Spain without leaving San Diego: the Alcazar Garden was patterned after the Alcazar palace gardens in Seville. Just beyond, the 200-foot California Tower sits atop the Museum of Man.

Welles used it and its dramatic tower as the principal features of the Xanadu estate in his 1941 classic, *Citizen Kane*. Inside, exhibits at this highly respected anthropological museum focus on Southwestern, Mexican, and South American cultures. Carved monuments from the Mayan city of Quirigua in Guatemala, cast from the originals in 1914, are particularly impressive. Exhibits might include examples of intricate beadwork from across the Americas, the history of Egyptian mummies, or the lifestyles of the Kumeyaay peoples, Native Americans who live in the San Diego area. Especially cool for kids is the hands-on Children's Discovery Center. ⊠ *California Bldg., 1350 El Prado, Balboa Park* ☎ *619/239–2001* ⊕ *www.museumofman.org* ⊠ *$12.50* ۞ *Daily 10–4:30.*

> **HISTORY REVEALED**
>
> While demurely posing as a butterfly garden today, the history behind the Zoro Garden is far racier. Tucked between the Casa de Balboa and the Fleet Center, this area showcased a nudist colony during the 1935–36 Exposition.

☾ **San Diego Natural History Museum.** There are 7.5 million fossils, dinosaur models, and even live reptiles and other specimens under this roof. Favorite exhibits include the Foucault Pendulum, suspended on a 43-foot cable and designed to demonstrate the Earth's rotation, and *Ocean Oasis,* the world's first large-format film about Baja California and the Sea of Cortés. Regional environment exhibits are highlighted, and traveling exhibits also make a stop here. Included in admission are 3-D films shown at the museum's giant-screen theater. Call ahead for information about films, lectures, and free guided nature walks. ⊠ *1788 El Prado, Balboa Park* ☎ *619/232–3821* ⊕ *www.sdnhm.org* ⊠ *$17; extra for special exhibits* ۞ *Sun.–Fri. 10–5, Sat. 9–5.*

☾ **San Diego Zoo.**

Fodor'sChoice
★
⇨ *See the highlighted listing in this chapter.*

★ **Spanish Village Art Center.** More than 250 local artists, including glassblowers, enamel workers, woodcarvers, sculptors, painters, jewelers, and photographers rent space in these red tile–roof studio-galleries that were set up for the 1935–36 exposition in the style of an old Spanish village, and they give demonstrations of their work on a rotating basis. Spanish Village is a great source for memorable gifts. ⊠ *1770 Village Pl., Balboa Park* ☎ *619/233–9050* ⊕ *www.spanishvillageart.com* ⊠ *Free* ۞ *Daily 11–4.*

★ **Spreckels Organ Pavilion.** The 2,400-bench-seat pavilion, dedicated in 1915 by sugar magnates John D. and Adolph B. Spreckels, holds the 4,518-pipe Spreckels Organ, the largest outdoor pipe organ in the world. You can hear this impressive instrument at one of the year-round, free, 2 pm Sunday concerts, regularly performed by civic organist Carol Williams and guest artists—a highlight of a visit to Balboa Park. On Monday evenings from late June to mid-August, internationally renowned organists play evening concerts. At Christmastime the park's Christmas tree and life-size Nativity display turn the pavilion into a seasonal wonderland. ⊠ *2211 Pan American Rd., Balboa Park* ☎ *619/702–8138* ⊕ *www.sosorgan.org.*

Continued on page 62

Polar bear, San Diego Zoo

LIONS AND TIGERS AND PANDAS: The World-Famous San Diego Zoo

From cuddly pandas and diving polar bears to 6-ton elephants and swinging great apes, San Diego's most famous attraction has it all. Nearly 4,000 animals representing 800 species roam the 100-acre zoo in expertly crafted habitats that replicate the animals' natural environments. While the pandas get top billing, there are plenty of other cool creatures to see here, from teeny-tiny mantella frogs to two-story-tall giraffes. But it's not all just fun and games. Known for its exemplary conservation programs, the zoo educates visitors on how to go green and explains its efforts to protect endangered species.

SAN DIEGO ZOO TOP ATTRACTIONS

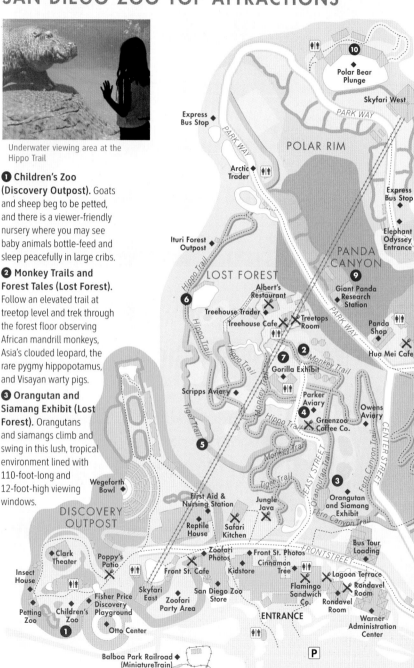

Underwater viewing area at the Hippo Trail

❶ Children's Zoo (Discovery Outpost). Goats and sheep beg to be petted, and there is a viewer-friendly nursery where you may see baby animals bottle-feed and sleep peacefully in large cribs.

❷ Monkey Trails and Forest Tales (Lost Forest). Follow an elevated trail at treetop level and trek through the forest floor observing African mandrill monkeys, Asia's clouded leopard, the rare pygmy hippopotamus, and Visayan warty pigs.

❸ Orangutan and Siamang Exhibit (Lost Forest). Orangutans and siamangs climb and swing in this lush, tropical environment lined with 110-foot-long and 12-foot-high viewing windows.

Polar Bear Plunge ❿

Skyfari West

PARK WAY

Express Bus Stop

PARK WAY

Arctic Trader

POLAR RIM

Express Bus Stop

Elephant Odyssey Entrance

Ituri Forest Outpost

PANDA CANYON

LOST FOREST

Albert's Restaurant

Giant Panda Research Station ❾

Hippo Trail

❻

Treehouse Trader

Treehouse Cafe

Treetops Room

Panda Shop

Hua Mei Cafe

PARK WAY

Hippo Trail

❼

Gorilla Exhibit

Monkey Trail

Scripps Aviary

Parker Aviary

Owens Aviary

Tiger Trail

❹

Greenzoo Coffee Co.

Hippo Trail

Monkey Trail

❺

Wegeforth Bowl

Monkey Trail

Tiger Trail

Orangutan Trail

EASY STREET

CENTER STREET

Fern Canyon Trail

❸ Orangutan and Siamang Exhibit

First Aid & Nursing Station

Jungle Java

DISCOVERY OUTPOST

Reptile House

Safari Kitchen

Bus Tour Loading

FRONT STREET

Clark Theater

Poppy's Patio

Zoofari Photos

Front St. Photos

Cinnamon Tree

Insect House

Front St. Cafe

Kidstore

Lagoon Terrace

Flamingo Sandwich Co.

Rondavel Room

Skyfari East

San Diego Zoo Store

Zoofari Party Area

Fisher Price Discovery Playground

Petting Zoo

Children's Zoo ❶

ENTRANCE

Rondavel Room

Warner Administration Center

Otto Center

Balboa Park Railroad (Miniature Train)

P

4 Scripps, Parker, and Owens Aviaries (Lost Forest). Wandering paths climb through the enclosed aviaries where brightly colored tropical birds swoop between branches inches from your face.

5 Tiger Trail (Lost Forest). The mist-shrouded trails of this simulated rainforest wind down a canyon. Tigers, Malayan tapirs, and Argus pheasants wander among the exotic trees and plants.

6 Hippo Trail (Lost Forest). Glimpse huge but surprisingly graceful hippos frolicking in the water through an underwater viewing

window and buffalo cavorting with monkeys on dry land.

7 Gorilla Exhibit (Lost Forest). The gorillas live in one of the zoo's bioclimatic zone exhibits modeled on their native habitat with waterfalls, climbing areas, and an open meadow. The sounds of the tropical rain forest emerge from a 144-speaker sound system that plays CDs recorded in Africa.

8 Sun Bear Forest (Asian Passage). Playful beasts claw apart the trees and shrubs that serve as a natural playground for climbing, jumping, and general merrymaking.

9 Giant Panda Research Station (Panda Canyon). An elevated pathway provides visitors with great access

Lories at Owen's Aviary

to the zoo's most famous residents in their side-by-side viewing areas. The adjacent discovery center features lots of information about these endangered animals and the zoo's efforts to protect them.

10 Polar Bear Plunge (Polar Rim). Watch polar bears take a chilly dive from the underwater viewing room. There are also Siberian reindeer, white foxes, and other Arctic creatures here. Kids can learn about the Arctic and climate change through interactive exhibits.

11 Elephant Odyssey. Get a glimpse of the animals that roamed Southern California 12,000 years ago and meet their living counterparts. The 7.5-acre, multispecies habitat features elephants, California condors, jaguars, and more.

12 Koala Exhibit (Outback). The San Diego Zoo houses the largest number of koalas outside Australia. Walk through the exhibit for photo ops of these marsupials from Down-Under curled up on their perches or dining on eucalyptus branches.

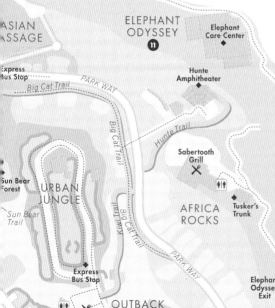

MUST-SEE ANIMALS

❶ GORILLA

This troop of primates engages visitors with their human-like expressions and behavior. The youngsters are sure to delight, especially when hitching a ride on mom's back. Up-close encounters might involve the gorillas using the glass partition as a backrest while peeling cabbage. By dusk the gorillas head inside to their sleeping quarters, so don't save this for your last stop.

❷ ELEPHANT

Asian and African elephants coexist at the San Diego Zoo. The larger African elephant is distinguished by its big flapping ears—shaped like the continent of Africa—which it uses to keep cool. An elephant's trunk has over 40,000 muscles in it—that's more than humans have in their whole body.

❸ GIANT PANDA

The San Diego Zoo is well-known for its giant panda research and conservation efforts, and has had five successful panda births. You'll likely see parents Bai Yun ("White Cloud") and Gao-Gao ("Big-Big") with their youngest baby Xiao Liwu ("little gift").

❹ KOALA

While this collection of critters is one of the cutest in the zoo, don't expect a lot of activity from the koala habitat. These guys spend most of their day curled up asleep in the branches of the eucalyptus tree—they can sleep up to 20 hours a day. Although eucalyptus leaves are poisonous to most animals, bacteria in koalas' stomachs allow them to break down the toxins.

❺ POLAR BEAR

The trio of polar bears is one of the San Diego Zoo's star attractions, and their brand-new exhibit gets you up close and personal. Visitors sometimes worry about polar bears living in the warm San Diego climate, but there is no cause for concern. The San Diego-based bears eat a lean diet, thus reducing their layer of blubber and helping them keep cool.

DID YOU KNOW?

Bamboo is the panda's dietary staple—they can consume 84 pounds of it a day—and the zoo grows 69 species of bamboo to ensure they have plenty of variety.

PLANNING YOUR DAY AT THE ZOO

Left: Main entrance of the San Diego Zoo. Right: Sunbear

PLANNING YOUR TIME

Plan to devote at least a half-day to exploring the zoo, but with so much to see it is easy to stay a full day or more.

If you're on a tight schedule, opt for the guided **35 minute bus tour** that lets you zip through three-quarters of the exhibits. However, lines to board the busses can be long, and you won't get as close to the animals.

Another option is to take the **Skyfari Aerial Tram** to the far end of the park, choose a route, and meander back to the entrance. The Skyfari trip gives a good overview of the zoo's layout and a spectacular view.

The **Elephant Odyssey**, while accessible from two sides of the park, is best entered from just below the Polar Rim. The extremely popular **Panda exhibit** can develop long lines, so get there early.

The zoo offers several entertaining **live shows** daily. Check the website or the back of the map handed out at the zoo entrance for the day's offerings and showtimes.

BEFORE YOU GO

■ To avoid ticket lines, purchase and print tickets online using the zoo's Web site.

■ To avoid excessive backtracking or a potential meltdown, plan your route along the zoo map before setting out. Try not to get too frustrated if you lose your way, as there are exciting exhibits around every turn and many paths intersect at several points.

■ The zoo offers a variety of program extras, including behind-the-scenes tours, backstage pass animal encounters, and sleepover events. Call in advance for pricing and reservations.

AT THE ZOO

■ Don't forget to explore at least some of the exhibits on foot—a favorite is the lush Tiger Trail.

■ If you visit on the weekend, find out when the Giraffe Experience is taking place. You can purchase leaf–eater biscuits to hand feed the giraffes!

■ Splurge a little at the gift shop: your purchases help support zoo programs.

■ The zoo rents strollers, wheelchairs, and lockers; it also has a first-aid office, a lost and found, and an ATM.

Fern Canyon, San Diego Zoo

GETTING HERE AND AROUND

The zoo is easy to get to, whether by bus or car.

Bus Travel: Take Bus No. 7 and exit at Park Boulevard and Zoo Place.

Car Travel: From Downtown, take Route 163 north through Balboa Park. Exit at Zoo/Museums (Richmond Street) and follow signs.

Several options help you get around the massive park: express buses loop through the zoo and the Skyfari Aerial Tram will take you from one end to the other. The zoo's topography is fairly hilly, but moving sidewalks lead up the slopes between some exhibits.

QUICK BITES

There is a wide variety of food available for purchase at the zoo from food carts to ethnic restaurants such as the Pan-Asian **Hua Mei Cafe.**

One of the best restaurants is **Albert's** ($), near the Gorilla exhibit, which features grilled fish, homemade pizza, and fresh pasta along with a full bar.

SERVICE INFORMATION

✉ 2920 Zoo Dr., Balboa Park

☎ 619/234–3153; 888/697–2632 Giant panda hotline

⊕ www.sandiegozoo.org

💲 $42 adult, $32 children (3-11) includes Skyfari and bus tour; 2-Visit Pass ($76 adult, $56 children age 3-11); zoo parking free

💳 AE, D, MC, V

🕐 July–Sept., daily 9–9; Oct.–June, daily 9–dusk. Hours may be extended for holidays and special events, and Children's Zoo and Skyfari ride may have reduced hours—check

SAN DIEGO ZOO SAFARI PARK

online or call for details.

About 45 minutes north of the zoo in Escondido, the 1,800-acre San Diego Zoo Safari Park is an extensive wildlife sanctuary where animals roam free—and guests can get close in escorted caravans and on backcountry trails. This park and the zoo operate under the auspices of the San Diego Zoo's nonprofit organization; joint tickets are available. ⇨ *See Chapter 15: North County and Environs for more information.*

Stairs lead down to the lush Palm Canyon, which has more than 58 species of palms.

WORTH NOTING

House of Pacific Relations. This is not really a house but a cluster of red tile–roof stucco cottages representing some 30 foreign countries. The word "pacific" refers to the goal of maintaining peace. The cottages, decorated with crafts and pictures, are open Sunday afternoons, when you can chat with transplanted natives and try out different ethnic foods. From the first Sunday in March through the last Sunday in October, folk-song and dance performances are presented on the outdoor stage around 2 pm—check the schedule at the park visitor center. Across the road from the cottages, but not affiliated with them, is the Spanish colonial–style **United Nations Building.** Inside, the United Nations Association's International Gift Shop, open daily, has reasonably priced crafts, cards, and books. ⊠ *2191 Pan American Pl., Balboa Park* ☏ *619/234–0739* ⊕ *www.sdhpr.org* ✉ *Free, donations accepted* ☉ *Sun. noon–4.*

☺ ★ **Marie Hitchcock Puppet Theater.** Performances incorporate marionettes, hand puppets, rod puppets, shadow puppets, and ventriloquism, while the stories range from traditional fairy tales to folk legends and contemporary puppet plays. Kids stare wide-eyed at the short, energy-filled productions. ⊠ *2130 Pan American Pl, Balboa Park* ☏ *619/544–9203* ⊕ *www.balboaparkpuppets.com* ✉ *$5* ☉ *Wed.–Sun., 1 or more shows each morning and afternoon.*

Marston House. George W. Marston (1850–1946), a San Diego pioneer and philanthropist who financed the architectural landscaping of Balboa Park—among his myriad other San Diego civic projects—lived in this 16-room home at the northwest edge of the park. Designed in

1905 by San Diego architects Irving Gill and William Hebbard, it's a classic example of the American Arts and Crafts style, which emphasizes simplicity and functionality of form. On the 5-acre grounds is a lovely English Romantic garden, as interpreted in California. The house may only be visited by guided tour. ⊠ *3525 7th Ave., Balboa Park* ☎ *619/298–3142* ⊕ *www.marstonhouse.org* ⊒ *$10* ⊙ *Thurs.– Mon. 10–4:30 in summer, Fri.–Mon. 10–4:30 in winter, guided tours every half-hr. Call for info about weekend specialty tours of gardens and historic 7th Ave.*

Miniature Railroad. Adjacent to the zoo parking lot and across from the carousel, a pint-size 48-passenger train runs a ½-mile loop through four tree-filled acres of the park. The engine of this rare 1948 model train is one of only 50 left in the world. ⊠ *2885 Zoo Pl., Balboa Park* ☎ *619/239–0512* ⊒ *$3* ⊙ *June–Aug., daily 11–6:30; Sept.–May, weekends and school holidays 11–4:30.*

Museum of Photographic Arts. World-renowned photographers such as Ansel Adams, Imogen Cunningham, Henri Cartier-Bresson, and Edward Weston are represented in the permanent collection, which includes everything from 19th-century daguerreotypes to contemporary photojournalism prints. The museum hosts excellent traveling exhibits, in addition to selections from their own collection. Photos rotate frequently so call ahead if you're interested in something specific. ⊠ *Casa de Balboa, 1649 El Prado, Balboa Park* ☎ *619/238–7559* ⊕ *www. mopa.org* ⊒ *$8* ⊙ *Tues.–Sun. 10–5; open til 9 Thurs. in summer.*

San Diego History Center. The San Diego Historical Society maintains its research library in the basement of the Casa de Balboa and organizes shows on the first floor. Permanent and rotating exhibits, which are often more lively than you might expect, survey local urban history after 1850, when California entered the Union. A 100-seat theater hosts public lectures, workshops, and educational programs, and a gift shop carries a good selection of books on local history as well as reproductions of old posters and other historical collectibles. ⊠ *Casa de Balboa, 1649 El Prado, Balboa Park* ☎ *619/232–6203* ⊕ *www.sandiegohistory. org* ⊒ *$6* ⊙ *Tues.–Sun. 10–5, open daily in summer.*

San Diego Automotive Museum. Even if you don't know a choke from a chassis, you're bound to admire the sleek designs of the autos in this impressive museum. On display are items from the museum's core collection of vintage motorcycles and cars, as well as a series of international rotating exhibits. *Back to the Future* fans will find a favorite in the 1981 silver Delorean. Even noncar buffs will love the *Fabulous Car of Louis Mattar*, which was ingeniously kitted out to set the cross-country endurance record in 1952 (6,320 miles nonstop from San Diego to New York City and back, refueling from a moving gas truck). A video display shows highlights such as Mattar and his co-drivers changing the tire while in motion and pouring a glass of water from the onboard tap. There's an ongoing automobile restoration program, and an extensive automotive research library. ⊠ *2080 Pan American Plaza, Balboa Park* ☎ *619/231–2886* ⊕ *www. sdautomuseum.org* ⊒ *$8* ⊙ *Daily 10–5.*

☼ **San Diego Hall of Champions.** In a 70,000-square-foot building, this museum celebrates local jock heroes as well as the Padres and Chargers sports teams with its collection of memorabilia, uniforms, paintings, photographs, and computer and video displays. In keeping with the progressive nature of the San Diego sports community, there are also skateboarding, surfing, and motorcross exhibits featuring local legends like Tony Hawk and Shaun White. ⊠ *Federal Bldg., 2131 Pan American Plaza, Balboa Park* ☎ *619/234–2544* ⊕ *www.sdhoc.com* ✆ *$8* ☽ *Daily 10–4:30.*

☼ **San Diego Model Railroad Museum.** When the impressive exhibits at this 27,000-square-foot museum are in operation, you can hear the sounds of chugging engines, screeching brakes, and shrill whistles. Local model railroad clubs built and maintain the four main displays, which represent California railroads in "miniature," with the track laid on scale models of San Diego County terrain. A Toy Train Gallery contains an interactive Lionel exhibit that includes a camera car hooked up to a TV set showing an engineer's-eye view of the layout. ⊠ *Casa de Balboa, 1649 El Prado, Balboa Park* ☎ *619/696–0199* ⊕ *www.sdmrm.org* ✆ *$8* ☽ *Tues.–Fri. 11–4, weekends 11–5.*

Timken Museum of Art. Though somewhat out of place architecturally, this small and modern structure, made of travertine imported from Italy, is a jewelbox. The museum houses works by major European and American artists as well as a superb collection of Russian icons. ⊠ *1500 El Prado, Balboa Park* ☎ *619/239–5548* ⊕ *www.timkenmuseum.org* ✆ *$5 suggested donation; Audio Tours $3* ☽ *Tues.–Sat. 10–4:30, Sun. 1:30–4:30.*

Old Town and Uptown

WORD OF MOUTH

"Another fun thing to do is to visit Old Town—and have some good Mexican food. One of the first missions founded in San Diego is also just above Old Town—the Father Junípero Serra Mission."

—Tomsd

GETTING ORIENTED

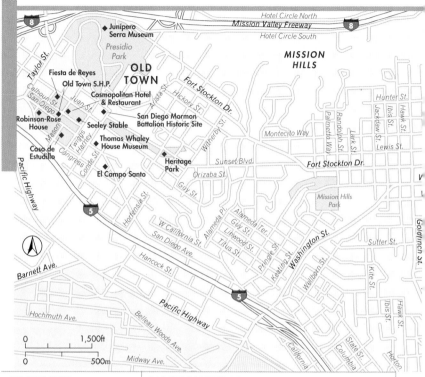

GETTING HERE

Old Town and Uptown are northwest and north of Balboa Park, respectively. Access to Old Town is easy thanks to the nearby Old Town Transit Center. Ten bus lines stop here, as do the San Diego Trolley and the Coaster commuter rail line. Two large parking lots linked to the Old Town Historic Park by an underground pedestrian walkway ease some of the parking congestion.

Uptown is best explored by car, although several bus routes do serve the area. Both metered street parking and pay-and-display lots are available.

TOP REASONS TO GO

Step back in time: Experience the early days of San Diego, from its beginnings as a remote military outpost and mission to the development of the first town plaza.

Architectural delights: Take an architectural journey through San Diego's history. Discover the pueblo- and clapboard-style structures of Old Town and the ornate Victorian gems in Heritage Park. Then head up the hill to view wonderfully preserved early-20th-century homes in Uptown.

Scare yourself silly: A nighttime visit to the Thomas Whaley House Museum, "the most haunted house in America," is sure to give you goose bumps.

Tortillas and margaritas: Enjoy the convivial atmosphere at one of the many Mexican eateries in Old Town.

Live like a local: Explore the vibrant shopping, dining, and nightlife of Uptown's unique neighborhoods.

PLANNING YOUR TIME

It takes about two hours to walk through Old Town. Try to time your visit to coincide with the free daily tours given by costumed park staff. They depart at 11 and 2 from the Robinson-Rose House Visitor Center and take about one hour. If you go to Presidio Park, definitely consider driving up the steep hill from Old Town.

The highlight of an Uptown tour is exploring the heart of Hillcrest, located at the intersection of University and 5th avenues. Plan to drive or catch a bus between neighborhoods, then explore on foot.

FESTIVALS

The Uptown neighborhoods host a variety of events throughout the year like free summer concerts at Trolley Barn Park. Hillcrest hosts the annual LGBT Pride event every July. In late summer, Cityfest rocks the neighborhood with live music, food stalls, and beer gardens. Old Town celebrates Cinco de Mayo and the Old Town Art Festival held in October.

QUICK BITES

Fiesta de Reyes snacks. If traveling back in time in Old Town has left you tired and hungry, Fiesta de Reyes has several options for a quick recharge. To the right when you enter from the plaza, La Panaderia serves sweet and savory empanadas as well as homemade *churros* (fried dough) and hot chocolate. Viva el Café, to the rear of the courtyard, has decadent desserts and specialty coffees. Between Friday and Sunday, the simple booth marked Street Tacos is good, too. ⊠ *4016 Wallace St., Old Town* ☎ *619/297–3100* ⊕ *www.fiestadereyes.com.*

Bread and Cie Café. Their delicious loaves are distributed around San Diego, but visitors to Hillcrest can go to the source. Pastries, soups, salads, sandwiches, and, of course, plenty of bread are served in a bustling atmosphere. Enjoy a cappuccino alfresco, or sit inside to watch the commotion from the open kitchen. ⊠ *350 University Ave., Hillcrest* ☎ *619/683–9322* ⊕ *www.breadandcie.com.*

Sightseeing
★★★★☆

Nightlife
★★★★☆

Dining
★★★★★

Lodging
★★☆☆☆

Shopping
★★★★☆

San Diego's Spanish and Mexican roots are most evident in Old Town and the surrounding hillside of Presidio Park. Visitors can experience settlement life in San Diego from Spanish and Mexican rule to the early days of U.S. statehood. Nearby Uptown is comprised of several smaller neighborhoods near downtown and around Balboa Park: the vibrant neighborhoods of Hillcrest, University Heights, and Mission Hills showcase their unique blend of historical charm and modern urban community.

OLD TOWN

Updated by
Claire Deeks
van der Lee

As the first European settlement in Southern California, **Old Town** began to develop in the 1820s. However, its true beginnings took place on a nearby hillside in 1769 with the establishment of a Spanish military outpost and the first of California's missions, San Diego de Alcalá. In 1774 the hilltop was declared a presidio reál, a fortress built by the Spanish empire, and the mission was relocated along the San Diego River. Over time, settlers moved down from the presidio to establish Old Town. A central plaza was laid out, surrounded by adobe and, later, wooden structures. San Diego became an incorporated U.S. city in 1850, with Old Town as its center. In the 1860s, however, the advent of Alonzo Horton's New Town to the southeast caused Old Town to wither. Efforts to preserve the area began early in the 20th century, and Old Town became a state historic park in 1968.

Today Old Town is a lively celebration of history and culture. The **Old Town San Diego State Historic Park** re-creates life during the early settlement, while San Diego Avenue buzzes with art galleries, gift shops, festive restaurants, and open-air stands selling inexpensive Mexican handicrafts.

TOP ATTRACTIONS

Fiesta de Reyes. North of San Diego's Old Town Plaza lies the area's unofficial center, built to represent a colonial Mexican plaza. This collection of shops and restaurants around a central courtyard in blossom with magenta bougainvillea, scarlet hibiscus, and other flowers in season reflect what it might have looked like in the early California days, from 1821 to 1872, complete with shops stocked with items reminiscent of that era. More than a dozen shops and restaurants line the plaza (Casa de Reyes is a great stop for a margarita and some chips and guacamole), and if you are lucky, you might catch a mariachi band or folklorico dance performance on the plaza stage—check the website for times and upcoming special events. ✉ *4016 Wallace St., Old Town* ☎ *619/297–3100* ⊕ *www. fiestadereyes.com* ⊙ *Shops 10–9 daily.*

Fodor'sChoice ★

WORD OF MOUTH

"Do plan on visiting Old Town (State Historic Park). Not for the shopping, but for the history. Great place to walk around, some good food, etc. This will give you a good overview of early history for this part of the country."
—sludick

Heritage Park. A number of San Diego's important Victorian buildings are the focus of this 7.8-acre park, up the Juan Street hill near Harney Street. The buildings, moved here and restored by Save Our Heritage Organization, include Southern California's first synagogue, a one-room Classical Revival structure built in 1889 for Congregation Beth Israel. The most interesting of the park's six former residences might be the Sherman-Gilbert House, which has a widow's walk and intricate carving on its decorative trim. It was built for real-estate dealer John Sherman in 1887 at the then-exorbitant cost of $20,000—indicating just how profitable the booming housing market could be. All the houses, some of which may seem surprisingly colorful, accurately represent the bright tones of the era. The synagogue and the Senlis Cottage are open to visitors daily from 9 to 5. The latter contains a small exhibit with information on the history and original locations of the houses. The McConaughy House hosts the Old Town Gift Emporium, a gift shop specializing in Victorian porcelain dolls (open Thursday–Tuesday 10–5). ✉ *2454 Heritage Park Row, Old Town* ☎ *858/565–3600* ⊕ *www.sdparks.org.*

Old Town San Diego State Historic Park. The six square blocks on the site of San Diego's original pueblo are the heart of Old Town. Most of the 20 historic buildings preserved or re-created by the park cluster around **Old Town Plaza,** bounded by Wallace Street on the west, Calhoun Street on the north, Mason Street on the east, and San Diego Avenue on the south. The plaza is a pleasant place to rest, plan your tour of the park, and watch passersby. San Diego Avenue is closed to vehicle traffic here.

Fodor'sChoice ★

Some of Old Town's buildings were destroyed in a fire in 1872, but after the site became a state historic park in 1968, reconstruction and restoration of the remaining structures began. Five of the original adobes are still intact. The tour pamphlet available at Robinson-Rose House gives details about all the historic houses on the plaza and in its vicinity; *a few of the more interesting ones are noted below.* Several reconstructed

4

Old Town celebrates Mexican culture with live music and entertainment at the Cinco de Mayo festival.

buildings serve as restaurants or as shops purveying wares reminiscent of those that might have been available in the original Old Town; **Racine & Laramie**, a painstakingly reproduced version of San Diego's first (1868) cigar store, is especially interesting. Free tours depart daily from the Robinson-Rose House at 11 and 2.

Casa de Estudillo. San Diego's first County Assessor, Jose Antonio Estudillo, built this home in 1827 in collaboration with his father, the commander of the San Diego Presidio, José Maria Estudillo. The largest and most elaborate of the original adobe homes, it was occupied by members of the Estudillo family until 1887. It was purchased and restored in 1910 by sugar magnate and developer John D. Spreckels, who advertised it in bold lettering on the side as "Ramona's Marriage Place." Spreckels's claim that the small chapel in the house was the site of the wedding in Helen Hunt Jackson's popular novel *Ramona* had no basis; that didn't stop people from coming to see it, however. ⊠ *4001 Mason St.*

Cosmopolitan Hotel and Restaurant. A Peruvian, Juan Bandini, built a hacienda on this site in 1829, and the house served as Old Town's social center during Mexican rule. Albert Seeley, a stagecoach entrepreneur, purchased the home in 1869, built a second story, and turned it into the Cosmopolitan Hotel, a way station for travelers on the daylong trip south from Los Angeles. It later served as a cannery before being revived (a few times over the years) as a hotel and restaurant. ⊠ *2660 Calhoun St.*

Robinson-Rose House. Facing Old Town Plaza, this was the original commercial center of Old San Diego, housing railroad offices, law offices, and the first newspaper press. Built in 1853 but in ruins at the end of the 19th century, it has been reconstructed and now serves as the park's visitor center. Inside are a model of Old Town as it looked in 1872, as well as various historic exhibits. Ghosts came with the rebuild, as the house is now considered haunted. Just behind the Robinson-Rose House is a replica of the Victorian-era Silvas-McCoy house, originally built in 1869. ✉ *4002 Wallace St.*

Seeley Stable. Next door to the Cosmopolitan Hotel, the stable became San Diego's stagecoach stop in 1867 and was the transportation hub of Old Town until 1887, when trains became the favored mode of travel. The stable houses horse-drawn vehicles, some so elaborate that you can see where the term "carriage trade" came from. Also inside are Western memorabilia, including an exhibit on the California vaquero, the original American cowboy, and a collection of Native American artifacts. ✉ *2630 Calhoun St.*

Also worth exploring: The San Diego Union Museum, Mason Street School, Wells Fargo History Museum, First San Diego Courthouse, Casa de Machado y Silvas Commercial Restaurant Museum, and the Casa de Machado y Stewart. Ask at the visitor center for locations. ✉ *Visitor Center (Robinson-Rose House), 4002 Wallace St., Old Town* ☎ *619/220–5422* ⊕ *www.parks.ca.gov* ✐ *Free* ☉ *Oct.–Apr., daily 10–4; May–Sept., daily 10–5; hrs may vary at individual sites.*

Presidio Park. The hillsides of the 50-acre green space overlooking Old Town from the north end of Taylor Street are popular with picnickers, and many couples have taken their wedding vows on the park's long stretches of lawn, some of the greenest in San Diego. The park offers a great ocean view from the top, and more than 2 miles of hiking trails below. It's a nice walk from Old Town to the summit if you're in good shape and wearing the right shoes—it should take about half an hour. You can also drive to the top of the park via Presidio Drive, off Taylor Street.

If you walk, look in at the **Presidio Hills Golf Course** on Mason Street. It has an unusual clubhouse that incorporates the ruins of Casa de Carrillo, the town's oldest adobe, constructed in 1820. At the end of Mason Street, veer left on Jackson Street to reach the **presidio ruins,** where adobe walls and a bastion have been built above the foundations of the original fortress and chapel. Also on-site is the 28-foot-high **Serra Cross,** built in 1913 out of brick tiles found in the ruins. Continuing up the hill, you will find the **Junípero Serra Musuem,** built at the sight of the original Mission San Diego de Alcalá and often mistaken for the Mission. Take Presidio Drive southeast and you'll come to the site of

---

AMERICA'S MOST HAUNTED

Built on a former gallows site in 1856, the Whaley House is one of 30 houses designated by the Department of Commerce to be haunted. Legend has it that the house is inhabited by seven spirits, making it the "most haunted house in America." Listen for the sound of heavy footsteps, said to belong to the ghost of Yankee Jim Robinson, a convict hanged on the site in 1852. Less ominous are sightings of the Whaley family's fox terrier scampering about the house.

4

Fort Stockton, built to protect Old Town and abandoned by the United States in 1848. Plaques and statues also commemorate the Mormon Battalion, which enlisted here to fight in the battle against Mexico. ⊠ *Taylor and Jackson Sts., Old Town* ⊕ *www.sdparks.org.*

★ **Thomas Whaley House Museum.** Thomas Whaley was a New York entrepreneur who came to California during the gold rush. He wanted to provide his East Coast wife with all the comforts of home, so in 1857 he had Southern California's first two-story brick structure built, making it the oldest double-story brick building on the West Coast. The house, which served as the county courthouse and government seat during the 1870s, stands in strong contrast to the Spanish-style adobe residences that surround the nearby historic plaza and marks an early stage of San Diego's "Americanization." A garden out back includes many varieties of prehybrid roses from before 1867. The place is perhaps most famed, however, for the ghosts that are said to inhabit it. Starting at 5 pm, admission is by guided tour offered every half hour with the last tour departing at 9:30 pm. The nighttime tours are geared more toward the supernatural aspects of the house than the daytime self-guided tour. ⊠ *2476 San Diego Ave., Old Town* ☎ *619/297–7511* ⊕ *www.whaleyhouse.org* ⌲ *$6 before 5 pm, $10 after 5* ◷ *Sept.–May, Sun.–Tues. 10–5, Thurs.–Sun. 10–9:30; June–Aug., daily 10–9:30* ◷ *Closed Wed. Sept.–May.*

WORTH NOTING

El Campo Santo cemetery. The old adobe-wall cemetery established in 1849 was, until 1880, the burial place for many members of Old Town's founding families—as well as for some gamblers and bandits who passed through town. Antonio Garra, a chief who led an uprising of the San Luis Rey Indians, was executed at El Campo Santo in front of the open grave he had been forced to dig for himself. These days the small cemetery is a peaceful stop for visitors to Old Town. Most of the markers give only approximations of where the people named on them are buried; some of the early settlers laid to rest at El Campo Santo actually reside under San Diego Avenue. ⊠ *North side of San Diego Ave. S, between Arista and Ampudia Sts., Old Town* ▭ *No credit cards.*

Junípero Serra Museum. The hill on which San Diego's original Spanish presidio (fortress) and California's first mission were perched is now the domain of a Spanish Mission–style museum established, along with Presidio Park, by department store magnate and philanthropist George Marston in 1929 to commemorate the history of the site from the time it was occupied by the Kumeyaay Indians through its Spanish, Mexican, and American periods. Artifacts include Kumeyaay baskets, Spanish riding gear, and an 18th-century cannon once used to protect Fort Guijarros down the hill in Old Town. The education room has hands-on stations where kids can grind acorns in metates (stones used for grinding grain), or dig for buried artifacts with archaeology tools. Ascend the tower to compare the view you'd have gotten before 1929 with the one you have today. The museum, now operated by the San Diego History Center, is at the north end of Presidio Park, near Taylor Street. ⊠ *2727 Presidio Dr., Old Town* ☎ *619/232–6203* ⊕ *www.sandiegohistory.org* ⌲ *$6* ◷ *Sept.–May, weekends 10–4; June–Aug., Fri.–Sun. 10–5; private tours on weekdays may be arranged in advance.*

CLOSE UP

California's Padre President

San Diego, the first European settlement in Southern California, was founded by Father Junípero Serra in July 1769. A member of the Franciscan order, Father Serra was part of a larger expedition chartered by King Charles III of Spain to travel north from Baja California and occupy the territory known as Alta California.

When they arrived in San Diego, the Spaniards found about 20,000 Kumeyaay Indians living in a hundred or so villages. The missionaries attempted to convert them to Christianity, and taught them agricultural and other skills so they could work what would become the missions' vast holdings.

Mission San Diego de Alcalá, established on a hillside above what is now Mission Valley, was the first of the 21 missions that the Franciscans built along the coast of California. After establishing the mission and presidio in San Diego, Serra and Portola moved on, founding the Mission San Carlos Borromeo and presidio at Monterey.

Father Serra, the padre president of California, established nine missions. Besides those at San Diego and Monterey, there were: San Antonio de Padua, 1771; San Gabriel, 1771; San Luis Obispo, 1772; Dolores, 1776; San Juan Capistrano, 1776; Santa Clara, 1777; and San Buenaventura, 1782. He personally oversaw the planning, construction, and staffing of each of these, and conferred the sacraments. His work took him from Carmel to locations up and down the length of California. It's estimated that during this period he walked more than 24,000 miles in visiting missions.

The missions comprised millions of acres and were in fact small self-sufficient cities with the church as the centerpiece. In addition to converting the Indians to Christianity and teaching them European ways, the padres managed farming, education, and industries such as candle making and tanning. San Diego is the southernmost mission, while the mission at Sonoma, San Francisco Solano, the last to be founded, in 1823, is the northernmost; each was established a day's walk—about 30 miles—from the previous one and was linked to El Camino Highway. The missions were the earliest form of lodging in the Golden State, known far and wide for their hospitality. You can trace the steps of Father Serra along El Camino Real by driving U.S. 101, the historic route that traverses coastal California.

Father Serra spent barely a year in San Diego before embarking on his journey to establish missions across California, but his presence left a lasting imprint. You can see some of the history at the Junípero Serra Museum and at Mission San Diego Alcalá.

—Bobbi Zane

San Diego Mormon Battalion Historic Site. Operated by the Church of Jesus Christ of Latter-day Saints, this engaging museum tells the story of the formation of the Mormon Battalion and their journey to San Diego. The battalion of just under 500 men left Council Bluffs, Iowa on July 20, 1846 for a grueling 6-month, roughly 2,000-mile infantry march during the Mexican-American war. Approximately 80 women and children accompanied the group. Upon their arrival in San Diego, members of the Battalion were involved in the development of Old Town. Opened in

early 2010 after a major remodel, the Mormon Battalion building features impressive set designs and multimedia exhibits. Guides in period costumes lead visitors through a series of rooms representing stages of the journey. Talking picture frames, and other interactive features keep things interesting. At the end of the tour, visitors can learn more about members of the

WORD OF MOUTH

"Hillcrest and Mission Hills are "Uptown" neighborhoods and older. I just like the way they feel. Houses look pretty nice and many are historic, like Craftsman and Spanish style."

—Cosmia

Battalion in the Research Room, or pan for gold out back. ⊠ *2510 Juan St., Old Town* ☎ *619/298–3317* ⊕ *www.oldtownsandiegoguide. com/2012/Mormon_battalion/* 🎟 *Free* ⊙ *Daily 9–9.*

HILLCREST

The large retro Hillcrest sign over the intersection of University and 5th avenues makes an excellent landmark at the epicenter of this vibrant section of Uptown. Strolling along University Avenue between 4th and 6th avenues from Washington Street to Robinson Avenue will reveal a mixture of retail shops and restaurants. National chains such as American Apparel and Pinkberry coexist with local boutiques, bookstores, bars, and coffee shops. A few blocks east, another interesting stretch of stores and restaurants runs along University Avenue to Normal Street. Long established as the center of San Diego's gay community, the neighborhood bustles both day and night with a mixed crowd of shoppers, diners, and partygoers. If you are visiting Hillcrest on Sunday between 9 and 2 be sure to explore the Hillcrest Farmers Market.

☾ ★ **Hillcrest Farmers Market.** One of San Diego's best farmers' markets, this weekly bazaar offers everything from vegan fruit pies and strawberry lemonade to homemade hummus and Turkish kabobs. A wide assortment of fresh produce and flowers are delivered straight from San Diego's farms. Several vendors dish up food to enjoy on the spot, making this an excellent choice for a quick lunch. ⊠ *3960 Normal St., between Blaine Ave. and Lincoln Ave., Hillcrest* ☎ *619/299–3330* ⊕ *www.hillcrestfarmersmarket.com* ⊙ *Sun. 9–2.*

Spruce Street Bridge. Constructed in 1912 by Edwin Capps, this 375-foot suspension bridge originally served as a passageway between isolated neighborhoods and trolley lines. Spanning across Kate Sessions Canyon (commonly referred to as Arroyo Canyon), today this wobbly bridge is considered one of San Diego's best-kept secrets, with its scenic and somewhat hair-raising stroll over treetops below. ⊠ *Spruce St. and 1st Ave., Hillcrest.*

MISSION HILLS

The route from Old Town to Hillcrest passes through the historic neighborhood of **Mission Hills** with its delightful examples of early-20th-century architecture. From the top of Presidio Park, take Presidio Drive into the heart of this residential area. A left on Arista Street and a right on Fort Stockton Drive takes you past wonderfully preserved Spanish Revival, Craftsman, and Prairie-style homes, to name a few. Many local residents fine-tune their green thumbs at the **Mission Hills Nursery** (✉ *1525 Ft. Stockton Dr.*), founded in 1910 by Kate Sessions, the "Mother of Balboa Park." Continuing on Fort Stockton Drive, a right on Goldfinch Street and a left on University Avenue will take you into the Hillcrest section of Uptown. For more information on this historic San Diego neighborhood, visit the Mission Hills Heritage Organization at ⊕ *www.missionhillsheritage.org.*

MISSION VALLEY

Although Mission Valley's charms may not be immediately apparent, it offers many conveniences to visitors and residents alike. One of the area's main attractions is the Fashion Valley mall, with its mix of high-end and mid-range retail stores and dining options, and movie theater. Mission Valley is also home to the San Diego Chargers stadium, and traffic is congested on game days and on most days during rush hour. Just beyond the stadium, the Mission Basilica San Diego de Alcalá provides a tranquil refuge from the surrounding suburban sprawl.

★ **Mission Basilica San Diego de Alcalá.** It's hard to imagine how remote California's earliest mission once must have been; these days, it's accessible by major freeways (I–15 and I–8) and by the San Diego Trolley. Mission San Diego de Alcalá, the first of a chain of 21 missions stretching northward along the coast, was established by Father Junípero Serra on Presidio Hill in 1769 and moved to this location in 1774. There was no greater security from enemy attack here: Padre Luis Jayme, California's first Christian martyr, was clubbed to death by the Kumeyaay Indians he was trying to convert in 1775. The present church is the fifth built on the site; it was reconstructed in 1931 following the outline of the 1813 church. It measures 150 feet long but only 35 feet wide because, without easy means of joining beams, the mission buildings were only as wide as the trees that served as their ceiling supports were tall. Father Jayme is buried in the sanctuary; a small museum named for him documents mission history and exhibits tools and artifacts from the early days. From the peaceful palm-bedecked gardens out back you can gaze at the 46-foot-high *campanario* (bell tower), the mission's most distinctive feature; one of its five bells was cast in 1802. ✉ *10818 San Diego Mission Rd., Mission Valley* ✚ *From I–8 east, exit and turn left on Mission Gorge Rd., turn left on Twain Rd. and mission will be on right* ☎ *619/281–8449* ⊕ *www.missionsandiego.com* 💳 *$3 suggested donation, $2 audio tour* ☾ *Daily 9–4:45.*

Gay-friendly Hillcrest is one of the hippest neighborhoods in San Diego.

UNIVERSITY HEIGHTS

Tucked between Hillcrest and North Park, this small but charming neighborhood is centered on Park Boulevard. The tree-lined street is home to several notable bars and restaurants, as well as the acclaimed LGBT Diversionary Theatre. Kids will love the playgrounds at Trolley Barn Park, just around the corner on Adams Avenue. The park is also home to free family concerts in the summer.

NORTH PARK

Named for its location north of Balboa Park, this evolving neighborhood is home to an exciting array of restaurants, bars, and shops. High-end condominiums and local merchants are often cleverly disguised behind historic signage from barbershops, bowling alleys, and theater marquees. The stretch of Ray Street near University Avenue is home to several small galleries, as well as the Ray at Night art walk, held the second Saturday of each month. Just around the corner on University Avenue lies the stunning 1920s-era Birch North Park Theatre, owned by the Lyric Opera San Diego. With a steady stream of new openings in the neighborhood, North Park is one of San Diego's top dining and nightlife destinations.

North Park Farmers' Market. Held rain or shine, this market features more than 40 vendors, locally grown produce, fresh flowers, arts and crafts, and an impressive selection of gourmet foods. ⊠ *Behind CVS, 3150 N. Park Way, North Park* ⊕ *www.northparkfarmersmarket.com* ⊙ *Thurs. 3–7.*

Mission Bay, Beaches, and SeaWorld

WORD OF MOUTH

"We got [to SeaWorld] for opening. Park was quiet and we got to ride Atlantis 3 times with no wait. My 3-year-old LOVED this ride. We got to 'pet' some lizards and check out some parrots. Then we just slowly meandered through the park . . . We had reservations for the 12:30 Dine with Shamu. The lunch was actually pretty good, and I really enjoyed the Shamu cookies."

—rizzo0904

GETTING ORIENTED

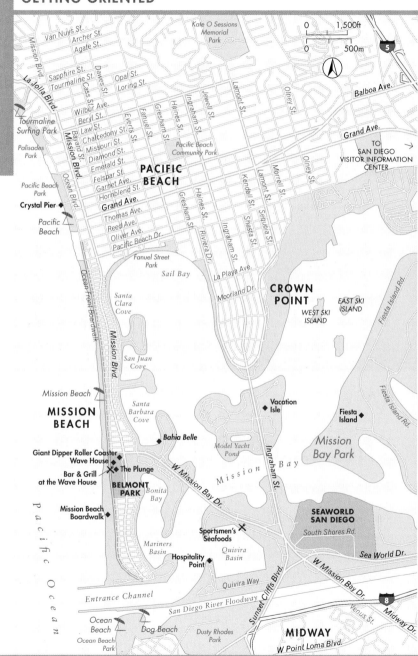

TOP REASONS TO GO

Sun and sand: With sand stretching as far as the eye can see, Mission and Pacific beaches represent the classic Southern California beach experience.

Bustling boardwalk: College kids partying at the bars, families grilling in front of their vacation homes, and kids playing in the sand—take in the scene with a stroll along the Mission Beach boardwalk.

Shamu mania: Even parents will find themselves falling in love with this charming orca whale at one of SeaWorld's spectacular shows.

Bayside delights: A quiet respite from the nearby beaches, Mission Bay is ringed with peaceful pathways, playgrounds, and parks.

Get out on the water: Catch a wave, paddle a kayak, or rev a Jet Ski at this irresistible water-sports playground.

QUICK BITES

Sportsmen's Sea Foods. This waterside eatery serves good fish-and-chips, seafood salads, and sandwiches to eat on the inelegant but scenic patio—by the marina, where sportfishing boats depart daily—or to take out to your chosen picnic spot. ✉ *1617 Quivira Rd., Mission Bay* ☎ *619/224–3551* ⊕ *www.sportsmensseafood.com.*

The Bar and Grill at the Wave House. This spot is a great place to grab a drink or meal while taking in the view of surfers on the nearby wave machine. ✉ *Mission Beach Boardwalk at Belmont Park, Mission Bay* ☎ *858/228–9304* ⊕ *www.wavehousesandiego.com.*

There is no shortage of dining options inside **SeaWorld**, from sandwiches at the **Seaport Market,** to Italian fare at **Mama Stella's Pizza Kitchen,** BBQ at the **Calypso Bay Smokehouse,** or baked goods at **Seaside Coffee and Bakery.**

GETTING HERE

SeaWorld, Mission Bay, and Mission and Pacific beaches are all served by public bus routes 8 and 9. Many local hotels offer shuttle service to and from SeaWorld. There is a free parking lot at Belmont Park, although it can quickly fill during busy times.

PLANNING YOUR TIME

You may not find a visit to SeaWorld fulfilling unless you spend at least half a day; a full day is recommended.

Belmont Park is open daily, but not all its rides are open year-round.

The Mission Beach Boardwalk and the miles of trails around Mission Bay are great for a leisurely bike ride. On foggy days, particularly in late spring or early summer, the beaches can be overcast in the morning with the fog burning off as the day wears on.

5

SEAWORLD SAN DIEGO

SeaWorld is best known as the home of beloved orca whale Shamu. One of the world's largest marine-life amusement parks, it continues to expand.

(above) Acrobatic dolphins perform at SeaWorld's Blue Horizons. (lower right) Shamu steals the show at One Ocean. (upper right) You can purchase food to feed the flamingos at Flamingo Cove.

The highlights are the large-arena entertainments and, with Shamu headlining, the signature show, **One Ocean,** brings down the house. **Blue Horizons** has dolphins, pilot whales, tropical birds, and aerialists together in a spectacular performance.

Most of the exhibits are walk-through marine environments such as **Shark Encounter,** where you come face-to-face with several species of sharks while passing through a 57-foot clear acrylic tube. **Wild Arctic** starts out with a simulated helicopter ride to the North Pole and features beluga whales, walruses, and polar bears.

The park also wows with its adventure rides like **Journey to Atlantis,** with a heart-stopping 60-foot plunge, and **Shipwreck Rapids,** where you careen down a river in an inner tube encountering waterfalls. SeaWorld's newest ride, **Manta,** is a thrilling coaster.

DISCOUNTS AND DEALS

The San Diego Zoo Combo Pass ($135 for adults, $105 for children ages 3 to 9) offers seven consecutive days of unlimited admission to SeaWorld, the San Diego Zoo, and the San Diego Safari Park. Look for SeaWorld specials at Mission Bay area hotels; some offer admission deals or free shuttle service to and from the park. Be sure to ask when you book.

SEAWORLD IN A DAY

The highlights of any visit to SeaWorld are the shows, so review the current performance schedule (available online or when you arrive at the park) and plan accordingly. Shows are fairly short—about 20 minutes—so you can see several.

SeaWorld is busiest in the middle of the day, so tackle the adventure rides either at the beginning or end of your visit. Coaster lovers will want to carve out time for the popular new **Manta** ride. Unless it's very hot, consider braving the soakers—**Journey to Atlantis, Shipwreck Rapids,** and sitting in the arenas' **Splash Zones**—in close secession, and then changing into dry clothes.

For an interactive experience, focus on the feeding stations and touch pools. The friendly bottlenose dolphins at **Dolphin Point** just might let you pet them while the hands-on **California Tide Pool** features San Diego's indigenous marine life. At the **Bat Ray Feeding** pool, the friendly rays pop up to the surface for snacks and a gentle pat on the head, while hungry sea lions await you at **Pacific Point.**

The standouts among the walk-through marine exhibits are the **Penguin** and **Shark Encounters, Turtle Reef,** and **Wild Arctic.** Those with tots 42 inches and under should head to the **Sesame Street Bay of Play.**

It's easy for your SeaWorld visit to become a very full day. Although saving either **One Ocean** or **Blue Horizons** for a finale can be great, if you get too tired you might end up missing a main attraction.

POPULAR ADD-ONS

The 30-minute **Dolphin Interaction Program** ($215) lets you feed, touch, and give behavior signals to bottlenose dolphins. A less expensive treat ($39 adults, $19 children) is the **Dine with Shamu** package, which includes a buffet lunch or dinner. The one-hour **Sea World Up Close Tour** ($16 adults, $14 children) takes you into backstage training areas.

TIPS

■ Pack a change of clothes for after the soaker rides and shows; you can rent lockers to stow belongings. And bring sunscreen and hats.

■ If you get your hand stamped when exiting the park, you can return later that same day.

■ Arrive at shows at least 30 minutes early to get front-row seats, and be prepared to get wet.

■ Steer kids to the **Under the Sun** gift shop, near the Calypso Smoke House, where all items are $10 or less.

■ Eating options include dining with Shamu next to the pool, or casual spots like the Seaside Coffee and Bakery or the Seaport Market.

SERVICE INFORMATION

✉ 500 SeaWorld Dr., near west end of I-8, Mission Bay ☎ 800/257-4268 ⊕ www.seaworld.com 🎟 $78 adults, $70 kids; parking $15 cars ⊙ Daily 10-dusk; extended hrs in summer.

Sightseeing
★★★★☆
Nightlife
★★★☆☆
Dining
★★☆☆☆
Lodging
★★★☆☆
Shopping
★☆☆☆☆

Mission Bay and the surrounding beaches are the aquatic playground of San Diego. The choice of activities available is astonishing, and the perfect weather makes you want to get out there and play. At the south end of the bay lies Sea-World, one of San Diego's most popular attractions. If you're craving downtime after all the activity, there are plenty of peaceful spots to relax and simply soak up the sunshine.

MISSION BAY

Mission Bay welcomes visitors with its protected waters and countless opportunities for fun. The 4,600-acre **Mission Bay Park** is the place for water sports like sailing, stand-up paddleboarding, and water-skiing. With 19 miles of beaches and grassy areas, it's also a great place for a picnic. And if you have kids, don't miss **SeaWorld**, one of San Diego's most popular attractions.

TOP ATTRACTIONS

Bahia Belle. At the dock of the Bahia Resort Hotel, on the eastern shores of West Mission Bay Drive, you can board this restored stern-wheeler for a sunset cruise of the bay and party until the wee hours. There's always music, mostly jazz, rock, and blues, and on Friday and Saturday nights the music is live. You can imbibe at the *Belle*'s full bar, which opens at 9:30 pm, but many revelers like to disembark at the Bahia's sister hotel, the Catamaran Resort, and have a few rounds before reboarding (the boat cruises between the two hotels, which co-own it, stopping to pick up passengers every half hour). Crusies after 9:30 pm are adults-only, but most cruises get a mixed crowd of families, couples, and singles. ⊠ *998 W. Mission Bay Dr., Mission Bay* ☎ *858/539–7779* ⊕ *www.sternwheelers.com/cruise* ⊠ *$10 for unlimited cruising; cruisers must be 21-plus after 9:30 pm; free for guests of Bahia and Catamaran hotels* ☉ *Sept.–Nov. and Feb.–May, Fri. and Sat. 6:30 pm–12:30 am, departures every hr on the ½ hr; June, Wed.–Sat.*

CLOSE UP

Planning a Day at the Beaches and Bay

A day spent at Mission Bay or the surrounding beaches can be as active or leisurely as you like.

If you want to play in the water, the bay is a great place to kayak, sail, or try some stand-up paddleboarding. If you're into surfing, be sure to check out the waves at **Crystal Pier** in Pacific Beach. A new kind of surfing experience is available at the **Wave House** at **Belmont Park**, where the Flow Rider lets you catch a continuous wave.

If you want to keep active on land, the Bayside Walk and Bike Path is a great place to jog or ride along the bay. Beach Cruiser bike rentals are widely available. For a more leisurely stroll and some people-watching, head to the **Mission Beach Boardwalk**. At the south end of Mission Beach try your hand at some typically Californian beach volleyball.

If you'd rather take it easy, just find a spot to lay out your towel anywhere along Mission or Pacific beach and soak up the sun. If you tire of the sand, enjoy a picnic at **Hospitality Point** or enjoy the view from one of the restaurants at Paradise Point Resort and Spa. As the day winds down, the happy-hour crowd is just heating up along Garnet Avenue in Pacific Beach. Alternatively, head to the Bahia Resort Hotel, where you can catch the **Bahia Belle** for a cruise around the bay.

If you are traveling with kids, a day at **SeaWorld** should be high on your list. There is plenty of family fun beyond SeaWorld, too. The protected beaches of the bay are popular spots for youngsters. The well-paved, peaceful Bayside Walk and Bike Path winds past picnic tables, grassy areas, and playgrounds, making it an ideal family spot. For a more lively contrast, cross the street to reach the Mission Beach Boardwalk, a classic boardwalk popular with young, hip surfers. At the south end lies **Belmont Park**, which includes an amusement park, the **Wave House**, and the **Giant Dipper** wooden roller coaster.

5

6:30 pm–12:30 am; July–Labor Day, daily 6:30 pm–12:30 am; closed Dec. yearly and Jan. in odd-numbered years.

★ **Belmont Park.** The once-abandoned amusement park between the bay and Mission Beach Boardwalk is now a shopping, dining, and recreation complex. Twinkling lights outline the **Giant Dipper,** an antique wooden roller coaster on which screaming thrill-seekers ride more than 2,600 feet of track and 13 hills (riders must be at least 4 feet, 2 inches tall). Created in 1925 and listed on the National Register of Historic Places, this is one of the few old-time roller coasters left in the United States. The **Plunge,** an indoor swimming pool, also opened in 1925, and was the largest—60 feet by 125 feet—saltwater pool in the world at the time (it's had freshwater since 1951). Johnny Weismuller and Esther Williams are among the stars who were captured on celluloid swimming here. Other Belmont Park attractions include a video arcade, a submarine ride, bumper cars, a tilt-a-whirl, and an antique carousel. The rock wall challenges both junior climbers and their elders. Belmont Park also has the most consistent wave in the county at the

Wave House, where the FlowRider provides surfers and bodyboarders a near-perfect simulated wave on which to practice their skills. ✉ *3146 Mission Blvd., Mission Bay* ☎ *858/488–1549 for rides, 858/228–9300 for pool* ⊕ *www.belmontpark.com* ✉ *Unlimited ride day package $27 for 48" and over, $16 for under 48"; pool $7; pool and fitness center $15* ☉ *Park opens at 11 daily, ride operation varies seasonally; pool open weekdays noon–4 and 8–10, weekends noon–8.*

★ **Mission Bay Park.** Mission Bay Park is San Diego's monument to sports and fitness. This 4,600-acre aquatic park has 27 miles of shoreline including 19 miles of sandy beaches. Playgrounds and picnic areas abound on the beaches and low grassy hills. On weekday evenings, joggers, bikers, and skaters take over. In the daytime, swimmers, water-skiers, windsurfers, anglers, and boaters—some in single-person kayaks, others in crowded powerboats—vie for space in the water. ✉ *2688 E. Mission Bay Dr., off I–5 at Exit 22 E. Mission Bay Dr., Mission Bay* ☎ *858/581–7602 park ranger's office* ⊕ *www.sandiego.gov/park-and-recreation/parks/missionbay* ✉ *Free.*

Mission Beach Boardwalk. The cement pathway lining the sand from the southern end of Mission Beach north to Pacific Beach is always bustling with activity. Cyclists ping the bells on their beach cruisers to pass walkers out for a stroll alongside the oceanfront homes. Vacationers kick back on their patios, while friends play volleyball in the sand. The activity picks up alongside Belmont Park and the Wavehouse, where people stop to check out the action on the FlowRider wave. ✉ *Alongside sand from Mission Beach Park to Pacific Beach, Mission Beach.*

🕓 **SeaWorld San Diego.**

Fodor's Choice
★   ⇨ *See the highlighted listing in this chapter.*

Vacation Isle. Ingraham Street bisects this island, providing two distinct experiences for visitors. The west side is taken up by the Paradise Point Resort & Spa, but you don't have to be a guest to enjoy the hotel's lushly landscaped grounds and bay-front restaurants. Boaters and jet-skiers congregate near the launch at **Ski Beach** on the east side of the island, where there's a parking lot as well as picnic areas and restrooms. Ski Beach is the site of the annual Bayfair (formerly called the Thunderboat Regatta), held in September. At the model yacht pond on the south side of the island, children and young-at-heart adults take part year-round in motorized miniature boat races. ✉ *Mission Bay.*

WORTH NOTING

Fiesta Island. The most undeveloped area of Mission Bay Park, this is popular with bird-watchers (there's a large protected nesting site for the California tern at the northern tip of the island) as well as with dog owners—it's the only place in the park where pets can run free. At Christmas the island provides an excellent vantage point for viewing the bay's Parade of Lights. In July the annual Over-the-Line Tournament, a competition involving a unique local version of softball, attracts thousands of players and oglers. ✉ *Access from East Mission Bay Dr., Mission Bay.*

DID YOU KNOW?

San Diego has 70 miles of coastline perfect for the time-honored tradition of building sandcastles. All you need is a pail, a shovel, and a little imagination.

Hospitality Point. Enjoy lunch in this pretty, secluded spot, which has a view of sailboats and yachts entering the open sea. At the entrance to Hospitality Point, the City of San Diego Mission Bay Park and Recreation Department office supplies area maps and other recreational information. ⊠ *2500 Quivira Ct., Mission Bay* ☎ *619/525–8213* ⊕ *www.sandiego.gov/park-and-recreation/parks/missionbay* ☉ *Weekdays 8–4:30.*

> **MISSION BAY WARNING**
>
> Swimmers at Mission Bay should note signs warning about water pollution; on occasions when heavy rains or other events cause pollution, swimming is strongly discouraged.

MISSION BEACH

Heading west on Mission Bay Drive to the ocean, the Giant Dipper roller coaster rises into view welcoming visitors to the **Belmont Park** amusement park and to **Mission Beach.** Mission Boulevard runs north along a two block–wide strip embraced by the Pacific Ocean on the west and the bay on the east. Mission Beach is a famous and lively fun zone for families and young people both; if it isn't party time at the moment, it will be five minutes from now. The pathways in this area are lined with vacation homes, many for rent by the week or month. Those fortunate enough to live here year-round have the bay as their front yard, with wide sandy beaches, volleyball courts, and—less of an advantage—an endless stream of sightseers on the sidewalk.

PACIFIC BEACH

North of Mission Beach is the college-packed party town of **Pacific Beach,** or "PB" as locals call it. The laid-back vibe of this surfer's mecca draws in free-spirited locals who roam the streets on skateboards and beach cruisers, in the local uniform of board shorts, bikinis, and baseball caps. Lining the main strip of Grand and Garnet avenues are tattoo parlors, smoke shops, vintage stores, and coffeehouses. The energy level peaks during happy hour, when PB's cluster of nightclubs, bars, and 150 restaurants open their doors to those ready to party.

TOP ATTRACTIONS

Crystal Pier. Stretching out into the ocean from the end of Garnet Avenue, Crystal Pier is Pacific Beach's landmark. A stroll to the end of the pier reveals fishermen hoping for a good catch, while surfers make catches of their own in the waves below. ⊠ *At end of Garnet Ave., Pacific Beach.*

6

La Jolla

WITH NORTHERN SAN DIEGO: CLAIREMONT AND KEARNY MESA

WORD OF MOUTH

"The Cove at La Jolla . . . reminds one of the South of France. From there you can easily wander around the very cute/upscale village of La Jolla."

—Tomsd

GETTING ORIENTED

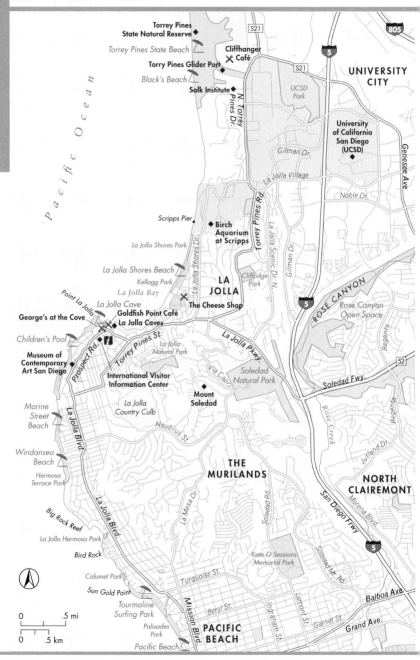

TOP REASONS TO GO

Promenade above the cove: The winding pathways above La Jolla Cove offer stunning views of the surf and sea lions below.

Shop 'til you drop: La Jolla's chic boutiques and galleries are San Diego's answer to Rodeo Drive. You may even spot a celebrity as you browse on Prospect Street and Girard Avenue.

Aquatic adventures: Hop in a kayak or strap on scuba gear to explore La Jolla's marine preserve.

Luxe living: Experience the good life at top-notch spas and restaurants. Or just gawk at multimillion-dollar mansions and their denizens running errands in Ferraris.

Torrey Pines State Beach and Reserve: Play the links, hike the trails, relax on the beach, or hang glide off the cliffs.

QUICK BITES

The Cheese Shop. Located in the heart of La Jolla Shores, this is a great place to grab a quick lunch or picnic provisions for the beach. The sandwiches are excellent, and kids will love the fresh-baked cookies and old-time candy selection. ⊠ 2165 Av. de la Playa, La Jolla ☎ 858/459–3921 ⊕ www.cheeseshoplajolla.com.

Goldfish Point Café. If you are looking for a casual breakfast or lunch overlooking La Jolla Cove, the Goldfish Point Café is sure to hit the spot without breaking the bank. ⊠ 1255 Coast Blvd., La Jolla ☎ 858/459–7407 ⊕ www.goldfishpointcafe.com.

George's at the Cove. This restaurant complex may be one of the best-known spots in La Jolla for its incredible views of La Jolla Cove. The main restaurant, **George's California Modern,** is an upscale affair; **Ocean Terrace** is a great for a casual meal. ⊠ 1250 Prospect St., La Jolla ☎ 858/454–4244 ⊕ www.georgesatthecove.com.

GETTING HERE

If you enjoy meandering, the best way to approach La Jolla from the south is to drive on Mission Boulevard through Mission and Pacific beaches, past the crowds of in-line skaters, bicyclists, and sunbathers. The congestion eases up as the street becomes La Jolla Boulevard. Road signs along La Jolla Boulevard and Camino de la Costa direct drivers and bicyclists past homes designed by respected architects such as Irving Gill. As you approach the village, La Jolla Boulevard turns into Prospect Street.

PLANNING YOUR TIME

La Jolla's highlights can be seen in a few hours with a visit to La Jolla Village and the cove followed by a scenic drive along the coast and up through Torrey Pines.

The village and La Jolla Cove are easily explored on foot, but it's a steep walk between the two. Parking can be tough, so don't hold out for a better spot. Greater La Jolla is best explored by car or bus route 30.

VISITOR INFORMATION

International Visitor Information Center. La Jolla branch of the International Visitor Information Center is a great resource for information and coupons. ⊠ 7966 Herschel Ave, Herschel at Prospect St., La Jolla ☎ 619/236–1212 ⊕ www.sandiego.org ⏱ Hrs vary by season, generally 11–4.

6

Sightseeing
★★★★☆
Nightlife
★★☆☆☆
Dining
★★★★☆
Lodging
★★★☆☆
Shopping
★★★★☆

La Jollans have long considered their village to be the Monte Carlo of California, and with good cause. Its coastline curves into natural coves backed by verdant hillsides covered with homes worth millions. La Jolla is both a natural and cultural treasure trove. The upscale shops, galleries, and restaurants of La Jolla Village satisfy the glitterati, while secluded trails, scenic overlooks, and abundant marine life provide balance and refuge.

Updated by
Claire Deeks
van der Lee

Although **La Jolla** is a neighborhood of the city of San Diego, it has its own postal zone and a coveted sense of class; the ultrarich from around the globe own second homes here—the seaside zone between the neighborhood's bustling downtown and the cliffs above the Pacific has a distinctly European flavor—and old-money residents maintain friendships with the visiting film stars and royalty who frequent the area's exclusive luxury hotels and private clubs. Development and construction have radically altered the once serene and private character of the village, but it has gained a cosmopolitan air that makes it a popular vacation resort.

The Native Americans called the site La Hoya, meaning "the cave," referring to the grottoes that dot the shoreline. The Spaniards changed the name to La Jolla (same pronunciation as La Hoya), "the jewel," and its residents have cherished the name and its allusions ever since.

Prospect Street and Girard Avenue, the village's main drags, are lined with expensive shops and office buildings. Through the years the shopping and dining district has spread to Pearl and other side streets.

East of La Jolla and well off the tourist trail, the inland neighborhoods of Clairemont and Kearny Mesa are the center of San Diego's Asian population and offer many interesting restaurants and specialty stores.

TOP ATTRACTIONS

Birch Aquarium at Scripps. Affiliated with the world-renowned Scripps Institution of Oceanography, this excellent aquarium sits at the end of a signposted drive leading off North Torrey Pines Road and has

MUSEUM OF CONTEMPORARY ART SAN DIEGO

✉ *700 Prospect St.,*
La Jolla ☏ *858/454–3541*
⊕ *www.mcasd.org* 🎫 *$10,*
good for one visit here and
at MCASD downtown within 7
days; free 3rd Thurs. of month
5–7 ◷ *Thurs.–Tues. 11–5;*
3rd Thurs. of month 11–7
◷ *Closed Wed.*

TIPS

■ Be sure to also check out MCASD's downtown branch; admission is good for seven days and valid at both locations. See Chapter 2: Downtown for MCASD's downtown branch.

■ Get in free the third Thursday of every month from 5 to 7.

■ Informative and insightful exhibit tours are offered free on weekends at 2, and on the third Thursday of the month at 6.

■ Head to the museum's X Store for unique cards and gifts.

■ The pleasant courtyard at the museum café is a great spot to relax and recharge.

Driving along Coast Boulevard, it is hard to miss the mass of watercraft jutting out from the rear of the Museum of Contemporary Art San Diego (MCASD) La Jolla location. *Pleasure Point* by Nancy Rubins is just one example of the mingling of art and locale at this spectacular oceanfront setting.

Highlights

The oldest section of La Jolla's branch of San Diego's contemporary art museum was originally a residence, designed by Irving Gill for philanthropist Ellen Browning Scripps in 1916. In the mid-1990s the compound was updated and expanded by architect Robert Venturi, who respected Gill's original geometric structure and clean Mission-style lines while adding his own distinctive touches. The result is a striking contemporary building that looks as though it's always been here.

The light-filled Axline Court serves as the museum's entrance and does triple duty as reception area, exhibition hall, and forum for special events, including the glittering Monte Carlo gala each September, attended by the town's most fashionable folk. Inside, the museum's artwork gets major competition from the setting: you can look out from the top of a grand stairway onto a landscaped garden that contains permanent and temporary sculpture exhibits as well as rare 100-year-old California plant specimens and, beyond that, to the Pacific Ocean.

California artists figure prominently in the museum's permanent collection of post-1950s art, but the museum also includes examples of every major art movement through the present—works by Andy Warhol, Robert Rauschenberg, Frank Stella, Joseph Cornell, and Jenny Holzer, to name a few. Important pieces by artists from San Diego and Tijuana were acquired in the 1990s. The museum also gets major visiting shows.

6

DID YOU KNOW?

Goldfish Point in La Jolla is named after the garibaldi damselfish, which resemble goldfish, found in these waters. The garibaldi is California's official marine fish.

sweeping views of the La Jolla coast below. More than 60 tanks are filled with colorful saltwater fish, and a 70,000-gallon tank simulates a La Jolla kelp forest. A special exhibit on sea horses features several examples of the species, plus mesmerizing sea dragons and a sea horse nursery. Besides the fish themselves, attractions include a gallery based on the institution's ocean-related research, and interactive educational exhibits on a variety of environmental issues. ✉ *2300 Expedition Way, La Jolla* 🕾 *858/534–3474* ⊕ *www.aquarium.ucsd.edu* 🖅 *$14* ⊙ *Daily 9–5; last entry at 4:30.*

LA JOLLA

☺ **La Jolla Caves.** It's a walk of 145 sometimes slippery steps down a tunnel to Sunny Jim, the largest of the caves in La Jolla Cove and the only one reachable by land. This is a one-of-a-kind local attraction, and worth the time if you have a day or two to really enjoy La Jolla. The man-made tunnel took two years to dig, beginning in 1902; later, a shop was built at its entrance. Today the Sunny Jim Cave Store, a throwback to that early shop, is still the entrance to the cave. The shop sells jewelry and watercolors by local artists. ✉ *1325 Coast Blvd. S, La Jolla* 🕾 *858/459–0746* ⊕ *www.cavestore.com* 🖅 *$4* ⊙ *Daily 10–5.*

Fodor's Choice **Museum of Contemporary Art San Diego (MCASD).**
★ ⇨ *See the highlighted listing in this chapter.*

Fodor's Choice **Torrey Pines State Natural Reserve.** *Pinus torreyana*, the rarest native pine
★ tree in the United States, enjoys a 1,700-acre sanctuary at the northern edge of La Jolla, and about 6,000 of these unusual trees, some as tall as 60 feet, grow on the cliffs here. The park is one of only two places in the world (the other is Santa Rosa Island, off Santa Barbara) where the Torrey pine grows naturally. The reserve has several hiking trails leading to the cliffs, 300 feet above the ocean; trail maps are available at the park station. Wildflowers grow profusely in spring, and the ocean panoramas are always spectacular. At Torrey Pines State Beach, just below the reserve, it's possible to walk south all the way past the lifeguard towers to Black's Beach when the tide is out, over rocky promontories carved by the waves (avoid the bluffs, however; they're unstable). **Los Peñasquitos Lagoon** at the north end of the reserve is one of the many natural estuaries that flow inland between Del Mar and Oceanside. It's a good place to watch shorebirds. Volunteers lead guided nature walks at 10 and 2 on most weekends. ✉ *N. Torrey Pines Rd. exit off I–5 onto Carmel Valley Rd. going west, then turn left (south) on Coast Hwy. 101, 12600 N. Torrey Pines Rd., La Jolla* 🕾 *858/755–2063* ⊕ *www. torreypine.org* 🖅 *Parking $10–$15* ⊙ *Daily 9–dusk.*

University of California at San Diego. The campus of one of the country's most prestigious research universities spreads over 1,200 acres of coastal canyons and eucalyptus groves. If you're interested in contemporary art, check out the **Stuart Collection of Sculpture**—18 thought-provoking, site-specific works by artists such as Nam June Paik, William Wegman, Niki de St. Phalle, Jenny Holzer, and others arrayed around the campus. UCSD's **Price Center** has a well-stocked, two-level bookstore—the largest in San Diego—and a good coffeehouse, Perks. Look for

6

the postmodern **Geisel Library**, named for longtime La Jolla residents Theodor "Dr. Seuss" Geisel and his wife, Audrey. For campus culture, vegan dishes, and live music, head to the **Che Café** located in Building 161, painted in bright murals. Bring quarters for the parking meters, or cash or a credit card for the parking structures, since free parking is only available on weekends. ⊠ *Exit I–5 onto La Jolla Village Dr. going west; take Gilman Dr. off-ramp to right and continue to information kiosk at campus entrance on Gilman Dr., La Jolla* 🕾 *858/534-4414 campus tour information* ⊕ *www.ucsd.edu* ⊗ *90-min campus tours Sun. at 2 from South Gilman Information Pavilion; reserve before noon Thurs.*

WORTH NOTING

Mount Soledad. La Jolla's highest spot can be reached by taking Nautilus Street to La Jolla Scenic Drive South, and then turning left. Proceed a few blocks to the park, where parking is plentiful and the views are astounding, unless the day is hazy. The top of the mountain is an excellent vantage point from which to get a sense of San Diego's geography: looking down from here you can see the coast from the county's northern border to the south far beyond downtown. ⊠ *6905 La Jolla Scenic Dr. S, La Jolla.*

Salk Institute. The world-famous biological-research facility founded by polio vaccine developer Jonas Salk sits on 27 clifftop acres. The twin structures that modernist architect Louis I. Kahn designed in the 1960s in consultation with Dr. Salk used poured concrete and other low-maintenance materials to clever effect. The thrust of the laboratory–office complex is outward toward the Pacific Ocean, an orientation accentuated by a foot-wide "Stream of Life" that flows through the center of a travertine marble courtyard between the buildings. Architects-to-be and building buffs enjoy the free tours of the property; register online two days in advance. You can, however, stroll at will through the dramatic courtyard—simultaneously monumental and eerie. ⊠ *10010 N. Torrey Pines Rd., La Jolla* 🕾 *858/453-4100* ⊕ *www.salk.edu* ⊠ *Free* ⊗ *Grounds open weekdays 8:30–5; architectural tours weekdays at noon (reservations required 2 business days in advance; see website for details).*

NORTHERN SAN DIEGO: CLAIREMONT AND KEARNY MESA

Located inland from La Jolla and north of Mission Valley, the neighborhoods of Clairemont and Kearny Mesa often fly under the radar of most visitors to San Diego. The shopping centers and restaurants of this area serve as a hub for San Diego's sizeable and diverse Asian population. Though these neighborhoods aren't traditional tourist destinations, those who do venture here will be rewarded as they dine at a myriad of authentic Asian restaurants, relax over a reflexology foot massage, or peruse the aisles of specialty grocery stores. An afternoon here reminds visitors that San Diego's cultural diversity does not come solely from its neighbor to the south.

Point Loma and Coronado

WITH HARBOR AND SHELTER ISLANDS, AND OCEAN BEACH

WORD OF MOUTH

"Coronado is such a great place to walk and/or bike. You can bike all over the island and it is so enjoyable—much nicer than driving around. You can pack a lunch and stop at any of the many parks, or the beach."

—nanabee

GETTING ORIENTED

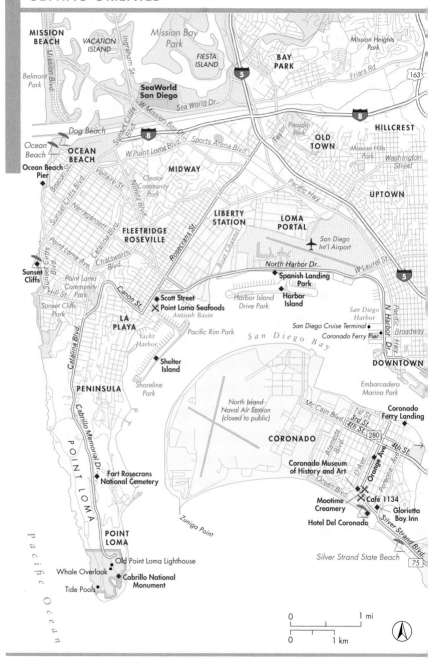

TOP REASONS TO GO

Point Loma's panoramic views: Take in the view from the mountains to the ocean at Cabrillo National Monument. Come evening, watch the sun go down at Sunset Cliffs.

The Hotel Del: As the grande dame of San Diego, the historic Hotel Del Coronado charms guests and visitors alike with her graceful architecture and oceanfront setting.

Boating paradise: San Diego's picturesque marinas are filled with sportfishing charters and ultraluxury yachts.

Sandy beaches: The long stretches of sand on Coronado are family-friendly, while Fido will love swimming at Ocean Beach's Dog Beach.

Military might: From the endless rows of white headstones at Fort Rosecrans National Cemetery to the roar of fighter jets over North Island Naval Air Station, San Diego's strong military ties are palpable.

QUICK BITES

Point Loma Seafoods. The freshest and tastiest fish to be found along Point Loma's shores comes from this shop behind the Vagabond Inn. The fish market sells the catches of the day; the adjacent take-out counter has prepared hot and cold food. ⊠ *2805 Emerson St., Point Loma* ☎ *619/223–1109* ⊕ *www.pointlomaseafoods.com.*

Cafe 1134. You can get a good curried tuna sandwich on French bread to accompany your espresso at this hip mini-bistro. ⊠ *1134 Orange Ave., Coronado* ☎ *619/437–1134* ⊕ *www.cafe1134.net.*

Mootime Creamery. For a sweet pick-me-up, try the rich ice cream, frozen yogurt, or sorbet made fresh daily at Mootime. Dessert nachos made with waffle-cone chips are an unusual addition to the sundae menu. Look for the statue of Elvis on the sidewalk in front. ⊠ *1025 Orange Ave., Coronado* ☎ *619/435–2422* ⊕ *www.nadolife.com/mootime.*

GETTING HERE

Bus 84 serves Cabrillo National Monument on Point Loma, although a transfer is required from Bus 28, near Shelter Island. For Harbor Island, the hearty can walk from the Embarcadero or catch a bus to the airport and walk from there.

Coronado is accessible via the arching blue 2.2-mile-long San Diego–Coronado Bay Bridge, which offers breathtaking views of the harbor and downtown. Alternatively, pedestrians and bikes can reach Coronado via the popular ferry service. Bus 904 meets the ferry and travels as far as Silver Strand State Beach. Bus 901 runs daily between the Gaslamp Quarter and Coronado.

PLANNING YOUR TIME

If you're interested in seeing the tide pools at Cabrillo National Monument, call ahead or check the weather page of the *Union-Tribune* to find out when low tide will occur. Scott Street, with its Point Loma Seafoods, is a good place to find yourself at lunchtime, and Sunset Cliffs Park is where you want to be at sunset.

A leisurely stroll through Coronado takes at least an hour, more if you stop to shop or walk along the family-friendly beaches. Whenever you come, if you're not staying overnight, remember to get back to the dock in time to catch the final ferry out at 9:30 (10:30 on weekends).

7

CABRILLO NATIONAL MONUMENT

Cabrillo National Monument marks the site of the first European visit to San Diego, made by 16th-century explorer Juan Rodríguez Cabrillo. Cabrillo landed at this spot, which he called San Miguel, on September 15, 1542. Today the 160-acre preserve with its rugged cliffs and shores and outstanding overlooks is one of the most frequently visited of all the national monuments.

Catching sight of a whale from the cliffs of Cabrillo National Monument can be a highlight of a wintertime visit to San Diego. More accessible sea creatures can be seen in the tide pools at the foot of the monument's western cliffs.

On land, trails lead down the hillside through sagebrush and cactus. Overlook points offer spectacular views from the desert mountains to downtown and beyond. The informative visitor center and the lighthouse give a historical perspective to this once-remote promontory.

(above) Point Loma from the water, as Cabrillo would have seen it in 1542. (lower right) Old Point Loma Lighthouse stood watch for 36 years. (upper right) Cabrillo's statue adorns the visitor center.

SERVICE INFORMATION

The visitor center, located next to the statue of Cabrillo, presents films and lectures about Cabrillo's voyage, the sea-level tide pools, and migrating gray whales.

⊠ *1800 Cabrillo Memorial Dr., Point Loma* ☎ *619/557-5450* ⊕ *www.nps.gov/cabr* 🖃 *$5 per car, $3 per person entering on foot or by bicycle, admission good for 7 days* ☉ *Park daily 9–5.*

A HALF DAY AT CABRILLO NATIONAL MONUMENT

A **statue of Cabrillo** overlooks downtown from a windy promontory, where people gather to admire the stunning panorama over the bay, from the snowcapped San Bernardino Mountains, 130 miles north, to the hills surrounding Tijuana to the south. The stone figure standing on the bluff looks rugged and dashing, but he is a creation of an artist's imagination—no portraits of Cabrillo are known to exist.

The moderately steep **Bayside Trail,** 2½ mile round-trip, winds through coastal sage scrub, curving under the cliff-top lookouts and taking you ever closer to the bay-front scenery. You cannot reach the beach from this trail, and must stick to the path to protect the cliffs from erosion and yourself from thorny plants and snakes—including rattlers. You'll see prickly pear cactus and yucca, fragrant sage, and maybe a lizard, rabbit, or hummingbird. The climb back is long but gradual, leading up to the old lighthouse.

Old Point Loma Lighthouse's oil lamp was first lighted in 1855 and was visible from the sea for 25 miles. Unfortunately, it was too high above the cliffs to guide navigators trapped in Southern California's thick offshore fog. In 1891 a new lighthouse was built 400 feet below. The restored old lighthouse is open to visitors. An exhibit in the Assistant Keepers Quarters next door tells the story of the Old Lighthouse, the daily lives of the keepers, how lighthouses work, and the role they played in the development of early maritime commerce along the West Coast. On the edge of the hill near the old lighthouse sits a refurbished radio room containing displays of U.S. harbor defenses at Point Loma used during World War II.

■ TIP→ Restrooms and water fountains are plentiful, but, except for vending machines at the visitor center, there's no food. Exploring the grounds consumes time and calories; pack a picnic and rest on a bench overlooking the sailboats.

WHALE-WATCHING

The western and southern cliffs of Cabrillo National Monument are prime whale-watching territory. A sheltered **viewing station** has wayside exhibits describing the great gray whales' yearly migration from Baja California to the Bering and Chukchi seas near Alaska. High-powered telescopes help you focus on the whales' waterspouts. Whales are visible on clear days from late December through early March, with the highest concentration in January and February. Note that when the whales return north in spring, they are too far out in the ocean to be seen from the monument.

TIDE POOLS

When the tide is low you can walk on the rocks around saltwater pools filled with starfish, crabs, anemones, octopuses, and hundreds of other sea creatures and plants. Tide pooling is best when the tide is at its lowest so call ahead or check tide charts online before your visit. Exercise caution on the slippery rocks.

Sightseeing
★★★☆☆
Nightlife
★☆☆☆☆
Dining
★★★☆☆
Lodging
★★★★☆
Shopping
★★★☆☆

Although Coronado is actually an isthmus, easily reached from the mainland if you head north from Imperial Beach, it has always seemed like an island and is often referred to as such. To the west, Point Loma protects the San Diego Bay from the Pacific's tides and waves. Both Coronado and Point Loma have stately homes, sandy beaches, private marinas, and prominent military installations. Nestled between the two, Harbor and Shelter islands owe their existence to dredging in the bay.

POINT LOMA

Updated by
Claire Deeks
van der Lee

The hilly peninsula of **Point Loma** curves west and south into the Pacific and provides protection for San Diego Bay. Its high elevations and sandy cliffs provide incredible views, and make Point Loma a visible local landmark. Its maritime roots are evident, from its longtime ties to the U.S. Navy to its bustling sport fishing and sailing marinas. The funky community of **Ocean Beach** coexists alongside the stately homes of **Sunset Cliffs** and the honored graves at **Fort Rosecrans National Cemetery.**

TOP ATTRACTIONS

Cabrillo National Monument.

Fodor's Choice
★
⇨ *See the highlighted listing in this chapter.*

Fort Rosecrans National Cemetery. In 1934, 8 of the 1,000 acres set aside for a military reserve in 1852 were designated as a burial site. About 100,000 people are now interred here; it's impressive to see the rows upon rows of white headstones that overlook Point Loma just north of the Cabrillo National Monument. Some of those laid to rest here were killed in battles that predate California's statehood; the graves of the 17 soldiers and one civilian who died in the 1874 Battle of San Pasqual between troops from Mexico and the United States are marked by a large bronze plaque. Perhaps the most impressive structure in the

Point Loma to Harbor Island Driving Tour

Take Catalina Boulevard all the way south to the tip of Point Loma to reach **Cabrillo National Monument**. North of the monument, as you head back into the neighborhoods of Point Loma, you'll see the white head-stones of **Fort Rosecrans National Cemetery**. Continue north on Catalina Boulevard to Hill Street and turn left to reach the dramatic **Sunset Cliffs**, at the western side of Point Loma near Ocean Beach. Park to tour the dramatic cliff tops and the boiling seas below, but be cautious because the cliffs can be unstable. Signs generally warn you where not to go. Head north on Sunset Cliffs Boulevard until you reach Newport Avenue, where you will make a left to enter the heart of **Ocean Beach**. If you have your dog with you, head north to **Ocean Beach's Dog Beach** or check out surfers from the **Ocean Beach Pier** off Niagara Avenue. Just before the pier, turn left onto New-port Avenue, OB's main drag.

Return to Sunset Cliffs Boulevard and backtrack south to take a left on Point Loma Avenue. Turn left at Canon Street, which leads toward the penin-sula's eastern (bay) side. Almost at the shore you'll see **Scott Street**, Point Loma's main commercial drag. Scott Street is bisected by Shelter Island Drive, which leads to **Shelter Island**. For another example of what can be done with tons of material dredged from a bay, go back up Shelter Island Drive, turn right on Rosecrans Street, another right on North Harbor Drive, and a final right onto **Harbor Island**.

cemetery is the 75-foot granite obelisk called the Bennington Monu-ment, which commemorates the 66 crew members who died in a boiler explosion and fire onboard the USS *Bennington* in 1905. ⊠ *Cabrillo Memorial Dr., Point Loma* ☎ *619/553–2084* ⊙ *Weekdays 8–4:30, weekends 9–5.*

★ **Sunset Cliffs.** As the name suggests, the 60-foot-high bluffs on the western side of Point Loma south of Ocean Beach are a perfect place to watch the sun set over the sea. To view the tide pools along the shore, use the staircase off Sunset Cliffs Boulevard at the foot of Ladera Street.

The dramatic coastline here seems to have been carved out of ancient rock. The impact of the waves is very clear: each year more sections of the cliffs are posted with caution signs. Don't ignore these warn-ings—it's easy to slip in the crumbling sandstone, and the surf can be extremely rough. The small coves and beaches that dot the coastline are popular with surfers drawn to the pounding waves. The homes along the boulevard—pink stucco mansions beside shingled Cape Cod–style cottages—are fine examples of Southern California luxury. ⊠ *Sunset Cliffs Blvd., Point Loma.*

WORTH NOTING

Scott Street. Running along Point Loma's waterfront from Shelter Island to the old Naval Training Center on Harbor Drive, this thoroughfare is lined with fishing charters and whale-watching boats. It's a good spot to watch fishermen (and women) haul marlin, tuna, and puny mackerel off their boats. ⊠ *Scott St., Point Loma.*

OCEAN BEACH

At the northern end of Point Loma lies the chilled-out, hippyesque town of Ocean Beach, commonly referred to as "OB." The main thoroughfare of this funky neighborhood is dotted with dive bars, coffeehouses, surf shops, and 1960s diners. OB is a magnet for everyone from surfers to musicians and artists. Newport Avenue, generally known for its boisterous bars, is also home to San Diego's largest antiques district. Fans of OB applaud its resistance to "selling out" to upscale development, whereas detractors lament its somewhat scruffy edges.

TOP ATTRACTIONS

Ocean Beach Pier. This T-shape pier is a popular fishing spot and home to the Ocean Beach Pier Café and a small tackle shop. Constructed in 1966, it is the longest concrete pier on the West Coast and a perfect place to take in views of the harbor, ocean, and Point Loma peninsula. Surfers flock to the waves that break just below. ⊠ *1950 Abbott St., Ocean Beach.*

SHELTER ISLAND

In 1950 San Diego's port director decided to raise the shoal that lay off the eastern shore of Point Loma above sea level with the sand and mud dredged up during the course of deepening a ship channel in the 1930s and '40s. The resulting peninsula, **Shelter Island,** became home to several marinas and resorts, many with Polynesian details that still exist today, giving them a retro flair. This reclaimed peninsula now supports towering palms and resorts, restaurants, and side-by-side marinas. The center of San Diego's yacht-building industry, boats in every stage of construction are visible in Shelter Island's yacht yards. A long sidewalk runs past boat brokerages to the hotels and marinas that line the inner shore, facing Point Loma. On the bay side, fishermen launch their boats and families relax at picnic tables along the grass, where there are fire rings and permanent barbeque grills. Within walking distance is the huge Friendship Bell, given to San Diegans by the people of Yokohama, Japan, in 1960 and the Tunaman's Memorial, a statue commemorating San Diego's once-flourishing fishing industry.

HARBOR ISLAND

Following the successful creation of Shelter Island, in 1961 the U.S. Navy used the residue from digging berths deep enough to accommodate aircraft carriers to build **Harbor Island**. Restaurants and high-rise hotels dot the inner shore of this 1½-mile-long man-made peninsula adjacent to the airport. The bay's shore is lined with pathways, gardens, and scenic picnic spots. On the east end point, **Island Prime and C-level Lounge** (*see Where to Eat*) has killer views of the downtown skyline.

WORTH NOTING

Spanish Landing Park. Across from the western end of Harbor Island, on the mainland's Spanish Landing Park, a bronze plaque marks the arrival in 1769 of a party from Spain that headed north from San Diego to conquer California. The group combined the crews of two ships, the *San Carlos* and the *San Antonio*, and a contingent that came overland from Baja California. Spanish Landing also houses the construction site for replica of the San Salvador galleon, currently being built in conjunction with the Maritime Museum. The project is expected to be complete by late 2013, at which point the galleon will sail to the Museum's Embarcadero location. As part of a beautification program, the city has begun installing whimsical artworks in this park, which is less visited than many city parks and therefore a quiet enclave in which to spend a peaceful hour or two. If you're hardy, you can walk from here to the Embarcadero, and then into the heart of downtown. ⊠ *Harbor Island.*

CORONADO

As if freeze-framed in the 1950s, Coronado's quaint appeal is captured in its old-fashioned storefronts, well-manicured gardens, and charming **Ferry Landing Marketplace.** The streets of Coronado are wide, quiet, and friendly, and many of today's residents live in grand Victorian homes handed down for generations. Naval Air Station North Island was established in 1911 on Coronado's north end, across from Point Loma, and was the site of Charles Lindbergh's departure on the transcontinental flight that preceded his famous solo flight across the Atlantic. Coronado's long relationship with the U.S. Navy and its desirable real estate have made it an enclave for military personnel; it's said to have more retired admirals per capita than anywhere else in the United States.

TOP ATTRACTIONS

Coronado Ferry Landing. This collection of shops at Ferry Landing is on a smaller scale than the Embarcadero's Seaport Village, but you do get a great view of the downtown San Diego skyline. The little bayside shops and restaurants resemble the gingerbread domes of the Hotel Del Coronado. **Bikes and Beyond** (☎ *619/435–7180 ⊕ hollandsbicycles. com*) rents bikes and surreys, perfect for riding through town and along Coronado's scenic bike path. ⊠ *1201 1st St., at B Ave., Coronado* ☎ *619/435–8895 ⊕ www.coronadoferrylandingshops.com.*

Fodor's Choice **Hotel Del Coronado.** The Del's distinctive red-tile roofs and Victorian gingerbread architecture have served as a set for many movies, political meetings, and extravagant social happenings. It's speculated that the Duke of Windsor may have first met Wallis Simpson here. Eleven presidents have been guests of the Del, and the film *Some Like It Hot*—starring Marilyn Monroe, Jack Lemmon, and Tony Curtis—used the hotel as a backdrop.

The Hotel Del, as locals call it, was the brainchild of financiers Elisha Spurr Babcock Jr. and H. L. Story, who saw the potential of Coronado's virgin beaches and its view of San Diego's emerging harbor. It opened in 1888 and became a National Historic Landmark in 1977.

Although the pool area is reserved for hotel guests, several surrounding dining patios make great places to sit back and imagine the scene during the 1920s, when the hotel rocked with good times. The History Gallery has photos from the Del's early days, and books elaborating on its history and that of Kate Morgan. Tours take place on Tuesday and Friday at 10:30, weekends at 2. Reservations are required. ✉ *1500 Orange Ave., at Glorietta Blvd., Coronado* ☎ *619/435–6611, 619/437–8788 tour reservations (through Coronado Visitor Center)* ⊕ *www.hoteldel. com* 🖾 *Tours $15.*

Orange Avenue. Coronado's business district and its villagelike heart, this is surely one of the most charming spots in Southern California. Slow-paced and very "local" (the city fights against chain stores), it's a blast from the past, although entirely up-to-date in other respects. The military presence—Coronado is home to the U.S. Navy Sea, Air and Land (SEAL) forces—is reflected in shops selling military gear and places like **McP's Irish Pub,** at No. 1107, the unofficial SEALs headquarters. ✉ *Orange Ave., near 9th St., Coronado.*

WORTH NOTING

Coronado Museum of History and Art. The neoclassical First Bank of Commerce building, constructed in 1910, holds the headquarters and archives of the Coronado Historical Association, a museum, the Coronado Visitor Center, the Coronado Museum Store, and Tent City Restaurant. The museum's collection celebrates Coronado's history with photographs and displays of its formative events and major sights. *Promenade Through the Past: A Brief History of Coronado and its Architectural Wonders,* available at the museum store, traces a 60-minute walking tour of the area's architecturally and historically significant buildings. A guided tour of them departs from the museum lobby on Wednesday mornings at 10:30 and costs $10 (reservations required). ✉ *1100 Orange Ave., at Park Pl., Coronado* ☎ *619/435–7242 or 619/437–8788 walking tour reservations* ⊕ *www.coronadohistory.org* 🖾 *$4 suggested donation* ⊙ *Weekdays 9–5, weekends 10–5.*

Glorietta Bay Inn walking tour. The former residence of John Spreckels, the original owner of North Island and the property on which the Hotel Del Coronado stands, is now a popular hotel. On Tuesday, Thursday, and Saturday morning at 11 it's the departure point for a fun and informative 1½-hour walking tour of a few of the area's 86 officially designated historic homes. It includes—from the outside only—some spectacular mansions and the Meade House, where L. Frank Baum, author of *The Wizard of Oz,* wrote additional Oz stories. ✉ *1630 Glorietta Blvd., Coronado* ☎ *619/435–3101, 619/435–5993 tour information* 🖾 *Tour $12.*

EN ROUTE

Chicano Park. San Diego's Mexican-American community is centered on Barrio Logan, under the San Diego–Coronado Bay Bridge on the downtown side. Chicano Park, spread along National Avenue from Dewey to Crosby streets, is the barrio's recreational hub. It's worth taking a short detour to see the huge murals of Mexican history painted on the bridge supports at National Avenue and Dewey Street; they're among the best examples of folk art in the city. ⚠ With its somewhat isolated location under the bridge, visiting after dark is not recommended. ✉ *National Ave. at S. Evans St., Barrio Logan.*

Where to Eat

WORD OF MOUTH

"If you go to the Prado (which I love), try their tres leches cake for
dessert. . . . It is the best version I've ever had. I would try to do
it for happy hour after the zoo."

—ncounty

Updated
by Maren
Dougherty

San Diego's proximity to Mexico makes it an attractive destination for anything wrapped in a tortilla, but there's so much more. While most of the top restaurants offer seasonal California fare, San Diego also boasts excellent ethnic cuisines available at all prices.

As elsewhere in the United States, the San Diego dining scene has moved toward using sustainable, locally sourced meat, seafood, and produce—and providing good value. This emphasis on affordability is often presented as early or late-night dining specials, but also extends to the wine lists, where smart sommeliers are offering more wines from value regions like France's Loire and Languedoc, and countries like Chile and South Africa.

Downtown is packed with restaurants, but many can be touristy, so it's a good to be selective. The übertrendy Gaslamp Quarter delights visitors looking for innovative concepts that also have nightlife appeal, while the gentrified Little Italy district has become a center for affordable Italian fare as well as surprises like English pubs and supper clubs with live music. Modern restaurants and cafés thrive in the East Village, amid the luxury condos near PETCO Park. Bankers Hill, just west of Balboa Park, is one of the hottest food destinations in the city, and most spots also have interesting cocktails.

The Uptown neighborhoods centered by Hillcrest—an urbane district with San Francisco flavor—are a mix of bars and independent restaurants. North Park, in particular, has a happening restaurant scene, with just about everything kind of cuisine you can think of, and laidback prices to boot. Mission Valley, a central area with many hotels and shopping malls, abounds with casual, family-friendly fare. And scenic La Jolla offers some of the best fine dining in the city.

Ethnic cuisine remains popular in the Gaslamp Quarter, Hillcrest, and Convoy Street in Kearney Mesa, which is a hub for Chinese, Korean, and Vietnamese fare. In Chula Vista you'll find authentic Mexican food, while Coronado—the peninsula city across San Diego Bay—has beachy neighborhood eateries and extravagant hotel dining rooms with dramatic water views.

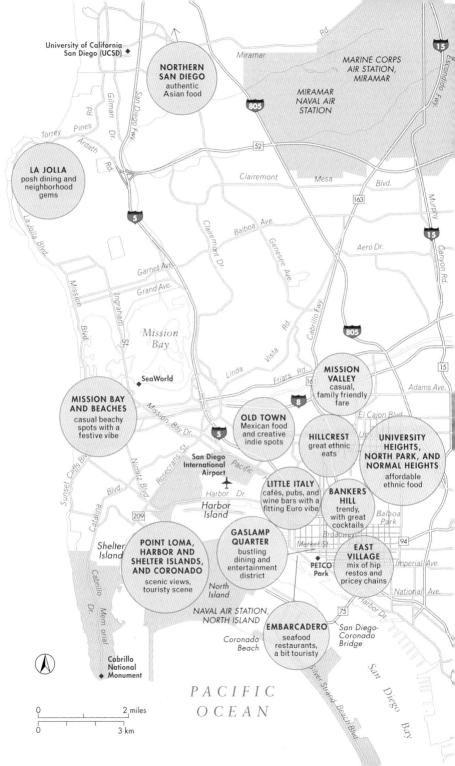

University of California
San Diego (UCSD)

MARINE CORPS
AIR STATION,
MIRAMAR

MIRAMAR
NAVAL AIR
STATION

**NORTHERN
SAN DIEGO**
authentic
Asian food

Miramar

Rd.

Escondido Fwy.

15

805

52

Clairemont   Mesa   Blvd.

Torrey
Pines   Gilman   San Diego Fwy.
Rd.   Dr.

Ardath
Rd.

163

LA JOLLA
posh dining and
neighborhood
gems

5

Balboa Ave.

Clairemont Dr.

Genesee Ave.

Aero Dr.

Murphy

15

Canyon Rd.

La Jolla Blvd.

Garnet Ave.

Ingraham St.

Grand Ave.

*Mission
Bay*

Linda   Vista   Rd.

Cabrillo Fwy.

Friars Rd.

16

805

15

Mission Blvd.

SeaWorld

8

**MISSION
VALLEY**
casual,
family friendly
fare

Adams Ave.

El Cajon Blvd.

**MISSION BAY
AND BEACHES**
casual beachy
spots with a
festive vibe

Mission Bay Dr.

5

OLD TOWN
Mexican food
and creative
indie spots

HILLCREST
great ethnic
eats

U

**UNIVERSITY
HEIGHTS,
NORTH PARK, AND
NORMAL HEIGHTS**
affordable
ethnic food

Sunset Cliffs Blvd.

Nimitz Blvd.

Rosecrans St.

San Diego
International
Airport

Pacific

LITTLE ITALY
cafés, pubs, and
wine bars with a
fitting Euro vibe

**BANKERS
HILL**
trendy,
with great
cocktails

Balboa
Park

Catalina
Blvd.

Harbor Dr.

Harbor
Island

Harbor Island

209

94

Shelter
Island

Cabrillo
Mem
orial
Dr.

**POINT LOMA,
HARBOR AND
SHELTER ISLANDS,
AND CORONADO**
scenic views,
touristy scene

**GASLAMP
QUARTER**
bustling
dining and
entertainment
district

Market St.

PETCO
Park

**EAST
VILLAGE**
mix of hip
restos and
pricey chains

Imperial Ave.

National Ave.

Broadway

North
Island

*NAVAL AIR STATION,
NORTH ISLAND*

75

EMBARCADERO
seafood
restaurants,
a bit touristy

San Diego-
Coronado
Bridge

Harbor Dr.

*Coronado
Beach*

Cabrillo
National
Monument

San Diego Bay

Silver Strand Beach Blvd.

*PACIFIC
OCEAN*

0   2 miles

0   3 km

SAN DIEGO DINING PLANNER

DINING HOURS

Unless otherwise noted, the restaurants listed in this guide are open daily for lunch and dinner. Lunch is typically served 11:30 am to 2:30 pm, and dinner service in most restaurants begins at 5:30 pm and ends at 10 pm, though a number of establishments serve until 11 pm or later on Friday and Saturday night.

RESERVATIONS

We mention reservations in reviews only when they're essential or not accepted. But reservations are usually a good idea—a venue may be booked solid or rented out for a special event, so it's best to call ahead. Especially for fine-dining restaurants, reserve as far ahead as you can, and reconfirm when you arrive in town.

WHAT TO WEAR

San Diego restaurants have given up trying to require dressy attire. It's a casual city for men and women alike, with designer jeans and a trendy top as the typical going-out uniform. A few dress-up places remain. Otherwise, a "come-as-you-are" attitude generally prevails.

CHILDREN

San Diego welcomes all kinds of diners, including children, though some of the more formal establishments and expense-account steak houses probably are inappropriate venues for kids. Children's menus can be found here and there, but staff at most establishments will cheerfully offer a few suggestions for the younger set if asked. The restaurants we recommend for families with children are marked with a ☺ symbol.

PARKING

With the boom of new apartments and condominiums in Little Italy, parking near many of its restaurants has become a problem. Try to find valet parking or a spot in a surface lot. Downtown, there's Parkade, a controlled-price public parking garage at the corner of 6th Avenue and K Street, which usually has ample parking even in the evening. There's also a local San Diego Trolley stop that's less than two blocks from Little Italy's India Street restaurant row. If you use the trolley to get to downtown and Gaslamp Quarter restaurants, you can avoid parking fees that may exceed $20 and valets who expect tips.

SMOKING

Smoking is banned in restaurants, but some permit it on their terraces.

PRICES

Meal prices in San Diego have caught up with those of other major metropolitan areas, despite the fact that the city's serious dining scene is still developing. Especially in districts like La Jolla, the Gaslamp Quarter, and Coronado, high rents and popularity with tourists lead to more expensive entrées. But with the economic downturn, many restaurants around town are offering extra value with fixed-price menus and early-dining specials.

Prices in the reviews are the average cost of a main course at dinner or, if dinner is not served, at lunch.

RESTAURANT REVIEWS

Listed alphabetically within neighborhoods. Use the coordinate (⊕ 1: B2) at the end of each listing to locate a site on the San Diego Dining and Lodging Atlas following this chapter.

DOWNTOWN

The East Village is one of the hippest areas of downtown, with its urbane mix of independent restaurants serving everything from French bistro fare and burgers to Thai food and artisan-baked bread. It's just east of the Gaslamp Quarter, which is known as much for the nightlife as the eateries. Many restaurants in the Gaslamp Quarter are pricey chains and tourist-driven concepts along 4th, 5th, and 6th avenues. We've selected just a few of the chains where the steaks and crab cakes are worth the splurge; most of the other picks are for local eateries that emphasize seasonal, locally sourced ingredients. They range from casual spots for burgers, sushi, and tacos to stylish restaurants serving fresh seafood, Italian cuisine, and aged steaks. North from downtown, Little Italy offers a mix of traditional pasta spots and trendy bar-restaurants.

GASLAMP QUARTER

$$$ ITALIAN

🍴 **BiCE Ristorante.** Go out for Italian in the Gaslamp Quarter and you risk getting caught in a tourist trap—BiCE Ristorante is an exception. Popular with locals and visitors, BiCE offers its refined, big-city style of Italian cuisine in a sleek downtown space. This dinner-only restaurant led by Italian-born chef Mario Cassineri offers a cheese-and-salumi bar, dishes like gnocchi with asiago cheese, veal with saffron risotto, and market fresh fish. Waiters deliver professional service and informed opinions on the extensive Italian wine list, while the bar features local artisanal and imported beers and appropriate cocktails like the Il Rutino, with Aperol and prosecco. [$] *Average main: $34* ✉ *425 Island Ave., Gaslamp Quarter* ☎ *619/239–2423* 🌐 *www.bicesandiego.com* 🕓 *No lunch* ⊕ *1:D5.*

$$$ SEAFOOD

🍴 **Blue Point Coastal Cuisine.** If there's a convention in town, Blue Point gets jammed with diverse diners who share a taste for sophisticated seafood. The menu swims with classics like crab cakes, mussels in tomato-fennel broth, and halibut crusted with breadcrumbs, herbs, and diced lobster meat. The small but serious oyster bar, which serves both raw and imaginatively prepared shellfish, is a warm-up for the menu of more seafood, plus chicken and steaks. The wine list is impressive, and the service is efficient and friendly. The airy dining room has gleaming woodwork and walls of windows looking onto 5th Avenue and Market Street, a prime corner for people-watching. [$] *Average main: $34* ✉ *565 5th Ave., Gaslamp Quarter* ☎ *619/233–6623* 🕓 *No lunch* ⊕ *1:E5.*

$$ SPANISH

Fodor's Choice ★

🍴 **Cafe Sevilla.** Sevilla moved into new digs in 2011, allowing a fresh look for this tapas bar, nightclub, and restaurant. Thursday through Sunday evenings, it's packed with youthful throngs who crowd the ground-floor bar for drinks, tapas, and live music. Others head to the downstairs club for classics from the Spanish kitchen and, on Saturday nights, professional flamenco dancing. The kitchen does a respectable job with the traditional shellfish and chicken paella (there are meat and other seafood versions,

BEST BETS FOR SAN DIEGO DINING

With hundreds of restaurants to choose from, how will you decide where to eat? We've selected our favorite restaurants by price, cuisine, and experience in the Best Bets list below. In the first column, Fodor's Choice properties represent the "best of the best" in every price category. Bon appétit!

Fodor'sChoice ★

Bencotto $$, p. 121
Bread & Cie $, p. 130
Café Chloe $$, p. 120
Cowboy Star $$$, p. 120
Cucina Urbana $$$, p. 125
Dumpling Inn $, p. 144
George's at the Cove $$$$, p. 140
The Kebab Shop $, p. 120
Mistral $$, p. 149
Nine-Ten $$$$, p. 141
Ortega's Bistro $$, p. 130
Sushi Ota $$$, p. 137
Taka $$, p. 119

By Price

$

Blue Water Seafood Market & Grill, p. 128
Bread & Cie, p. 130
El Zarape, p. 132
The Kebab Shop, p. 120
Lucha Libre, p. 129

Saffron Noodles, p. 131

$$

Barbarella, p. 139
Bencotto, p. 121
BO-Beau, p. 146
Café Chloe, p. 120
Jsix, p. 116
Mistral, p. 149
Taka, p. 119

$$$

Cowboy Star, p. 120
Nobu, p. 118
Searsucker, p. 119
Sushi Ota, p. 137

$$$$

George's at the Cove, p. 140
Morton's, The Steakhouse, p. 118
Nine-Ten, p. 141

By Cuisine

AMERICAN

A.R. Valentien, p. 139
Craft & Commerce, p. 122
Bankers Hill, p. 124
Jimmy's Famous American Tavern, p. 146
Jsix, p. 116
Nine-Ten, p. 141
Searsucker, p. 119
Starlite, p. 129

ASIAN

Dae Jang Keum Korean BBQ, p. 144
Harney Sushi, p. 129
Saffron Noodles, p. 131
Sushi on the Rock, p. 143

CAFÉS

Azucar, p. 147
Bread & Cie, p. 130
Café Chloe, p. 120
Michele Coulon Dessertier, p. 141

CHINESE

China Max, p. 144
Dumpling Inn, p. 144
Emerald Chinese Seafood Restaurant, p. 145

DESSERTS

Café Chloe, p. 120
Karen Krasne's Extraordinary Desserts, p. 122
Michele Coulon Dessertier, p. 141
Viva Pops, p. 134

FRENCH

Bertrand at Mister A's, p. 125
BO-Beau, p. 146
Farm House Cafe, p. 132

INDIAN

Royal India, p. 119

ITALIAN

Barbarella, p. 139
BiCE Ristorante, p. 113
Cucina Urbana, p. 125
Pizzeria Arrivederci, p. 131

JAPANESE

Hane Sushi, p. 126
Sushi Diner, p. 144
Sushi Ota, p. 137
Taka, p. 119

LATIN/MEXICAN

El Zarape, p. 132
Isabel's Cantina, p. 135
Lucha Libre, p. 129
Ortega's Bistro, p. 130

MEDITERRANEAN

The Kebab Shop, p. 120
Mama's Bakery & Lebanese Deli, p. 133
Mistral, p. 149

PIZZA

Pizzicato Pizza, p. 126
URBN Coal Fired Pizza, p. 133

SEAFOOD

Blue Water Seafood Market & Grill, p. 128
El Pescador, p. 140
Fish Market, p. 123
The Oceanaire Seafood Room, p. 118

STEAKHOUSES

Cowboy Star, p. 120
Morton's, The Steakhouse, p. 118
Puerto La Boca, p. 122

VEGETARIAN

Kous Kous Moroccan Bistro, p. 130
Lanna, p. 137
Saffron Noodles, p. 131
Starlite, p. 129
Tender Greens, p. 147

By Experience

BRUNCH

Café Chloe, p. 120
Farm House Cafe, p. 132
Hash House A Go Go, p. 130
Nine-Ten, p. 141

BUSINESS MEALS

Ave 5, p. 124
Bali Hai, p. 148
Bankers Hill, p. 124
George's at the Cove, p. 140
Truluck's, p. 143

COCKTAILS

Bankers Hill, p. 124
Craft & Commerce, p. 122
Searsucker, p. 119
Starlite, p. 129

DINING WITH KIDS

Hodad's, p. 148
Ortega's Bistro, p. 130
Pizzeria Arrivederci, p. 131
Rimel's Rotisserie, p. 142
Tartine, p. 150
Tender Greens, p. 147

GOOD FOR GROUPS

Barrio Star, p. 125
Dae Jang Keum Korean BBQ, p. 144
Red Pearl Kitchen, p. 118
Royal India, p. 119
URBN Coal Fired Pizza, p. 133

HOTEL DINING

A.R. Valentien, p. 139
Jsix, p. 116
Mistral, p. 149
Nine-Ten, p. 141

OUTDOOR DINING

1500 Ocean, p. 148
Café Chloe, p. 120
Osteria Romantica, p. 142
The Prado, p. 124
Starlite, p. 129

PRETHEATER

Ave 5, p. 124
Bankers Hill, p. 124
Café Chloe, p. 120
RA Sushi Bar Restaurant, p. 118

ROMANTIC

Bertrand at Mister A's, p. 125
BO-Beau, p. 146
Chez Loma, p. 149
George's at the Cove, p. 140
Mistral, p. 149
Whisknladle, p. 143

SINGLES SCENE

George's at the Cove, p. 140
JRDN, p. 137
RA Sushi Bar Restaurant, p. 118
Red Pearl Kitchen, p. 118

TRENDY

Bankers Hill, p. 124
Craft & Commerce, p. 122
Jsix, p. 116
Neighborhood, p. 121
Nobu, p. 118
Prepkitchen, p. 142
Searsucker, p. 119

WATER VIEWS

Bali Hai, p. 148
Fish Market, p. 123
George's at the Cove, p. 140
JRDN, p. 137
Marine Room, p. 141
Mistral, p. 149

WINE LISTS

1500 Ocean, p. 148
A.R. Valentien, p. 139
George's at the Cove, p. 140
Mistral, p. 149
Vela, p. 119

8

too); other good choices are the highly flavorful baked rabbit and the roasted pork tenderloin. A new favorite is a trio of dramatically presented *brochetas,* or skewers, of spiced shrimp, Spanish sausage, and steak with mushrooms and onions. [$] *Average main: $20* ✉ *353 5th Ave., Gaslamp Quarter* ☎ *619/233–5979* 🌐 *www.cafesevilla.com* 🕘 *No lunch* ✥ *1:E5.*

$$$ MEXICAN 🍴 **Candelas.** The scents and flavors of imaginative Mexican cuisine with a European flair permeate this handsome, romantic restaurant and nightspot in the shadow of San Diego's tallest residential towers. Candles glow everywhere around the small, comfortable dining room and lounge. Fine openers such as black bean soup and greens with sautéed tomatoes give way to main courses like salmon stuffed with Brie and crab meat. Drinks are half price during happy hour from 5 to 9 pm Sunday through Thursday and 5 to 7 pm on Friday and Saturday. [$] *Average main: $28* ✉ *416 3rd Ave., Gaslamp Quarter* ☎ *619/702–4455* 🌐 *www.candelas-sd.com* ✍ *Reservations essential* 🕘 *No lunch* ✥ *1:D5.*

$ IRISH 🍴 **The Field.** A family-run pub decorated with paraphernalia from an Irish farm, the Field has character to spare. Diners enjoy solid meals of Irish stew, corned beef and cabbage, Gaelic steak with an Irish whisky–peppercorn sauce or, best of all, the *boxty*: a lacy but substantial potato pancake served crisp and hot with such fillings as sage-accented chicken or Irish bacon and cheese. As the evening wears on, the crowd grows younger, livelier, louder, and sometimes rowdier. A traditional Irish breakfast is served on weekends, and there's dancing and live music many nights of the week. The terrace is a particularly popular spot for dinner. [$] *Average main: $15* ✉ *544 5th Ave., Gaslamp Quarter* ☎ *619/232–9840* 🌐 *www.thefield.com* 🕘 *No breakfast weekdays* ✥ *1:D5.*

$$ AMERICAN 🍴 **Jsix.** Creative and carefully prepared seafood reigns on this menu that reflects the diverse flavors found along the West Coast from Mexico to Washington. Chef Christian Graves uses locally sourced, sustainably raised meats and seafood in dishes such as the tarragon and Dijon mussels and seared albacore with avocado puree. Nonseafood options include butternut squash ravioli, chicken with green garlic–bacon risotto, and a pork chop with rosemary garlic potatoes. The cheeses, salami, and house-made pickles are excellent. Desserts are made with equal care, and the bar boasts cocktails made with seasonal fruit. The eclectic decor includes blown-glass pendant lights, a series of culinary paintings by a local artist, and a dramatically backlighted bar. [$] *Average main: $23* ✉ *616 J St., Gaslamp Quarter* ☎ *619/531–8744* 🌐 *www.jsixrestaurant.com* ✥ *1:E5.*

$ INDIAN 🍴 **Monsoon.** An exceptionally attractive restaurant, Monsoon delights diners with features such as a waterfall on the back wall that splashes soothingly in the background, not to mention the excellent food. The menu offers many dishes not easily found at local Indian eateries, including a sweetly spiced mango soup, banana curry, and lamb curry. Everything is spiced to taste, and baked-to-order breads should not be missed. A plentiful buffet is served at lunchtime daily and for dinner on Monday. Folding doors allow some tables to share the outdoor atmosphere of the terrace, but at a peaceful distance from the sidewalk. [$] *Average main: $17* ✉ *729 4th Ave., Gaslamp Quarter* ☎ *619/234–5555* 🌐 *www.monsoonrestaurant.com* ✥ *1:D4.*

ICE CREAM AND CHOCOLATE SHOP

NOW APPEARING: GREAT! HOT FUDGE SUNDAES

GHIRARDELLI

CHOCOLATE SHOP

SUGAR RUSH

The Gaslamp Quarter has many touristy chain restaurants but there are also spots worth seeking out. Check our listings for suggestions.

$$$$ ✕ **Morton's, The Steakhouse.** In the soaring Harbor Club towers near both
STEAKHOUSE the San Diego Convention Center and the Gaslamp Quarter, Morton's
teems with conventioneers out for a night on the town. Bar 12-21, named
for the month and day that the first Morton's restaurant opened in 1978,
offers an extensive list of original cocktails and tasty appetizers such as
filet mignon sliders. For the main event, the restaurant excels at classic steak-house fare: bone-in rib eye, New York strip steak, and mixed
grills such as filet mignon with shrimp. Expect a treat: Morton's knows
how to put on a superb spread that takes the concept of indulgence to
new heights. $ *Average main: $40* ✉ *Harbor Club, 285 J St., Gaslamp
Quarter* ☎ *619/696–3369* ⊕ *www.mortons.com* ☾ *No lunch* ✛ *1:D5.*

$$$ ✕ **Nobu.** This outpost of Nobu Matsuhisa's restaurant empire in the
JAPANESE Hard Rock Hotel is known for inventive and fresh sushi and hot dishes
created with a modern Japanese-Peruvian flair. The sexy if rather noisy
room with scorched ash wood treatments and jade-green walls makes a
cool space to enjoy Nobu classics like raw white fish *tiradito* (the Peru-
vian equivalent of sashimi) with yuzu citrus, lobster in wasabi sauce, or
succulent black cod with miso glaze. If you're feeling adventurous, let
the sushi chef's whims guide you through a delicious *omakase*, or tasting
menu—just be sure to tell them what you'd like to spend. More than a
few diners have ended up with a surprise bill in the hundreds. $ *Aver-
age main: $28* ✉ *Hard Rock Hotel, 207 5th Ave., Gaslamp Quarter*
☎ *619/814–4124* ⊕ *www.noburestaurants.com* ☾ *No lunch, except
during major conventions* ✛ *1:E5.*

$$$ ✕ **The Oceanaire Seafood Room.** Engineered to recall an ocean liner from
SEAFOOD the 1940s, the decor at Oceanaire may be a bit contrived but the food—
and the classic cocktails are spot on. Expect the freshest oysters and
sashimi, and a carefully prepared menu of up to 25 daily "fresh catches,"
with specialties ranging from utterly convincing Maryland crab cakes
and oysters Rockefeller to richly stuffed California sole, a luxurious one-
pound pork chop, and irresistible hash brown potatoes. The menu might
also include the deliciously hot, spice-fired "angry" pink snapper. Service
tends to be casual in San Diego, which makes the professional staff here
all the more notable. $ *Average main: $31* ✉ *400 J St., Gaslamp Quarter*
☎ *619/858–2277* ⊕ *www.theoceanaire.com* ☾ *No lunch* ✛ *1:D5.*

$$ ✕ **RA Sushi Bar Restaurant.** Clad in T-shirts with flirty slogans, the attrac-
JAPANESE tive servers challenge a young clientele to strive for a sexy attitude at
this small, intimate space carved out of a former department store. Two
ultrahip bars—one for cocktails, one for sushi, both for being seen—
fuel the popularity, bolstered by a dining-room menu from which you
can make a meal out of the many appetizers, such as sesame chicken
wings, assorted sashimi, and scallops in spicy "dynamite" sauce. Other-
wise, choose from the sushi combination plates, panko-breaded chicken
katsu, salmon with garlic green beans, and hearty noodle dishes. With
snacks and drinks for $3–$8, the Monday to Saturday happy hour is
one of the best in downtown. $ *Average main: $22* ✉ *474 Broadway,
Gaslamp Quarter* ☎ *619/321–0021* ⊕ *www.rasushi.com* ✛ *1:D3.*

$ ✕ **Red Pearl Kitchen.** Vivid red Venetian plaster walls, a loungey vibe, and
ASIAN a widely varied menu of pan-Asian fare make Red Pearl Kitchen stand
out among San Diego's other, more generic, Asian restaurants. Here,

diners embark on a culinary journey with dishes like pineapple and Kobe beef satay, crab spring rolls, spicy meatballs, and steamed pork buns, all of which are designed for sharing. Pair them with sake and wine, or creative cocktails. It's a great for a group. On weekends the bar and lounge are dominated by exuberant twentysomethings—and the service can be spotty. $ *Average main: $17* ✉ *440 J St., Suite 108, Gaslamp Quarter* ☎ *619/231–1100* ⊕ *www.redpearlkitchen.com* ✛ *1:D5.*

$$ ✕ **Royal India.** Experience cuisine once reserved for royalty as broth-
INDIAN ers Sam and Jag Kambo lovingly re-create their mother's north Indian recipes. Everything from the mint chutney to the smoky tomato sauce that graces the chicken *tikka masala* is made from scratch. Dining here is first-rate, whether it's the daily lunch buffet or the sumptuous dinners that include sizzling chili-lemon chicken kebabs, indulgent lamb korma, and garlic naan. Elegant but comfortable decor is highlighted by a carved antique maple bar, stunning chandeliers, and golden arches from a palace in Jodhpur. Don't miss the imported Indian beers, mango martinis, or desserts, including mango mousse and rice pudding redolent of warm spices. $ *Average main: $20* ✉ *329 Market St., Gaslamp Quarter* ☎ *619/269–9999* ⊕ *www.royalindia.com* ✛ *1:D5.*

$$$ ✕ **Searsucker.** The much-hyped first restaurant from *Top Chef* finalist
AMERICAN Brian Malarkey opened in summer 2010 and has maintained its buzz ever since, attracting patrons with its fun urban decor and experimental dishes like swordfish with drunken cherries and beef cheeks over goat cheese dumplings. The flavor combinations are mostly successful, particularly when paired with comfort-food sides like bacon grits and grilled asparagus. Chef Malarkey adds to the lively vibe when he makes his rounds to chat with diners. $ *Average main: $30* ✉ *611 5th Ave., Gaslamp Quarter* ☎ *619/233–7327* ⊕ *www.searsucker.com* ⌛ *Reservations essential* ✛ *1:E4.*

$$ ✕ **Taka.** It may be on a prominent corner, but the pristine fish imported
JAPANESE from around the world and the creative presentations are what attracts
Fodor's Choice the crowds each night. Start with one of the sushi chef's appetizers,
★ perhaps the monkfish liver with ponzu, some slices of tender hamachi sashimi, or a special box-press sushi with shrimp, tuna, and crab topped with pickled seaweed and caviar. Hot dishes include salmon teriyaki and an East-meets-West-style New York steak. The restaurant is a favorite with Japanese visitors. $ *Average main: $20* ✉ *555 5th Ave., Gaslamp Quarter* ☎ *619/338–0555* ⊕ *www.takasushi.com* ☾ *No lunch* ✛ *1:E5.*

$ ✕ **The Tin Fish.** On the rare rainy San Diego day, the staff can take it
SEAFOOD easy at this eatery less than 100 yards from the PETCO Park baseball stadium, where half of the 100-odd seats are outdoors—otherwise the whole place is pretty much always jammed. Musicians entertain some evenings, making this a lively spot for dinners that range from grilled and fried fish to seafood burritos and tacos. The quality here routinely surpasses that at grander establishments. Hours vary whether it's baseball season or not, but the Tin Fish usually stays open until 8 pm Sunday through Thursday, and generally until 11 on Friday and Saturday. $ *Average main: $10* ✉ *170 6th Ave., Gaslamp Quarter* ☎ *619/238–8100* ⊕ *www.tinfishgaslamp.com* ⌛ *Reservations not accepted* ✛ *1:E5.*

$$ ✕ **Vela.** The name means "sail" in Latin, and this restaurant in the Hil-
ECLECTIC ton Bayfront hotel concentrates on cuisine and wines from coastal areas

8

around the globe but really runs the gamut. Served with delicious views of the bay, dishes range from arugula and peach salad to braised short ribs and seasonal preparations of salmon and scallops. Lunch brings burgers and pulled pork along with many vegan and gluten-free options. Quiet and business-appropriate, the restaurant has well-trained staff and decor set off by striking light fixtures with an ocean motif. [$] *Average main: $25* ✉ *1 Park Blvd., Gaslamp Quarter* ☎ *619/321–4284* 🌐 *www.hiltonsandiegobayfront.com* ✍ *Reservations essential* ✥ *1:E6.*

$$$ FRENCH 🍴 **The Westgate Room.** Normandy-born chef Fabrice Hardel oversees the preparation of three meals a day at the Westgate Hotel, writing seasonal menus that mix French and Asian flavors. At dinner you're likely to find specials like grilled salmon with spring onions and shiitake mushrooms, as well as classics like Dover sole meunière and New York steak with potato gratin. Chandeliers, white linen tablecloths, and fresh flowers create a classic fine dining atmosphere. The $42 Sunday brunch in the opulent Le Fontainebleau Room—with made-to-order crepes, omelets, and seafood dishes—is one of the best in town. [$] *Average main: $29* ✉ *Westgate Hotel, 1055 2nd Ave., Gaslamp Quarter* ☎ *619/557–3655* 🌐 *www.westgatehotel.com* ✥ *1:D3.*

EAST VILLAGE

$$ FRENCH Fodor's Choice ★ 🍴 **Café Chloe.** The intersection of 9th and G is the meeting point for San Diego's café society, thanks to the superchic and friendly Café Chloe. Surrounded by luxury high-rises, hotels, and boutiques, this pretty Parisian spot is frequented by the locals for breakfast, lunch, dinner, and weekend brunch. Whole wheat pancakes with sour-cherry sauce are an excellent way to start the day; lunch might mean a smoked trout and apple salad or a casserole of macaroni, pancetta, and Gorgonzola; and dinner highlights include duck confit or steak frites. Enjoy wines by the glass, imported teas, and coffee with desserts like seasonal fruit tarts or chocolate pot de crème. It's a particularly lovely place to spend the afternoon. [$] *Average main: $21* ✉ *721 9th Ave., East Village* ☎ *619/232–3242* 🌐 *www.cafechloe.com* ✥ *1:E4.*

$$$ STEAKHOUSE Fodor's Choice ★ 🍴 **Cowboy Star.** Executive chef Victor Jimenez cooks up porterhouses for two and grass-fed fillets along with fluffy mashed potatoes, glazed carrots, and garlic-sautéed spinach at this modern, urban steak house with a tongue-in-cheek cowboy theme. It's not a place for line dancing or peanut shelling: servers wear stylish plaid shirts and the wood-and-brick decor has leather accents and photography that recalls the Old West. Non–steak eaters can tuck into dishes like scallops with spiced kumquats and halibut with summer squash. The high-back booths are comfy; so are the chef's counter and the bar, where mixologists shake up strong bourbon cocktails. The drink selections include artisanal brews paired with the steaks. Street parking is usually available. [$] *Average main: $32* ✉ *640 10th Ave., East Village* ☎ *619/450–5880* 🌐 *www.thecowboystar.com* ⏲ *Closed Mon. No lunch Sun.* ✥ *1:E4.*

$ GREEK Fodor's Choice ★ 🍴 **The Kebab Shop.** Easy to find in Europe but rare in San Diego are kebab shops: fast-food Mediterranean eateries where roasted meats and falafel are served on plates of rice or wrapped in flatbread for consumption at all hours of the day. This East Village shop doesn't have much competition, but that doesn't mean it's not first-rate. The lamb is spicy and filling, and fresh tabouli and Greek salads round out the meals. For a delicious meal on the go, order the *döner* box: a choice of spiced lamb, marinated chicken, or falafel, accompanied by fries or rice, fresh veggies, and creamy garlic yogurt sauce. $ *Average main: $7* ⊠ *630 9th Ave., East Village* ☎ *619/525–0055* ⊕ *www.thekebabshop. com* ⚞ *Reservations not accepted* ✛ *1:E4.*

$
AMERICAN

✕ **Neighborhood.** There's no ketchup in the house—the young owners (inspired by the famous Father's Office in Los Angeles) don't want anything to mar the flavor of their perfectly seasoned burgers topped with pickled daikon or spicy Cajun sauce, and served on artisanal buns. Also highly recommended are the smoked, porter-braised beef ribs, the chorizo corn dogs, and the fennel frites with white balsamic vinegar. Wash any of it down with one of the many artisan beers such as Delirium Tremens on tap and Pliny the Elder, Belgian triple ale aged in Jim Beam casks, or wines by the glass. ■ **TIP →** There's a hidden, speakeasy-style bar in the back that's open at night. $ *Average main: $10* ⊠ *777 G St., East Village* ☎ *619/446–0002* ⊕ *www.neighborhoodsd.com* ⚞ *Reservations not accepted* ✛ *1:E4.*

LITTLE ITALY

$$
AMERICAN

✕ **Anthology.** Executive chef Todd Allison seeks to create fare that's as finely tuned as the music at this modern three-level supper club with a top-floor patio and wonderful acoustics. Contemporary jazz, rock, and blues music is played live here by artists including Diane Schuur, Brian McKnight, and Joe Sample. Stick to simple choices such as the mussels, short rib sliders, Caesar salad, and bananas Foster cake. Check the schedule in advance; the venue is closed on most Mondays and some other nights for private events. $ *Average main: $24* ⊠ *1337 India St., Little Italy* ☎ *619/595– 0300* ⊕ *www.anthologysd.com* ☾ *Closed most Mon.* ✛ *1:C3.*

$$
ITALIAN
Fodor'sChoice
★

✕ **Bencotto.** The Northern Italian team behind Bencotto opened a fine-dining restaurant in Milan and a bistro called Salumeria Rosi in New York before developing this sophisticated addition to Little Italy. Diners linger over wine and meat platters at the friendly bar and the more intimate upstairs dining room. Small plates designed for sharing include fried saffron risotto balls and sliced cantaloupe with prosciutto, but the real draws are the fresh pastas made daily in-house that include Gorgonzola-filled gnocchi, various ravioli, and squid-ink fettuccine. The pastas can be topped with a choice of sauces and chicken, shrimp, or meatballs. ■ **TIP →** Parking can be challenging but the Little Italy valet service is available after 6 pm. $ *Average main: $18* ⊠ *750 W. Fir St., Little Italy* ☎ *619/450–4786* ⊕ *www.lovebencotto.com* ☾ *Closed Mon. (except in summer)* ✛ *1:C2.*

$$
ITALIAN

✕ **Buon Appetito.** This charmer serves old world–style cooking in a casual environment. For a more relaxed meal, choose a table on the sidewalk; inside, the dining room is livelier, and jammed with art and fellow diners. Baked eggplant in a mozzarella-topped tomato sauce is a dream of a dish—in San Diego, tomato sauce doesn't get better than this. Other options worth considering include the sea bass in mushroom sauce, a hearty cioppino, and an expert osso bucco. There are affordable and varied wines to pair with everything. The young Italian waiters' good humor makes this a fun experience. $ *Average main: $17* ⊠ *1609 India St., Little Italy* ☎ *619/238–9880* ⊕ *www.buonappetito.signonsandiego.com* ✛ *1:C2.*

8

$ MODERN HAWAIIAN 🍴 **Craft & Commerce.** Winner of the 2011 Grand Orchid, one of San Diego's top design awards, Craft & Commerce is one of the several hip, tasty, and not-so-Italian restaurants to open in Little Italy the past few of years. Early in the evening, a young after-work crowd mingles at the bar with well-crafted cocktails and mini bacon-wrapped corn dogs. Dinner brings gastropub fare like fried chicken with buttermilk slaw, mussels, and a thick burger with red onion confit. It can get quite crowded on nights and weekends; go at lunch for a more relaxed vibe and a better look at the award-winning funky decor. [$] *Average main: $12* ✉ *675 W. Beech St., Little Italy* ☎ *619/269–2202* 🌐 *www.craft-commerce.com* ✍ *Reservations not accepted* ✥ *1:C2.*

$$ SOUTHWESTERN 🍴 **Indigo Grill.** Chef-partner Deborah Scott infuses her contemporary Southwestern cuisine with inspirations from Mexico to Alaska at this fun, upbeat restaurant. The broad terrace gets cool breezes—which do nothing to moderate the chilies that heat dishes such as a stacked beet salad, pecan-crusted trout, and salmon roasted on a wooden plank. Creative desserts like the coconut crème brûlée is so generous in size that it can easily satisfy two. The vibe is quieter during Sunday brunch, but the morning entrées, which include frittatas, chocolate bacon pancakes, and tamales with caramelized onions, are excellent. [$] *Average main: $26* ✉ *1536 India St., Little Italy* ☎ *619/234–6802* 🌐 *www.indigogrill.com* ⏲ *No lunch* ✥ *1:C2.*

$ CAFÉ 🍴 **Karen Krasne's Extraordinary Desserts.** For Paris-perfect cakes, tarts, and pots-de-crème, not to mention delicious and unusual breakfasts, lunches, and light dinners, head to this branch of Karen Krasne's pastry shop and café, a few blocks east of India Street, which is Little Italy's main drag. The converted commercial space has soaring ceilings and is serene and casual. The shop also sells artisanal cheeses, private-blend teas, and made-on-premises chocolates and ice creams. The panini sandwiches are creative and filling. The original shop is near Balboa Park, at 2929 5th Avenue. [$] *Average main: $13* ✉ *1430 Union St., Little Italy* ☎ *619/294–7001* 🌐 *www.extraordinarydesserts.com* ✍ *Reservations not accepted* ✥ *1:C2.*

$$$ ITALIAN 🍴 **Po Pazzo Bar and Grille.** An eye-catching creation from leading Little Italy restaurateurs Joe and Lisa Busalacchi, Po Pazzo earns its name, which means "a little crazy," by mixing a lively bar scene with a restaurant that serves modern Italian fare. It's sort of like a steak house with an accent, offering attractive salads and pasta dishes, as well as a top-notch presentation of steaks Sinatra style (with mushrooms, tomatoes, and onions) and Sicilian rib-eye steak that defines richness. Live music on weekends makes this a lively destination, so head elsewhere if you're looking for intimate conversations. [$] *Average main: $29* ✉ *1917 India St., Little Italy* ☎ *619/238–1917* 🌐 *www.popazzo.com* ✥ *1:C2.*

$$ ARGENTINE 🍴 **Puerto La Boca.** Named for a waterfront neighborhood in Buenos Aires that was home to generations of newly arrived Italian immigrants, this handsome restaurant is at the gateway to an area filling up with trendy boutiques, including a Harley-Davidson showroom. Like the cooking in Buenos Aires, the menu here marries the traditional Argentine love of beef—and lots of it—with traditional Italian recipes and techniques. A long list of sizable steaks is crowned

by the *parrillada*, a feast of beef cuts, sausage, sweetbreads, and chicken, meant to be shared by at least two people. The sliced tomatoes in a creamy Roquefort sauce are the perfect way to start the meal. If you're not in the mood for beef, try the unusual "Bombonera" pizza with prosciutto, heart of palm, and olives. $ *Average main: $25* ✉ *2060 India St., Little Italy* ☎ *619/234–4900* ⊕ *www. puertolaboca.com* ⊘ *No lunch Sun.* ✛ *1:C1.*

$$ ITALIAN

× **Trattoria Fantastica.** Sicilian flavors abound on the trattoria menu here, highlighted by such offerings as a salmon salad at lunch, linguine with clams, and the pasta *palermitana*—rigatoni with spicy sausage, olives, capers, and marinara sauce. The seafood pastas are particularly popular, as are the robust, well-seasoned pizzas baked in the stone oven. There is a pastry shop and gelateria at the front of the restaurant; head farther back for the rustic Italian dining room and the romantic courtyard. Call ahead if you want to score a table in the courtyard, and keep this in mind as a snack break for beautiful pastries, remarkable gelato, and freshly brewed Italian coffees. There's live piano music Friday through Sunday nights. $ *Average main: $20* ✉ *1735 India St., Little Italy* ☎ *619/234–1735* ⊕ *www.trattoriafantastica.com* ✛ *1:C2.*

EMBARCADERO

$$ SEAFOOD ☾

× **Fish Market.** Fresh mesquite-grilled, steamed, and skewered fish and shellfish are the specialty at this informal restaurant. There's also an excellent shellfish bar that serves crab cocktails and steamed clams. The Monday through Thursday happy hour means specials on snacks like oysters and smoked trout quesadillas, as well as drink deals. The view is stunning: enormous plate-glass windows look directly out onto the harbor. A more formal restaurant upstairs, Top of the Market, is expensive but worth the splurge, and is the place to find such rarities as Pacific swordfish with pumpkin risotto and ricotta salata. $ *Average main: $21* ✉ *750 N. Harbor Dr., Embarcadero* ☎ *619/232–3474 Fish Market, 619/234–4867 Top of the Market* ⊕ *www.thefishmarket. com* ✛ *1:A4.*

$$ ECLECTIC

× **Roy's Restaurant.** The modern and inviting space that is Roy's Restaurant overlooks the marina, and showcases chef Roy Yamaguchi's version of Hawaiian cuisine, fused with French techniques and flourishes. Inventive sushi such as a delicious surf-and-turf roll draped in Kobe beef give way to delicate lobster potstickers and Szechuan baby back ribs. Entrées run from the original macadamia-crusted mahimahi in lobster-studded beurre blanc sauce to beef short ribs. Desserts, like a hot chocolate soufflé, are served with island-style warmth. ■**TIP**➜ Parking is available in the San Diego Marriott Marquis and Marina garage for $8 with validation. $ *Average main: $24* ✉ *333 W. Harbor Dr., Embarcadero* ☎ *619/239–7697* ⊕ *www.roysrestaurant.com* ✛ *1:C5.*

8

BALBOA PARK AND BANKERS HILL

BALBOA PARK

There are a lot of food carts and small cafés in Balboa Park, but the Prado is the only sit-down restaurant worth visiting.

$$$
ECLECTIC
✕ **The Prado.** The striking Spanish-Moorish interior of this lovely restaurant in the historic House of Hospitality on Balboa Park's museum row has painted ceilings and elaborate glass sculptures. It also brings a contemporary menu to an area where picnic lunches or hot dogs from a nearby cart are the usual options. The bar is a fashionable pre- and post-theater destination for light nibbles with Latin, Italian, and Asian flavors and creative drinks; in the dining room, reliable dishes range from lunchtime grilled mahimahi tacos and a fancy pressed salad of baby arugula, strawberries, dried figs, and asiago cheese to saffron-scented lobster paella and roasted sea bass. $ *Average main: $30* ✉ *1549 El Prado, Balboa Park* ☎ *619/557–9441* ⊕ *www. pradobalboa.com* ⊗ *No dinner Mon.* ✛ *2:F6.*

BANKERS HILL

The recent influx of new condo dwellers to this neighborhood just west of Balboa Park has attracted the attention of several independent restaurateurs who are among the best in the city, and the area has become the next up-and-coming dining neighborhood in San Diego. San Diegans have long visited the area for classics like the circa-1970s Bertrand at Mister A's but now you can also find standout French, Asian, and Italian food mixed in with divey bars, old Chinese food haunts, and delis.

$$
AMERICAN
✕ **Ave 5.** In a brick-walled space that feels a bit like an art gallery, San Diego native and chef-owner Colin MacLaggan serves American cuisine with a French twist for dinner and Sunday brunch. In the evening, start with the crispy calamari or the baked Camembert salad with pecans, grapefruit, and honey vinaigrette. Excellent mains include grilled salmon with quinoa, lamb burger with truffle fries, and glazed short rib. The restaurant is known for cocktails such as the signature Ave 5, crafted with house-made blueberry tonic and vodka or gin. Desserts shine as well; the fromage blanc cheesecake is not to be missed. $ *Average main: $19* ✉ *2760 5th Ave., Bankers Hill* ☎ *619/542–0394* ⊕ *www.avenue5restaurant.com* ⊗ *Closed Mon.* ✛ *2:D6.*

$$
AMERICAN
✕ **Bankers Hill.** The living wall of succulents on the front patio hints at Bankers Hill's focus on fresh, thoughtfully prepared cuisine. Inside, the updated take on a bar and grill features open-beam ceilings and a zinc bar serving craft beers and sassy cocktails like the Conquistador, a mix of tequila, blood orange liqueur, jalapeño, and cilantro. Located on a quiet stretch of Bankers Hill, the restaurant draws a sophisticated, after-work crowd for happy hour drinks and eats. Dinner standbys—mostly comfort food with contemporary flair—include the crispy BBQ pork tacos, deviled eggs, and truffled french fries. $ *Average main: $19* ✉ *2202 4th Ave., Bankers Hill* ☎ *619/231–0222* ⊕ *www.bankershillsd. com* ⊗ *No lunch* ✛ *1:D5.*

Pepper-crusted tuna is a popular dish at Ave 5 in Bankers Hill.

$ 🍴 **Barrio Star.** In a colorful, airy Bankers Hill space, chef Isabel Cruz of
MEXICAN Isabel's Cantina and up-and-coming chef Todd Camburn put a fresh, distinctive, and rather refined spin on classic Mexican fare. After an afternoon at nearby Balboa Park, swing by for happy hour margaritas and tacos or feast on grilled sweet corn slathered in spicy lime butter, tortilla soup with cotija cheese, slow-roasted pork carnitas tacos with house-made tortillas, flourless Mexican chocolate cake, and Latin-inspired cocktails. On weekends, Barrio Star opens at 9 am for breakfasts of tamales, tortas, and blackberry pancakes. [$] *Average main: $12* ✉ *2706 5th Ave., Bankers Hill* ☎ *619/501–7827* 🌐 *www.barriostar.com* ✥ *2:D6.*

Fodor's Choice ★

$$$$ 🍴 **Bertrand at Mister A's.** Restaurateur Bertrand Hug's sumptuous 12th-
FRENCH floor dining room offers serene decor, contemporary paintings, and a view that stretches to Mexico, making it perfect for a sunset cocktail. It's a popular destination for wedding anniversaries, power lunches, and other significant meals. Chef Stephane Voitzwinkler creates luxurious seasonal dishes such as duck confit, sauteéed scallops with risotto, and grilled lamb chops with braised artichokes. The dessert list encompasses a galaxy of sweets. Service, led by the charming Hug, is expert and attentive. [$] *Average main: $36* ✉ *2550 5th Ave., 12th fl., Bankers Hill* ☎ *619/239–1377* 🌐 *www.bertrandatmisteras.com* ✍ *Reservations essential* ⏲ *No lunch weekends* ✥ *2:D6.*

$$$ 🍴 **Cucina Urbana.** Proprietor Tracy Borkum's casual and stylish Cal-
ITALIAN Italian spot remains one of the most popular tables in town. Everything is reasonably priced, and diners can pop into the retail wine room, select a bottle, and drink it with dinner for a modest corkage fee. The ricotta gnudi bathed in brown butter and fried sage are the best yet; fried squash blossoms sing; and polenta boards mixed tableside are creative

Fodor's Choice ★

and satisfying. Also good are the lasagna, the short rib pappardelle, and the goat cheese and toasted almond ravioli. Sit at the cozy bar and watch the chefs turn out bubbly, thin-crust pizzas topped with wild mushroom and taleggio cheese or pancetta fried egg and potatoes, or find a spot at the main bar for a clever cocktail crafted from seasonal fruit and Italian liqueurs. $ *Average main: $26* ✉ *505 Laurel St., Bankers Hill* ☎ *619/239–2222* ⊕ *www.cucinaurbana.com* ⚟ *Reservations essential* ✛ *2:E6.*

$$ ✗ **Hane Sushi.** An airy and open room with a fresh Japanese aesthetic is
JAPANESE   the setting for pristine and contemporary sushi by Roger Nakamura, who spent years learning his craft from Yukito Ota of San Diego's beloved Sushi Ota restaurant. Though Hane (pronounced "hah-nay") is trendier than Ota and offers nonsushi options like kobe beef carpaccio, sushi purists will be happy with the toro, uni, golden eye snapper, and special delicacies imported from Japan. The sweet shrimp is local, arriving fresh from "a little guy carrying a bucket," as staff say. Modernists will like the creative rolls and specialty cocktails. $ *Average main: $20* ✉ *2760 5th Ave., Bankers Hill* ☎ *619/260–1411* ⊗ *Closed Mon. No lunch weekends* ✛ *2:E6.*

$ ✗ **Marketplace Deli.** Don't be put off by the retro sign out front, the
AMERICAN   Marketplace Deli is a surprisingly modern and well-stocked grocery, wine shop, and liquor store. It's a lunchtime favorite for people from area offices and Balboa Park because of the amazingly varied and affordable sandwiches and salads made daily. Local favorites include the California sandwich with turkey, avocado, bacon, and sprouts; the Albacore Melt; and the Greek salad. $ *Average main: $5* ✉ *2601 5th Ave., Bankers Hill* ☎ *619/239–8361* ⊕ *www.marketplacedeli. menutoeat.com* ⊗ *No dinner* ✛ *2:E6.*

$ ✗ **Pizzicato Pizza.** Almost everything at Pizzicato, an East Coast phenom-
ITALIAN   enon that got its start in Portland, is made fresh daily, from the dough for the gourmet pizzas to the salads. Lunchtime brings panini stuffed with Tuscan meatballs, as well as grilled vegetable salads and lunch specials for under $8. Popular pizzas include the four-cheese with sausage and mushrooms; a Thai-style pizza with shrimp, peanut sauce, and roasted sweet peppers; and the *molto carne* with prosciutto, pepperoni, and Italian sausage. $ *Average main: $8* ✉ *2420 5th Ave., Bankers Hill* ☎ *619/232–9000* ⊕ *www.pizzicatopizza.com* ✛ *2:D6.*

OLD TOWN AND UPTOWN

Hillcrest and the nearby Uptown district, formed by the neighborhoods of University Heights, Normal Heights, and North Park, are a mecca for affordable and diverse ethnic dining and entertainment. Most of these spots are independently owned by restaurateurs who are on-site to make sure their customers are happy. Hillcrest is an easy walking neighborhood that's open to everyone but is considered the center of San Diego's gay community. The other Uptown neighborhoods are known for their hip and health-conscious eateries, where you'll have no problem finding vegan and gluten-free entrées served with the city's finest craft beers.

CLOSE UP

Where to Refuel Around Town

San Diego has a few homegrown chains as well as many stand-alone eateries that will amiably fill you up without demanding too much cash in return.

Burger Lounge
(⊕ *www.burgerlounge.com*) specializes in juicy burgers made from grass-fed beef—besides skipping grain, the cows were also raised without growth hormones or antibiotics. Locations in Kensington (⊠ *4116 Adams Ave.* ☎ *619/584–2929*), Coronado (⊠ *922 Orange Ave.* ☎ *619/435–6835*), Gaslamp (⊠ *528 5th Ave.* ☎ *619/955–5727*), La Jolla (⊠ *1101 Wall St.* ☎ *858/456–0196*), and Little Italy (⊠ *1608 India St.* ☎ *619/237–7878*) share a retro-mod orange and white decor and hearty side dishes like onion rings and house-made french fries, sodas, and malts. The turkey burgers are equally flavorful.

A vast and varied homegrown chain specializing in seafood is the **Brigantine** (multiple locations, see ⊕ *www.brigantine.com*), which offers a cozy atmosphere and a menu that ranges from fish tacos to fresh oysters, grilled swordfish with avocado butter, and wok-charred ahi tuna in every corner of San Diego County. The happy hours at any of the Brigantine (aka "The Brig" to locals) restaurants are popular for the oysters and fish tacos.

The Mission, a local minichain open only for breakfast and lunch, has three locations: Mission Beach (⊠ *3795 Mission Blvd.* ☎ *858/488–9060*), North Park (⊠ *2801 University Ave.* ☎ *619/220–8992*), and the East Village (⊠ *1250 J St.* ☎ *619/232–7662*). They all fulfill their mission as a breakfast-and-lunch destination (there's no service after 3 pm) with

a menu that runs the gamut from banana-blackberry pancakes to a Zen breakfast complete with tofu and brown rice, to creative black-bean burritos and a smoked turkey sandwich. Or if you're in the mood for excellent Mexican-style comfort fare, head to **Achiote** (⊕ *www.achioterestaurants. com*) in San Ysidro (⊠ *4119 Camino de la Plaza* ☎ *619/690–1494*) and Otay Mesa (⊠ *2110 Birch Rd.* ☎ *619/482–0307*)—the omelet with chipotle cream sauce is muy rico. Sushi lovers should head to **Harney Sushi** in Old Town (⊠ *3964 Harney St.* ☎ *619/295–3272*) and Oceanside (⊠ *301 Mission Ave.* ☎ *760/967–1820* ⊕ *www.harneysushi.com*) for California-style sushi and superfresh fish with a rocking atmosphere that includes DJ booths and a sexy modern Asian design.

If there's something for everyone at the Mission, the statement is equally true of San Diego's enormously popular **Sammy's Woodfired Pizza** (multiple locations; see ⊕ *www. sammyspizza.com*) chain. With convenient outlets in La Jolla, Mission Valley, and the Gaslamp Quarter, Sammy's makes friends with oversize salads, a vast selection of pizzas, entrées, and pastas, and the fun "messy sundae," which lives up to its name.

Besides chains, keep these streets or neighborhoods in mind for refueling: funky Ocean Beach, famed for its easygoing breakfast places; Little Italy (India Street), with endless Italian options; and Hillcrest in the vicinity of the 5th Avenue–University Avenue intersection, a buffet of international cuisines. If you want Asian, Convoy Street in Kearny Mesa is the place to go.

8

The historic adobe buildings clustered in the center of Old Town are where California first started; it's the first permanent encampment of Spanish settlers. Obviously, it's Mexican food that reigns here, though many of the restaurants that were once independently owned have become very commercial. Still, Old Town offers a few choices for affordable and authentic cuisine. Heaping dishes of enchiladas, tacos, and carnitas (slow-cooked pork) can be found at any of the lively spots along San Diego Avenue and at Fiesta de Reyes, a cluster of shops and eateries by the Old Town Historic Park.

> **OLD VINES**
>
> Napa and Sonoma counties in Northern California might get all the publicity when it comes to wine, but California viticulture got its start in San Diego—in Old Town to be exact. There are no vines there anymore, but Wine Cabana (✉ 2539 Congress St. ☎ 619/574–9463) offers cozy cabanas for sneaking away from the tourist trail and relaxing with a glass of California Chardonnay.

Mission Valley, east of Balboa Park is the shopper's paradise, where big-box restaurants cater to refueling shoppers on their way to or from one of the area's massive malls—Fashion Valley and Westfield Mission Valley—which are just blocks apart. Mission Valley also includes the Hotel Circle area of San Diego, which includes plenty of tourist and business hotels, and a large golf course that can be seen from Interstate 8, the east–west freeway that feeds into Mission Valley. The area isn't known for groundbreaking cuisine, but it has lots of satisfying casual and fast-casual spots.

OLD TOWN

$ ✕ **Blue Water Seafood Market & Grill.** Take one bite of the fresh, perfectly

SEAFOOD   grilled fish at this seafood spot and you'll forget about the no-frills decor. Placing an order at the counter is a three-step process. First, choose the type of fish (mahimahi, swordfish, and seared ahi are popular). Next, tell them how you want your fish seasoned (lemon butter, garlic butter, teriyaki, or chipotle). Finally, decide whether you'd like it served as a sandwich, over salad, or on a plate with rice. Check the prices prior to ordering because they fluctuate according to market availability. The kids' menu has chicken fingers and grilled cheese for seafood-averse little ones. $ Average main: $11 ✉ 3667 India St., Old Town ☎ 619/497–0914 ⊕ www.bluewaterseafoodsandiego.com ⌦ Reservations not accepted ✛ 2:C5.

$$$ ✕ **El Agave.** The area is a bit touristy so you might not expect to find

MEXICAN   such authentic regional Mexican fare at this comfortably upmarket restaurant. Standout options include quesadillas filled with mushrooms, baked halibut in chipotle sauce with rice and vegetables, and chicken in a slow-simmered mole sauce. There are more than 2,000 tequilas to choose from, displayed throughout the brick-walled space (even on shelves suspended from the ceiling), which make El Agave the largest "tequileria" in the United States. The collection includes artisanal tequilas dating to the 1930s and some infused with jalapeño chilies. $ Average main: $30 ✉ 2304 San Diego Ave., Old Town ☎ 619/220–0692 ⊕ www.elagave.com ✛ 2:A4.

$$ JAPANESE 🍴 **Harney Sushi.** People in the know come here for super-fresh California-style sushi and modern Asian cuisine served in a sexy atmosphere with a live DJ spinning popular music and R&B favorites. The walls are lined with high-end modern Asian art and moody lighting throughout; there's also a heated outdoor patio. Inventive sushi rolls include the Rolls Royce with lobster tempura and the sweet and spicy Lightning Roll with shrimp tempura, spicy tuna, and baked black cod. Open until midnight every night, Harney is perfect for late-night dining and cocktails. [$] *Average main: $20* ✉ *3964 Harney St., Old Town* ☎ *619/295–3272* 🌐 *www.harneysushi.com* 🕑 *No lunch weekends* ✣ *2:A4.*

$ MEXICAN Fodor's Choice ★ 🍴 **Lucha Libre.** On any given weekday at lunch, you're sure to see a line of locals from nearby offices waiting for their favorite Lucha Libre picks—and the food here is worth the wait. Named for a form of Mexican wrestling that often involves brightly colored masks, the restaurant's hot-pink walls and shiny booths create a fun and family-friendly atmosphere. There is an array of gourmet tacos and burritos on the menu; the Surfin' California burrito packed with grilled steak, shrimp, french fries, avocado, and chipotle sauce is a favorite. There are also many meatless options. [$] *Average main: $7* ✉ *1810 W. Washington St., Old Town* ☎ *619/296–8226* 🌐 *www.tacosmackdown.com* ✣ *2:B5.*

$ MEXICAN 🍴 **Miguel's Cocina Old Town.** Located on Old Town's main drag, Miguel's has a covered terrace with a fireplace as well as a spacious, family-friendly dining room. The kitchen offers Mexican brick-oven entrées like an achiote and citrus-marinated pork roast and jumbo shrimp stuffed with jack cheese and wrapped with bacon. For a true Old Town dining experience, share a plate of carnitas: slow-roasted pork with tortillas and salsa fresca. The margarita list includes flavors like prickly pear, pomegranate, and habanero-lime. Wine, mojitos, and margaritas are $5 during the daily 2–6 pm happy hour. [$] *Average main: $13* ✉ *2444 San Diego Ave., Old Town* ☎ *619/298–9840* 🌐 *www.brigantine.com/miguels_cocina* ✣ *2:A4.*

$ AMERICAN 🍴 **Starlite.** This trendy 21-and-over establishment attracts a diverse and discerning crowd to a somewhat quiet stretch of India Street with its solid seasonal fare and understated midcentury vibe. At the center of the intimate, award-winning interior is a chandelier made of stainless steel tubes cut to reveal soft, twinkling lights. Chef Kathleen Wise covers the gamut of comfort food from Belgian-style fries and marinated olives to organic macaroni and cheese, juicy roasted chicken, and a fish of the day paired with mushrooms and bitter greens. Cocktails are just as creative and seasonal as the cuisine; in hot weather the Starlite Mule in a copper cup is the perfect way to cool off. Brunch is served on Sunday. [$] *Average main: $16* ✉ *3175 India St., Old Town* ☎ *619/358–9766* 🌐 *www.starlitesandiego.com* ✣ *2:C6.*

HILLCREST

$$ INDIAN 🍴 **Bombay Exotic Cuisine of India.** Notable for its sultry, elegant dining room, complete with a waterfall, Bombay employs a chef whose generous hand with lush local produce gives each course a colorful freshness reminiscent of California cuisine, though the flavors definitely hail from India. Try the tandoori lettuce-wrap appetizer and any of the stuffed *kulchas* (stuffed flatbreads). The unusually large selection of curries

8

may be ordered with meat, chicken, fish, or tofu. The curious should try the *dizzy noo shak*, a sweet and spicy banana curry. The lunch buffet, served every day from 11 to 2:30, is an excellent way to sample a variety of delicacies. [$] *Average main: $19* ✉ *3960 5th Ave., Hillcrest* ☎ *619/297–7777* 🌐 *www.bombayrestaurant.com* ✥ *2:D4.*

$ CAFÉ Fodor's Choice ★ 🍴 **Bread & Cie.** There's an East Coast air to this artsy urban bakery and café known for being one of San Diego's first and best artisanal bread bakers. Owner Charles Kaufman is a former New Yorker and a filmmaker, and he gave Bread & Cie a sense of theater by putting bread ovens imported from France at center stage. Warm focaccia covered in cheese and vegetables, crusty loaves of black olive bread, bear claws, gourmet granola with Mediterranean yogurt, and first-rate cinnamon rolls are served from daybreak to sunset; lunch time also brings options like house-made quiche and panini filled with pastrami, turkey, and pesto, or Brie and honey. [$] *Average main: $7* ✉ *350 University Ave., Hillcrest* ☎ *619/683–9322* 🌐 *www.breadandcie.com* ⏲ *No dinner* ✥ *2:D4.*

$$ AMERICAN 👶 🍴 **Hash House A Go Go.** Expect to wait an hour or more for weekend breakfast at this splashy Hillcrest eatery, where the walls display photos of farm machinery and other icons of Middle America, although the menu takes a Southern-accented look at national favorites. The supersize portions are notable; at breakfast, huge platters carpeted with fluffy pancakes sail out of the kitchen, while at noon customers favor the overflowing chicken pot pies crowned with flaky pastry. The parade of old-fashioned good eats continues at dinner with hearty meat and seafood dishes, including sage-flavored fried chicken, bacon-studded waffles, and meatloaf stuffed with roasted red pepper, spinach, and mozzarella with a side of mashed potatoes. [$] *Average main: $22* ✉ *3628 5th Ave., Hillcrest* ☎ *619/298–4646* 🌐 *www.hashhouseagogo.com* ⏲ *Closed Mon. night* ✥ *2:D5.*

$$ MOROCCAN 🍴 **Kous Kous Moroccan Bistro.** Settle into the low-cushioned seating and let the sensual atmosphere of the dining room, draped in imported fabrics and hung with Moroccan lanterns, transport you to somewhere far away for the evening. Moroccan-style couscous makes a tasty bed for a variety of dishes by chef Moumen Nouri including tagines with chicken, merguez sausage, or vegetables, grilled skewers loaded with meat, and salads like *khizzou* of roasted carrots with ginger. The food is flavorful without being spicy. The strawberries with orange flower water are a delicious way to end the meal. Set-price Moroccan feasts are available, starting at $22 per person. [$] *Average main: $17* ✉ *3940 4th Ave., Hillcrest* ☎ *619/295–5560* 🌐 *www.kouskousrestaurant.com* ⏲ *No lunch* ✥ *2:D4.*

$$ MEXICAN 👶 Fodor's Choice ★ 🍴 **Ortega's Bistro.** Californians have long flocked to Puerto Nuevo, the "lobster village" south of San Diego in Baja California, so when a member of the family that operates several Puerto Nuevo restaurants opened Ortega's, it became an instant sensation. The draw is no-nonsense, authentic Mexican fare, and the specialty of choice is a whole lobster prepared Baja-style (steamed then grilled) and served with superb beans, rice, and made-to-order tortillas. But there are other fine options, too, including melt-in-your-mouth carnitas (slow-cooked

pork), made-at-the-table guacamole, and grilled tacos filled with *huit-lacoche* corn mushrooms and Mexican herbs. The pomegranate margaritas are a must, as is the special red salsa if you like authentic spice. $ *Average main: $18 ⊠ 141 University Ave., Hillcrest* ☎ *619/692–4200* ⊕ *www.ortegasbistro.com* ✛ *2:D4.*

$ ✕ **Pizzeria Arrivederci.** The superhot oven in this restaurant, which is
ITALIAN   run by a native of Sorrento, adds an authentic toasty flavor to pizzas
↻   topped with forest mushrooms and smoky *scamorza* cheese, and to
the *alla messicana,* a Mexican-style pie whose topping includes pork
sausage, cilantro, and crushed red peppers. The list of imaginative pizzas
is long (yes, you can get a pepperoni pizza, too), but there are also
expertly made pastas such as farfalle in a creamy vodka sauce with
smoked salmon, and lobster ravioli. Start with a well-priced glass or
bottle of wine and a plate of roasted peppers with anchovies or the
shrimp and white-bean salad with arugula. The young waiters from
Italy treat guests well. $ *Average main: $14 ⊠ 3789 4th Ave., Hillcrest*
☎ *619/542–0293* ⊕ *www.arrivederciristorante.com* ✛ *2:D4.*

$ ✕ **Saffron Noodles.** Outdoor tables on a narrow sidewalk and inexpen-
THAI   sive prices make this and the neighboring Saffron Thai Grilled Chicken
takeout worth a short detour from Old Town. The simple menu has
spicy and mild noodle soups; stir-fried noodles with chicken, beef, pork,
or shrimp; and a couple of uncommon Vietnamese and Thai-Indian
noodle dishes bathed with aromatic sauces: the spicy "Eslam" dish is
made of wide rice noodles stir-fried with chicken or tofu in a sauce of
turmeric, lemongrass, and chilies. The Saffron Noodles restaurant has
a minimalist look but is sunny and comfortable. Go next door for to-go
boxes of the namesake grilled half chicken served with jasmine rice,
tart-sweet cucumber salad, and savory house-made peanut sauce. $ *Average main: $8 ⊠ 3731 India St., Hillcrest* ☎ *619/574–7737* ⊕ *www.*
saffronsandiego.com ⌲ *Reservations not accepted* ✛ *2:B5.*

MISSION VALLEY

$ ✕ **King's Fish House.** This warehouse-size restaurant is wildly popular
SEAFOOD   with shoppers at Mission Valley's many malls, owing to extremely
↻   friendly and efficient service, tanks filled with lively lobsters, and a
daily-changing menu with a fine selection of freshly shucked oysters.
Specialties include New Orleans–style barbecued shrimp and a New
England clambake complete with red potatoes and sweet corn on the
cob. Seasonal fish and shellfish are char-grilled, deep-fried, sautéed,
steamed, or skewered, and the menu obliges meat eaters with a convincing cheeseburger, roasted chicken, and grilled sirloin. When jammed, the
scene recalls a train station—and sounds like one, too. $ *Average main:*
$17 ⊠ 825 Camino de la Reina N, Mission Valley ☎ *619/574–1230*
⊕ *www.kingsfishhouse.com* ✛ *2:E2.*

$ ✕ **Mr. Peabody's Burgers & Ale.** Burgers and beer are an unbeatable com-
AMERICAN   bination anywhere, but especially within a stone's throw of the pricey
Fashion Valley mall. Friendly and informal, this bustling eatery is fine
for kids during lunch, but perhaps not after that. The attractions range
from the domestic, microbrew, and imported beers and juicy half-pound
burgers to a variety of tacos like ones with seasoned ground turkey and
a satisfying, gently priced rib-eye steak. Order a basket of excellent

fries or onion rings for the table, but not both, because the portions are beyond huge. [$] *Average main: $10* ✉ *6110 Friars Rd., Mission Valley* ☎ *619/542–1786* ✍ *Reservations not accepted* ✣ *2:B2.*

$ AMERICAN 👍 🍴 **Ricky's Restaurant.** Chain restaurants haven't driven out all of San Diego's old-line family dining spots, and this unpretentious place, opened in 1968 on the quiet fringe of Mission Valley, remains dear to the city's heart. A traditional three-meals-daily restaurant, Ricky's serves big portions of unassuming, well-prepared, all-American cooking, like steak with all the trimmings for $16, but it's really famed for breakfast, when savory corned-beef hash and fluffy strawberry Dutch baby and oven-baked omelets are the rule. The spectacular apple pancake, a soufflé-like creation that takes 20 minutes to bake, arrives piping hot and is irresistible to the last molecule of molten cinnamon sugar. Ricky's popularity never wanes. [$] *Average main: $13* ✉ *2181 Hotel Circle S, Mission Valley* ☎ *619/291–4498* ✣ *2:B3.*

$ AMERICAN 🍴 **The Zodiac.** Men like to lunch at this elegant room in the luxurious Neiman Marcus department store as much as the ladies, who enjoy cool chardonnay and the restaurant's complimentary chicken consommé and hot popovers with strawberry butter. Healthy seafood-topped salads abound, but they get serious competition from the likes of a dressy lobster club sandwich, salmon with couscous, and filet mignon. The desserts are as self-indulgent as some of the well-heeled patrons. This is by far the best place to dine in Fashion Valley, which is universally regarded as San Diego's leading shopping center. [$] *Average main: $18* ✉ *Neiman Marcus, Fashion Valley, 7027 Friars Rd., Mission Valley* ☎ *619/542–4450* ⏲ *No dinner* ✣ *2:C2.*

UNIVERSITY HEIGHTS

$ MEXICAN 🍴 **El Zarape.** There's a humble air to this cozy Mexican taqueria, but one bite of the signature scallop tacos and you'll realize something special is happening in the kitchen. Inside the satiny corn tortilla, seared bay scallops mingle with tangy white sauce and shredded cheese. Or perhaps you'll prefer sweet pieces of lobster meat in oversize quesadillas, burritos filled with chiles rellenos, or the original beef, ham, and pineapple Aloha burrito. No matter, nearly everything is fantastic at this busy under-the-radar eatery. Mexican beverages, including the sweet-tart hibiscus-flower drink *jamaica* (pronounced ha-ma-ike-ah)and the cinnamon rice drink *horchata,* and house-made flan and rice pudding round out the menu. [$] *Average main: $6* ✉ *4642 Park Blvd., University Heights* ☎ *619/692–1652* 🌐 *www.elzarape.menutoeat.com* ✣ *2:F3.*

$ FRENCH 🍴 **Farm House Cafe.** Chef Olivier Biouteau and his wife, Rochelle, are living their dream of owning a French country restaurant—but in San Diego. Escargot risotto, savory flatbreads, fettuccini with lamb, and even a perfect burger paired with affordable wines are among the delights that await. It's a cozy room, so call ahead; regulars like to fill the seats at the bar. The dinner and Sunday brunch menus change seasonally but many of the sweets stay the same. Save room for the almond panna cotta, butterscotch pot de crème with cookies, or Olivier's chocolate truffles. [$] *Average main: $18* ✉ *2121 Adams Ave., University Heights* ☎ *619/269–9662* 🌐 *www.farmhousecafesd.com* ⏲ *Closed Mon.* ✣ *2:F3.*

NORTH PARK

North Park is a young, hip neighborhood, about a 10-minute drive from Downtown, past Balboa Park. It's popular among locals but not as much for tourists because it's less convenient than many other San Diego neighborhoods. You won't find million-dollar views or nightclubs with bottle service, but North Park has some of the best and most eclectic food in San Diego. It's hard to think of a style of food not found here. Starting at the intersection of University Avenue and 30th Street, it's possible to walk in any direction and find inexpensive spots serving French, vegetarian, Mexican, Hawaiian, Southern, and Asian cuisines, as well as dessert cafés, wine bars, gastropubs, and gourmet coffee and tea houses. If you're in town on the 30th of the month, head to North Park for the monthly 30th on 30th night, when area eateries have food and drink specials, such as $2 wines and $3 appetizers.

SAN DIEGO'S BOUNTY

Sunny San Diego is one of the premier agricultural areas in the country. Visit a farmers' market and have a taste: spring is the season for cherimoyas and strawberries, summer brings peaches and boysenberries, autumn is the time for apples and pears, and winter is abundant with tangerines and grapefruit. There's a different market every day of the week; check the list of farmers' markets around the county at 🌐 *www.sdfarmbureau.org.*

$$ AMERICAN 🍴 **The Linkery.** The menu at this earthy farm-to-table-style restaurant reads like a Who's Who of seasonal produce and the area's top organic farms. A changing roster of house-made sausages such as chicken-mushroom, *kaisekreiner* (spicy Vienna-style pork sausage with cheese), and smoky poblano pork lends the casual restaurant its name, but there's vegetarian fare, too, including a carrot ginger soup and marinated eggplant burgers. Entrées include grass-fed skirt steak with purple potato mash and gnocchi with peppers. Every night has a different themed special, from Monday's sausage night to fish fry Fridays, Saturday's lowcountry boil, and Sunday's choucroute. The well-chosen wine and beer list includes cask-conditioned ales. [$] *Average main: $23* ✉ *3794 30th St., North Park* ☎ *619/255–8778* 🌐 *www.thelinkery.com* ✥ *2:G4.*

$ MIDDLE EASTERN 🍴 **Mama's Bakery & Lebanese Deli.** This little house converted into a restaurant serves some of the best authentic Lebanese fare in San Diego County. The key is the *sajj*, a superheated oven that's used to cook the herbed flatbread of the same name. The warm *sajj* bread might be wrapped around garlicky marinated chicken, hummus, and vegetables, or made into the Manakeesh Ultimate, a combination of yogurt cheese, herbs, tomatoes, olives, and fresh mint. Try the hearty seasoned ground beef "kafta" plate that includes house-made hummus, basmati rice, green salad, and pita bread. For dessert, don't resist the buttery baklava filled with cashews or pistachio nuts. [$] *Average main: $9* ✉ *4237 Alabama St., North Park* ☎ *619/688–0717* 🌐 *www.mamasbakery.net* ✍ *Reservations not accepted* ⏰ *No dinner weekends* ✥ *2:F3.*

$ PIZZA 🍴 **URBN Coal Fired Pizza.** A few blocks east of 30th Street (North Park's restaurant row), this 5,000-square-foot warehouse is a chic and casual pizza spot. Hip young locals chow down on coal-fired New Haven–style pies, fresh salads, and cheese boards. Try the carbalicious mashed potato pizza pie topped with pancetta, fresh mozzarella, and Parmesan. Linger with a local brew or a craft cocktail off the extensive drink list. It's a good space for groups so the atmosphere can get quite festive. $ *Average main: $8* ✉ *3085 University Ave., North Park* ☎ *619/255–7300* ⊕ *www.urbnnorthpark.com* ⊘ *No lunch Mon.* ✛ *2:H4.*

NORMAL HEIGHTS

$

CAFÉ

⊙

✕ **Viva Pops.** Frozen treats are elevated to an art form at this colorful shop in the Adams Avenue corridor where owner Lisa Altmann creates popsicles from organic seasonal fruits. The nectarine-basil and strawberry pops shine in summer; cool weather brings flavors like pomegranate, pineapple chili, blood orange, and creamy passion fruit; the popular Mexican chocolate and lavender-lemonade are available year-round. Be sure to bring cash, as they don't accept credit cards. $ *Average main: $3* ✉ *3330 Adams Ave., Normal Heights* ☎ *619/795–1080* ⊕ *www.ilovevivapops.com* ▭ *No credit cards* ⊘ *Closed Mon. and Tues.* ✛ *2:H2.*

MISSION BAY, BEACHES, AND SEAWORLD

This sprawling area, which includes Pacific Beach, is all about great views of the water, sandy beaches, and relaxation. Most of the restaurants here are casual spots that diners can visit in T-shirts and board shorts or little sundresses and flip-flops. Food available here is similarly laid-back. Burgers and tacos are easy to find, but so are sushi, Mexican, and Thai food. Many of the restaurants here are bars at heart that serve food and quickly transform around 9 pm, but several venues including JRDN, Isabel's Cantina, and Gringo's serve food that's notable.

MISSION BAY

$$

SEAFOOD

⊙

✕ **Red Marlin.** The bright, modern space in the Hyatt Regency Mission Bay has soaring ceilings and large bay windows overlooking the water. The outdoor deck has fire pits and more of a lounge feel. Start with a pot of clams steamed with bacon and garlic, or a blue crab cake with preserved lemon and a salad, then move on to seared sea scallops with heirloom tomatoes or a grilled filet mignon. The kids' menu has turkey sandwiches on whole wheat, oatmeal, carrot sticks, and other healthy options along with the standard chicken nuggets. ▥ **TIP➔** During the summer, linger outside to catch the SeaWorld fireworks show (schedule available at www.seaworldparks.com). $ *Average main: $26* ✉ *1441 Quivira Rd., Mission Bay* ☎ *619/221–4868* ⊕ *www.hyatt.com/gallery/redmarlin* ✛ *3:C6.*

PACIFIC BEACH

$

CARIBBEAN

✕ **Andrés Restaurant.** For more than two decades, Andrés was San Diego's sole outpost for savory Cuban and Puerto Rican cuisine. In a nondescript building in the Morena Boulevard home-furnishings district near Pacific Beach, it's still not much to look at, but the enclosed-patio dining room is comfortable, and servers smile as they place heaped-high plates of breaded steak, roast pork, and grilled marinated fish in front of impressed diners. For Cuban home cooking at its best, order

JRDN (pronounced Jordan) in the Tower23 Hotel is a great spot for a sunset dinner.

the *picadillo*, a ground-beef hash with bold and piquant flavors and avoid the often-overcooked pollo asado. All entrées are accompanied by oceans of delicious black beans and mountains of rice. Nothing ever changes here, which is just how the regulars like it. $\boxed{\$}$ *Average main: $12 ✉ 1235 Morena Blvd., Pacific Beach* ☎ *619/275–4114* ⊕ *www.andresrestaurantsd.com* ✛ *3:E6.*

$$ ✕ **Caffe Bella Italia.** Contemporary northern Italian cooking as prepared ITALIAN in Italy is the rule at this simple dinner-only restaurant about a mile from the ocean. It's one of the more romantic places you'll find in Pacific Beach, especially on the candlelit outdoor patio, but jeans and flip-flops are perfectly acceptable. Popular choices from the menu include Neapolitan-style squid ink ravioli stuffed with lobster, pizzas baked in a wood-fired oven, and entrées like chicken breast sautéed with Marsala wine and mushrooms, or slices of rare filet mignon tossed with herbs and topped with arugula and Parmesan shavings. Impressive daily specials might include options like beet-stuffed ravioli in creamy saffron sauce. $\boxed{\$}$ *Average main: $21 ✉ 1525 Garnet Ave., Pacific Beach* ☎ *858/273–1224* ⊕ *www.caffebellaitalia.com* ☾ *No lunch* ✛ *3:C5.*

$ ✕ **Isabel's Cantina.** A funky mix of Asian and Latin fare mingles on the ECLECTIC inventive menu at this popular beachy restaurant created by chef and cookbook author Isabel Cruz. A huge teak Buddha reposes coolly in one corner, playing yin to the yang of spicy Latin-inspired fare. You can start the day early here with coconut French toast, soy-chorizo scramble with black beans, and healthy egg-white dishes. Lunch and dinner dishes include crispy wontons with ahi tuna, chicken lettuce wraps, and grilled salmon with house-made salsas. For a night away from the rowdy Pacific Beach bars, go here for espresso drinks and desserts

Talking Tacos

Even though terms like taco, burrito, enchilada, and tostada are as common as macaroni and cheese to San Diegans, don't count on any residents to agree on where to find the best ones. That's because tacos are as individual as spaghetti sauce and come in endless variations from small, authentic Mexico City–style tacos to Cal-Mex versions in crunchy shells topped with cheddar cheese.

The most traditional style of taco features a small soft corn tortilla pressed from corn masa dough and filled with shredded beef, carne asada (roasted beef), braised tongue in green sauce, spicy marinated pork, or deep-fried fish or seafood. Tortillas made from white flour are out there, too, but they're not nearly as tasty.

Garnishes usually include a drizzle of salsa and a squeeze of tart Mexican lime (a small citrus similar to the Key lime that's juicier than the large lime commonly found in the United States), along with chopped cilantro and onion. Whole radishes topped with lime juice and a sprinkle of salt are served on the side.

Mama Testa's (⊠ 1417 University Ave., Suite A, Hillcrest ☎ 619/298–8226 ⊕ www.mamatestataqueria. com ✛ 2:E4) shows the diversity of regional Mexican tacos with ones that are fried, steamed, and grilled. The salsa bar, which offers at least eight different selections including a spicy peanut salsa, is unparalleled. The restaurant's name (a suggestive double entendre in Spanish) and the colorful decor inspired by Mexican lucha libre wrestling and loteria are all part of the fun.

If you can't make it across the border, check out **Tacos El Gordo**, a well-known Tijuana taco franchise that has branches in Chula Vista (⊠ 689 H St. ☎ 619/691–8848) and National City (⊠ 1940 Highland Ave. ☎ 619/474–5033). Carne asada and seasoned pork adobada tacos on small freshly made tortillas are popular, but El Gordo also offers more exotic fillings like sesos (brain) or tripa (intestines). Look for their distinctive red-and-white sign, since there are imitators.

Most casual San Diego restaurants offer some version of the fish taco, either with batter-fried white fish or grilled fish topped with a mayonnaise-based tangy white sauce, shredded cabbage, lime, and salsa. A combination plate almost always includes seasoned rice and beans, either soupy or refried beans that are smooth and creamy thanks to the addition of lots of fat. Both styles of beans are crowned with melted shredded cheese and usually support a small raft of shredded lettuce dabbed with a bit of sour cream. Any empty spaces (you shouldn't see more of the plate than the rim) will be hidden by the preferred combination of tacos, enchiladas, chiles rellenos, and burritos.

What are those? Enchiladas can be filled with cheese, chicken, or beef and topped with savory, mostly mild red or green chili sauce. Chiles rellenos are mild, deep-fried peppers stuffed with cheese and then baked in tomato and chili sauce. Burritos are flour tortillas filled with beans, rice, and shredded meat. Breakfast burritos typically contain eggs, cheese, and potatoes and are often served all day.

like sautéed bananas and decadent flourless chocolate cake. $\boxed{\text{\$}}$ *Average main: $14* ✉ *966 Felspar St., Pacific Beach* ☎ *858/272–8400* ⊕ *www. isabelscantina.com* ✣ *3:C5.*

$$$
AMERICAN

✕ **JRDN.** With some 300 seats, this ocean-facing restaurant (pronounced Jordana), in the beach-chic boutique-style Tower23 Hotel might sound overwhelming, but the seating is divided between a long, narrow outdoor terrace and a series of relatively intimate indoor rooms. Chef David Warner prepares modern steak house fare including chops and steaks with sauces of the diner's choosing, lightened with lots of seasonal produce and a raw bar menu. Weekend brunch and lunch have a similar appeal, with dishes like crab cake eggs Benedict with citrus hollandaise, a blackened mahimahi sandwich, and a summer melon salad. On Friday and Saturday the bar is the place to see and be seen in Pacific Beach for under-thirty types, and it's jammed after 9 pm. $\boxed{\text{\$}}$ *Average main: $33* ✉ *Tower 23 Hotel, 723 Felspar St., Pacific Beach* ☎ *858/270–5736* ⊕ *www.jrdn.com* ✣ *3:B5.*

$
AMERICAN

✕ **Kono's Surf Club Café.** Kono's in Pacific Beach lures the locals with an outdoor patio and ocean views, but the last thing you'll want to do after eating one of Kono's massive breakfast burritos is slip into a bikini. There's a reason for the expression "burrito belly"—but it's a small price to pay for brazenly overindulgent pleasure. They're open till 2 pm weekdays, and till 3 pm on the weekends. $\boxed{\text{\$}}$ *Average main: $7* ✉ *704 Garnet Ave., Pacific Beach* ☎ *858/483–1669* ⊗ *No dinner* ✣ *3:B5.*

$
THAI

✕ **Lanna.** There are always colorful fresh flowers in this Thai restaurant on the eastern edge of Pacific Beach, and the food is similarly fresh and vibrant. There are a number of house specialties not found elsewhere, such as "Talay Thai," a batter-fried fish fillet topped with a green-apple salad, onions, and cashews; spice-braised duck in a deep, dark, wonderfully fragrant red curry sauce; and "Spicilicious Seafood," a mix of shrimp, squid, mussels, and scallops stir-fried in a chili-garlic sauce. The kitchen demonstrates considerable talent, and servers are prompt and gracious. $\boxed{\text{\$}}$ *Average main: $12* ✉ *4501 Mission Bay Dr., Pacific Beach* ☎ *858/274–8424* ⊕ *www.lannathaicuisine.com* ✣ *3:D4.*

$$$
JAPANESE
Fodor's Choice
★

✕ **Sushi Ota.** Wedged into a minimall between a convenience store and a looming medical building, Sushi Ota's location might seem less than auspicious but it helps to know that San Diego–bound Japanese businesspeople frequently call for reservations before boarding their trans-Pacific flights. Look at the expressions on customers' faces as they leave and you can see the satisfied glows that result from dining on San Diego's best sushi. Besides the usual California roll and tuna and shrimp sushi, there are specialties that change daily such as sea urchin or surf clam sushi, a soft-shell crab roll, or the *omakase* tasting menu. Note that Japanese speakers tend to get the best spots, and servers can be abrupt. ▥ **TIP→** There's additional parking behind the mall. $\boxed{\text{\$}}$ *Average main: $30* ✉ *4529 Mission Bay Dr., Pacific Beach* ☎ *858/270–5670* ⚲ *Reservations essential* ⊗ *No lunch Sat.–Mon.* ✣ *3:D4*

8

CLOSE UP

Dining with a View in La Jolla

It's a "sad but truism" that many restaurants with great views serve food that isn't so hot. Many less-than-dedicated operators figure that the gorgeous vista will help make up for any deficiencies in the flavor department. Here are some exceptions to that rule:

George's Ocean Terrace (✉ 1250 Prospect St. ☎ 858/454-4244 ✛ 3:A2), part of the George's at the Cove complex, is one of the busiest spots in the village and for good reason: the casual bistro has an expansive view of the ocean, where you can glimpse boats and sometimes whales. Order a bowl of their signature black bean, broccoli, and chicken soup; Asian-style chicken wings; or garlic-roasted shrimp.

For a more upscale experience, head downstairs to **George's California Modern**, which offers excellent high-end fare. Chef Trey Foshee's menu offers seasonal dishes like local-catch grilled octopus salad with tzatziki sauce; and scallop, lemon, and tarragon ravioli. ✛ 3:A2

Tucked into a hillside above the cove, **Brockton Villa** (✉ 1235 Coast Blvd. ☎ 858/454-7393 ✛ 3:B2) serves three meals a day, but they excel at brunch and lunch when ocean views are best. Snag a seat by the fireplace and order the soufflé-like Coast Toast or an artichoke and asparagus omelet.

Cody's La Jolla (✉ 8030 Girard Ave. ☎ 858/459-0040 ✛ 3:A2) serves up a slice of ocean view along with American fare like voluminous omelets and grilled chicken sandwiches with Gruyère and crisp pancetta.

At **Goldfish Point Cafe** (✉ 1255 Coast Blvd. ☎ 858/459-7407 ✛ 3:B2) the menu is very light, limited to coffee, teas, pastries, and a few sandwiches. But it's easily the most affordable romantic spot in La Jolla. They also welcome dogs with free treats and a bowl of water.

LA JOLLA AND NORTHERN SAN DIEGO

Some of the area's top gems in the culinary sense are found in La Jolla. The best create fine Californian, Italian, Asian, and French cuisine that showcases San Diego's abundant local produce and seafood. The enclave is also packed with fun spots that attract lots of tourists year-round but there are many neighborhood favorites on the side streets that offer good food and inviting decor. The ocean-view restaurants along Prospect Street are very popular, so it's important to plan ahead if you want to secure a table.

To work up an appetite, stroll the streets and meander through art galleries, walk along La Jolla Cove, or take a hike down the bluff to the beach. The "view" restaurants are tempting, but be wary of committing to a full meal at ones that aren't mentioned here as you'll take your chances with the quality of the food.

Although mostly an industrial and residential area that doesn't attract many tourists, Kearny Mesa and Clairemont offer a diversity of small independent and ethnic restaurants. If you've rented a car, it's worth the 15-minute drive from downtown or the beaches to experience parts of the city where you won't find surfers or fish tacos. Convoy Street—the commercial heart of the busy Kearny Mesa area—is the unofficial Asian Restaurant Row of San Diego, and presents a comprehensive selection of Chinese, Korean, and Vietnamese restaurants, a number of which qualify as "Best in Class." West of Kearny Mesa is Clairemont, where you'll also find ethnic restaurants and grocery stores. Good food can be found very affordably here—just don't be put off by the simple interiors and the service, which sometimes can seem somewhat abrupt or offhand due to cultural and language differences.

LA JOLLA

$$$$ AMERICAN Fodor's Choice ★

🍴 **A.R. Valentien.** Known for his insistence on in-season, fresh-today produce and seafood, chef Jeff Jackson writes menus daily for this cozy room in the luxurious, Craftsman-style Lodge at Torrey Pines. His take on food combinations is simultaneously simple and inventive, as demonstrated in appetizers of smoked trout with potatoes and turnips, and porcini mushroom and chestnut soup with bacon and apple. In addition to the à la carte menu, a nightly three-course tasting menu explores the day's market through the eyes of the talented chef. At lunch on the outdoor terrace, consider the "Drugstore" hamburger: a grilled patty is placed on top of lettuce, tomato, and condiments, and is then topped with cheese before being steamed to perfection on its sesame seed bun. [$] *Average main: $35* ✉ *11480 N. Torrey Pines Rd., La Jolla* ☎ *858/777–6635* 🌐 *www.arvalentien.com* ⏲ *No breakfast weekdays* ✣ *3:B1.*

$$ ITALIAN

🍴 **Barbarella.** With the sunny patio brightened by year-round blooms and the menu of casual Cal-Italian fare, it's not hard to see why Barbarella is such a favorite. For locals, the other part of the charm is owner Barbara Beltaire, who works the room joking with regulars, perhaps even swiping a french fry or two. The warm, woodsy room is accented with original work by local artists and a mosaic-tile pizza oven decorated by the late French sculptor, Niki de Saint Phalle. The seasonal menu ranges from crispy wild-mushroom pizzas, mussels, and zucchini fritti in a silver cup, to oversize burgers topped with marinated red onions and blue cheese, and a whole stone-roasted fish of the day. Barbarella is packed on weekends, so reservations are a must. [$] *Average main: $21* ✉ *2171 Ave. de la Playa, La Jolla* ☎ *858/454–7373* 🌐 *www.barbarellarestaurant.com* ✣ *3:B2.*

$ ITALIAN

🍴 **Barolo.** This quiet, candlelit restaurant in the Golden Triangle's Renaissance Towne Center is a family-run alternative to the many chains of the inland La Jolla area. The menu is fairly basic but tasty Italian, with specialties like veal scallops with mushrooms, and pear-and-sundried-tomato-stuffed ravioli. The mixed-greens salad with shrimp and avocado nicely kicks off a meal that may go on simply to a sausage pizza, homemade gnocchi with pesto, chicken Marsala, or grilled salmon. Ask for a banquette table and enjoy the suave, eager-to-please service. Portions are big but it's worth saving some to leave room for the tiramisu. [$] *Average main: $15* ✉ *8935 Towne Center Dr., La Jolla* ☎ *858/622–1202* 🌐 *www.barolos.com* ⏲ *No lunch weekends* ✣ *3:E1.*

$$$
ASIAN

✕ **Café Japengo.** Shiny black surfaces and bamboo trees accent the interior of this Pacific Rim restaurant that serves Asian-inspired cuisine with many North and South American touches. The grilled beef yakitori and the *char siu* duck salad are guaranteed to wake up your taste buds. There's also a selection of grilled, wood-roasted, and wok-fried entrées—try the braised short ribs with risotto or the miso butterfish. The sushi is always fresh, and many regard this as the liveliest sushi bar in town. Service can be slow, but the pace in the bar, crowded with young locals on the make, is fast and energetic. If you savor quiet, avoid weekend evenings. $ *Average main: $31 ⊠ Aventine Center, 8960 University Center La., La Jolla* ☎ *858/450–3355* ⊕ *www. cafejapengo.com* ☉ *No lunch weekends* ✛ *3:D1.*

$
SEAFOOD
Fodor's Choice
★

✕ **El Pescador.** This low-key fish market and café in the heart of La Jolla village is popular with locals for its simply prepared fresh fish. Try a filet—maybe halibut, swordfish, salmon, or tuna—lightly grilled and perched on a soft torta roll with shredded lettuce, tomato, and onions. Other choices include ceviche, sashimi plates, Dungeness crab salad, sautéed mussels with sourdough bread, and excellent fish tacos. Seats are few, and tables often end up being shared, but the food is worth the wait. ■**TIP**➔ Order fish sandwiches to go for a tasty oceanfront picnic at La Jolla Cove. $ *Average main: $15 ⊠ 627 Pearl St., La Jolla* ☎ *858/456–2526* ⊕ *www.elpescadorfishmarket.com* ⚭ *Reservations not accepted* ✛ *3:A2.*

$
AMERICAN

✕ **Elijah's.** You don't go to a deli for the atmosphere, you for the food, and Elijah's is just what you'd expect: towering sandwiches, blintzes, and specialties like the "mish-mosh" soup that combines noodles, matzo balls, and shredded crepes in a big bowl of steaming chicken broth. Count on hearty breakfasts, reliable chopped liver, and dinners like chicken-in-the-pot and savory beef brisket. The restaurant makes impressive Reuben sandwiches, a combination of corned beef or pastrami, sauerkraut, Swiss cheese, and Thousand Island dressing on rye bread. Service is quick and friendly. One of San Diego's best art-movie theaters is 50 feet away. $ *Average main: $12 ⊠ 8861 Villa La Jolla Dr., La Jolla* ☎ *858/455–1461* ⊕ *www.elijahsrestaurant.com* ✛ *3:D1.*

$$$$
AMERICAN
Fodor's Choice
★

✕ **George's at the Cove.** La Jolla's oceanfront destination restaurant includes three dining areas: **California Modern** on the bottom floor, **George's Bar** in the middle, and **Ocean Terrace** on the roof. Hollywood types and other visiting celebrities can be spotted at California Modern, the sleek main dining room with its wall of windows. Simple preparations of fresh seafood, beef, and lamb reign on the menu, which chef Trey Foshee enlivens with produce from local specialty growers. Give special consideration to roasted Niman Ranch pork loin with maitake mushrooms, smoked Maine lobster with squash blossoms, and the legendary fish tacos. For a more casual and inexpensive experience, go to the indoor/outdoor George's Bar, where you can get tacos and watch a sports game, or head upstairs to the outdoor-only Ocean Terrace for spectacular views of La Jolla Cove. ⑤ *Average main: $39* ✉ *1250 Prospect St., La Jolla* ☎ *858/454–4244* ⊕ *www.georgesatthecove.com* ⚲ *Reservations essential* ✦ *3:B2.*

$ ✕ **JK Burgers & Hot Dogs.** If you're looking for a good messy burger or a

AMERICAN hot dog with all the fixings, head to JK for filling and affordable fare. The casual decor features paintings and photos by San Diego artists and photographers. On the Fido-friendly patio or inside, chow down on Chicago-style Vienna-brand beef hot dogs dressed in mustard, onion, relish, chopped tomatoes, tiny hot peppers, celery salt, and dill pickles— but never ketchup. The menu also includes fish-and-chips and turkey burgers as well as juicy Italian beef sandwiches, chili cheeseburgers, and barbecued ribs. ⑤ *Average main: $9* ✉ *8935 Towne Center Dr., La Jolla* ☎ *858/622–0222* ⊕ *www.jkburgers.com* ⚲ *Reservations not accepted* ⊘ *No dinner Sun.* ✦ *3:E1.*

$$$$ ✕ **Marine Room.** Gaze at the ocean from this venerable La Jolla Shores

FRENCH mainstay and, if it's during an especially high tide, feel the waves race across the sand and crash against the glass. This fine-dining restaurant is built for romance: you might even witness a marriage proposal or a wedding on the beach. Long-term executive chef Bernard Guillas takes a bold approach to combining ingredients and his creative seasonal menus score with "trilogy" plates that combine three meats, sometimes including game, in distinct preparations. Exotic ingredients show up in a variety of dishes, among them Absinthe butter–basted lobster tail, tangerine-glazed organic tofu, and rack of lamb with mission fig compote. ⑤ *Average main: $35* ✉ *2000 Spindrift Dr., La Jolla* ☎ *866/644– 2351* ⊕ *www.marineroom.com* ⚲ *Reservations essential* ✦ *3:B2.*

$ ✕ **Michele Coulon Dessertier.** The desserts are magnificent at this small,

CAFÉ charming shop in the heart of La Jolla, where dessertier Michele Coulon

ⓒ confects wonders, using organic produce and imported chocolate. Moist chocolate-chip scones, a *Gateau Aileen* (sponge cake layered with buttercream and fresh organic berries), a berry-frangipane tart, and a decadent chocolate mousse cake are just a few examples of the treats you'll find. There are also usually several gluten-free items available. This is not just a place for dessert, however. Lunch is served Monday through Saturday (the store is open 9 to 4), and the simple menu includes quiche Lorraine and salads. ⑤ *Average main: $11* ✉ *7556 Fay Ave., Suite D, La Jolla* ☎ *858/456–5098* ⊕ *www.dessertier.com* ⚲ *Reservations not accepted* ⊘ *Closed Sun. No dinner* ✦ *3:A2.*

$$$$ ✕ **Nine-Ten.** In the sleek, contemporary dining room that occupies the

AMERICAN ground floor of the Grande Colonial Hotel, acclaimed chef (and 2011

Fodor's Choice *Iron Chef* challenger) Jason Knibb serves satisfying seasonal fare at

★ breakfast, lunch, and dinner. The downtown La Jolla location is ideal for travelers but it's just as much a locals spot, attracting professionals for power lunches and foodies for the excellent food. At night the perfectly executed menu may include tantalizing appetizers like Jamaican jerk pork belly or lamb sugo and mains such as a roasted leg of rabbit stuffed with Swiss chard, lemons, raisins, and cumin, or beef short ribs braised with Alesmith stout and served with root vegetables. Standout desserts include cilantro basil cake and strawberry sorbet with candied kumquats. Three- and five-course prix-fixe menus are available for the whole table. [$] *Average main: $36* ✉ *Grande Colonial Hotel, 910 Prospect St., La Jolla* ☎ *858/964–5400* 🌐 *www.nine-ten.com* ✣ *3:A2.*

$ ITALIAN 🍴 **Osteria Romantica.** The name means "Romantic Inn," and with a sunny location a few blocks from the beach in La Jolla Shores, the look suggests a trattoria in Italy. The kitchen's wonderfully light hand shows up in the tomato sauce that finishes the scampi and other dishes, and in the pleasing Romantica salad garnished with figs and walnuts. Savory pasta choices include lobster-filled *mezzelune* (half moons) in saffron sauce, and wonderfully rich spaghetti *alla carbonara*. The breaded veal cutlets crowned with chopped arugula and tomatoes are a popular main course. The warm, informal service suits the neighborhood. [$] *Average main: $17* ✉ *2151 Ave. de la Playa, La Jolla* ☎ *858/551–1221* 🌐 *www.osteriaromantica.com* ✣ *3:B2.*

$ AMERICAN 🍴 **Prepkitchen.** If you're looking for a less expensive La Jolla option, head to this gem, known to fans as "PK." The low-key sister restaurant to Whisk'n'ladle (also in La Jolla) offers a seasonal menu of soups, sandwiches, and mains, with standouts like the salmon with roasted corn, fusilli Bolognese, and a flavorful house-cured pastrami sandwich served with house-made potato chips. At weekend brunch, try chilaquiles, a delicious dish of chipotle chicken, fried eggs, and crème fraîche. If you'd rather picnic than dine in, family meals meant to feed 4–5 people are available for takeout. [$] *Average main: $17* ✉ *7556 Fay Ave., La Jolla* ☎ *858/875–7737* 🌐 *www.prepkitchen.com* ✍ *Reservations not accepted* ✣ *3:A2.*

$$ SEAFOOD 👶 🍴 **Rimel's Rotisserie.** This comfy spot is a good choice for families and, unless you opt for the market-priced "fresh catches" and the grass-fed filet mignon from the owner's Home Grown Meats shop, it's more affordable than many of the restaurants in pricy La Jolla. Many items come in under $12, such as grilled mahimahi tacos (served with a powerful green chili-garlic salsa), grain-fed chicken grilled on a mesquite-fire rotisserie, and "steaming rice bowls" that are actually plates spread with jasmine rice, wok-cooked vegetables, and grilled seafood with a variety of vegetables. [$] *Average main: $22* ✉ *1030 Torrey Pines Rd., La Jolla* ☎ *858/454–6045* 🌐 *www.rimelsrestaurants.com* ✣ *3:B2.*

$$ ASIAN 🍴 **Roppongi Restaurant and Sushi Bar.** The Asian-accented global menu at Roppongi was a hit from the moment it opened. The contemporary dining room, done in wood tones and accented with a tropical fish tank, Buddhas, and other Asian statuary, has rows of comfortable booths perfect for small groups. Order the imaginative Euro-Asian tapas as appetizers, or combine them for a full meal along with sake or a refreshing ginger mojito. Equally delicious are the crispy tofu, the pan-seared scallops on potato pancakes, and the Mongolian duck quesadilla. Well-executed entrées include short ribs with thai basil glaze and macadamia-crusted mahimahi with mango chutney. Purists should go elsewhere, but the sushi bar offers delicious specialty rolls. [$] *Average main: $22* ✉ *875 Prospect St., La Jolla* ☎ *858/551–5252* 🌐 *www.roppongiusa.com* ✣ *3:A2.*

$ ✕ **Sushi on the Rock.** There's something fun about Sushi on the Rock,
SUSHI   from the young friendly chefs to the comically named California-style
Fodor'sChoice   sushi specialties, like the Slippery When Wet roll featuring tempura
★   shrimp, eel, crab, and cucumber. There are many original rolls to choose
from, including the Barrio Roll stuffed with tuna, cilantro, and spicy
tomato salsa; the Ashley Roll that pairs seared tuna with soft-shell crab
and tangy whole-grain mustard sauce; and the Bruce Lee, with spicy
crab, tuna, and avocado. The Japanese-inspired dishes, including pot
stickers and an Asian-style Caesar salad are also good, as is the lobster
mac and cheese. This popular spot, which has a patio with an ocean
view, gets busy in the late afternoon with people wanting to grab a
seat for the daily happy hour (5–6:30). $ *Average main: $16* ⊠ *1025
Prospect St., #250, La Jolla* ☎ *858/459–3208* ⊕ *www.sushiontherock.
com* ⌲ *Reservations not accepted* ✛ *3:B2.*

$$$ ✕ **Tapenade.** Named after the Provençal black-olive-and-anchovy paste,
FRENCH   Tapenade specializes in the fresh cuisine of the south of France, and the
food fits perfectly with the unpretentious, light, and airy room, lined
with 1960s French movie posters, in which it's served. Fresh ingredients,
a delicate touch with sauces, and an emphasis on seafood characterize
the menu, which changes frequently. If you're lucky, it may include wild
boar stewed in red wine, lobster with white corn sauce flavored with
Tahitian vanilla, pan-gilded sea scallops, and desserts like chocolate
fondant and profiteroles. The two-course "Riviera Menu" served at
lunch for $21.95 is a steal. $ *Average main: $30* ⊠ *7612 Fay Ave., La
Jolla* ☎ *858/551–7500* ⊕ *www.tapenaderestaurant.com* ⊗ *No lunch
weekends* ✛ *3:B2.*

$$$ ✕ **Truluck's.** This Southern-style seafood restaurant with reasonably
SEAFOOD   priced fish, steaks, and international wines has live piano music nightly.
Menu standouts include Alaskan king crab legs and miso-glazed seabass
with cucumber slaw. Monday is all-you-can-eat stone crab claws and
side dishes. The crab fried rice is so popular and plentiful that some
guests order it as an entrée. For dessert, go for the carrot cake or the
Chocolate Sack, a bed made of chocolate and stuffed with enough
delicious pound cake, fresh berries, and warm chocolate to satisfy a
crowd. $ *Average main: $30* ⊠ *8990 University Center La., La Jolla*
☎ *858/453–2583* ⊕ *www.trulucks.com* ✛ *3:D1.*

$$ ✕ **Whisknladle.** This hip, popular eatery that doubles as a fashion show
SEAFOOD   of La Jolla ladies who lunch has earned national acclaim with its combi-
Fodor'sChoice   nation of casual comfort and a menu of ever-changing local fare. In nice
★   weather, request a patio table when reserving. Appetizers include dishes
like heirloom tomato salad and savory flatbreads that change daily. Larger
plates feature local halibut with Chino Farms vegetables or crab tortel-
lini. And the bar is worth a visit, too, with its original menu of cocktails
like the tamarind margarita, cucumber honey mimosa, and pomegranate
mojito. $ *Average main: $23* ⊠ *1044 Wall St., La Jolla* ☎ *858/551–7575*
⊕ *www.whisknladle.com* ⌲ *Reservations essential* ✛ *3:A2.*

$$ ✕ **Zenbu.** There's a cool California vibe at this cozy, moodily lit sushi-
SUSHI   and-seafood restaurant that serves some of the freshest fish in town.
Restaurateur Matt Rimel runs a commercial fishing company and uses
his connections to bring in seafood from all over the world that excels,

8

whether raw or cooked. Seasonal specialties include buttery *otoro* (tuna belly) and local sea urchin fresh from its spiny shell. Sushi, which can be pricey, ranges from simple nigiri to beautiful sashimi plates and original rolls like the Salmon Spider, which combines soft-shell crab with fresh salmon. Cooked dishes run from noodle bowls and grass-fed Montana prime sirloin seared at the table on a hot stone, to whole fried rockfish or spicy "dynamite" lobster. $ *Average main: $20* ⊠ *7660 Fay Ave., La Jolla* ☎ *858/454–4540* ⊕ *www.zenbusushi.com* ☽ *No lunch* ✛ *3:B2.*

CLAIREMONT

$ ✕ **Sushi Diner.** With Rastafari flags, surfer videos on loop, and Bob Mar-
SUSHI   ley–inspired sushi rolls, chef/owner Daisuke makes it clear that this is a place to chill. The tiny and always bustling restaurant has a loyal following of locals who don't mind waiting for tables because of the friendly service, inexpensive sushi, and tasty island-inspired extras like Spam fried rice. Vegetarians won't have a problem here; there are several veggie rolls, tofu dishes, and meatless appetizers. ▟ **TIP➔** During the 4–7 happy hour, many appetizers and hand rolls are 99¢ with the purchase of a beer. $ *Average main: $10* ⊠ *7530 Mesa College Dr., Clairemont* ☎ *858/565–1179* ⊕ *www.sushidiner1.com* ⌂ *Reservations not accepted* ☽ *Closed Sun. No lunch Sat.* ✛ *3:G4.*

KEARNY MESA

$ ✕ **China Max.** This good-looking Convoy Street eatery has won multi-
CHINESE   tudes of loyal fans, not only because of the quality, variety, and authenticity of the cooking, but because a value-priced, late-supper menu is offered nightly from 9 to 11. Dishes not to be missed from the House Special menu include the lettuce "taco" stuffed with stir-fried shrimp, country-style *mei fun* noodles, dumplings filled with shrimp paste and Chinese chives, and pan-fried lamb chops in black-pepper sauce. Fish tanks teem with seafood, all market priced. The dim sum dumplings and pastries served at lunch may be San Diego's best. $ *Average main: $15* ⊠ *4698 Convoy St., Kearny Mesa* ☎ *858/650–3333* ⊕ *www. chinamaxsandiego.com* ✛ *3:G3.*

$$ ✕ **Dae Jang Keum Korean BBQ.** Follow the smell of smoky BBQ to this
KOREAN   casual, family-run Korean BBQ spot, a block off Convoy Street. Patrons gather in booths around tabletop grills to cook seasoned short ribs, pork belly, and beef brisket for $20–$25 per person, though you can also order from the plentiful menu of authentic Korean dishes prepared in the kitchen. Beer, wine, and soju (a vodka-like Korean liquor) are available. Service is friendly but can be slow; prepare for a leisurely feast. $ *Average main: $22* ⊠ *7905 Engineer Rd., Kearny Mesa* ☎ *858/573–2585* ✛ *3:H3.*

$ ✕ **Dumpling Inn.** Modest, family-style, and delicious, this is in some ways
CHINESE   the most likable of Convoy Street's Asian restaurants. The tiny establish-
☾   ment loads its tables with bottles of aromatic and spicy condiments for
Fodor's Choice   the boiled, steamed, and fried dumplings that are the house specialty—the
★   pork and chive are particularly good. After dumplings, you can move on to simple options like the honey-glazed shrimp, or more elaborate ones, like mini braised pork shank. Ask about daily specials, such as shredded pork in plum sauce served on a sea of crispy noodles. You can bring your

own wine or beer; the house serves only tea and soft drinks. $ *Average main: $9* ✉ *4619 Convoy St., #F, Kearny Mesa* ☎ *858/268–9638* ☾ *Closed Mon.* ✛ *3:G3.*

$$ ✕ **Emerald Chinese Seafood Restaurant.** Tucked away in a rather run-down looking strip mall, Emerald is nevertheless sought out by those who look for elaborate, carefully prepared, and sometimes costly seafood dishes. Even when the restaurant is full to capacity with 300 diners, the noise level is moderate and conversation flows easily among families and other groups ordering from the banquet menu. Market-priced—and that can be high—lobsters, clams, and fish reside in tanks until the moment of cooking. Simple preparations flavored with scallions, black beans, and ginger are among

CHINESE

WHEN THE GRUNIONS RUN

A generations-old San Diego tradition is heading to the beach during certain high tides—preferably when the moon is full—to hunt grunion. These small, barely edible fish come ashore during mating periods and "run" on the beach, causing great excitement among spectators. As the fish flop across the sand in search of adventure (as it were), bold individuals chase them down and scoop up a few with their hands—catching them by any other means is illegal. Beach-area businesses and eateries often know the date of the next run.

the most worthy. Other recommended dishes include beef with Singapore-style satay sauce, honey-walnut shrimp, baked chicken in five spices, Peking duck, and, at lunch, the dim sum. $ *Average main: $20* ✉ *3709 Convoy St., Suite 101, Kearny Mesa* ☎ *858/565–6888* ✛ *3:H4.*

$$ ✕ **Pampas Argentine Grill.** The focus of the menu at this steakhouse just a few blocks east of the Convoy Street restaurant row is meat, grilled and served with zesty chimichurri sauce. Choices include rib eye, filet mignon, and strip steaks, along with marinated boneless chicken, lamb, and the seafood of the day. Reasonably priced and served for two or more, the "Parrillada Pampas" is a grilled-at-the-table mixed-grill feast of beef, spicy sausage, and sweetbreads. The spacious, lively restaurant is gently lighted and decorated with paintings that strive for the romance of the tango. There's live music on weekends—and a tango the last Friday of the month. $ *Average main: $23* ✉ *8690 Aero Dr., Kearny Mesa* ☎ *858/278–5971* ⊕ *www.pampasrestaurant.com* ☾ *No dinner Mon. No lunch weekends* ✛ *3:H4.*

ARGENTINE

$ ✕ **Phuong Trang.** One of the most popular Vietnamese restaurants in San Diego, the menu at Phuong Trang offers hundreds of appetizers, soups, noodle dishes, and main courses, which can make choosing a meal a bewildering process. Waiters steer you to tasty, moderately adventurous offerings like fried egg rolls, char-grilled shrimp paste wrapped around sugarcane, beef in grape leaves, and fresh spring rolls filled with pork and shrimp, but if you're feeling adventurous there are plenty of less mainstream options as well. And if you just want a simple meal, you can't go wrong with broken rice and a grilled pork chop. The large, relatively spare dining room gets packed, especially on weekends, but service is speedy, if sometimes curt. $ *Average main: $8* ✉ *4170 Convoy St., Kearny Mesa* ☎ *858/565–6750* ✍ *Reservations not accepted* ✛ *3:G3.*

VIETNAMESE

POINT LOMA, OCEAN BEACH, HARBOR AND SHELTER ISLANDS, AND CORONADO

Point Loma has a storied history as the center of the tuna-fishing industry and is developing into an area of charming neighborhood restaurants. In recent years, a couple of places have opened that specialize in simple, high-quality fare showcasing local ingredients. But most restaurants in Point Loma and on Harbor and Shelter islands are casual neighborhood spots or eateries with great views that cater to tourists and sailing enthusiasts.

Coronado is a picturesque community filled with neat wood-frame homes, the historic turrets of the Hotel Del Coronado, and one of the most beautiful beaches in the area. Though there are exceptions, many restaurants here rely on a steady stream of tourist traffic, so often the cuisine is adequate and somewhat expensive but not stellar.

POINT LOMA

$$ FRENCH   ✕ **BO-Beau.** Near Point Loma, on the outskirts of Ocean Beach, a neighborhood better-known for fish tacos and dive bars, this warm, romantic bistro evokes a French farmhouse setting. Executive Chef Katherine Humphus refined her skills at French Laundry and New York's wd-50 before joining the Cohn Restaurant Group to craft a French-inspired menu of soups, woodstone oven flatbreads, mussels, and other bistro classics. Go traditional with *boeuf bourguignon* or spice it up with a flatbread topped with roasted beets, jalapenos, and goat cheese, and a side of crispy brussel sprouts. Service is friendly and reliable. ⑤ *Average main: $19* ⊠ *4996 W. Point Loma Blvd., Point Loma* ☎ *619/224–2884* ⊕ *www.bobeaukitchen.com* ☺ *No lunch* ✛ *4:B1.*

$ AMERICAN ⓒ Fodor's Choice ★   ✕ **Jimmy's Famous American Tavern.** Jimmy's is a standout in the wave of recent gastropubs, and while the food is the main draw here, the decor—industrial meets Americana—has an appealing straightforwardness, too. Head through the garage-style doors for a patio seat with a water view or opt for a cozy booth. The menu features elevated takes on backyard BBQ that include the Jimmy, a 10-ounce burger topped with pimento cheese, applewood smoked bacon, and jalapeño jelly. The buttermilk fried chicken breast and jalapeño deviled eggs are also worth a try. The short rib hash at Sunday brunch is stellar. ⑤ *Average main: $16* ⊠ *4990 N. Harbor Dr., Point Loma* ☎ *619/226–2103* ⊕ *www.j-fat.com* ✛ *4:B1.*

$ BARBECUE Fodor's Choice ★   ✕ **Phil's BBQ.** At peak dining hours, the line can be hours long for diners craving Phil's baby back ribs, the pulled pork, or the huge, crispy onion rings. Adding to the restaurant's reputation and allure is the fact that one of the specialties, the El Toro tri-tip sandwich, was included in Travel Channel celebrity Adam Richman's 2012 list of America's best sandwiches. But don't let the crowds dissuade you: phone in for carry-out, sit at the bar, or bring the family during mid-afternoon for a messy, char-grilled introduction to barbecue heaven. ⑤ *Average main: $14* ⊠ *3750 Sports Arena Blvd., Point Loma* ☎ *619/226–6333* ⊕ *www.philsbbq.net* ⚄ *Reservations not accepted* ☺ *Closed Mon.* ✛ *4:B1.*

$ AMERICAN 🍴 **Sessions Public.** From the short rib sliders, duck confit Thai summer rolls, and rib-eye fries on the menu to the stuffed ducks adorning the walls it's clear this is no vegetarian joint. Opened by Point Loma native Abel Kaase, this neighborhood restaurant draws a young crowd that's more hipster than hippie. The menu features farm-to-table fare and 20 craft beers on tap each day. Highlights include the mussels, the certified Angus beef natural burger topped with gouda and arugula, and duck-fat fries served with garlic aioli. Sunday brunch is fun and casual with a special morning cocktail menu. **TIP→ For postdinner drinks, pop over to the adjacent Catalina Lounge, a favorite local dive bar with cheap drinks and friendly bartenders.** [$] *Average main: $14* ✉ *4204 Voltaire St., Point Loma* ☎ *619/756–7715* 🌐 *www.sessionspublic.com* 🕓 *No lunch Mon.–Thurs.* ✥ *4:B1.*

A FISH TALE

From the 1930s to the early '70s, San Diego was the capitol of the American tuna-fishing industry. Visit Point Loma to see the remnants of the fishing industry or stop by Whole Foods for a sample of this favorite fish canned by American Tuna, a company formed by six local fishing families who only use poles—not nets—to catch premium albacore tuna in a sustainable way.

$ AMERICAN Fodor's Choice ★ 🍴 **Tender Greens.** "Farm-fresh ingredients served up with little fuss" is the ethos behind this casual cafeteria-style spot in Liberty Station. It's very popular at lunch but the line moves quickly. Expect big salads like seared tuna Niçoise; Fra' Mani salami with shaved fennel, pecorino, and arugula; or chipotle chicken salad. Naturally raised beef and chicken are roasted and then tucked into sandwiches or served as a dinner plate with vegetables. Wine and house-made desserts round out the menu. [$] *Average main: $13* ✉ *2400 Historic Decatur Rd., Point Loma* ☎ *619/226–6254* 🌐 *tendergreensfood.com* ✥ *4:C1.*

$ ITALIAN 🍴 **The Venetian.** The spacious back room of this casual but intimate neighborhood restaurant is actually a sheltered garden that you can enjoy in any weather. The menu leans mostly toward southern Italian cuisine, with house specialties like shrimp puttanesca, and bow-tie pasta tossed with prosciutto, peas, and mushrooms in a rose-tinted cream sauce. The well-priced selection of veal, chicken, and seafood dishes is excellent, but many regulars settle for the lavishly garnished antipasto salad and one of the tender-crusted pizzas. [$] *Average main: $15* ✉ *3663 Voltaire St., Point Loma* ☎ *619/223–8197* 🌐 *www.venetian1965.com* 🕓 *No lunch Fri.–Sun.* ✥ *4:B1.*

OCEAN BEACH

$ CUBAN 🍴 **Azucar.** For a taste of Cuba in San Diego, head to this casual bakery. Ideal for a quick meal before shopping or hitting the beach, the friendly café offers morning specialties such as raspberry scones with passion fruit icing, ham quiche, and *café con leche* (sweet Cuban espresso with hot milk). For lunch, try the slow-roasted pork sandwich with plantain chips. There are some tables, but it's a tiny spot so many customers opt to order food to-go. [$] *Average main: $7* ✉ *4820 Newport Ave., Ocean Beach* ☎ *619/523–2020* 🌐 *www.iloveazucar.com* 🕓 *No dinner* ✥ *4:B1.*

$ ✕ **Hodad's.** No, it's not a flashback.
AMERICAN   The 1960s live on at this fabu-
🐣   lously funky burger joint, where
the walls are covered with license
plates and the amiable servers
covered with tattoos. Still, this is
very much a family place, and the
clientele often includes toddlers
and octogenarians. Huge burgers
are the thing, loaded with onions,
pickles, tomatoes, lettuce, and condiments, and so gloriously messy
that you might wear a swimsuit so
you can stroll to the beach for a

bath afterward. The minihamburger is a good option if you're looking
for moderation—the double bacon cheeseburger is the opposite. For
sides, go for the onion rings or the seasoned potato wedges. $ Aver-
age main: $9 ⊠ 5010 Newport Ave., Ocean Beach 🕾 619/224–4623
⊕ hodadies.com ⊹ 4:B1.

SHELTER ISLAND

$$ ✕ **Bali Hai.** This kitschy-classy waterfront restaurant is loved as much
HAWAIIAN   for the strong, sugary drinks served in tiki mugs as it is for the gor-
Fodor'sChoice   geous views of the San Diego Bay and the downtown skyline. One
★   of few restaurants within walking distance of Shelter Island hotels,
Bali Hai's menu has Hawaiian, Asian, and Californian influences,
with an emphasis on seafood. Standouts include the Hawaiian tuna
poke stack, crispy spring rolls, and seared diver scallops with glazed
pork belly. Lounge seating accommodates groups while tables by the
window are ideal for quiet, romantic dinners. $ Average main: $23
⊠ 2230 Shelter Island Dr., Shelter Island 🕾 619/222–1181 ⊕ www.
balihairestaurant.com ⊹ 4:C2.

HARBOR ISLAND

$$$$ ✕ **Island Prime and C Level.** This sizable eatery on the shore of Harbor
AMERICAN   Island is two restaurants in one: the extravagant, dinner-only Island
Prime, and the much less formal (but not inexpensive) lunch-and-dinner
C Level, which has a choice terrace. Both venues tempt with unrivaled
views of downtown San Diego's ever-growing skyline. Island Prime's
splurge-worthy menu includes rosemary-crusted rib eye; a trio of fil-
lets topped with blue cheese, wild mushrooms, and blue crab; and
salmon with linguini. Lunch is the best time at C Level, which serves
hearty pastas, sandwiches, and salads. Reservations are strongly sug-
gested for Island Prime; C Level doesn't take them. $ Average main:
$36 ⊠ 880 Harbor Island Dr., Harbor Island 🕾 619/298–6802 ⊕ www.
islandprime.com ⊹ 4:F1.

CORONADO

$$$$ ✕ **1500 Ocean.** The fine-dining restaurant at Hotel Del Coronado, right
AMERICAN   on the beach, offers a memorable evening showcasing the best organic
and naturally raised ingredients the region has to offer. Select ingredi-
ents come straight from the hotel's herb and produce garden. Sublimely

subtle dishes include the colorful succotash with sweet corn, heirloom tomatoes, squash blossoms, and Sauvignon Blanc; and diver scallops with roasted corn, grilled apricots, and Chardonnay. The elegant interior of the restaurant evokes a posh cabana; the terrace has ocean views. An excellent international wine list and clever desserts and artisanal cheeses complete the experience. $ *Average main: $36* ⌂ *Hotel Del Coronado, 1500 Orange Ave., Coronado* ☎ *619/522–8490* ⊕ *www. hoteldel.com/1500-ocean.aspx* ⌕ *Reservations essential* ⊗ *Closed Sun. and Mon. No lunch* ✛ *4:G6.*

$$
FRENCH

✕ **Chez Loma.** A favorite with guests at nearby Hotel Del Coronado, this restaurant is tucked away on a side street, in a historic Victorian house. The menu has a French bistro focus, with carefully prepared *boeuf bourguignon* and lamb shank with a light coffee and chocolate infusion, but Spanish influences can be found in shared plates like octopus and potatoes with spicy tomato sauce. The solid selection of desserts includes gingerbread and chocolate pot de crème. Chez Loma's menu and atmosphere are not kid-friendly. $ *Average main: $23* ⌂ *1132 Loma Ave., Coronado* ☎ *619/435–0661* ⊗ *No lunch* ✛ *4:G6.*

$
AMERICAN
☺

✕ **Coronado Brewing Company.** The carefully crafted beers, such as the Islander Pale Ale (IPA) and Mermaid's Red Ale, are good by themselves, but they're also the perfect accompaniment to bratwurst and beer-battered onion rings, served in huge portions. There's indoor seating, a pair of sidewalk terraces and, best of all, a walled garden that provides a quiet haven from the bustle of Orange Avenue. Simple choices are the wisest, from the Philadelphia-style steak sandwich to wood-fired pizzas to fish tacos with chipotle sour cream. It may be a brewery, but it's still popular with families. $ *Average main: $12* ⌂ *170 Orange Ave., Coronado* ☎ *619/437–4452* ⊕ *www. coronadobrewingcompany.com* ✛ *4:H4.*

$$
INTERNATIONAL
Fodor's Choice
★

✕ **Mistral.** Named after the warm wind that blows across southern France and Italy, the fine-dining, dinner-only restaurant at Loews Coronado Bay Resort focuses on southern French and northern Italian cuisine built around naturally raised meats and organic local produce. Fifth-generation French chef Patrick Ponsaty presents a menu that ranges from arugula salad with figs and lavender honey, to grilled prime beef tenderloin and salmon with lobster emulsion. A well-edited wine list and house-made desserts like profiteroles with Valrhona chocolate sauce and vanilla ice cream complete the experience. The decor plays up the sweeping views of the bay visible from every table. $ *Average main: $24* ⌂ *Loews Coronado Bay Resort, 4000 Coronado Bay Rd., Coronado* ☎ *619/424–4000* ⊕ *www.dineatmistral.com* ⊗ *Closed Sun. and Mon. No lunch* ✛ *4:H6.*

$$$
AMERICAN

✕ **Sheerwater.** This casual but pricey all-day dining room is the primary restaurant at Hotel Del Coronado. A spacious, breeze-swept terrace offers extraordinary ocean views, while the indoor room can be on the noisy side, especially when families are present. The menu offers a local take on all-American fare, with dishes such as lobster bisque with avocado-mango salsa, and splits the entrée list between meats like filet mignon with *beurre blanc* or truffled béarnaise sauce, and seafood offerings such as baked salmon and halibut. Chicken fingers, pizza, and other

8

standard kids' menu options are served with a choice of baby carrots or french fries. [$] *Average main: $28* ✉ *Hotel Del Coronado, 1500 Orange Ave., Coronado* ☎ *619/435–6611* 🌐 *www.hoteldel.com* ⊕ *4:G6.*

$ FRENCH 🐾 🍴 **Tartine.** There's always a dish of water for canine pals on the terrace of this French-inspired café a block from San Diego Bay. Popular sandwiches include ham-and-Brie slathered with grain mustard, or Gorgonzola cheese, walnuts, mache, and sliced pears. Clever salads and soups round out the daytime menu. Dinner brings a bruschetta of the day, capellini with pomodoro sauce, bistro salad, and specials like chicken under a brick with butternut squash risotto. The stars of the menu are the house-made desserts such as lemon tarts and double-chocolate bread pudding. Continental breakfast commences at 6 am when quiche and just-baked pastries silently command, "Eat me!" This may be Coronado's best bet for casual but stylish fare. [$] *Average main: $15* ✉ *1106 1st St., Coronado* ☎ *619/435–4323* 🌐 *www.tartinecoronado.com* ⊕ *4:H4.*

Where to Eat and Stay in San Diego

KEY

- ☐ *Hotels*
- ■ *Restaurants*
- ▦ *Restaurant in Hotel*
- ✥ *following dining and lodging reviews indicates a map-grid coordinate*

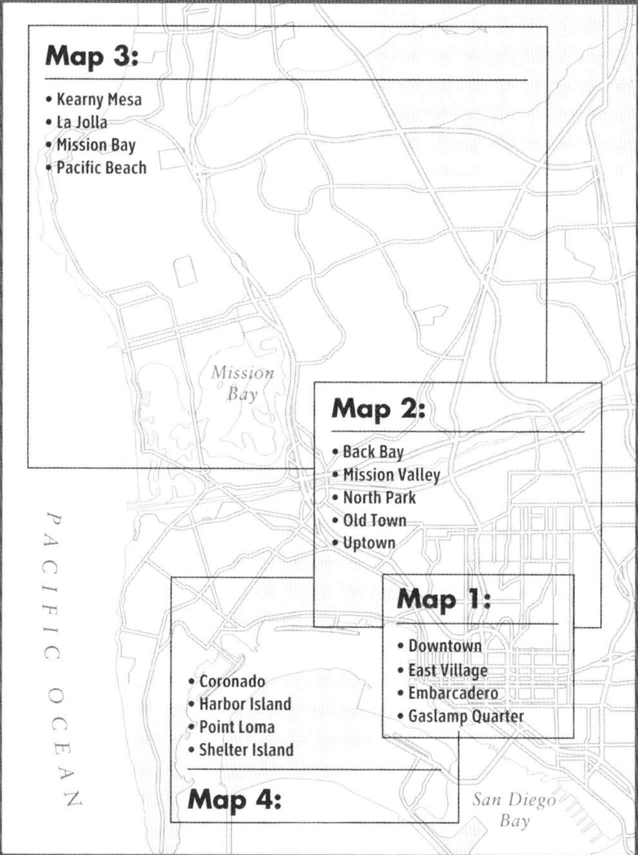

Map 3:
• Kearny Mesa
• La Jolla
• Mission Bay
• Pacific Beach
Mission Bay
Map 2:
• Back Bay
• Mission Valley
• North Park
• Old Town
• Uptown
PACIFIC OCEAN
Map 1:
• Downtown
• East Village
• Embarcadero
• Gaslamp Quarter
• Coronado
• Harbor Island
• Point Loma
• Shelter Island
Map 4:
San Diego Bay

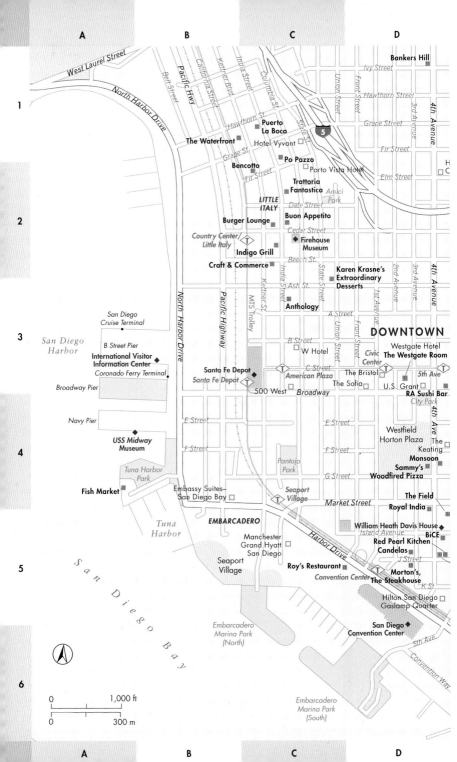

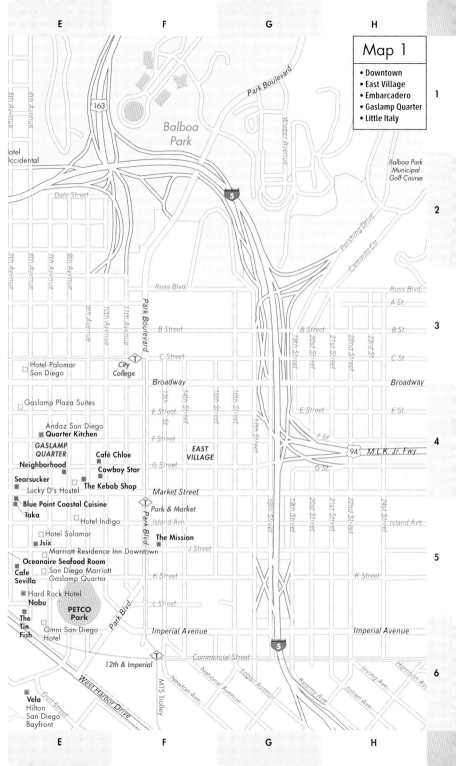

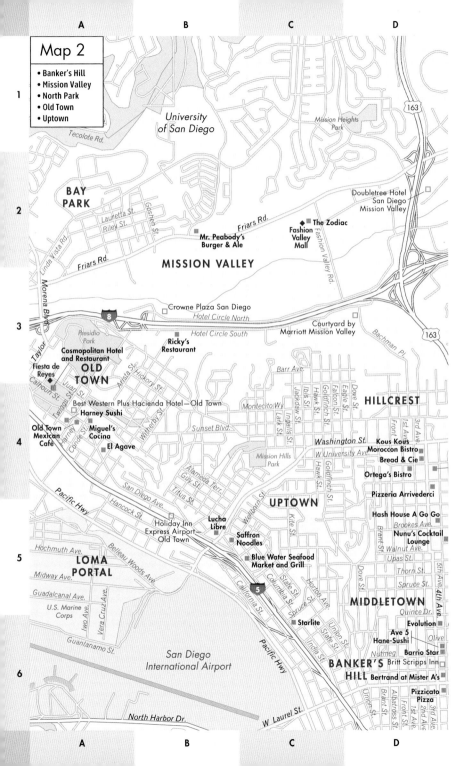

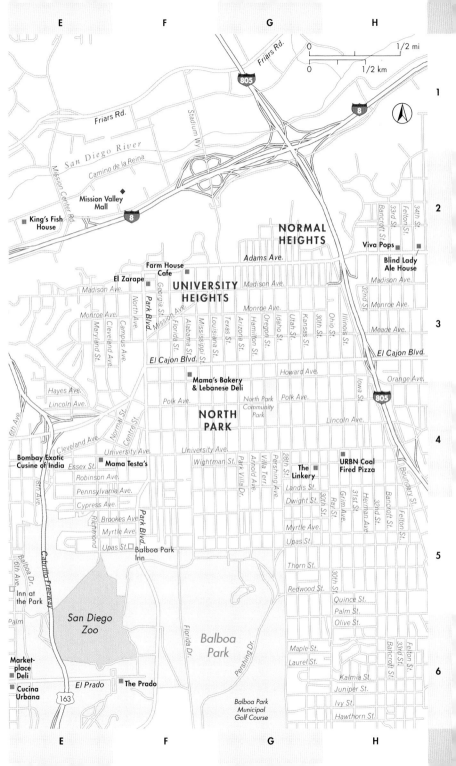

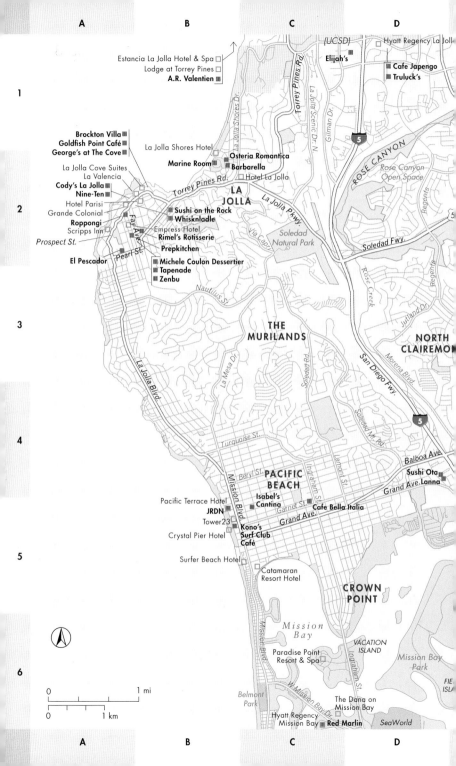

A B C D

(UCSD)

Hyatt Regency La Joll

Elijah's

■ Cafe Japengo
■ Truluck's

1

Estancia La Jolla Hotel & Spa ☐
Lodge at Torrey Pines ☐
A.R. Valentien ■

Brockton Villa ■
Goldfish Point Café ■
George's at The Cove ■
La Jolla Shores Hotel

La Jolla Cove Suites
La Valencia
Cody's La Jolla ■
Nine-Ten ■
Hotel Parisi
Grande Colonial
Roppongi ■
Scripps Inn

Prospect St.

El Pescador ■

La Jolla Shores Dr.

Marine Room ■

Torrey Pines Rd.

Osteria Romantica
Barbarella ■
☐ Hotel La Jolla

**LA
JOLLA**

Sushi on the Rock ■
Whisknladle ■

Empress Hotel
Rimel's Rotisserie ■

Prepkitchen ■

Michele Coulon Dessertier ■
Tapenade ■
Zenbu ■

Fay Ave.

Pearl St.

Nautilus St.

La Jolla Pkwy.

Via Capri

*Soledad
Natural Park*

Torrey Pines Rd.

La Jolla Scenic Dr. N.

Gilman Dr.

La Jolla Scenic Dr.

Hyatt Regency La Joll

2

ROSE CANYON

*Rose Canyon
Open Space*

Regents

Soledad Fwy.

Rose Creek

Regents

3

**THE
MURILANDS**

La Mesa Dr.

Soledad Rd.

San Diego Fwy.

Morena Blvd.

Jutland Dr.

**NORTH
CLAIREMO**

La Jolla Blvd.

4

Turquoise St.

Beryl St.

**PACIFIC
BEACH**

Garnet St.

Ingraham St.

Lamont St.

Soledad Mt. Rd.

Balboa Ave.

Sushi Ota ■
Grand Ave. **Lanna**

5

Pacific Terrace Hotel
JRDN ■
Tower23 ☐
Crystal Pier Hotel

**Isabel's
Cantina** ■

**Kono's
Surf Club
Café** ■

Mission Blvd.

Cafe Bella Italia

Grand Ave.

Surfer Beach Hotel

Catamaran
Resort Hotel ☐

**CROWN
POINT**

Ingraham St.

*VACATION
ISLAND*

*Mission Bay
Park*

6

0 ——— 1 mi

0 ——— 1 km

*Belmont
Park*

Mission Blvd.

*Mission
Bay*

Paradise Point
Resort & Spa ☐

W. Mission Bay Dr.

Hyatt Regency
Mission Bay ☐ **Red Marlin** ■

The Dana on
Mission Bay ☐

SeaWorld

*FIE
ISLA*

A B C D

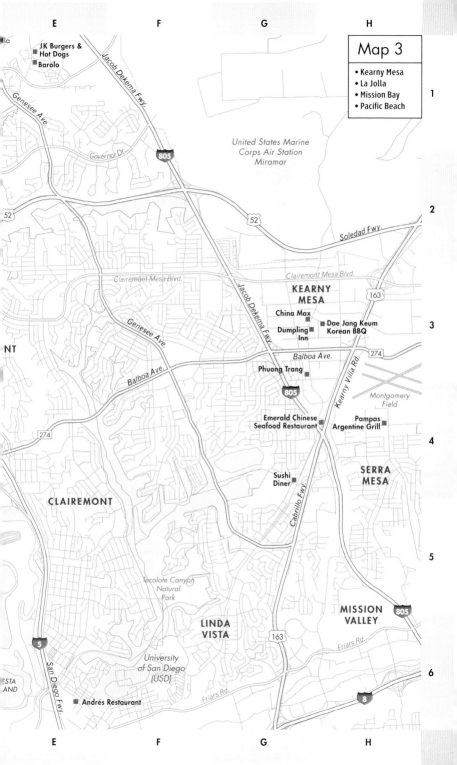

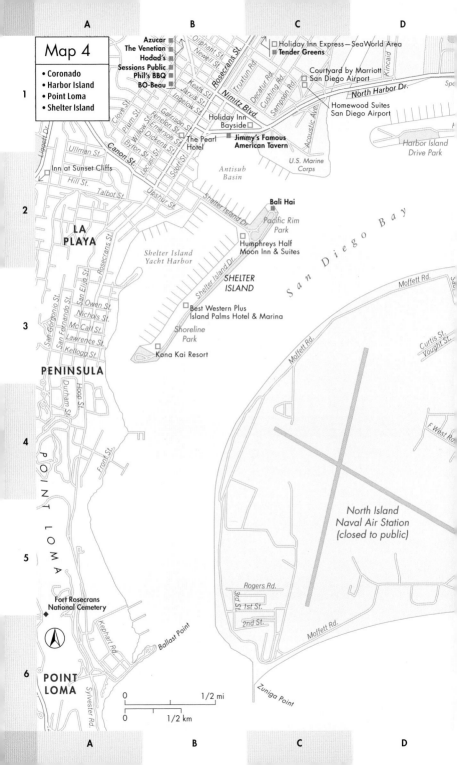

Map 4

- Coronado
- Harbor Island
- Point Loma
- Shelter Island

A1
Azucar
The Venetian
Hodad's
Sessions Public
Phil's BBQ
BO-Beau

Holiday Inn Express—SeaWorld Area
Tender Greens

Courtyard by Marriott
San Diego Airport

Homewood Suites
San Diego Airport

Holiday Inn
Bayside

The Pearl
Hotel

Jimmy's Famous
American Tavern

U.S. Marine
Corps

Inn at Sunset Cliffs

Harbor Island
Drive Park

*Antisub
Basin*

LA
PLAYA

Bali Hai

*Pacific Rim
Park*

Humphreys Half
Moon Inn & Suites

*Shelter Island
Yacht Harbor*

**SHELTER
ISLAND**

San Diego Bay

Best Western Plus
Island Palms Hotel & Marina

*Shoreline
Park*

Kona Kai Resort

PENINSULA

*North Island
Naval Air Station
(closed to public)*

P O I N T   L O M A

Fort Rosecrans
National Cemetery

Rogers Rd.

Ballast Point

POINT
LOMA

Zuniga Point

Streets: Oliphant St., Newell St., Rosecrans St., Truxtun Rd., Decatur Rd., Cushing Rd., Kincaid, North Harbor Dr., Keats St., Jarvis St., Ingelow St., Nimitz Blvd., Sampson St., Acoustic Ave., Clove St., Plum St., Willow St., Garrison St., Fenelon St., Emerson St., Dickens St., Byron St., Sims St., Scott St., Canon St., Ullman St., Hill St., Talbot St., Ueshur St., Shelter Island Dr., Rosecrans St., San Elijo St., San Gorgonio St., San Fernando St., Owen St., Nichols St., McCall St., Lawrence St., Kellogg St., Hugo St., Durham St., Front St., Moffett Rd., Curtis St., Vought St., F. West Rd., Kephart Rd., 3rd St., 1st St., 2nd St., Sylvester Rd.

0   1/2 mi
0   1/2 km

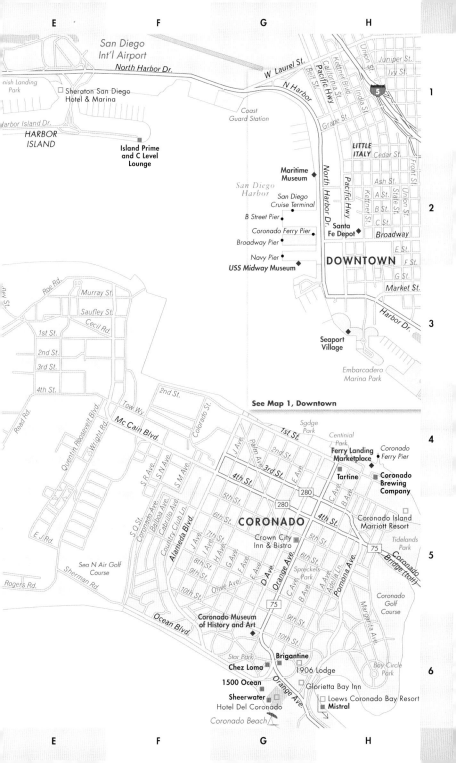

Where to Stay

WORD OF MOUTH

"We had a blast staying at Hotel Indigo. The view and the bar on the 9th floor is fabulous. Petco Park is smack in view."

—SOCALOC

Updated
by Maren
Dougherty

In San Diego, you could plan a luxurious vacation, staying at a hotel with 350-thread-count sheets, wall-mounted flat screens, and panoramic Pacific views. But with some flexibility—maybe opting for a partial-view room with standard TVs—it's possible to experience the city's beauty at half the price.

Any local will tell you two things about San Diego: No. 1, the weather really is perfect; and No. 2, the area's neighborhoods and beach communities offer great diversity, from lively urban vacations to laid-back beachfront escapes. In action-packed downtown, luxury hotels battle it out by offering the nicest perks, including outdoor infinity pools, in-room iPod docks, chauffeured rides in SUVs, and passes to the hotels' hip weekend parties. There are also hostels and some budget-friendly options in and near Little Italy.

You'll need a car if you stay outside downtown, but the coastal communities are rich with lodging options. Across the bridge, Coronado's hotels and resorts offer access to a stretch of glistening white sand that's often recognized as one of the best beaches in the country. La Jolla offers many romantic, upscale ocean-view hotels and some of the area's best restaurants and specialty shopping. But it's easy to find a water view in any price range: surfers make themselves at home at the casual inns and budget stays of Pacific Beach. If you're planning to fish, check out hotels located near the marinas in Shelter Island, Point Loma, or Coronado.

For families, Uptown, Mission Valley, and Old Town are close to Sea-World and the San Diego Zoo, offering good-value accommodations with extras like sleeper sofas and video games. Mission Valley is ideal for business travelers; there are plenty of well-known chain hotels with conference space, modern business centers, and kitchenettes for extended stays.

When your work (or sightseeing) is done, join the trendsetters flocking to downtown's Gaslamp Quarter for its hip restaurants and rooftop hotel bars that rival L.A.'s stylish scenes.

WHERE SHOULD I STAY?

	Neighborhood Vibe	Pros	Cons
Downtown	Downtown's hub is the Gaslamp Quarter, an action-packed area with many hotels, boutiques, restaurants, and clubs. Little Italy and Embarcadero areas are quieter.	Close to food and nightlife options for every age and taste. Quick walk or trolley ride to convention center. Won't need a car to get to many attractions.	Streets can be congested and noisy at night, particularly in the Gaslamp Quarter and East Village. Overnight parking is expensive.
Uptown and Old Town	Quieter area north of downtown with more budget-friendly hotels. Old Town has a busy stretch of Mexican restaurants and historic sites.	Central location that's close to Balboa Park and major freeways. Good for business travelers. More inexpensive dining options.	Limited nightlife options. Feels more removed from San Diego's beachy feel. Mission Valley area lacks character; it's filled with malls and car lots.
Mission Bay, Beaches, and SeaWorld	Relaxed and casual beachside area with many resorts, golf courses, and parks. Largest man-made aquatic park in the country.	Right on the water. Can splurge on Jet Skis and other water sports or stick to BBQs and public playgrounds. Close to SeaWorld.	Resorts are spaced far apart, and area is somewhat removed from central San Diego. Watch for high resort fees and other not-so-obvious charges.
La Jolla	The "jewel" of San Diego, an affluent coastal area with a small-town atmosphere. Has a range of luxury hotels and a few value choices.	Gorgeous views. Close or right on the beach. Some of the best seafood restaurants and high-end shopping in the state. Safe area for walking.	Often congested, and parking can be nearly impossible in summer. Very expensive area. Has few hotels that cater to children.
Point Loma and Coronado with Harbor and Shelter Islands	Areas by the bay have historic and resort hotels, beaches, and tourist-oriented restaurants. Coronado and Point Loma are more residential, home to many military families.	Great views of the city, bay, and beaches. Near the airport. Convenient for boaters. Hotels tend to be family-friendly, with large rooms and pools.	Isolated from the rest of the city; you'll spend significant time commuting to other parts of San Diego, such as La Jolla and Balboa Park.

9

PLANNING

LODGING STRATEGY

Where should I stay? With hundreds of San Diego hotels in dozens of neighborhoods, it may seem like a daunting question. But fret not—our expert writers and editors have done most of the legwork. The selections here represent the best this sunny paradise has to offer—from the best budget motels to the sleekest boutique hotels. Scan "Best Bets" for our top recommendations by price and experience. Or find a review quickly in the listings—search by neighborhood, then alphabetically. Happy hunting!

PARKING

Given the distances between attractions and limited public transportation routes, a car is almost a necessity for visitors to San Diego. That being said, a vehicle can significantly add to your expenses if you stay

BEST BETS FOR SAN DIEGO LODGING

Fodor's offers a selective listing of quality lodging experiences. Here we've compiled our top recommendations. The very best properties—in other words, those that provide a particularly remarkable experience in their price range—are designated in the listings with a Fodor's Choice logo.

Fodor's Choice ★

By Price

By Experience

in the ritzier areas. Overnight parking in Coronado, La Jolla, and downtown's Gaslamp Quarter can be as high as $35 per night; in Uptown and Mission Bay it usually runs $10 to $15.

NEED A RESERVATION?

Book well in advance, especially if you plan to visit in summer, which is the busy season for most hotels. In spring and fall, conventions and sports events can fill every downtown hotel room. When you make reservations, ask about specials. Hotel packages are your best bet; deals range from arts and culture escapes to relaxing spa weekends. Check hotel websites for Internet specials, and try to call a hotel directly; sometimes your effort will result in a lower rate. Several properties in the Hotel Circle area of Mission Valley offer reduced rates and even free tickets to the San Diego Zoo and other attractions. Many hotels also promote discounted weekend packages to fill rooms after convention and business customers leave town. Since the weather is great year-round, don't expect substantial discounts in winter. You can save on hotels and attractions by visiting the San Diego Convention and Visitors Bureau website (⊕ *www.sandiego.org*) for a free Vacation Planning Kit with a Travel Value Coupon booklet.

STAYING WITH KIDS

San Diego is a great year-round family destination. The area is full of hotels suited to a family's budget and/or recreational needs, and many allow kids under 18 to stay free with their parents. You'll find the most choices and diversity in and around Mission Bay, which is close to Sea-World, beaches, parks, and Old Town. Many Mission Bay hotels offer SeaWorld packages or discounts. Another central choice is Mission Valley, which has kid-friendly malls, movie theaters, and hotels. Some resorts offer full- or half-day programs for kids that include swimming, arts and crafts, and trips to the Birch Aquarium. These programs are usually available only in summer and some holiday weekends. Look for "children's programs" within the italicized service information below each lodging review if these services are important to you. Properties that are especially family-friendly are marked with ☺ throughout the chapter.

SERVICES

Downtown hotels once catered primarily to business travelers, though the new boutique hotels are attracting hip leisure travelers to the area, while those at Mission Bay, in coastal locations such as Carlsbad and Encinitas, and at inland resort areas offer golf and other sports facilities, spa services, children's activities, and more.

If a particular amenity is important to you, ask for it; many hotels will provide extras on request. Also double-check your bill at checkout. These days, hotels are fond of tacked-on charges such as a "mini-bar restocking fee" or cleaning charges for smokers. If a charge seems unreasonable, ask to remedy it at checkout. If you're traveling with pets, note that pet policies do change and some hotels require substantial cleaning fees of $50 to $100. A cautionary note to smokers: some hotels are entirely smoke-free, meaning even smoking outdoors is frowned on or prohibited.

PRICES

The lodgings we list run from bare-bones basic to lavishly upscale. Note that even in the most expensive areas, you can find affordable rooms. High season is summer, and rates are lowest in fall. If an ocean view is important, request it when booking, but be aware that it will cost significantly more than a non-ocean-view room.

Prices in the reviews are the lowest cost of a standard double room in high season. For expanded hotel reviews, facilities, and current deals, visit Fodors.com.

HOTEL REVIEWS

Listed alphabetically within neighborhoods. Use the coordinates (✛ 2:F3) after property names or reviews to locate the property on the San Diego Dining and Lodging Atlas. The first number after the ✛ symbol indicates the map number. Following that is the property's coordinate on the map grid.

DOWNTOWN

Lively downtown is San Diego's hotel hub, with everything from budget chains to boutique and business hotels. Here's a part of Southern California where you won't need a car; you can walk or take the trolley to Seaport Village, the Embarcadero, the convention center, galleries and coffeehouses, and the Horton Plaza shopping center. Smack in the middle of downtown is the Gaslamp Quarter where you'll find nightlife options for every night of the week, ranging from 1920s-style jazz lounges to posh multilevel clubs.

GASLAMP QUARTER

$
HOTEL
500 West. The historic Armed Services YMCA Building houses this upscale hostel suitable for backpackers and other budget-minded travelers. **Pros:** near shops and restaurants; good value; kitchen. **Cons:** small rooms; few double rooms; no air-conditioning. $ *Rooms from: $59* ⊠ *500 W. Broadway, Gaslamp Quarter* ☎ *619/234–5252 or 866/500–7533* ⊕ *www.500westhotel.com* ⌇ *259 rooms* ⫿ *No meals* ✛ *1:C3.*

$$$
HOTEL
Fodor'sChoice
★
Andaz San Diego. The former Ivy Hotel was rebranded in 2010 as the luxury, Hyatt-managed Andaz, whose new owners nixed the snobbery but kept the style. **Pros:** luxurious rooms; thriving nightlife scene; friendly service. **Cons:** noisy on weekends; not a good choice for families. $ *Rooms from: $288* ⊠ *600 F St., Gaslamp Quarter* ☎ *619/849–1234* ⊕ *www.sandiego.andaz.hyatt.com* ⌇ *142 rooms, 17 suites* ⫿ *No meals* ✛ *1:E4.*

$$
HOTEL
The Bristol. Pop art by Peter Max and Andy Warhol sets a mod 1960s tone at this splashy boutique hotel. **Pros:** modern rooms; centrally located; good value. **Cons:** few amenities, somewhat seedy area. $ *Rooms from: $159* ⊠ *1055 1st Ave., Gaslamp Quarter* ☎ *619/232–6141 or 888/745–4393* ⊕ *www.thebristolsandiego.com* ⌇ *102 rooms* ⫿ *No meals* ✛ *1:D3.*

$
HOTEL
Gaslamp Plaza Suites. One of San Diego's first "skyscrapers," this 11-story structure that's on the National Register of Historic Places was built in 1913. **Pros:** historic building; good location a block from

Hard Rock Hotel

The Sofia Hotel

Versailles Room, Westgate Hotel

Horton Plaza; well priced. **Cons:** books up early; smallish rooms. $ *Rooms from: $122* ✉ *520 E St., Gaslamp Quarter* ☎ *619/232–9500 or 800/874–8770* ⊕ *www.gaslampplaza.com* ⤴ *12 rooms, 52 suites* ❘❍❘ *Breakfast* ✛ *1:E4.*

$$
HOTEL
Fodor'sChoice
★

🛏 **Hard Rock Hotel.** Self-billed as a hip playground for rock stars and people who want to party like them, the Hard Rock is conveniently located near PETCO Park overlooking glimmering San Diego Bay. **Pros:** central location; great scene; luxurious rooms. **Cons:** pricey drinks; some attitude. $ *Rooms from: $204* ✉ *207 5th Ave., Gaslamp Quarter* ☎ *619/702–3000 or 866/751–7625* ⊕ *www.hardrockhotelsd.com* ⤴ *244 rooms, 176 suites* ❘❍❘ *No meals* ✛ *1:E5.*

$$
HOTEL
☾

🛏 **Hilton San Diego Bayfront.** Not your typical Hilton, this modern 30-story hotel overlooking San Diego Bay strives for a boutique feel. **Pros:** close to the convention center and PETCO Park; new rooms. **Cons:** pricey dining options; not as family-friendly as other area hotels. $ *Rooms from: $215* ✉ *1 Park Blvd., Gaslamp Quarter* ☎ *619/564–3333* ⊕ *www. hiltonsdbayfront.com* ⤴ *1,160 rooms, 30 suites* ❘❍❘ *No meals* ✛ *1:E6.*

$$$
HOTEL

🛏 **Hilton San Diego Gaslamp Quarter.** The moment you experience the cozy lounge spaces and wood accents of the Hilton's modern and sophisticated lobby, you realize this isn't your run-of-the-mill chain hotel. **Pros:** nice decor; upscale lofts; near restaurants and shops. **Cons:** noisy area; pricey parking. $ *Rooms from: $289* ✉ *401 K St., Gaslamp Quarter* ☎ *619/231–4040 or 800/445–8667* ⊕ *www.hiltongaslamp.com* ⤴ *240 rooms, 13 suites, 30 lofts* ❘❍❘ *No meals* ✛ *1:D5.*

$$
HOTEL
☾

🛏 **Hotel Palomar San Diego.** Now a member of the Kimpton Hotel group, the Palomar (formerly the Sè San Diego) retains its luxurious ambience. **Pros:** new rooms; centrally located; luxury amenities. **Cons:** expensive parking; Saltbox restaurant is pricey and needs improvement. $ *Rooms from: $208* ✉ *1047 5th Ave., Gaslamp Quarter* ☎ *619/515–3000* ⊕ *www. hotelpalomar-sandiego.com* ⤴ *146 rooms, 37 suites* ❘❍❘ *No meals* ✛ *1:E3.*

$$$
HOTEL
☾
Fodor'sChoice
★

🛏 **Hotel Solamar.** The hip Solamar is best known for its pool-side rooftop bar, LoungeSix, and stylish lobby decor. **Pros:** great restaurant; attentive service; upscale rooms. **Cons:** busy valet parking; bars are crowded and noisy on weekends. $ *Rooms from: $242* ✉ *435 6th Ave., Gaslamp Quarter* ☎ *619/819–9500 or 877/230–0300* ⊕ *www.hotelsolamar.com* ⤴ *217 rooms, 16 suites* ❘❍❘ *No meals* ✛ *1:E5.*

$$
HOTEL

🛏 **The Keating Hotel.** The Keating's 120-year-old historic exterior looks nothing like its sexy interior, remade into a hotel in 2006. **Pros:** great location; boutique hotel. **Cons:** street noise; industrial-feeling rooms; small lobby. $ *Rooms from: $196* ✉ *432 F St., Gaslamp Quarter* ☎ *619/814–5700 or 877/753–2846* ⊕ *www.thekeating.com* ⤴ *26 rooms, 9 suites* ❘❍❘ *No meals* ✛ *1:D4.*

$$
HOTEL

🛏 **Marriott Residence Inn Downtown.** A home away from home for urbanites, the all-suites hotel opened in November 2009. **Pros:** spacious rooms; central location; pet-friendly. **Cons:** no room service; pricey valet-only parking will add up quickly during an extended stay. $ *Rooms from: $219* ✉ *356 6th Ave., Gaslamp Quarter* ☎ *619/487–1200* ⊕ *www.marriott.com/sanrg* ⤴ *240 suites* ❘❍❘ *Breakfast* ✛ *1:E5.*

$$
HOTEL

🛏 **Omni San Diego Hotel.** Business travelers who also want to catch a baseball game flock to this modern masterpiece that occupies the first

21 floors of a 32-story high-rise overlooking PETCO Park. **Pros:** great views; good location; modern setting. **Cons:** busy; crowded during baseball season. [$] *Rooms from: $224* ✉ *675 L St., Gaslamp Quarter* ☎ *619/231–6664 or 800/843–6664* 🌐 *www.omnihotels.com* 🛏 *478 rooms, 33 suites* 🍴 *No meals* ⊕ *1:E6.*

$$$ HOTEL **San Diego Marriott Gaslamp Quarter.** The 22-story Marriott sits amid the Gaslamp's restaurants and boutiques, near a trolley station, the convention center, and PETCO Park. **Pros:** good views; modern decor; central location. **Cons:** rooftop bar can get rowdy; no pool. [$] *Rooms from: $249* ✉ *660 K St., Gaslamp Quarter* ☎ *619/696–0234* 🌐 *www.sandiegogaslamphotel.com* 🛏 *291 rooms, 15 suites* 🍴 *No meals* ⊕ *1:E5.*

$$ HOTEL Fodor's Choice ★ **The Sofia Hotel.** This stylish and centrally located boutique hotel has small rooms, but clever details help guests feel pampered. **Pros:** upscale room amenities; historic building; near shops and restaurants. **Cons:** busy area; small rooms. [$] *Rooms from: $209* ✉ *150 W. Broadway, Gaslamp Quarter* ☎ *619/234–9200 or 800/826–0009* 🌐 *www.thesofiahotel.com* 🛏 *211 rooms, 4 suites* 🍴 *No meals* ⊕ *1:D3.*

$$ HOTEL **U.S. Grant.** Stepping into the regal U.S. Grant not only places you in the lap of luxury but also transports you back in time. **Pros:** modern rooms; great location; near shopping and restaurants. **Cons:** small elevators; some reports of trouble with a/c units. [$] *Rooms from: $199* ✉ *326 Broadway, Gaslamp Quarter* ☎ *619/232–3121 or 800/325–3589* 🌐 *www.usgrant.net* 🛏 *223 rooms, 47 suites* 🍴 *No meals* ⊕ *1:D3.*

$$$ HOTEL **W Hotel.** Come here for the trendy decor, upscale rooms, and central location between Gaslamp and Little Italy. **Pros:** large lobby that's fun for people watching; modern rooms; nice spa. **Cons:** expensive parking; not centrally located. [$] *Rooms from: $235* ✉ *421 W. B St., Gaslamp Quarter* ☎ *619/398–3100* 🌐 *www.whotels.com/sandiego* 🛏 *253 rooms, 5 suites* 🍴 *No meals* ⊕ *1:C3.*

$$$ HOTEL Fodor's Choice ★ **Westgate Hotel.** A modern high-rise near Horton Plaza hides San Diego's most opulent old-world-style hotel. **Pros:** elegant rooms; grand lobby, near shopping. **Cons:** formal atmosphere; mandatory facility fee. [$] *Rooms from: $280* ✉ *1055 2nd Ave., Gaslamp Quarter* ☎ *619/238–1818 or 800/221–3802* 🌐 *www.westgatehotel.com* 🛏 *215 rooms, 8 suites* 🍴 *No meals* ⊕ *1:D3.*

EAST VILLAGE

$$ HOTEL **Hotel Indigo.** Smart-looking spaces and great service for the business traveler are the hallmarks of the Indigo chain of modern hotels. **Pros:** close to restaurants and bars; new rooms. **Cons:** no pool; somewhat noisy neighborhood. [$] *Rooms from: $172* ✉ *509 9th Ave., East Village* ☎ *619/727–4000* 🌐 *www.hotelindigo.com/sandiego* 🛏 *210 rooms, 5 suites* 🍴 *No meals* ⊕ *1:E5.*

$ B&B/INN **Lucky D's Hostel.** A quick walk from PETCO Park and downtown bars, this no-frills hostel is a good fit for travelers content with shared bathrooms and the sounds of late-night partiers stumbling home. **Pros:** solo travelers can easily find friends here; central location; free dinner on some nights. **Cons:** can get very hot in summer; noisy; no on-site parking. [$] *Rooms from: $62* ✉ *615 8th Ave., East Village* ☎ *619/595–0000* 🌐 *www.luckydshostel.com* 🛏 *35 dorms, 5 private rooms* 🍴 *Some meals* ⊕ *1:E4.*

9

W Hotel

LITTLE ITALY

$
B&B/INN

Hotel Vyvant. You'll find more amenities at other downtown hotels but it's hard to beat this property's value and charm. **Pros:** good location; historic property; welcoming staff. **Cons:** some shared baths; no parking. *$ Rooms from: $139 ⊠ 505 W. Grape St., Little Italy ☎ 619/230–1600 or 800/518–9930 ⊕ www.littleitalyhotel.com ➫ 21 rooms, 2 suites ❑ Breakfast ✚ 1:C1.*

$
HOTEL

Porto Vista Hotel & Suites. A $15 million renovation turned this former budget motel into a contemporary hotel-motel with two additional buildings, a stylish restaurant and lounge, and a fitness center. **Pros:** new decor in common areas, some guest rooms, and the fitness center; airport shuttle. **Cons:** spotty service; small rooms, some still in need of updating. *$ Rooms from: $145 ⊠ 1835 Columbia St., Little Italy ☎ 619/544–0164 or 855/504–8986 ⊕ www.portovistasandiego.com ➫ 189 rooms, 22 suites ❑ No meals ✚ 1:C2.*

EMBARCADERO

$$
HOTEL

Embassy Suites–San Diego Bay. The front door of each spacious, contemporary suite here opens out onto a 12-story atrium. **Pros:** new bathrooms; harbor-facing rooms have spectacular views; spacious accommodations; good location. **Cons:** busy area; wildly varying rates. *$ Rooms from: $190 ⊠ 601 Pacific Hwy., Embarcadero ☎ 619/239–2400 or 800/362–2779 ⊕ www.sandiegobay.embassysuites.com ➫ 337 suites ❑ Breakfast ✚ 1:B4.*

$$$
HOTEL

Manchester Grand Hyatt San Diego. Primarily for business travelers, this hotel between Seaport Village and the convention center is San Diego's largest, and its 33- and 40-story towers make it the West

Coast's tallest waterfront hotel. **Pros:** great views; conference facilities; good location. **Cons:** very busy; some rooms dated. [$] *Rooms from: $235* ✉ *1 Market Pl., Embarcadero* ☎ *619/232–1234 or 800/233–1234* 🌐 *www.manchestergrand.hyatt.com* 🛏 *1,530 rooms, 95 suites* 🍴 *No meals* ✥ *1:C5.*

BALBOA PARK AND BANKERS HILL

BANKERS HILL

$ HOTEL 🏨 **Inn at the Park.** Antique furniture, ornate mirrors, and the original 1926 ceiling grace the lobby of this historic hotel (formerly the Park Manor Suites) within walking distance of Balboa Park. **Pros:** spacious rooms; evening entertainment; full kitchens. **Cons:** no a/c; valet parking only. [$] *Rooms from: $159* ✉ *525 Spruce St., Bankers Hill* ☎ *619/291–0999* 🌐 *www.shellhospitality.com/Inn-at-the-Park* 🛏 *82 suites* 🍴 *Breakfast* ✥ *2:E5.*

OLD TOWN, MISSION VALLEY, AND NORTH PARK

San Diego's Uptown area is close to the San Diego Zoo and Balboa Park, and includes the neighborhoods of Hillcrest, Mission Hills, Bankers Hill, North Park, and University Heights. There are few hotels, but the area offers pedestrian-friendly shopping and hip dive bars.

Dense with Mexican eateries, Old Town is the place to be for quick and easy access to house-made tortillas. The neighborhood is also home to historic adobe shops and museums. East of Old Town is Mission Valley, a suburban maze of freeways, shopping centers, and Hotel Circle, where many spacious and inexpensive lodging options are located.

OLD TOWN

$ HOTEL 👶 🏨 **Best Western Plus Hacienda Hotel–Old Town.** Perched on a hill in the heart of Old Town, this hotel is known for its expansive courtyards, outdoor fountains, and maze of stairs that connect eight buildings of guest rooms. **Pros:** airport shuttle; well-maintained outdoor areas. **Cons:** some rooms need renovating; complicated layout. [$] *Rooms from: $149* ✉ *4041 Harney St., Old Town* ☎ *619/298–4707* 🌐 *www.haciendahotel-oldtown.com* 🛏 *178 rooms, 21 suites* 🍴 *No meals* ✥ *2:A4.*

$$ B&B/INN 🏨 **The Cosmopolitan Hotel.** With antique furniture, pull-chain toilets, and a veranda overlooking Old Town State Historic Park, the Cosmo offers guests a taste of Victorian-era living. **Pros:** historic charm; huge suites; romantic. **Cons:** no TVs; public or street parking only. [$] *Rooms from: $175* ✉ *2660 Calhoun St., Old Town* ☎ *619/297–1874* 🌐 *www.oldtowncosmopolitan.com* 🛏 *6 rooms, 4 suites* 🍴 *Some meals* ✥ *2:A4.*

$ HOTEL 🏨 **Holiday Inn Express Airport–Old Town.** Already an excellent value for Old Town, this cheerful property throws in such perks as a free breakfast buffet. **Pros:** good location; hot continental breakfast; few add-on fees. **Cons:** some freeway noise; few nightlife options. [$] *Rooms from: $95* ✉ *1955 San Diego Ave., Old Town* ☎ *619/543–1130 or 800/315–2621* 🌐 *www.hiexpress.com* 🛏 *116 rooms, 7 suites* 🍴 *Breakfast* ✥ *2:B5.*

Family-Friendly Hotels

Got kids in tow? San Diego is designed for family fun; the year-round sunny, warm weather ensures lots of play days. The focus is on outdoor activities, such as surfing or swimming, but be sure to spend a day at Balboa Park's gardens, museums, and IMAX theater. Many hotels let kids under 18 stay free—just ask. And check into kids' activity programs, family-size suites, in-room Nintendo, or kitchenettes. Shop around for hotel packages, which often include tickets to local attractions.

Some of the high-end properties have special programs for kids; most occur in summer, some year-round. The famous **Hotel Del Coronado** has tons of activities, from surfing lessons and kayak tours to foosball and karaoke in "VIBZ," a year-round hangout for teens ages 13–17. The **Loews Coronado Bay Resort** has welcome gifts for children, a kids-only pool, a game library, and special menus. Some recreational fun is offered seasonally, such as sunset sails and gondola rides. And kids can bring their pets.

Across the bay, resorts on family-friendly Mission Bay cater to young ones. The **Catamaran Resort Hotel** holds science camps for kids ages 5–12. Offered daily in summer, the workshops focus on a range of topics, including the diversity of sea life and the physics of beach cruisers. At the **Lodge at Torrey Pines'** library, kids over age 12 can play pool or watch movies borrowed from the concierge; it's open from 8 am until 11 pm.

Smaller hotels in Mission Valley and La Jolla may not have organized programs but several offer extra amenities for kids and teens; the Courtyard by Marriott Mission Valley has a Nintendo Wii system in the lobby and board games that kids can borrow from the front desk.

MISSION VALLEY

$ **Courtyard by Marriott Mission Valley.** Amenities abound for families seeking a fun and casual base for trips to SeaWorld and the zoo. **Pros:** easy freeway access to area attractions; good value; nice perks for families and business travelers. **Cons:** few stores and restaurants in walking distance; halls can be noisy with kids. $ *Rooms from: $134* ✉ *595 Hotel Circle S, Mission Valley* ☎ *619/291–5720* ⊕ *www.courtyardsd. com* ⤵ *309 rooms, 8 suites* ⦿ *No meals* ⊹ *2:D3.*

HOTEL
☾
Fodor's Choice
★

$$ **Doubletree Hotel San Diego Mission Valley.** Near the Fashion Valley shopping mall and adjacent to the Hazard Center—which has a seven-screen movie theater, four major restaurants, and more than 20 shops—the Doubletree is also convenient to Route 163 and I-8. **Pros:** stellar service; large rooms; good for fitness buffs. **Cons:** dated bathrooms; unimpressive views. $ *Rooms from: $199* ✉ *7450 Hazard Center Dr., Mission Valley* ☎ *619/297–5466 or 800/222–8733* ⊕ *www.doubletree.com* ⤵ *300 rooms, 3 suites* ⦿ *No meals* ⊹ *2:D2.*

HOTEL

$ **Crowne Plaza San Diego.** Clean and comfortable, the Crowne Plaza may not have the frills of downtown hotels and coastal resorts, but it's a reliable pick for budget-minded families. **Pros:** near shopping; free shuttles; lush grounds. **Cons:** near freeway; dated public areas. $ *Rooms from: $126*

HOTEL

2270 Hotel Circle N, Mission Valley 619/297–1101 *www. cp-sandiego.com* 406 rooms, 11 suites *No meals* 2:B3.

NORTH PARK

$
B&B/INN

Balboa Park Inn. This budget guesthouse occupies four Spanish colonial–style 1915 residences connected by courtyards. **Pros:** good value; convenient location; continental breakfast. **Cons:** no parking; no on-site services; busy area. *Rooms from: $99* 3402 Park Blvd., North Park 619/298–0823 or 800/938–8181 *www. balboaparkinn.com* 26 suites *Breakfast* 2:F5.

$$$
B&B/INN
Fodor's Choice
★

Britt Scripps Inn. A block west of Balboa Park, this inn occupies the former mansion of the Scripps newspaper family. **Pros:** intimate; historic building; upscale amenities. **Cons:** far from nightlife; some street noise. *Rooms from: $255* 406 Maple St., North Park 888/881–1991 *www.brittscripps.com* 9 rooms *Breakfast* 2:D6.

MISSION BAY, BEACHES, AND SEAWORLD

Mission Bay Park, with its beaches, bike trails, boat-launching ramps, golf course, and grassy parks—not to mention SeaWorld—is a haven of hotels and resorts. Smaller hotels, motels, and hostels can be found nearby in Mission Beach and Pacific Beach. These coastal communities are popular among local twentysomethings for the many inexpensive dining and nightlife possibilities. The streets are also filled with surf shops and boutiques for picking up flip-flops, sundresses, and other beachy souvenirs. You can't go wrong with any of these beachfront areas, as long as the frenzied crowds at play don't bother you.

MISSION BAY

$$
RESORT

The Dana on Mission Bay. The modern-chic earth-tone lobby of this bay resort will make you feel like you've arrived somewhere much more expensive. **Pros:** water views; many outdoor activities. **Cons:** some rooms need renovation; not centrally located. *Rooms from: $159* 1710 W. Mission Bay Dr., Mission Bay 619/222–6440 or 800/445–3339 *www.thedana.com* 259 rooms, 12 suites *No meals* 3:C6.

$$
RESORT

Hyatt Regency Mission Bay Spa & Marina. This modern property has many desirable amenities, including balconies with excellent views of the garden, bay, ocean, or swimming pool courtyard. **Pros:** modern decor; great pet program; water views; 120-foot waterslides in pools, plus kiddie slide. **Cons:** slightly hard to navigate surrounding roads; thin walls; not centrally located. *Rooms from: $209* 1441 Quivira Rd., Mission Bay 619/224–1234 or 800/233–1234 *www.missionbay. hyatt.com* 354 rooms, 76 suites *No meals* 3:C6.

9

Courtyard by Marriott Mission Valley

Andaz San Diego

Britt Scripps Inn

$$$ RESORT 👪 🏨 **Paradise Point Resort & Spa.** The beautiful landscape of this 44-acre resort on Vacation Isle has been the setting for a number of movies. **Pros:** water views; pools; good service. **Cons:** not centrally located; summer minimum stays; motel-thin walls; parking and resort fees. [$] *Rooms from: $250* ✉ *1404 Vacation Rd., Mission Bay* ☎ *858/274–4630 or 800/344–2626* 🌐 *www.paradisepoint.com* 🛏 *462 cottages* 🍴 *No meals* ✣ *3:C6.*

MISSION BEACH

$$ RESORT 👪 🏨 **Catamaran Resort Hotel.** Tiki torches light the way through grounds thick with tropical foliage to the six two-story buildings and the 14-story high-rise in Mission Bay. **Pros:** spa; bay views; many activities for kids. **Cons:** not centrally located; dated room decor. [$] *Rooms from: $189* ✉ *3999 Mission Blvd., Mission Beach* ☎ *858/488–1081 or 800/422–8386* 🌐 *www.catamaranresort.com* 🛏 *262 rooms, 50 suites* 🍴 *No meals* ✣ *3:C5.*

PACIFIC BEACH

$$ HOTEL 🏨 **Crystal Pier Hotel and Cottages.** Crystal Pier, a Pacific Beach landmark, had its grand opening in 1927; 10 years later, the first of the blue-and-white cottages were built. **Pros:** ocean view; historic lodgings; free parking. **Cons:** few amenities; no air-conditioning in most; reservations fill up fast. [$] *Rooms from: $175* ✉ *4500 Ocean Blvd., Pacific Beach* ☎ *800/748–5894 or 858/483–6983* 🌐 *www.crystalpier.com* 🛏 *23 cottages, 6 suites* 🍴 *No meals* ✣ *3:B5.*

$$$$ RESORT 🏨 **Pacific Terrace Hotel.** Travelers love this terrific beachfront hotel and the ocean views from most rooms; it's a perfect place for watching sunsets over the Pacific. **Pros:** beach views; large rooms; friendly service. **Cons:** busy and sometimes noisy area; lots of traffic. [$] *Rooms from: $400* ✉ *610 Diamond St., Pacific Beach* ☎ *858/581–3500 or 800/344–3370* 🌐 *www.pacificterrace.com* 🛏 *61 rooms, 12 suites* 🍴 *No meals* ✣ *3:B5.*

$$ HOTEL 🏨 **Surfer Beach Hotel.** Choose this place for its great location—right on bustling Pacific Beach. **Pros:** beach location; ocean-view rooms; pool. **Cons:** dated rooms; no air-conditioning. [$] *Rooms from: $169* ✉ *711 Pacific Beach Dr., Pacific Beach* ☎ *858/483–7070 or 866/251–2764* 🌐 *www.surferbeachhotel.com* 🛏 *53 rooms, 16 suites* 🍴 *No meals* ✣ *3:C5.*

$$$ HOTEL 🏨 **Tower23.** A neomodern masterpiece with a beachy vibe, this boutique hotel is a favorite of the young and young-at-heart. **Pros:** beach views; central location; hip decor. **Cons:** no pool; busy area. [$] *Rooms from: $249* ✉ *723 Felspar St., Pacific Beach* ☎ *866/869–3723 or 858/270–2323* 🌐 *www.t23hotel.com* 🛏 *38 rooms, 6 suites* 🍴 *No meals* ✣ *3:B5.*

LA JOLLA

Multimillion-dollar homes line the beaches and hillsides of beautiful and prestigious La Jolla, a community about 20 minutes north of downtown. La Jolla Shores is a mile-long sandy beach that gets crowded in summer with kayakers, sunbathers, and students in scuba-diving classes. The village—the heart of La Jolla—is chockablock with expensive boutiques, art galleries, restaurants, and a grassy beachfront park that's popular for picnics and weddings. It may have an upscale European air, but don't despair if you're not driving up in an Aston Martin: this vacation spot has sufficient lodging choices for every budget.

$$ ⚟ **Empress Hotel.** Less glitzy than neighboring lodging options in La
HOTEL Jolla, the five-story Empress attracts business travelers and couples looking for a basic but comfortable place to stay. **Pros:** well-trained staff; near shops and restaurants; quiet street. **Cons:** not exciting for kids; some travelers report that noise carries between the thin walls. ⓢ *Rooms from: $159* ✉ *7766 Fay Ave., La Jolla* ☎ *858/454–3001 or 888/369–9900* ⊕ *www.empress-hotel.com* ⤳ *69 rooms, 4 suites* ⦶ *Breakfast* ✛ *3:A2.*

$$ ⚟ **Estancia La Jolla Hotel & Spa.** With its rambling California mission–
RESORT style architecture and brilliant gardens, this resort on what once was a famous equestrian ranch exudes rustic elegance. **Pros:** upscale rooms; nice spa; landscaped grounds. **Cons:** mandatory resort fees; not centrally located. ⓢ *Rooms from: $209* ✉ *9700 N. Torrey Pines Rd., La Jolla* ☎ *858/550–1000 or 877/437–8262* ⊕ *www.estancialajolla.com* ⤳ *200 rooms, 10 suites* ⦶ *No meals* ✛ *3:B1.*

$$$ ⚟ **Grande Colonial.** This white wedding cake–style hotel in the heart of
HOTEL La Jolla village has ocean views and charming European details that
Fodor's Choice include chandeliers, mahogany railings, and French doors. **Pros:** near
★ shopping; near beach; superb restaurant. **Cons:** somewhat busy street; no fitness center. ⓢ *Rooms from: $229* ✉ *910 Prospect St., La Jolla* ☎ *858/454–2181 or 877/792–8053* ⊕ *www.thegrandecolonial.com* ⤳ *52 rooms, 41 suites* ⦶ *No meals* ✛ *3:A2.*

$$ ⚟ **Hotel La Jolla.** Kimpton Hotels relaunched this hotel in 2012 with
HOTEL a coastal-chic design and a new 11th-floor restaurant, Cusp Dining & Drinks. **Pros:** new rooms; stunning views from the higher floors. **Cons:** tiny gym; valet parking only. ⓢ *Rooms from: $209* ✉ *7955 La Jolla Shores Dr., La Jolla* ☎ *858/459–0261 or 800/941–1149* ⊕ *www. hotellajolla.com* ⤳ *106 rooms, 4 suites* ⦶ *No meals* ✛ *3:C2.*

$$$ ⚟ **Hotel Parisi.** Soothing spa music and Asian art create a Zen-like atmo-
HOTEL sphere in the lobby of this La Jolla hotel favored by celebrities and other travelers who value privacy. **Pros:** upscale amenities; wellness services; centrally located. **Cons:** one-room "suites"; not appropriate for children. ⓢ *Rooms from: $249* ✉ *1111 Prospect St., La Jolla* ☎ *858/454– 1511* ⊕ *www.hotelparisi.com* ⤳ *29 suites* ⦶ *Breakfast* ✛ *3:B2.*

$$ ⚟ **Hyatt Regency La Jolla.** Popular among business travelers, this Hyatt
HOTEL is in the Golden Triangle area, about 10 minutes from the beach and the village of La Jolla. **Pros:** many restaurants; modern rooms; upscale amenities. **Cons:** busy hotel; not centrally located. ⓢ *Rooms from: $218* ✉ *Aventine Center, 3777 La Jolla Village Dr., La Jolla* ☎ *800/233–1234 or 858/552–1234* ⊕ *www.hyattregencylajolla.com* ⤳ *395 rooms, 24 suites* ⦶ *No meals* ✛ *3:D1.*

$$ ⚟ **La Jolla Cove Suites.** It may lack the charm of some properties in this
HOTEL exclusive area, but this motel with studios and suites (some with spacious oceanfront balconies) gives its guests the same first-class views of La Jolla Cove at lower rates. **Pros:** good value; ocean views; some large rooms. **Cons:** dated rooms; busy street. ⓢ *Rooms from: $179* ✉ *1155 Coast Blvd., La Jolla* ☎ *858/459–2621 or 888/525–6552* ⊕ *www. lajollacove.com* ⤳ *25 rooms, 90 suites* ⦶ *Breakfast* ✛ *3:B2.*

Lodge at Torrey Pines

Grande Colonial

LODGING ALTERNATIVES

APARTMENT RENTALS

Travelers planning on more than a weekend with Shamu can find a variety of apartment and hotel options suitable for extended stays. Some of these properties also work well for larger families and groups looking for shared accommodations with full kitchens and eating areas.

If you're sticking to hotels, many properties with suites offer special weekly and monthly rates, especially during the off-season. Downtown's new **Marriott Residence Inn** has studios and one-bedroom suites with full-size refrigerators and two-burner stoves. **Homewood Suites San Diego Airport** offers a similar setup; the hotel also has two-bedroom suites and offers complimentary grocery shopping service and light dinner receptions on weeknights. Less expensive options include **Hotel Occidental**, a no-frills spot near Balboa Park, and downtown's **500 West**, both of which promote excellent deals for weekly stays. Long-term guests at 500 West have access to a shared kitchen, laundry facilities, and social hostel-like common areas. Lastly, another option downtown is **Lucky D's Hostel**, perfect for international students and young travelers looking for an inexpensive place to stay for a week or two.

Oakwood Apartments rents comfortable furnished apartments in several popular neighborhoods with maid service and linens; there's a one-week to 30-day minimum stay depending on locations. Parking can be difficult in some of these areas, so be sure to ask about private parking and any associated fees.

Many travelers recommend the online **Vacation Rentals by Owner** (VRBO) directory for condos and beach houses that owners rent directly to individuals. There are some risks involved, but VRBO offers money-back guarantees, which prevents much of the online fraud that plagues other sites like Craigslist.

Oakwood Apartments (☎ 877/902–0832 ⊕ www.oakwood.com). **San Diego Sunset Vacation Rentals** (☎ 858/488–5204 ⊕ www. sandiegosunsetvacationrentals.com). **San Diego Vacation Rentals** (☎ 800/222–8281 ⊕ www.sdvr.com). **Vacation Rentals by Owner** (⊕ www.vrbo.com).

BED-AND-BREAKFASTS

San Diego is known more for its resorts and chain properties, but the city has several bed-and-breakfasts, most of which are in private homes and are well maintained and accommodating. Travelers hoping to stay in the Uptown neighborhoods near Balboa Park may find that bed-and-breakfasts are their best bet because there are few recommendable hotels but many activities and restaurants within walking distance. The San Diego Bed & Breakfast Guild lists a number of high-quality member inns. The Bed & Breakfast Directory for San Diego, maintained by a guild member, covers San Diego County.

Bed & Breakfast Directory for San Diego (☎ 619/523–1300 ⊕ www.bandbguildsandiego.org). **California Association of Bed and Breakfast Inns** (☎ 800/373–9251 ⊕ www.cabbi.com).

$$$
HOTEL

La Jolla Shores Hotel. One of San Diego's few hotels actually on the beach, this property is part of La Jolla Beach and Tennis Club. **Pros:** on beach; great views; quiet area. **Cons:** not centrally located; some rooms are dated. $ *Rooms from: $289* ⊠ *8110 Camino del Oro, La Jolla* ☎ *858/459–8271 or 877/346–6714* ⊕ *www.ljshoreshotel.com* ⤳ *127 rooms, 1 suite* ✛ *3:B2.*

$$$$
HOTEL

La Valencia. This pink Spanish-Mediterranean confection drew Hollywood film stars in the 1930s and '40s with its setting and views of La Jolla Cove. **Pros:** upscale rooms; views; near beach. **Cons:** standard rooms are tiny; lots of traffic outside. $ *Rooms from: $320* ⊠ *1132 Prospect St., La Jolla* ☎ *858/454–0771 or 800/451–0772* ⊕ *www. lavalencia.com* ⤳ *82 rooms, 15 villas, 15 suites* ⦿ *No meals* ✛ *3:B2.*

$$$$
RESORT
Fodor's Choice
★

Lodge at Torrey Pines. This beautiful Craftsman-style lodge sits on a bluff between La Jolla and Del Mar and commands a coastal view. **Pros:** spacious upscale rooms; good service; Torrey Pines Golf Club on property. **Cons:** not centrally located; expensive. $ *Rooms from: $400* ⊠ *11480 N. Torrey Pines Rd., La Jolla* ☎ *858/453–4420 or 800/995–4507* ⊕ *www. lodgetorreypines.com* ⤳ *164 rooms, 6 suites* ⦿ *No meals* ✛ *3:B1.*

$$
B&B/INN

Scripps Inn. You'd be wise to make reservations well in advance for this small, quiet inn tucked away on Coast Boulevard; its popularity with repeat visitors ensures that it's booked year-round. **Pros:** beach access; intimate feel; inexpensive parking. **Cons:** thin walls; motel layout; busy area. $ *Rooms from: $220* ⊠ *555 S. Coast Blvd., La Jolla* ☎ *858/454–3391* ⊕ *www.scrippsinn.com* ⤳ *7 rooms, 7 suites* ⦿ *Breakfast* ✛ *3:A2.*

POINT LOMA AND CORONADO WITH HARBOR AND SHELTER ISLANDS

Coronado feels like something out of an earlier, more gracious era, making it a great getaway. The clean white beaches are some of the best in the state, and they're rarely crowded. But if you plan to see many of San Diego's attractions, you'll spend significant time commuting across the bridge or riding the ferry.

Harbor Island and Shelter Island, two man-made peninsulas between downtown and Point Loma, have grassy parks, tree-lined paths, and views of the downtown skyline. Closer to downtown, Harbor Island is less than five minutes from the airport. Shelter Island is next to Point Loma, a hilly community that's home to Cabrillo National Monument and a naval base.

POINT LOMA

$$
HOTEL

Courtyard by Marriott San Diego Airport. Close to the restaurants and shops of Liberty Station, this family-friendly hotel spares travelers the extra fees charged by most downtown and coastal lodgings. **Pros:** modern rooms; near airport; friendly service. **Cons:** unimpressive views. $ *Rooms from: $200* ⊠ *2592 Laning Rd., Point Loma* ☎ *619/221–1900 or 888/236–2427* ⊕ *www.marriott.com* ⤳ *197 rooms, 3 suites* ⦿ *No meals* ✛ *4:C1.*

$$
HOTEL

Holiday Inn Bayside. If SeaWorld and the San Diego Zoo aren't enough to sap kids of their energy, the outdoor activities at this hotel across from San Diego Bay fishing docks should do the trick. **Pros:** great for

9

Hotel Del Coronado

1906 Lodge

kids; close to airport. **Cons:** dated lobby and common areas; not centrally located. [$] *Rooms from: $170* ✉ *4875 N. Harbor Dr., Point Loma* ☎ *619/224–3621 or 800/315–2621* 🌐 *www.holinnbayside.com* 🛏 *234 rooms, 10 suites* 🍴 *No meals* ✣ *4:C1.*

$ HOTEL 👶 🏨 **Holiday Inn Express–SeaWorld Area.** In Point Loma near the West Mission Bay exit off I–8, this is a surprisingly cute and quiet lodging option despite proximity to bustling traffic. **Pros:** near SeaWorld; kids eat free; good service. **Cons:** not a scenic area; somewhat hard to find. [$] *Rooms from: $144* ✉ *3950 Jupiter St., Point Loma* ☎ *619/226–8000 or 800/320–0208* 🌐 *www.seaworldhi.com* 🛏 *68 rooms, 2 suites* 🍴 *Breakfast* ✣ *4:C1.*

$$ HOTEL 👶 Fodor's Choice ★ 🏨 **Homewood Suites San Diego Airport.** Families and business travelers on long trips will benefit from the space and amenities at this all-suites hotel. **Pros:** warm staff; free parking; close to paths for joggers and bikers. **Cons:** often crowded dining room; far from nightlife. [$] *Rooms from: $185* ✉ *2576 Laning Rd., Point Loma* ☎ *619/222–0500* 🌐 *www.homewoodsuites.com* 🛏 *150 suites* 🍴 *Multiple meal plans* ✣ *4:C1.*

$$ HOTEL 🏨 **Inn at Sunset Cliffs.** Here you really do hear the sound of waves crashing against the shore. **Pros:** romantic; breathtaking views; friendly staff. **Cons:** exterior is slightly run-down; no elevator. [$] *Rooms from: $175* ✉ *1370 Sunset Cliffs Blvd., Point Loma* ☎ *619/222–7901 or 866/786–2543* 🌐 *www.innatsunsetcliffs.com* 🛏 *24 rooms* 🍴 *No meals* ✣ *4:A2.*

$ HOTEL Fodor's Choice ★ 🏨 **The Pearl Hotel.** This previously vintage motel received a makeover, turning it into a retro-chic beach hangout decorated with kitschy lamps and original art by local children. **Pros:** near marina; restaurant on-site (dinner only). **Cons:** not centrally located; one bed in rooms. [$] *Rooms from: $119* ✉ *1410 Rosecrans St., Point Loma* ☎ *619/226–6100* 🌐 *www.thepearlsd.com* 🛏 *23 rooms* 🍴 *No meals* ✣ *4:B1.*

SHELTER ISLAND

$$ HOTEL 👶 🏨 **Best Western Plus Island Palms Hotel & Marina.** If you have a boat to dock, this waterfront inn is a good choice—the adjacent marina has guest slips. **Pros:** near water; great room views; free tennis; free parking. **Cons:** somewhat confusing area; average-size rooms; can be noisy. [$] *Rooms from: $159* ✉ *2051 Shelter Island Dr., Shelter Island* ☎ *619/222–0561 or 800/922–2336* 🌐 *www.islandpalms.com* 🛏 *167 rooms, 60 suites* 🍴 *No meals* ✣ *4:B3.*

$$ RESORT 🏨 **Humphreys Half Moon Inn & Suites.** This sprawling South Seas–style resort has grassy open areas with palms and tiki torches; many of the rooms have water views. **Pros:** water views; near marina; free admission to Backstage Live music club. **Cons:** vast property; not centrally located. [$] *Rooms from: $159* ✉ *2303 Shelter Island Dr., Shelter Island* ☎ *619/224–3411 or 800/542–7400* 🌐 *www.halfmooninn.com* 🛏 *128 rooms, 54 suites* 🍴 *No meals* ✣ *4:B2.*

$ RESORT 🏨 **Kona Kai Resort.** This 11-acre property blends Hawaiian and Mediterranean styles—the rooms are well appointed, if a bit small, and most have balconies with views of either the adjacent marina or San Diego Bay. **Pros:** quiet area; near marina; water views. **Cons:** not centrally located; small rooms; spotty service. [$] *Rooms from: $119* ✉ *1551 Shelter Island Dr., Shelter Island* ☎ *619/221–8000 or 800/566–2524* 🌐 *www.resortkonakai.com* 🛏 *124 rooms, 5 suites* 🍴 *No meals* ✣ *4:B3.*

HARBOR ISLAND

$$ **Sheraton San Diego Hotel & Marina.** Of this property's two high-rises, the
HOTEL smaller, more intimate Bay Tower has larger rooms, with separate areas
suitable for business entertaining; the more recently renovated Marina
Tower has better sports facilities. **Pros:** water views; near marina and
airport; free airport shuttle. **Cons:** not centrally located; some rooms
show wear. $ *Rooms from: $209* ⊠ *1380 Harbor Island Dr., Har-
bor Island* ☎ *619/291–2900 or 888/625–5144* ⊕ *www.sheraton.com*
⤳ *1,001 rooms, 52 suites* ⦿ *Some meals* ✥ *4:E1.*

CORONADO

$$ **1906 Lodge.** Smaller but no less luxurious than the sprawling beach
B&B/INN resorts of Coronado, this lodge welcomes couples for romantic retreats
Fodor's Choice two blocks from the ocean. **Pros:** welcoming staff; historic property; free
★ underground parking. **Cons:** too quiet for families; no pool. $ *Rooms
from: $209* ⊠ *1060 Adella Ave., Coronado* ☎ *619/437–1900 or
866/435–1906* ⊕ *www.1906lodge.com* ⤳ *6 rooms, 11 suites* ⦿ *Some
meals* ✥ *4:G6.*

$$$ **Coronado Island Marriott Resort.** Near San Diego Bay, this snazzy hotel
RESORT has rooms with great downtown skyline views. **Pros:** spectacular views;
☾ on-site spa; close to water taxis. **Cons:** not in downtown Coronado;
difficult to find. $ *Rooms from: $249* ⊠ *2000 2nd St., Coronado*
☎ *619/435–3000 or 800/543–4300* ⊕ *www.marriotthotels.com/sanci*
⤳ *273 rooms, 27 suites* ⦿ *No meals* ✥ *4:H5.*

$ **Crown City Inn & Bistro.** On Coronado's main drag close to shops, res-
B&B/INN taurants, and the beach, this two-story motor inn is one of the island's
best deals. **Pros:** affordable; on-site restaurant; complimentary bikes;
public park across street. **Cons:** few amenities; somewhat dated rooms;
a hike from downtown. $ *Rooms from: $109* ⊠ *520 Orange Ave.,
Coronado* ☎ *619/435–3116* ⊕ *www.crowncityinn.com* ⤳ *35 rooms*
⦿ *No meals* ✥ *4:G5.*

$$ **Glorietta Bay Inn.** The main building on this property is an Edwardian-
HOTEL style mansion built in 1908 for sugar baron John D. **Pros:** great views;
friendly staff; close to beach. **Cons:** mansion rooms are small; lots of
traffic nearby. $ *Rooms from: $189* ⊠ *1630 Glorietta Blvd., Coronado*
☎ *619/435–3101 or 800/283–9383* ⊕ *www.gloriettabayinn.com* ⤳ *100
rooms* ⦿ *Breakfast* ✥ *4:G6.*

$$$$ **Hotel Del Coronado.** The Victorian-style "Hotel Del" is as much of
RESORT a draw today as it was when it opened in 1888. **Pros:** romantic; on
☾ the beach; hotel spa. **Cons:** some rooms are small; expensive dining;
Fodor's Choice hectic public areas. $ *Rooms from: $310* ⊠ *1500 Orange Ave., Coro-
★ nado* ☎ *800/468–3533 or 619/435–6611* ⊕ *www.hoteldel.com* ⤳ *679
rooms, 43 villas, 35 cottages* ⦿ *No meals* ✥ *4:G6.*

$$ **Loews Coronado Bay Resort.** You can park your boat at the 80-slip
RESORT marina of this romantic retreat set on a secluded 15-acre peninsula
☾ on the Silver Strand. **Pros:** great restaurants; lots of activities; lobby
worth lingering in. **Cons:** far from anything; confusing layout. $ *Rooms
from: $219* ⊠ *4000 Coronado Bay Rd., Coronado* ☎ *619/424–4000 or
800/815–6397* ⊕ *www.loewshotels.com/Coronado-Bay-Resort* ⤳ *402
rooms, 37 suites* ⦿ *No meals* ✥ *4:H6.*

Nightlife

WORD OF MOUTH

"Although you are not planning on 'Girls Gone Wild' nightlife, you and some 20-something friends would be bored in La Jolla. Mission Beach or Pacific Beach for sure I would suggest. Stay close to Garnet Ave., or Grand Ave. or Mission Bay Dr. Go to La Jolla for the day, eat dinner there, shop, etc. but IMHO, don't stay there."

—lollylo25

Updated by
Seth Combs

A couple of decades ago, San Diego scraped by on its superb daytime offerings. When the city's smattering of neighborhood dives and dance clubs got stale, locals fled town for late-night benders in L.A. or Las Vegas. Those sleepy-after-dark days are over; San Diego now sizzles when the sun goes down. Of particular interest to beer lovers, the city has become internationally acclaimed for dozens of breweries, beer pubs, and festivals.

The most obvious destination for visitors is the Gaslamp Quarter, a 16-block former red-light district gone glam. The debauchery is slightly more modest these days—or at least legal, anyway. Between the Gaslamp and neighboring East Village, there's truly something for everyone, from secretive speakeasies to big, bangin' dance clubs and chic rooftop lounges to grimy dives. If you're staying in the Gaslamp, it's the perfect place to party. Some of the hotels even have their own happening scenes. If you're driving from elsewhere, prepare to pay. Your best options: parking lots (prices start at $20) or valet (at some restaurants and clubs). If you don't mind a long trek—in other words, leave the stilettos at home—you can usually score spots 10 or more blocks from the action. Meters are free after 6 pm.

The epicenter of gay culture is Hillcrest, where you'll find bars and clubs catering primarily to the LGBT crowd—though everyone is welcome. East of Hillcrest is North Park, where hip twenty- and thirtysomethings hang out at edgy scenester hotspots (though locals complain that upscale new arrivals on the nightlife scene are ruining the underground vibe). Nearby South Park and University Heights also have a few cool offerings. A cab from downtown to any of these 'hoods costs about $15.

Pacific Beach tends to draw college kids who don't know when to say when, while Ocean and Mission beaches pull laid-back surfers and their cohort. La Jolla, for the most part, is a snooze if you're in the mood to booze late at night.

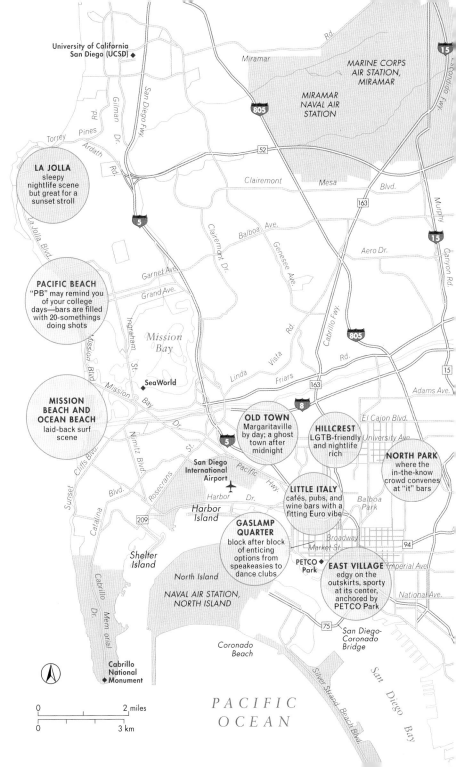

Californians love their independent cafés and coffeehouses. San Diego's got plenty, especially in the Hillcrest and North Park neighborhoods in Uptown. Many offer tasty fare (from light pastries to full meals) alongside every possible caffeinated concoction. Some offer terrific live entertainment, too. And, if a coffee buzz isn't the kind you're looking for, a handful also serve wine and beer. Hookah (also known as *shisha*) lounges are another popular bar alternative.

There are also nightlife destinations outside of town, in North County: Belly Up, in Solana Beach, has a killer sound system and attracts some big national names. The cover can be steep depending on the performer, but the laid-back vibe and strong drinks almost always attract a crowd. (For more info look in the North County destination listings.)

PLANNING

THE LOWDOWN

All glammed up and ready for a big night on the town? Here are a few things to keep in mind:

Step outside to smoke. San Diegans who smoke have had to do it on the street since 1998, although you'll occasionally catch smokers covertly lighting up in crowded venues. You can usually smoke on open-air patios or just outside the front door, but look for posted rules to be sure.

What to wear. California casual doesn't cut it at a few of the Gaslamp's swankier spots. Dress codes vary, but the more common no-no's are sneakers, shorts, and baseball caps.

Last call for alcohol. The last chance for nightcaps is theoretically 2 am, but most bars stop serving around 1:30. Listen for the bartender's announcement.

WHAT'S GOING ON?

Don't just wander the streets looking for action. A little research will lead you in the right direction.

Scour the entertainment section of the city's daily paper, the *San Diego Union-Tribune* (⊕ *www.utsandiego.com*), as well as the paper's more nightlife-heavy sister site DiscoverSD (⊕ *www.discoversd.com*), for event listings and editorial suggestions. Of San Diego's two alternative-weeklies, the *Reader* (⊕ *www.sandiegoreader.com*) offers the most thorough online listings, covering everything from tiny shows to huge festivals. *San Diego CityBeat* (⊕ *sdcitybeat.com*) clues locals in to the edgiest underground events.

San Diego magazine (⊕ *www.sandiegomagazine.com*) is a mainstream read for all walks of life; *Riviera* (⊕ *sandiego.modernluxury.com*) is younger, more upscale, and au courant. Both glossy monthlies have calendar sections and tips on topics such as haute nightlife attire and the hottest DJs.

Head to *Happy Hour* magazine (⊕ *happyhourmagonline.com*) or King of Happy Hour (⊕ *kingofhappyhour.com*) for happy-hour reviews and how-to tips, and SDDialedIn (⊕ *sddialedin.com*) for concert and music listings.

TOP NIGHTLIFE EXPERIENCES

Real relaxation: Bask in the warm weather, drink in hand, on one of the city's many open-air, rooftop bars.

Pedal power: Dance the night away in the Gaslamp Quarter then make a pedicab bicyclist do all the work to get you home. Just be sure to ask about prices upfront—the unregulated fares range from $5 to $15 for a short ride, depending on the driver.

Be a scenester: Order a shot of whiskey and a PBR while watching a future "It" band at The Casbah or Soda Bar.

C'mon, get happy: Pretend you're a local and grab the happy-hour drink deals with the working stiffs—it's a great excuse to tie one on while the sun's still shining.

Sports night: Swing by Bar Basic for a giant pizza and a pitcher of beer before the big game at PETCO Park.

NIGHTLIFE BY NEIGHBORHOOD

DOWNTOWN

GASLAMP QUARTER
BARS

Altitude Sky Lounge. Location is everything at this sophisticated lounge on the roof of the 22-floor San Diego Marriott Gaslamp Quarter. The views of the downtown skyline and PETCO Park will give you a natural high. ⊠ *660 K St., Gaslamp Quarter* ☎ *619/446–6086* ⊕ *www.altitudeskylounge.com.*

barleymash. A gigantic newcomer to the Gaslamp can resemble either a raucous club or a sports bar, depending on what night you're there. But the drinks are strong and reasonably priced, and the reclaimed wood decor makes for an intimate atmosphere, even when the DJs are spinning mostly Top 40. ⊠ *600 5th Ave., Gaslamp Quarter* ☎ *619/255–7373* ⊕ *www.barleymash.com.*

Dick's Last Resort. The surly waitstaff and abrasive service at this dive bar chain are part of the gimmick, and it works: fun-loving partiers pile into the barnlike space for live music, a solid beer list, and buckets of greasy grub. True to its name, this is a suitable "last resort" after a long night of drinking. ⊠ *345 4th Ave., Gaslamp Quarter* ☎ *619/231–9100* ⊕ *www.dickslastresort.com.*

Hard Rock Hotel. A-list wannabes (and a few real celebs) gather in two bars, the loungey 207 off the lobby and the rooftop Float. If you're here at the right time, be sure to check out the latter's Intervention and Wintervention daytime parties, which feature some of the world's biggest DJ names. Maybe you can't be a rock star, but you might as well party like one. Just be prepared to spend like one, too. ⊠ *207 5th Ave., Gaslamp Quarter* ☎ *619/764–6924* ⊕ *hardrockhotelsd.com.*

10

Altitude Sky Lounge, atop the Marriott Gaslamp Quarter, keeps things hot with fire pits on chilly nights.

Fodor's Choice
★ **Ivy Rooftop and Ivy Nightclub.** Here are lively and chill versions of San Diego nightlife on the same premises. Thrill seekers should head to the chicly cavernous Ivy Nightclub, while those in search of romance should head straight to the Ivy Rooftop, where they can sip cocktails poolside while gazing at gorgeous people or views of the city—both are abundant. ⊠ *600 F St., Gaslamp Quarter* ☎ *619/814–2055* ⊕ *ivyentertainmentsandiego.com.*

★ **La Puerta.** This Mexican-theme bar and restaurant is great for late-night eats (the kitchen is open until 1 am), but also has DJs seven nights a week and some of the best margaritas in the city. If you're looking for an unrivaled tequila selection, there are literally hundreds to choose from. ⊠ *560 4th Ave., Gaslamp Quarter* ☎ *619/696–3466* ⊕ *www. lapuertasd.com.*

LOUNGEsix. The trendy poolside bar on the fourth floor of the swank Hotel Solamar is a sexy spot to people-watch while sipping sangria or chili–mango margaritas and noshing on snacks from the "slow food" menu. On cool evenings, reserve a cabana or warm up next to one of the roaring fire pits. ⊠ *435 6th Ave., Gaslamp Quarter* ☎ *619/531–8744* ⊕ *www.jsixrestaurant.com.*

Palomar Rooftop Lounge. The fourth-floor rooftop of the Hotel Palomar remains a go-to spot for posh party people who don't mind dropping big money for a poolside cabana. Note, though, that the music shuts down after midnight. Those looking for a more nuanced and romantic setting should seek out the plush leather couches and craft cocktails at the lobby-side Saltbox bar. ⊠ *1047 5th Ave., Gaslamp Quarter* ☎ *619/515–3000* ⊕ *www.hotelpalomar-sandiego.com.*

CLOSE UP

Cocktails with a View

Combine sun and socializing at these rocking outdoor bars.

ROOFTOP BARS
Altitude Skybar (Gaslamp Quarter)

Ivy Rooftop at the Andaz San Diego (Gaslamp Quarter)

Firehouse PB (Pacific Beach)

LOUNGEsix (Gaslamp Quarter)

Stingaree (Gaslamp Quarter)

Top of the Park (Hillcrest)

OUTDOOR PATIOS
Dick's Last Resort (Gaslamp Quarter)

Humphrey's by the Bay (Shelter Island)

JRDN (Pacific Beach)

Lei Lounge (University Heights)

Moondoggies (Pacific Beach)

Pacific Beach Bar & Grill (Pacific Beach)

The Pearl Hotel (Point Loma)

Shakespeare Pub & Grille (Mission Hills)

Starlite (Mission Hills)

Urban Mo's (Hillcrest)

The Vine (Ocean Beach)

Patrick's II. Patrons enjoy live jazz, blues, soul, and rock in this intimate Irish-theme setting, although actual Irish music is—ironically—somewhat rare. ⊠ *428 F St., Gaslamp Quarter* ☎ *619/233–3077* ⊕ *www.patricksii.com.*

Prohibition. This underground jazz lounge lives up to its name with a slinky speakeasy style. Red lighting, dark wood, and leather tufted couches provide a cozy 1920s/'30s-inspired backdrop to the live jazz on weekends. ⊠ *548 5th Ave., Gaslamp Quarter* ☎ *619/663–5485* ⊕ *prohibitionsd.com.*

★ **The Propagandist.** A nice break from what can be a crazy Downtown scene, this basement speakeasy has a decor that includes church pews and World War II–style propaganda posters, as well as superlative craft cocktails, indie-rock bands, and edgy DJs on some nights. ⊠ *835 5th Ave., Gaslamp Quarter* ☎ *619/238–7117.*

Quality Social. It's been open several years, but this large, industrial-designed space recently got a shot in its proverbial after-dark arm thanks to a new booker who's been bringing in the best local DJs to spin a mix of house and electro remixes. What you won't hear? The sign on the side of the DJ booth says it all: "No Hip-Hop. No Dubstep. No LMFAO." ⊠ *789 6th Ave., Gaslamp Quarter* ☎ *619/501–7675* ⊕ *www.qualitysocial.com.*

★ **Side Bar.** One of San Diego's premier clubs has a "more is more" decor and an attitude to match. Painted birdcages hang from the loft ceiling and DJs spin from inside a giant cage, which also provides sturdy scaffolding for female go-go dancers on weekends. The black-clad chandeliers and mismatched velvet couches (including one that once belonged to Paris Hilton) get an additional visual pop from the nudie paintings lining the walls. Fancy martinis are a must, and if you get hungry after

10

last call, step next door to get some NYC-style pizza at Ciro's, open till 3 am. ⊠ *536 Market St., Gaslamp Quarter* 🕾 *619/696–0946* ⊕ *www. sidebarsd.com.*

Tivoli. Rumor has it that Wyatt Earp himself threw back a whiskey or two at the oldest bar in the Gaslamp, way before the walls were lined with neon beer signs. Perhaps old age accounts for the grungy veneer, but that doesn't stop locals from hitting this dive for $9 pitchers of PBR and hot dogs. The jukebox and pool table keep the unruly in check. Is that a spittoon in the corner? ⊠ *505 6th Ave., Gaslamp Quarter* 🕾 *619/232–6754* ⊕ *www.tivolibargrill.com.*

WORD OF MOUTH

"Tivoli's downtown is one of the oldest bars in SD. Waterfront in Little Italy is another dive beauty. You could go the other way and hit Shelter Island and do the Brigantine with the great everyday happy hour and the $3 fish tacos are awesome. Good crowd but not that many TVs."

—ksucat

Whiskey Girl. A major stop on the bachelorette party circuit sports a spiffy karaoke and photo booth, a Pop Art–inspired interior, and DJs spinning '80s and Top 40 almost every night. This is also a solid choice for grabbing some bar grub and watching a game. ⊠ *702 5th Ave., Gaslamp Quarter* 🕾 *619/236–1616* ⊕ *www.whiskeygirl.com.*

Yard House. It's a chain, yes, but you can't really go wrong with more than 100 beers on tap—billed as the world's largest selection of draft beer. With a backdrop of classic rock and an unbeatable downtown location, Yard House goes the distance. ⊠ *1023 4th Ave., Gaslamp Quarter* 🕾 *619/233–9273* ⊕ *www.yardhouse.com.*

WINE BARS

The Grape. Swing by this narrow, Parisian-style wine bar before or after dinner. The mile-long wine list and lively ambience make up for the overly themed decor. Skip the unremarkable nibbles. ⊠ *823 5th Ave., Gaslamp Quarter* 🕾 *619/238–8010* ⊕ *www.thegrapebar.com.*

Fodor's Choice ★ **Vin de Syrah.** This "spirit and wine cellar" sends you down a rabbit hole (or at least down some stairs) to a whimsical spot straight out of Alice in Wonderland. Behind a hidden door (look for a handle in the grass wall), you'll find visual delights (grapevines suspended from the ceiling, vintage jars with flittering "fireflies," cozy chairs nestled around a faux fireplace and pastoral vista) that rival the culinary ones—the wine list is approachable and the charcuterie boards are exquisitely curated. ▨ **TIP→** It's worth it to try the cocktails, especially if bar manager Adam Stemmler is on duty. ⊠ *901 5th Ave., Gaslamp Quarter* 🕾 *619/234–4166* ⊕ *www.syrahwineparlor.com.*

COFFEEHOUSES

Fumari Hookah Lounge. This relaxed café is a dark and cozy spot for smoking from a water pipe—the richly flavored tobaccos are worth the exorbitant price tag (around $20 for a bowl, except during the nightly happy hour 7–8). The chill ambience makes it easy to hang out and blow smoke rings all night, and desserts, coffee, and beer are also on offer. ⊠ *330 G St., Gaslamp Quarter* 🕾 *619/501–0613* ⊕ *www.fumari.com.*

COMEDY AND CABARET

American Comedy Co. At this underground space modeled after the legendary comedy clubs in New York, there's not a bad seat in the house—which is especially great since the venue pulls in some of the hugest names in stand-up comedy. ⊠ *818 6th Ave., Gaslamp Quarter* ☎ *619/795–3858* ⊕ *www.americancomedyco.com.*

DANCE CLUBS

★ **Fluxx.** Arguably the hottest club in the Gaslamp, this Vegas-style, multitheme space is packed to the gills on weekends with pretty people dancing to house and electro music and dropping major cash at the bar. ▉ **TIP→** Get here early for a lower cover and to avoid the epic lines that snake around the block. ⊠ *500 4th Ave., Gaslamp Quarter* ☎ *619/232–8100* ⊕ *www.fluxxsd.com.*

★ **Sevilla.** For more than two decades, Cafe Sevilla and the Sevilla nightclub have brought a Latin flavor to the Gaslamp Quarter through a mix of contemporary and traditional Spanish and Latin American music. Get fueled up at the tapas bar before venturing downstairs for dancing. Salsa lessons during the week provide an especially memorable experience. ⊠ *353 5th Ave., Gaslamp Quarter* ☎ *619/233–5979* ⊕ *sevillanightclub.com.*

★ **Stingaree.** One could argue that Stingaree was the Gaslamp's first megaclub and, almost a decade later, it's still going strong. Guests can enjoy electro and Top 40 in the main nightclub, a smashing three-story space with translucent "floating" staircases and floor-to-ceiling water walls. Dress nicely. The air of exclusivity at this hangout is palpable, and to reinforce the point, the drink prices are steep. ⊠ *454 6th Ave., at Island St., Gaslamp Quarter* ☎ *619/544–9500* ⊕ *www.stingsandiego.com.*

Fodor's Choice ★ **Voyeur.** This tiny club will leave you gasping for air—and loving it. The space may be small and stifling, but compensations include the creepy-cool decor (a mashup of skull/guns/Gothic weird stuff), a can't-hide bathroom in line with the club's name, a mesmerizing LED wall, gorgeous go-go girls, and cutting-edge electronic acts like MSTRKRFT and Bloody Beetroots. ⊠ *755 5th Ave., Gaslamp Quarter* ☎ *619/756–7678* ⊕ *voyeursd.com.*

OFF THE BEATEN PATH

Kava Lounge. This free-spirited underground dance club is a favorite of the nightlife-lovin' counterculture. You're likely see the next big thing in electronic music here, and DJs spin everything from downtempo to breakbeat. Organic cocktails keep sweaty bodies cool when the dance floor heats up. ⊠ *2812 Kettner Blvd., Middletown* ☎ *619/543–0933* ⊕ *www.kavalounge.com.*

PIANO BARS

The Shout! House. Dueling pianos and interactive, rock-and-roll sing-alongs make for a festive, even boisterous, evening here, but be sure to make reservations or come early to snag the best seats. ⊠ *655 4th Ave., Gaslamp Quarter* ☎ *619/231–6700* ⊕ *www.theshouthouse.com.*

Fodor's Choice ★ **Westgate Hotel Plaza Bar.** The old-money surroundings, including leather-upholstered seats, marble tabletops, and a grand piano, supply one of the most elegant and romantic settings for a drink in San Diego. ⊠ *1055 2nd Ave., Gaslamp Quarter* ☎ *619/557–3650* ⊕ *www.westgatehotel.com.*

10

For a bit of history, check out the Waterfront in Little Italy, San Diego's oldest bar.

ROCK, POP, HIP-HOP, FOLK, AND BLUES CLUBS

★ **House of Blues.** The local branch of the renowned music chain is decorated floor to ceiling with colorful folk art and features three different areas to hear music. There's something going on here just about every night of the week, and Sunday's gospel brunch is one of the most praiseworthy events in town. Can we get a hallelujah? ✉ *1055 5th Ave., Gaslamp Quarter* ☎ *619/299–2583* ⊕ *www.houseofblues.com.*

OFF THE
BEATEN
PATH

The Casbah. This small club near the airport, the unofficial headquarters of the city's indie music scene, has a national reputation for showcasing up-and-coming acts of all genres. Nirvana, Smashing Pumpkins, and the White Stripes all played here on the way to stardom. ✉ *2501 Kettner Blvd., Middletown* ☎ *619/232–4355* ⊕ *www.casbahmusic.com.*

EAST VILLAGE

BARS

Bar Basic. This spot is always bustling, in part because it's *the* place to be seen for Padres fans or anyone else attending events at PETCO Park. True to its name, Basic reliably dishes up simple pleasures: strong drinks and hot, coal-fired pizza. The garage-style doors roll up and keep the industrial-chic former warehouse ventilated during the balmy summer. ✉ *410 10th Ave., East Village* ☎ *619/531–8869* ⊕ *www.barbasic.com.*

East Village Tavern & Bowl. Twelve bowling lanes means no more hauls to the suburbs to channel one's inner Lebowski. Lane rental is pricey during prime times, but reasonable if you consider that some nearby clubs charge a Jackson just for admission, though reservations are definitely recommended. From the expansive bar area you can watch sports on 33 flat screens, and the satellite radio plays an assortment of alt- and classic rock. ⊠ *930 Market St., East Village* ☎ *619/677–2695* ⊕ *www. tavernbowl.com.*

El Dorado. El Dorado means "The Gold," and that's exactly what this hip hangout—part trendy club, part sophisticated speakeasy—has brought to a dodgy strip of downtown. The Western saloon–theme comes with creative drinks, cute bartenders, and in-demand local (and sometimes national) DJs and bands. Save your own gold with a $5 happy hour that runs from 7 till 9 pm. ⊠ *1030 Broadway, East Village* ☎ *619/237–0550* ⊕ *eldoradobar.com.*

Monkey Paw. What was once a notorious dive bar attracts hipsters and grizzled locals alike for a vast selection of craft beers (some brewed on-site), shuffleboard, and cheesesteaks that hit the spot no matter the hour. ⊠ *805 16th St., East Village* ☎ *619/358–9901* ⊕ *www. monkeypawbrewing.com.*

PIANO BARS

Fodor'sChoice ★ **Noble Experiment.** Speakeasy-style bars have been popping up all over San Diego, and the trend is impeccably realized in this quaint but decidedly swank cocktail lounge hidden in the back of a burger restaurant. Once customers find the hidden door (hint: look for the stack of kegs), they can bask in one of the plush leather booths while enjoying intricately crafted drinks that are second to none in the city. ⚠ Warning: Reservations are almost always a must, so be sure to call ahead. ⊠ *777 G St., East Village* ☎ *619/888–4713* ⊕ *nobleexperimentsd.com.*

LITTLE ITALY

BARS

Fodor'sChoice ★ **The Waterfront Bar & Grill.** It isn't really *on* the waterfront, but San Diego's oldest bar was once the hangout of Italian fishermen. Most of the collars are now white, and patrons enjoy an excellent selection of beers, along with chili, burgers, fish-and-chips, and other great-tasting grub, including fish tacos. Get here early, as there's almost always a crowd. ⊠ *2044 Kettner Blvd., Little Italy* ☎ *619/232–9656* ⊕ *www. waterfrontbarandgrill.com.*

BREWPUBS

Karl Strauss' Brewing Company. San Diego's first mircobrewery now has multiple locations, but the original one remains a staple. This locale draws an after-work crowd for pints of Red Trolley Ale and later fills with beer connoisseurs from all walks of life to try Karl's latest concoctions. Beer-to-go in half-gallon "growlers" is very popular, and the German-inspired pub food is above average. ⊠ *1157 Columbia St., Little Italy* ☎ *619/234–2739* ⊕ *www.karlstrauss.com.*

10

COFFEEHOUSES

Extraordinary Desserts. A delicious visual treat, with a lacy, laser-cut metal facade and elegant teak patio, also satisfies every sort of culinary craving, from savory to sweet and everything in between. The wine, beer, and bubbly list is très chic, too. ⌂ *1430 Union St., Little Italy* ☎ *619/294–7001* ⊕ *www.extraordinarydesserts.com.*

JAZZ CLUBS

Fodor's Choice ★ **Anthology.** The Rat Pack would love the fine-tuned acoustics in this classy, three-floor joint, one of the best-sounding music clubs in the city. Jazz acts are the mainstay, although the repertoire also includes folk and rock, and the club has hosted Ozomatli as well as Herb Alpert. ⌂ *1337 India St., Little Italy* ☎ *619/595–0300* ⊕ *www.anthologysd.com.*

NIGHT BAY CRUISES

Hornblower Cruises. Take a dinner-dance cruise aboard the *Lord Hornblower*—the trip comes with fabulous views of the San Diego skyline, as well as a three-course meal. ⌂ *Grape St. Pier, 1800 N. Harbor Dr., Little Italy* ☎ *888/467–6256* ⊕ *www.hornblower.com.*

Flagship Cruises and Events. Flagship Cruises welcomes guests aboard with a glass of champagne as a prelude to nightly dinner-dance and holiday cruises. ⌂ *1050 N. Harbor Dr., Little Italy* ☎ *619/522–6155* ⊕ *www.flagshipsd.com.*

EMBARCADERO

BARS

★ **The Lion's Share.** Hemingway would have loved this exquisitely designed brick-and-wood bar that serves up equally exquisite craft cocktails that, while pricey, are definitely made for sipping. The place attracts a sophisticated crowd and is highly recommended for those looking to impress a special someone. ⌂ *629 Kettner Blvd., Embarcadero* ☎ *619/564–6924* ⊕ *lionssharesd.com.*

Top of the Hyatt. This lounge at the Manchester Grand Hyatt crowns the tallest waterfront building in California, affording great views of San Diego Bay, including Coronado to the west, Mexico to the south, and Point Loma and La Jolla to the north. It's pricey and pretentious (don't you dare wear flip-flops), but this champagne-centric bar is great for catching a sunset or celebrating an anniversary. ⌂ *1 Market Pl., Embarcadero* ☎ *619/232–1234* ⊕ *manchestergrand.hyatt.com.*

COFFEEHOUSES

Upstart Crow. A bookstore and coffeehouse in one is tucked into downtown's charming Seaport Village. The secluded upstairs space is ideal for chatting or flipping through the book you just bought. Irreverent gifts are sold, too. ⌂ *835C W. Harbor Dr., Embarcadero* ☎ *619/232–4855* ⊕ *upstartcrowtrading.com.*

HEY, BIG SPENDER

You can dress to impress and bat your eyelashes, but unless you're a supermodel or a pro athlete, at the most exclusive of San Diego's clubs and lounges just about the only way to bypass a long queue or nab a corner booth is to arrange for bottle service. Just be forewarned: a lowly bottle of Jack Daniels will run you about $250.

BALBOA PARK AND BANKERS HILL

BANKERS HILL
COFFEEHOUSES
Café Bassam. A Parisian-inspired coffee-sipping experience is complete with quirky decor, about 150 teas, and a selection of wine. It's open until midnight most nights. ⊠ *3088 5th Ave., Bankers Hill* ☎ *619/557–0173* ⊕ *www.cafebassam.com.*

OLD TOWN AND UPTOWN

OLDTOWN
BARS
El Agave Tequileria. The bar of this restaurant named for the cactus whose sap is distilled into tequila stocks hundreds of top-shelf brands that are as sip-worthy as the finest cognac. ⊠ *2304 San Diego Ave., Old Town* ☎ *619/220–0692* ⊕ *www.elagave.com.*

O'Hungry's. This landmark saloon is famous for its yard-long beers and live music. The seafaring decorative scheme inside is quite a contrast to the Mexican-theme Old Town San Diego State Historic Park just outside the doors. Be sure to drink up quickly—O'Hungry's closes weekdays at 9 and weekends at 11. ⊠ *2547 San Diego Ave., Old Town* ☎ *619/298–0133* ⊕ *www.ohungrys.com.*

HILLCREST
BARS
Nunu's. This retro-cool hangout with stiff cocktails might be one of the most popular bars in très gay Hillcrest, but don't expect a glitzy facade. The intentionally dated decor sits within the tatty walls of a white-brick box that probably hasn't had a face-lift since the LBJ administration. ⊠ *3537 5th Ave., Hillcrest* ☎ *619/295–2878* ⊕ *nunuscocktails.com.*

COFFEEHOUSES
Fodor'sChoice
★
Extraordinary Desserts. This café lives up to its name, which explains why there's often a line, despite the ample seating. Paris-trained Karen Krasne turns out award-winning cakes, tortes, and pastries of exceptional beauty. The Japanese-theme patio invites you to linger over yet another coffee drink. A second location is in Little Italy. ⊠ *2929 5th Ave., Hillcrest* ☎ *619/294–2132* ⊕ *www.extraordinarydesserts.com.*

Filter Coffee House. A colorful cast of Hillcrest locals crowds this place, open until 3 am on weekends, to get their caffeine buzz going before heading to the clubs. The comfy couches and relaxed atmosphere certainly help, not to mention the fact that they also serve beer and wine. ⊠ *1295 University Ave., Hillcrest* ☎ *619/299–0145* ⊕ *www.filtersandiego.com.*

GAY NIGHTLIFE
Fodor'sChoice
★
Baja Betty's. Although it draws plenty of gay customers, this low-key but elegant space with chandeliers and soft lighting is popular with just about everyone in the Hillcrest area (and their pets are welcome, too). The bar staff stocks more than 100 brands of tequila and mixes plenty of fancy cocktails. ⊠ *1421 University Ave., Hillcrest* ☎ *619/269–8510* ⊕ *bajabettyssd.com.*

10

San Diego On Tap

The secret is out: San Diego is the nation's best beer town. In addition to more than 30 local breweries, San Diego has a stretch of beer-nerd heaven nicknamed the Belgian Corridor (30th Street in North/South Park). You can find all styles of beer in San Diego, from the meek to the mighty, but many local brewers contend that the specialty is the big, bold Double IPA (also called an Imperial IPA). It's an India Pale Ale with attitude—and lots of hops. Nearly every local brewery has its own version.

Bars with the best microbrew selection: Blind Lady Ale House, Hamilton's Tavern, Live Wire, O'Brien's, Toronado.

Best fests: Want one location and a seemingly endless supply of beer? Try the Belgian Beer Fest (March), the San Diego Festival of Beers (September ⊕ www.sdbeerfest.org), San Diego Beer Week (November ⊕ www.sdbw.org), and the Strong Ale Fest (December). ⊕ www.sandiegobrewersguild.org has more listings.

Best way to sample it all: Sign up for Brewery Tours of San Diego (⊕ www.brewerytoursofsandiego.com) to sample the best craft beers without a second thought about directions or designated drivers.

SAN DIEGO'S BEST BREWERIES

You can also head to the source, where beer is brewed. These are outside of the city center, but worth the trek for beer aficionados.

AleSmith Brewing Co. This artisanal microbrewery offers tastings at its out-of-the-way locale in the Miramar area. Visitors can tour the entire brewery for free on the last Saturday of every month. ⊠ 9368 Cabot Dr.,

Scripps Ranch ☎ 858/549–9888 ⊕ alesmith.com.

Fodor's Choice★ **Alpine Brewing Co.** Well worth the mountain drive, this family-owned operation may be itty-bitty, but it's also a big champ: brewmaster Pat McIlhenney has won national and international kudos and took the title of the fifth-best brewery in the nation from Beer Advocate. Tasters are a buck each, or fill a growler for future imbibing. If they're on tap, don't pass up Duet, Pure Hoppiness, or Exponential Hoppiness. Alpine recently opened a pub a few doors down where you can taste flights of their various beers. ⊠ 2351 Alpine Blvd., Alpine ☎ 619/445–2337 ⊕ www.alpinebeerco.com.

Ballast Point Brewing Co. This isn't the best location for a casual visit, but if you're in the Miramar/Scripps Ranch area, swing by for a tasting. Otherwise, look for their offerings at local brewpubs—the Sculpin IPA and Wahoo wheat beer are especially good. ⊠ 10051 Old Grove Rd., Scripps Ranch ☎ 858/695–2739 ⊕ www.ballastpoint.com.

Stone Brewing World Gardens and Bistro. The Big Daddy of San Diego craft brewing was founded by a couple of basement beer tinkerers in 1996; the company now exports its aggressively hoppy beers—instantly identifiable by their leering gargoyle labels—to bars and stores across the nation. Stone's monumental HQ is off the beaten path, but worth a visit for its free tours (with free tasters at the end!), vast on-tap selection (not just Stone beers), and excellent bistro eats. ⊠ 1999 Citracado Pkwy., Escondido ☎ 760/294–7866 ⊕ www.stonebrew.com.

Martinis Above Fourth. This swank lounge presents live piano, comedy, and cabaret on weekends to a friendly crowd. Swill cocktails inside or on the patio, and consider a meal afterward in the restaurant serving contemporary American fare. ✉ *3940 4th Ave., 2nd fl., Hillcrest* ☎ *619/400–4500* ⊕ *www.martinisabovefourth.com.*

Rich's. The dancing and music here are some of the best in the city, making Rich's popular not only with gay men but also plenty of lesbians and straight revelers. ✉ *1051 University Ave., Hillcrest* ☎ *619/295–2195* ⊕ *www.richssandiego.com.*

★ **Top of the Park.** Held only on Friday evenings, this festive after-work cocktail party on the rooftop of the Park Manor Suites hotel is de rigueur with the locals, especially gay men. It's a great way to kick off the weekend, and the views of downtown and Balboa Park are stupendous. ✉ *525 Spruce St., Hillcrest* ☎ *619/291–0999* ⊕ *www. shellhospitality.com/en/Inn-at-the-Park.*

Urban Mo's Bar and Grill. Cowboys gather for line dancing and two-stepping on the wooden dance floor—but be forewarned, yee-hawers, it can get pretty wild on Western nights. There are also Latin, hip-hop, and drag revues but the real allure is in the creative drinks ("Gone Fishing"—served in a fishbowl, for example) and the breezy patio where love (or something like it) is usually in the air. ✉ *308 University Ave., Hillcrest* ☎ *619/491–0400* ⊕ *www.urbanmos.com.*

WINE BARS

★ **Wine Steals.** This room crackles with excitement on busy nights—you can actually hear the din of conversation from half a block away. A wide assortment of reasonably priced wines draws patrons in, and the freshly baked pizza keeps them in top form for imbibing. Check out the other locations in the East Village, Point Loma, and Cardiff. ✉ *1243 University Ave., Hillcrest* ☎ *619/295–1188* ⊕ *www.winestealssd.com.*

MISSION HILLS

BARS

Aero Club. Named for its proximity to the airport, this watering hole draws in twenty- and thirtysomethings with its pool tables, dominoes, and 20 beers on tap (including a few local brews). Drinks are cheap, which makes this a popular place to fuel up before heading downtown. Don't miss the cool fighting warplanes mural. ✉ *3365 India St., Mission Hills* ☎ *619/297–7211* ⊕ *www.aeroclubbar.com.*

10

Shakespeare Pub & Grille. This Mission Hills hangout captures all the warmth and camaraderie of a traditional British pub—except here you can enjoy consistently sunny weather on the sprawling patio. The bar hands pour from a long list of imported ales and stouts, and the early hours for big matches make this *the* place to watch soccer. ✉ *3701 India St., Mission Hills* ☎ *619/299–0230* ⊕ *www.shakespearepub.com.*

COFFEEHOUSES

Gelato Vero Caffe. A youthful crowd gathers here for authentic Italian ice cream, espresso, and a second-floor view of the downtown skyline. The place is usually occupied by regulars who stay for hours at a time. ✉ *3753 India St., Mission Hills* ☎ *619/295–9269.*

PIANO BARS

Fodor's Choice ★ **Starlite.** Bar-goers are dazzled by Starlite's award-winning interior design, which includes rock walls, luxe leather booths, and a massive mirror-mounted chandelier. A hexagonal wood-plank entryway leads to a sunken white bar, where sexy tattooed guys and girls mix creative cocktails, such as the signature Starlite Mule, served in a copper mug. An iPod plays eclectic playlists ranging from old-timey jazz and blues to obscure vintage rock (and DJs are on hand on certain evenings). During warmer months, procuring a spot on the outside wood-decked patio is an art form. ⊠ *3175 India St., Mission Hills* ☎ *619/358–9766* ⊕ *www.starlitesandiego.com.*

> **NECTAR OF THE HIPSTER?**
>
> The Starlite Mule—a potent signature concoction of organic vodka, ginger beer, bitters, and fresh lime juice—is just one of the reasons people pack it in at this hard-to-find hotspot (look for the sign).

UNIVERSITY HEIGHTS

BREWPUBS

★ **Blind Lady Ale House.** Enjoy sublime pairings of two of the best things on the planet: pizza and beer. The pizzas are old world and organic, with house-made chorizo and other quality ingredients, and the beer selection—while succinct—is out of this world. Good luck, though, snagging a seat at one of the picnic tables at this popular hangout, which is decorated in resourced materials, from old wooden floors used as wall paneling to a giant '60s-era Hamm's beer billboard. ⊠ *3416 Adams Ave., University Heights* ☎ *619/255–2491* ⊕ *www.blindladyalehouse.com.*

Small Bar. True to its name, this University Heights pub is, well, pint-size, but the beer selection is huge. This means that on any given night the place is packed with aficionados and novices alike vying to try old favorites and new additions. ⊠ *4628 Park Blvd., University Heights* ☎ *619/795–7998* ⊕ *www.smallbarsd.com.*

NORTH PARK

BARS

★ **Bar Pink.** Cheap drinks, loud music, and a hip crowd explain the line that's usually waiting outside this divey bar co-owned by Rocket From the Crypt frontman John "Speedo" Reis. ⊠ *3829 30th St., North Park* ☎ *619/564–7194* ⊕ *www.barpink.com.*

★ **Hamilton's Tavern.** More commonly known simply as Hammy's, this bar has one of the best beer lists in town. On the ceiling, lights strung between old beer taps twinkle as bright as the eyes of the suds-lovers who flock here. In between pours, grab something from Hammy's kitchen—people come from all over for the wings and burgers. ⊠ *1521 30th St., South Park* ☎ *619/238–5460* ⊕ *hamiltonstavern.com.*

Live Wire. A tried-and-true authentic dive just on the border of the trendy North Park neighborhood lures pierced and tattooed kids in their twenties. A wide-ranging (and very loud) jukebox and TVs screening movies or music videos are the main entertainment, unless you count the people-watching. The cocktails as well as the excellent beers

A night out at Bar Pink may leave you seeing pink elephants, the bar's mascots.

come in pint glasses, so pace yourself; the police lie in wait on nearby side streets. ✉ *2103 El Cajon Blvd., North Park* ☎ *619/291–7450* ⊕ *www.livewirebar.com.*

★ **Seven Grand.** This whiskey lounge is a swanky addition to an already thriving North Park nightlife scene and a welcome alternative to the neighboring dives and dance clubs. Live jazz, a tranquil atmosphere, and a bourbon-loving craft cocktail list keep locals flocking. ✉ *3054 University Ave., North Park* ☎ *619/269–8820* ⊕ *www.sevengrandbars.com.*

True North. Many long-established locals hate this sports bar, eyeing the beefy bouncers and backwards baseball cap–wearing "bros" as a pox on their neighborhood's hip vibe. Yes, True North may be more Pacific Beach than North Park, but it has a sun-soaked patio and the tastiest tater-tots in town. ✉ *3815 30th St., North Park* ☎ *619/291–3815* ⊕ *www.truenorthtavern.com.*

Toronado. One of San Diego's favorite gathering spots for hop-heads is named in honor of the San Francisco beer bar of the same name. The beer list—both on tap and by the bottle—is hard to beat. The place can get noisy, but the food—a mix of burgers and American-style comfort food—more than makes up for it. ✉ *4026 30th St., North Park* ☎ *619/282–0456* ⊕ *www.toronadosd.com.*

BREWPUBS

Tiger! Tiger!. A communal vibe prevails at this wood, metal, and brick gastropub, where patrons sit at picnic tables to schmooze and sip from one of the dozens of carefully selected craft and micro brews on tap. ✉ *3025 El Cajon Blvd., North Park* ☎ *619/487–0401* ⊕ *www. tigertigertavern.com.*

COFFEEHOUSES

Claire de Lune. High ceilings and huge arched windows give the redesigned, historic Odd Fellows building in North Park a funky charm. There are sofas and armchairs for lounging as well as tables for studying. Local musicians and poets take the stage on various nights. ✉ *2906 University Ave., North Park* ☎ *619/688–9845* ⊕ *www. clairedelune.com.*

COMEDY AND CABARET

Lips. Patrons enjoy their dinner while drag queens entertain (a $3 to $5 per-person cover charge will be added to your check). The place is always a hit for birthdays and bachelorette parties, but fair warning to the conservative—the scene can get raunchy. The motto, "where the men are men and so are the girls," says it all. ✉ *3036 El Cajon Blvd., North Park* ☎ *619/295–7900* ⊕ *lipssd.com.*

DANCE CLUBS

★ **Whistle Stop Bar.** Here's a place to get your groove on to indie, electro, and hip-hop, plus live bands on Friday. This tiny-but-banging locals' favorite just a few minutes from downtown gets hot and crowded, and the dance floor is always happening on Saturday. Plus, the cover's usually five bucks. ✉ *2236 Fern St., South Park* ☎ *619/284–6784.*

GAY NIGHTLIFE

★ **Red Fox Steak House.** Referred to as Red Fox Room by those in the know, this dimly lighted lounge is dearly loved by locals, and not just the seniors who flock here to sing Sinatra tunes to tickled ivories and the occasional impromptu horn section. ✉ *2223 El Cajon Blvd., North Park* ☎ *619/297–1313* ⊕ *www.redfoxsd.com.*

NORMAL HEIGHTS

BARS

★ **Polite Provisions.** Spiked milk shakes and malts enhance the vintage drugstore feel of this hotspot on the border of North Park and Normal Heights. The craft beer selection is admirably large, and taps spew readymade cocktails. ✉ *4696 30th St., Normal Heights* ☎ *619/640–2500.*

Soda Bar. Don't be fooled by the name. Soda is in short supply at this off-the-beaten-path music venue that has earned a reputation as the place to see up-and-coming bands or grab a potent cocktail. ✉ *3615 El Cajon Blvd., Normal Heights* ☎ *619/255–7224* ⊕ *www.sodabarmusic.com.*

COFFEEHOUSES

Lestat's Coffee Shop. One of the few San Diego coffee shops that's open 24 hours a day, this Normal Heights mainstay also has a great selection of baked goods and a neighboring music venue that stages acoustic and comedy acts seven days a week. ✉ *3343 Adams Ave., Normal Heights* ☎ *619/282–0437* ⊕ *www.lestats.com.*

GET ON THE LIST

Spend your cash on cocktails, not steep covers. Visit the websites of the places you plan to check out, and look for "guest list" links. You can often land on VIP lists just by emailing the clubs or promoters. Be on the lookout for catches, though, like having to arrive to an event extra early.

GAY NIGHTLIFE

Lei Lounge. This fabulous tropical-theme lounge provides a minivacation, with cabanas, fire pits, palm trees, froufrou cocktails, tasty tapas, and DJ-spun music during Sunday brunch. It's paradise for an afternoon or evening—or both. ⊠ *4622 Park Blvd., University Heights* ☎ *619/813–2272* ⊕ *www.leilounge.com.*

MISSION BAY AND THE BEACHES

MISSION BAY
NIGHT BAY CRUISES

Bahia Belle. This Mississippi-style stern-wheeler offers relaxing evening cruises along Mission Bay that include cocktails, dancing, karaoke, and live music. Cruises run from Wednesday through Sunday in early summer, daily in July and August, and Friday and Saturday in winter (there are no cruises in December). The $10 fare is less than most nightclub covers, but if you are choosey about the company you keep, remember, these floating bars are known as "booze cruises" for a reason. ⊠ *998 W. Mission Bay Dr., Mission Bay* ☎ *858/539–7779* ⊕ *www.bahiahotel.com.*

PACIFIC BEACH
BARS

Bar West. Bar West brings downtown flavor to style-starved PB. Though clean-lined and attractive, the bar is packed with the usual suspects (collegiates and beach crowd), and the dance floor is a sweaty meat market on weekends. ⊠ *959 Hornblend St., Pacific Beach* ☎ *858/273–9378* ⊕ *barwestsd.com.*

Firehouse PB. Despite attempts at a South Beach chic in the heart of Pacific Beach, the late-night oontz-oontz house music and run-of-the-mill food make this place feel like a bad episode of *Miami Vice.* Still, the craft cocktails are solid, and you can linger on the rooftop lounge for an on-fire happy hour with an ocean view. ⊠ *722 Grand Ave., Pacific Beach* ☎ *858/274–3100* ⊕ *www.firehousepb.com.*

★ **JRDN.** This contemporary lounge (pronounced "Jordan") occupies the ground floor of Pacific Beach's chicest boutique hotel, Tower23, and offers a more sophisticated vibe in what is a very party-happy neighborhood. Sleek walls of windows and an expansive patio overlook the boardwalk. ⊠ *723 Felspar St., Pacific Beach* ☎ *858/270–5736* ⊕ *www. t23hotel.com.*

Moondoggies. This recently revamped relaxed hangout welcomes Gidget wannabes, as well as a mixed, laid-back crowd of people who don't mind shoulder bumps or beer spills. The large and airy space has a sports-bar feel heightened by the dozens of TVs in every available spot, many showing surf and skate videos that remind you that the beach is only two blocks away. ⊠ *832 Garnet Ave., Pacific Beach* ☎ *858/483–6550* ⊕ *www.moondoggies.com.*

Pacific Beach Bar & Grill. Only a block away from the beach, this popular nightspot has a huge outdoor patio, so you can enjoy star-filled skies as you party. The lines here on weekends are generally the longest of any club in Pacific Beach. There's plenty to see and do, from billiards and satellite TV sports to an interactive trivia game. The grill takes orders until 1 am, so this is a great place for a late-night snack. ⊠ *860 Garnet Ave., Pacific Beach* ☎ *858/272–4745* ⊕ *pbbarandgrill.com.*

RT's Longboard Grill. A young, tanned crowd comes to schmooze and booze under the indoor palapas that give this lively bar a south-of-the-border feel. ⊠ *1466 Garnet Ave., Pacific Beach* ☎ *858/270–4030* ⊕ *longboardgrill.com.*

BREWPUBS

Tap Room. Beachside locals have been clamoring for an authentic beer bar and certainly got one with this place. Hoppy choices are in the hundreds and the food is better than average bar food. ⊠ *1269 Garnet Ave., Pacific Beach* ☎ *858/274–1010* ⊕ *www.sdtaproom.com.*

COFFEEHOUSES

Zanzibar Café. This cozy, dimly lighted spot along Pacific Beach's main strip is a great place to mellow out and eavesdrop, or just to watch the club-hopping singles make their way down the street. ⊠ *976 Garnet Ave., Pacific Beach* ☎ *858/272–4762* ⊕ *www.zanzibarcafe.com.*

LA JOLLA AND KEARNEY MESA

BARS

Manhattan of La Jolla. Lovingly referred to as the "Manhattan Lounge" by locals, this underrated and largely undiscovered bar neighbors the Italian steak house inside the Empress Hotel. It feels like the type of place that the Rat Pack would have frequented, thanks to a dark, old-school interior that's perfect for sipping martinis and whispering sweet-nothings. ⊠ *7766 Fay Ave., La Jolla* ☎ *858/459–0700* ⊕ *www.manhattanoflajolla.com.*

The Spot. Nightlife can be kind of sleepy in affluent La Jolla, but in-the-know locals keep this bar buzzing on any given night thanks to powerful cocktails and bar grub that's served late into the evening. ⊠ *1005 Prospect St., La Jolla* ☎ *858/459–0800* ⊕ *www.thespotonline.com.*

★ **Whaling Bar & Grill.** Nestled inside the historic La Valencia Hotel, this upscale but unpretentious bar and grill is a nice place for a romantic nightcap or a martini served up by an expert staff that won't skimp on the liquor. ⊠ *1132 Prospect St., La Jolla* ☎ *858/459–0800* ⊕ *www. lavalencia.com.*

COFFEEHOUSES

Living Room Coffee. The La Jolla outpost of this local coffee chain is open until midnight and sports a full bar, which means that customers can spend a pleasant evening sipping a true-blue Irish coffee complete with whiskey at one of the many tables or couches. ⊠ *1010 Prospect St., La Jolla* ☎ *858/459–1187* ⊕ *www.livingroomcafe.com.*

COMEDY AND CABARET

Comedy Store La Jolla. Like its sister establishment in Hollywood, this club hosts some of the best national touring and local talent. Cover charges range from nothing on open-mike nights to $20 or more for national acts. Seating is at bistro-style table, and a two-drink minimum applies for all shows. ⊠ *916 Pearl St., La Jolla* ☎ *858/454–9176* ⊕ *lajolla.thecomedystore.com.*

Stop for happy hour drinks at Pacific Beach's sleek JRDN lounge.

ROCK, POP, HIP-HOP, FOLK, AND BLUES CLUBS

Ché Café. This good old-fashioned bastion of counterculture at University of California at San Diego presents some of the edgiest music around. The all-ages café is also home to a restaurant serving vegan and vegetarian food, and although the crowd skews very young and the vibe is decidedly punk-rock, that doesn't stop old fogeys (read: anyone over 25) from joining in the fun. ⊠ *Bldg. 161, UCSD campus, La Jolla* ⊕ *thechecafe.blogspot.com.*

KEARNEY MESA

BARS

O'Brien's. The self-proclaimed "Hoppiest Place on Earth" makes up for its tacky interior (pleather executive chairs?) with a world-class beer list. This must-visit mecca for hardcore beer lovers is hidden among the Asian-oriented strip malls of Kearny Mesa, about 15 minutes north of downtown. ⊠ *4646 Convoy St., Kearny Mesa* ☎ *858/715–1745* ⊕ *obrienspub.net.*

10

POINT LOMA, OCEAN BEACH, AND CORONADO

POINT LOMA

BARS

Brigantine. The most popular of this local chain's seven outposts offers scenic harbor views and a happy hour that can't be beat. Try the fish tacos—they're among the best in San Diego and go particularly well with a frosty margarita. ⊠ *2725 Shelter Island Dr., Point Loma* ☎ *619/224–2871* ⊕ *www.brigantine.com.*

★ **The Pearl Hotel.** Step into late '60s Palm Springs, with shag carpet, clean lines, and lots of wood accents. The lobby bar is almost as fabulous as the outdoor pool area, where inflatable balls bob in illuminated water and vintage flicks show on a huge screen. And feel free to drink to excess. After 10 pm, when the bar closes, you can stay over at a discounted $79 "play and stay" rate if there are any rooms available. ⊠ *1410 Rosecrans St., Point Loma* ☎ *619/226–6100* ⊕ *www.thepearlsd.com.*

COFFEEHOUSES

Living Room. This coffee shop in an old house has creaky wooden floors and plenty of cubbyholes for the college students who are regulars here. Not far from the water, it's a great place to catch a caffeine buzz before walking along Shelter Island. There are several other locations, including popular branches in Old Town and La Jolla. ⊠ *1018 Rosecrans St., Point Loma* ☎ *619/222–6852* ⊕ *www.livingroomcafe.com.*

OCEAN BEACH

BARS

Pacific Shores. This bar isn't going for classy with its acid-trip mermaid mural, but hey, it's OB—a surf town populated by leftovers from the '60s, man. A laid-back but see-and-be-seen crowd congregates here for relatively inexpensive drinks (no beers on tap, though), pool games, and pop and rock tunes on the jukebox. ⊠ *4927 Newport Ave., Ocean Beach* ☎ *619/223–7549.*

WINE BARS

The Vine. Alongside a small-plates food menu, this romantic little wine bar serves a solid selection of moderately priced wines by the glass. Grab a seat on the patio, order a cheese plate, and raise a toast as your wine opens up in the tangy sea air. ⊠ *1851 Bacon St., Ocean Beach* ☎ *619/222–8463* ⊕ *theobvine.com.*

ROCK, POP, HIP-HOP, FOLK, AND BLUES CLUBS

Winston's. This Ocean Beach rock club in a former bowling alley hosts local bands, reggae groups, and, occasionally, 1960s-style bands. The crowd, mostly locals, is typically mellow but can get rowdy. ⊠ *1921 Bacon St., Ocean Beach* ☎ *619/222–6822* ⊕ *www.winstonsob.com.*

SHELTER ISLAND

ROCK, POP, HIP-HOP, FOLK, AND BLUES CLUBS

Humphrey's by the Bay. From June through September this dining and drinking oasis surrounded by water hosts the city's best outdoor jazz, folk, and light-rock concert series and is the stomping ground of such musicians as the Cowboy Junkies and Chris Isaak. The rest of the year the music moves indoors for first-rate jazz, blues, and more. ⊠ *2241 Shelter Island Dr., Shelter Island* ☎ *619/224–3577* ⊕ *www. humphreysconcerts.com.*

The Arts

WORD OF MOUTH

"I would really suggest going to Balboa Park . . . lots of artsy and cultural things going on and it's just plain beautiful. Also, there is an outdoor theater that sometimes hosts various free concerts where you can bring a picnic and wine and sit and enjoy the music & people watching. If you like theaters—there is the Globe theater."

—losangelestraveller

Updated by
Seth Combs

Locals like to gripe about the arts scene in San Diego. Some even believe that we're culturally anemic because of a countywide overdose on sunshine—who wants to sit inside and paint (or act or dance) when it's so beautiful out nearly every day? But the city does have a thriving arts scene, featuring both seasoned heavyweights and up-and-comers.

San Diego's theater scene may be regional, but it's a breeding ground for Broadway-bound productions. Some of the more notable exports include *Jersey Boys,* The Who's *Tommy, Dirty Rotten Scoundrels,* and *Memphis.*

The world-class Old Globe Theatre, which recently expanded with its $22-million, state-of-the-art Conrad Prebys Theatre Center, stages everything from Shakespeare to Dr. Seuss's *How the Grinch Stole Christmas.* La Jolla Playhouse, founded in 1947 by Gregory Peck, has hosted more than 40 world premieres, and marquee actors such as Neil Patrick Harris and Holly Hunter have stood in its spotlight.

San Diego's dance scene is nothing to scoff at, either. In addition to thoroughly respectable ballet troupes—City Ballet and California Ballet Company—the city's modern movers are making waves.

In the visual arts arena, San Diego's stellar reputation is spreading regionally and beyond. Area galleries combine international artists with locally grown talent, while collectors from around the world get in on the buying action, most notably at the annual Art San Diego Contemporary Art Fair. Every year, the San Diego Art Prize gives a nod to a select group of established and emerging artists—some of international acclaim—while the Orchids and Onions doles out best of (and worst of) awards for architecture.

TOP ARTS EXPERIENCES

11

Arts free-for-all: Summertime means free concerts, movies, and theater throughout the county.

Puppet strings: Your kids might not care for Shakespeare at the Old Globe, but you can introduce them to great acting at Balboa Park's Marie Hitchcock Puppet Theatre.

Gallery gathering: Before you visit, scour gallery websites or places like *www.sdcitybeat.com* or *www.sezio. org* for upcoming openings, which usually include a spread of sips and snacks—and art, of course.

San Diego Film Festival: This five-day festival in September is a must for film lovers and celebrity spotters—a day pass will get you in to some of San Diego's most glamorous parties.

THE ARTS PLANNER

TICKETS

San Diego Art + Sol. You can scan arts listings and book tickets through San Diego Art + Sol, which is produced by a partnership of organizations, including the City of San Diego Commission for Arts and Culture and the San Diego Convention & Visitors Bureau. ⊕ *www.sandiego.org*.

Book tickets well in advance, preferably at the same time you make hotel reservations. Outlets selling last-minute tickets do exist, but you risk paying top rates or getting less-than-choice seats—or both.

Arts Tix. You can buy advance tickets, many at half price, to theater, music, and dance events at Arts Tix. ✉ *28 Horton Plaza, 3rd Ave. and Broadway, Gaslamp Quarter* ☎ *858/381–5595* ⊕ *www.sdartstix.com*.

Ticketmaster. Ticketmaster sells tickets to many performances, as well as to select museum exhibitions. Service charges vary according to the event, and most tickets are nonrefundable. ☎ *800/745–3000* ⊕ *www. ticketmaster.com*.

GALLERY AND MUSEUM NIGHTS

Museums and galleries in San Diego host monthly nighttime events meant to lure the city's culturati—especially of the younger variety.

The San Diego Museum of Art hosts an occasional sundown series called **Culture & Cocktails** (☎ *619/232–7931* ⊕ *www.sdmart.org*) to coincide with major new exhibitions. For a $15 admission, visitors can enjoy cocktails and nibbles, DJs and live entertainment, and a cool artsy twenty- and thirtysomething crowd.

The San Diego Museum of Contemporary Art Downtown (⊕ *www. mcasd.org*) ups the artsy ante with its long-running Thursday Night Thing—aka **TNT**—a boisterous three-times-a-year happening with drinks, live entertainment, and thematically related activities.

Oceanside Museum of Art (⊕ *www.oma-online.org*) has also gotten in on the nighttime action with **Art After Dark,** a now-and-again event for the North County set.

Up in Solana Beach, the third Thursday of the month brings **Cedros Gallery Nights.** Galleries and boutiques keep their doors open, and locals head out to mingle.

DANCE

Whether you fancy *rond de jambes* or something a bit more modern, San Diego's scene is *en pointe* for dance fans.

★ **California Ballet Company.** The company performs high-quality contemporary and classical works September–May at the **Civic Theatre** (*3rd Ave. and B St., Downtown* ☎ *619/570–1100*). The *Nutcracker* is staged annually around the holiday season. ⊕ *www.californiaballet.org.*

Balboa Theatre. This historic landmark hosts ballet, music, plays and even stand-up comedy performances. ✉ *868 4th Ave., Downtown* ☎ *619/570–1100* ⊕ *www.sandiegotheatres.org.*

City Ballet. The ballet holds performances at the **Spreckels Theatre** and a few other area venues from November through May. At Christmastime, they dance a mean *Nutcracker.* ✉ *Spreckels Theatre, 121 Broadway, Downtown* ☎ *858/272–8663* ⊕ *www.cityballet.org.*

FILM

Cinephiles will find plenty of options in San Diego, from free outdoor summer screenings to film fests in the fall.

Landmark Theatres. Known for first-run foreign, art, American independent, and documentary offerings, Landmark operates three theaters in the San Diego area. **La Jolla Village Cinemas** is a modern multiplex set in a shopping center. **Hillcrest Cinemas** (✉ *3965 5th Ave., Hillcrest*) is a posh multiplex right in the middle of Uptown's action. **Ken Cinema** (✉ *4061 Adams Ave., Kensington*) is considered by many to be the last bastion of true avant-garde film in San Diego. It plays a roster of art and revival films that changes regularly (many programs are double bills). ☎ *619/819–0236* ⊕ *www.landmarktheatres.com.*

Museum of Photographic Arts. In its 226-seat theater, the museum runs a regular film program that includes classic American and international cinema by prominent filmmakers, as well as the occasional late-night screenings of cult classics. Each MoPA screening is preceded by an informative introduction from the museum staff. ✉ *1649 El Prado, Balboa Park* ☎ *619/238–7559* ⊕ *www.mopa.org.*

Reuben H. Fleet Science Center. Movies about space, science, and nature are shown on the gigantic IMAX screen here. ✉ *1875 El Prado, Balboa Park* ☎ *619/238–1233* ⊕ *www.rhfleet.org.*

★ **San Diego Asian Film Festival.** More than a decade old, this fest (usually held in November) is now the largest Asian-theme festival on the West Coast and includes parties, Q&A sessions with directors, and hundreds of films from more than 20 countries. Most of the screenings are held at the Ultrastar Mission Valley theater (✉ *7510 Hazard Center Dr.*), but there are also special features screened throughout San Diego County. ✉ *7510 Hazard Center Dr., Mission Valley* ☎ *619/400–5911* ⊕ *www.sdaff.org.*

The Spreckels Organ Pavilion in Balboa Park hosts free Monday night concerts in the summer.

San Diego Film Festival. Usually held in late September, this festival screens local, national, and international entries at the **Gaslamp Theater** (✉ *701 5th Ave., Gaslamp Quarter*), as well as the **Museum of Contemporary Art-La Jolla** (✉ *700 Prospect St., La Jolla*). The city's glitterati—as well as a few Hollywood celebs—love to rub shoulders at the fest's films, panels, and finale fête. ✉ *10981 San Diego Mission Rd., Suite 112, Mission Valley* ☎ *619/582–2368* ⊕ *sdfilmfest.com.*

Sherwood Auditorium. The 500-seat auditorium at the Museum of Contemporary Art hosts foreign and classic film series and special cinema events. ✉ *700 Prospect St., La Jolla* ☎ *858/454–3541* ⊕ *www.mcasandiego.org.*

GALLERIES

Sure, surf art is popular 'round these parts, but you can also view (and purchase) world-class, cutting-edge collectibles.

Alexander Salazar Fine Art. The gallery's namesake has practically taken up an entire block of downtown to show off local and international contemporary artists in a gallery (✉ *640 Broadway*), as well as a giant exhibition and auction space (✉ *1040 7th Ave.*) and an artist's studio (✉ *635 Broadway*). The gallery also recently expanded to La Jolla (✉ *1162 Prospect St.*). ✉ *640 Broadway, Gaslamp Quarter* ☎ *619/531–8996* ⊕ *www.alexandersalazarfineart.com.*

Industry Showroom. This large space in downtown serves both as a workspace for local designers and artists, and as a storefront showroom to show off their wares. ✉ *525 5th Ave., Gaslamp* ☎ *619/701-2162* ⊕ *industryshowroom.com.*

★ **Quint Contemporary Art.** For more than 30 years, art lovers and museum directors have snagged new pieces from established locals as well as international contemporary artists at this La Jolla mainstay. If you're in town at the time of one of the gallery's openings, you can schmooze with San Diego art royalty. ✉ *7547 Girard Ave., La Jolla* ☎ *858/454–3409* ⊕ *quintgallery.com.*

Scott White Contemporary Art. The local spot to see the next big thing in contemporary art, this gallery has shown the works of many artists who went on to fill museums. ✉ *7655 Girard Ave., Suite 101, La Jolla* ☎ *858/255–8574* ⊕ *www.scottwhiteart.com.*

The Studio Arts Complex. Several artist studios and fine-art galleries are in this building, including **Perry L. Meyer Fine Art** (☎ *619/358–9512* ⊕ *www.plmeyerfineart.com*). ✉ *2400 Kettner Blvd., Little Italy.*

Subtext Gallery. This cute little gallery sells some fantastic pop, surrealist, and comic book–inspired art often from real up-and-coming artists and illustrators. Be sure to peruse the fantastic selection of zines and coffee-table books. ✉ *2479 Kettner Blvd., Little Italy* ☎ *619/546–8800* ⊕ *subtextgallery.com.*

Thumbprint Gallery. This quaint little gallery brings a little edge to otherwise sleepy La Jolla, showing off some of the best lowbrow and street artists in the city. This is a great place to purchase something truly unique for a low price. ✉ *920 Kline St., La Jolla* ☎ *858/354–6294* ⊕ *www.thumbprintgallerysd.com.*

MUSIC

San Diego can rightfully toot its horn: the local symphony and opera are on par with the nation's top regional offerings.

★ **Balboa Theatre.** This renovated theater offers a variety of performances including ballet, music, plays, and even stand-up comedy. In addition to architectural splendor, the space offers unsurpassed sound. ✉ *868 4th Ave., Gaslamp Quarter* ☎ *619/570–1100* ⊕ *www.sandiegotheatres.org.*

Fodor's Choice **Copley Symphony Hall.** The great acoustics here are surpassed only by the
★ incredible Spanish baroque interior. Not just the home of the San Diego Symphony Orchestra, the renovated 2,200-seat 1920s-era theater has also hosted major stars like Elvis Costello, Leonard Cohen, and Sting. ✉ *750 B St., Downtown* ☎ *619/235–0804* ⊕ *www.sandiegosymphony.org.*

Cricket Wireless Amphitheatre. The largest concert venue in town, the amphitheater can accommodate 20,000 concertgoers with reserved seats and lawn seating. It presents top-selling national and international acts during its late-spring to late-summer season. ✉ *2050 Entertainment Cir., Chula Vista* ☎ *619/671–3600* ⊕ *www.cricketwirelessamphitheatre.net.*

Humphreys Concerts by the Bay. This waterfront, outdoor venue stages intimate shows from big-name national acts from April into October. There's not a bad seat in the house, but those who don't want to pay the sometimes big ticket prices can catch the concert by renting a canoe or boat and parking it in the adjacent bay for a one-of-a-kind view. ✉ *2241 Shelter Island Dr., Point Loma* ☎ *800/745–3000* ⊕ *humphreysconcerts.com.*

DID YOU KNOW?

Before reopening in 2008, the Balboa Theatre had many lives. Originally built in 1924, it screened films from Mexico as Teatro Balboa, then housed sailors during World War II.

★ **La Jolla Athenaeum Music & Arts Library.** The Athenaeum is a membership-supported, nonprofit library with an exceptional collection of books, periodicals, CDs, and other media related to arts and music. It also hosts intimate jazz, chamber music, and the occasional folk concert throughout the year. ⊠ *1008 Wall St., La Jolla* ☎ *858/454–5872* ⊕ *ljathenaeum.org.*

The Loft at UCSD. This quaint, comfortable performance space inside the Price Center on the University of California San Diego campus hosts intimate music concerts, spoken word programs, film screenings, and culinary events. ⊠ *Price Center East, 9500 Gilman Dr., 4th fl., La Jolla* ☎ *858/534–4090* ⊕ *theloft.ucsd.edu.*

Open-Air Theatre. Top-name rock, reggae, and popular artists give summer concerts under the stars at this theater in the middle of the San Diego State University campus. ⊠ *San Diego State University, 5500 Campanile Dr., College Area* ☎ *619/594–6947.*

Orchestra Nova San Diego. From September to May, a 35-plus member ensemble performs classics, pop, and a signature *Messiah* concert in a number of different venues, including St. Paul's Cathedral downtown, Sherwood Auditorium in La Jolla, and Qualcomm Hall in Sorrento Valley. ☎ *858/350–0290* ⊕ *www.orchestranova.org.*

★ **San Diego Opera.** Drawing international performers, the opera's season runs January–April. Past performances have included *Die Fledermaus, Faust, Idomeneo,* and *La Bohème,* plus solo concerts by such talents as Renee Fleming. ⊠ *Civic Theatre, 3rd Ave. and B St., Downtown* ☎ *619/533–7000* ⊕ *www.sdopera.com.*

San Diego Symphony Orchestra. The orchestra's events include classical concerts and summer and winter pops, nearly all of them at Copley Symphony Hall. The outdoor Summer Pops series is held on the Embarcadero, on North Harbor Drive beyond the convention center. ⊠ *Box office, 750 B. St., Downtown* ☎ *619/235–0800* ⊕ *www.sandiegosymphony.org.*

Sherwood Auditorium. A 500-seat venue in La Jolla campus of the Museum of Contemporary Art, the auditorium hosts classical and jazz events as well as the occasional rock or experimental music concert. ⊠ *700 Prospect St., La Jolla* ☎ *858/454–3541* ⊕ *www.mcasd.org.*

★ **Spreckels Organ Pavilion.** Home of a giant outdoor pipe organ donated to the city, the beautiful Spanish baroque pavilion hosts concerts by civic organist Carol Williams and guest organists on most Sunday afternoons and on Monday evenings in summer. Local military bands, gospel groups, and barbershop quartets also perform here. All shows are free. ⊠ *Balboa Park* ☎ *619/702–8138* ⊕ *sosorgan.com.*

Spreckels Theatre. A landmark theater erected in 1912, the Spreckels hosts comedy, dance, theater, and concerts. Good acoustics and old-time elegance make this a favorite local venue. ⊠ *121 Broadway, Downtown* ☎ *619/235–9500* ⊕ *www.spreckels.net.*

Valley View Casino Center. Big-name concerts are held at this historic arena with room for 13,000-plus fans. ⊠ *3500 Sports Arena Blvd., Sports Arena* ☎ *619/224–4171* ⊕ *valleyviewcasinocenter.com.*

The Lamb's Players Theater presented Tim Slover's *Joyful Noise*, about the creation of Handel's *Messiah*.

Viejas Arena. Located on the San Diego State campus, the Viejas Arena attracts big-name musical and comedy acts to its 12,500-person facility. ✉ *San Diego State University, 5500 Canyon Crest Dr., College Area* ☎ *619/594–6947.*

THEATER

With the Old Globe Theatre and La Jolla Playhouse, San Diego's theater scene is a local star—and a major player for page-to-stage and Broadway-bound productions.

Coronado Playhouse. This cabaret-type theater near the Hotel Del Coronado stages regular dramatic and musical performances. ✉ *1835 Strand Way, Coronado* ☎ *619/435–4856* ⊕ *www.coronadoplayhouse.com.*

Cygnet's Old Town Theatre. A 248-seat theater operated by Cygnet Theatre Company, this is one of the more interesting small San Diego theater groups. Catch local takes on edgy classics like *Sweeney Todd* and *Little Shop of Horrors.* ✉ *4040 Twiggs St., Old Town* ☎ *619/337–1525* ⊕ *www.cygnettheatre.com.*

Diversionary Theatre. San Diego's premier gay and lesbian company presents a range of original works that focus on LGBT themes. ✉ *4545 Park Blvd., Suite 101, University Heights* ☎ *619/220–0097* ⊕ *www.diversionary.org.*

★ **Ion Theatre Company.** The little theater company that could, most of Ion's unique and sometimes controversial productions now take place in the quaint BLKBOX Theatre in Hillcrest and have included productions of *Gypsy* and *Topdog/Underdog.* ✉ *3704 6th Ave., Hillcrest* ☎ *619/600–5020* ⊕ *iontheatre.com.*

Fodor's Choice **La Jolla Playhouse.** Under the artistic direction of Christopher Ashley, the
★ playhouse presents exciting and innovative plays and musicals on three
stages. Many Broadway shows—among them *Memphis, Tommy,* and
Jersey Boys—have previewed here before their East Coast premieres.
⊠ *University of California at San Diego, 2910 La Jolla Village Dr., La
Jolla* ☎ *858/550–1010* ⊕ *www.lajollaplayhouse.org.*

★ **Lamb's Players Theatre.** The theater's regular season of five mostly uplift-
ing productions runs from February through November. It also stages
an original musical, *Festival of Christmas,* in December. The company
has two performance spaces, the one used for most productions in Coronado, and the Horton Grand Theatre in the Gaslamp Quarter. ⊠ *1142
Orange Ave., Coronado* ☎ *619/437–6000* ⊕ *www.lambsplayers.org.*

Marie Hitchcock Puppet Theater. Amateur and professional puppeteers and
ventriloquists entertain here five days a week. The cost is just a few
dollars for adults and children alike. If you feel cramped in the 200-
seat theater, don't worry; the shows rarely run longer than a half hour.
⊠ *2130 Pan American Rd., Balboa Park* ☎ *619/544–9203* ⊕ *www.
balboaparkpuppets.com.*

Mo`olelo Performing Arts Company. Staging three productions over the year
at the 10th Avenue Theatre in downtown, this company is committed to
performances by newer playwrights as well as more obscure works by old
masters. ⊠ *930 10th Ave., Downtown* ☎ *619/342–7395* ⊕ *moolelo.net.*

North Coast Repertory Theatre. A diverse mix of comic and dramatic
works is shown in the 194-seat space. The emphasis is on contemporary
productions, but the theater has been known to stage some classics, too.
⊠ *987 Lomas Santa Fe Dr., Suite D, Solana Beach* ☎ *858/481–1055*
⊕ *www.northcoastrep.org.*

Fodor's Choice **The Old Globe.** This complex, comprising the Sheryl and Harvey White
★ Theatre, the Lowell Davies Festival Theatre, and the Old Globe Theatre,
offers some of the finest theatrical productions in Southern California. Theater classics such as *The Full Monty* and *Dirty Rotten Scoundrels,* both of which went on to Broadway, premiered on these famed
stages. The Old Globe presents the family-friendly *How the Grinch
Stole Christmas* around the holidays, as well as a renowned summer
Shakespeare Festival with three to four plays in repertory. ⊠ *1363 Old
Globe Way, Balboa Park* ☎ *619/234–5623* ⊕ *www.oldglobe.org.*

★ **San Diego Civic Theatre.** In addition to being the home of the San Diego
Opera, the theater presents musicals and other major Broadway-style
touring productions throughout the year. ⊠ *1100 3rd Ave., Downtown*
☎ *619/570–1100* ⊕ *www.sandiegotheatres.org.*

Starlight Musical Theatre. A summertime favorite, the Starlight performs
a series of musicals performed in an outdoor amphitheater mid-June
to early October. Because of the theater's proximity to the airport,
actors often have to freeze midscene while a plane flies over. ⊠ *Starlight Bowl, 2005 Pan American Plaza, Balboa Park* ☎ *619/232–7827*
⊕ *starlighttheatre.org.*

Beaches

WORD OF MOUTH

"Everybody agrees that La Jolla is a wonderful place to spend a couple of hours. The beach is wide, sandy, excellent for a long barefoot walk. The cliffs have bizarre rocks, coves, amazing views, and a wide array of wildlife. There is the Children's Pool, a small sandy beach which is now occupied by a large horde of seals."

—Echnaton

SAN DIEGO'S BEST BEACHES

Step aside, Caribbean. Move over, Hawaii. San Diego's in the house! This unique Southern California city stands out for its clean waters, natural beauty, and easygoing charm. And thanks to high terrain that melds with the sea, its coastline delivers endless visual drama.

(above) Pacific Beach is the place to party. (lower right) Sea lions at the Children's Pool. (upper right) The U.S. Open Sandcastle Competition at Imperial Beach takes place annually in July or August.

With more than 50 miles of beach, there's a perfect stretch of sand for everyone. San Diego is a popular surfing area, but even nonsurfers appreciate the cool, refreshing waters and the delights of snorkeling. Most beaches are family-friendly, but some attract more specific crowds. Ocean Beach has a hipster feel, while Pacific Beach is a magnet for partiers. The North County lays claim to the choicest surfing spots, and Black's Beach attracts a smattering of nudists. Each beach here charms in a different way, so be sure to check out more than one.

BEACH BONFIRE

Just because the sun went down doesn't mean it's time to go home. Nothing compares to sitting around a crackling fire as the evening breeze ushers in whiffs of the sea. Fires are allowed only in fire rings, which you can find at **Ocean Beach, Mission Beach, Pacific Beach,** and **La Jolla Shores.** Revelers snap up ring slots quickly in summer; stake your claim early by filling one with wood and setting your gear nearby.

BEST BEACHES FOR . . .

OCEAN VIEWS

The view at **Sunset Cliffs** in Point Loma is dramatic and heart-achingly beautiful. Look for the few picnic tables that are positioned near the edge of the cliffs. **Torrey Pines State Natural Reserve** also provides fantastic views from its 300-foot-high cliffs.

ROMANCE

For a beautiful secluded spot, head to the lone shacklike hut that's nestled among the rocks at La Jolla's **Windansea Beach.** At **Fletcher Cove** in Solana Beach, look for the single bench overlooking the sea at the beach entrance.

KIDS

Despite its name, the **Children's Pool** isn't a great spot to take your kids to swim, but they'll love watching the seals and sea lions that populate its waters. **La Jolla Shores** is popular for the gentle waves in its swimmer's section, and **Mission Bay's** serene inlets make for shallow swimming pools.

OCEAN WALK

The Hotel Del Coronado on **Coronado Beach** makes the perfect backdrop to a walk along silky sand stretching toward the horizon. **Silver Strand** and **Imperial Beach** are also lovely.

AFTER-BEACH DRINKS

Pacific Beach's Garnet Street is home to the neighborhood's liveliest bars. College students head to Garnet on Friday and Saturday nights; at other times, it's a laid-back scene. **Pacific Beach Bar and Grill** and **Moondoggies** attract a younger crowd, while the **Silver Fox** is the quintessential dive bar.

BEST BEACH EATS

Living Room. This eatery is within walking distance of La Jolla Cove. Look for a table in back, where an open window lets in the fresh ocean air. ✉ *1010 Prospect St., La Jolla* ☎ *858/459–1187* ⊕ *www.livingroomcafe.com.*

Sbicca's. Not far from the shores of Del Mar, the upscale Sbicca's is famous for its roast chicken. ✉ *215 15th St., Del Mar* ☎ *858/481–1001* ⊕ *sbiccadelmar.com.*

Pizza Port. One of three branches, this combination pizzeria-brewery in Solana Beach is prized by North County locals for original pies like the seafood-laden Pizza Solana as well as house-brewed stout and cream ales. ✉ *135 N. Hwy. 101, Solana Beach* ☎ *858/481–7332* ⊕ *www.pizzaport.com.*

Las Olas. One of the best oceanfront Mexican restaurants in North County, Las Olas is across the street from the beach at Cardiff-by-the-Sea. Have a margarita or a grilled lobster before going to watch the surfers. ✉ *2655 S. Coast Hwy. 101, North County* ☎ *760/942–1860* ⊕ *www.lasolasmex.com.*

LA JOLLA'S BEACHES AND BEYOND

La Jolla (pronounced La Hoya) means "the jewel" in Spanish and appropriately describes this small, affluent village and its beaches. Some beautiful coastline can be found here, as well as an elegant upscale atmosphere.

(above) La Jolla is synonymous with beautiful vistas. (lower right) The view from Coast Highway 101 in Carlsbad is spectacular. (upper right) Hike down to the beach from Torrey Pines.

Conveniently located between North County and the Mission and South bays, La Jolla is easily accessible from downtown San Diego and North County. It's worth it to rent a car so you can sample the different beaches along the coast. The town's trademark million-dollar homes won't disappoint either—their cliff-side locations make them an attractive backdrop to the brilliant views of the sea below. Downtown La Jolla is more commercialized, with high-end stores great for browsing. La Jolla Shores, a mile-long beach, lies in the more residential area to the north. Above all, the beach and cove are La Jolla's prime charms—the cove's seals and underwater kelp beds are big draws for kayakers and nature lovers.

IN THE BUFF

Some people just don't like tan lines. Black's Beach is one of the largest clothing-optional beaches in the United States. The chances of running into naked beachgoers of all ages are higher at the north end, and Black's is properly secluded and difficult to get to. The members of Black's Beach Bares (⊕ *www. blacksbeach.org*) chronicle their brand of free-spirited nudism on their website.

COAST HIGHWAY 101

The portion of Coast Highway 101 that runs south from North County into La Jolla is one of San Diego's best drives. Start at South Carlsbad beach at Tamarack Avenue and continue through Leucadia, Encinitas, Cardiff-by-the-Sea, Solana Beach, Del Mar, and, finally, La Jolla. Any turn west will take you toward the beach. The drive offers intermittent glimpses of the sea; views from Carlsbad and Cardiff are especially beautiful. The grand finale is at Torrey Pines, where the waves roll into the misty, high-bluffed beach.

12

THE CLIFFS AT TORREY PINES

The ocean views from the 300-foot-high sandstone cliffs atop Torrey Pines State Natural Reserve are vast and exquisite. To reach the cliffs, hike one of the short trails that lead from the visitor center. Perch along the sandy edge, and let your legs dangle. If you're lucky, you may see dolphins swimming along the shore or surfers riding a break.

SEALS AT THE CHILDREN'S POOL

In the last decade, much of La Jolla's harbor seal population has made itself at home at the Children's Pool beach, prompting concerns about water contamination due to the seals' waste. Swimmers were told to avoid the pools; in 2004, one irked swimmer took legal action, claiming that the pool is for children and snorkelers, who benefit from the shallow waters—not for the seals. Animal rights groups argued that the seals should be protected in their chosen habitat. After legal and other clashes over the matter, in 2012 the California Coastal Commission approved the installation of a rope barrier to provide a buffer between the seals and beachgoers and divers.

LA JOLLA COVE WALK AND SHOP

If you're not keen on dipping your toes in the water (or even the sand, for that matter), head over to La Jolla Cove, an ideal spot for strolling and shopping with a view. Park at any of the available metered spaces on Girard Avenue in downtown La Jolla and browse the Arcade Building, built in the Spanish Mission style. Make your way toward the cove by following the signs, or simply walk toward any patches of ocean you see. Look for the gazebos that dot the edge of the cove; they make great photo ops.

WATER SPORTS

One of the most popular water activities is kayaking along the caves and snorkeling among the kelp beds near the cove at the Underwater Ecological Reserve. Kayak rental shops offer special outings that include midnight moonlight kayaking and the chance to dive among the leopard sharks that roam La Jolla's waters. Don't worry; the sharks are harmless.

Updated by
Amanda
Knoles

California's entire coastline enchants, but the state's southernmost region stands apart when it comes to sand, surf, and sea. Step out of the car and onto the beach to immediately savor its allure: smell the fresh salty air, feel the plush sand at your feet, hear waves breaking enticingly from the shore, and take in the breathtaking vistas.

San Diego's sandstone bluffs offer spectacular views of the Pacific as a palette of blues and greens: there are distant indigo depths, emerald coves closer to shore, and finally, the mint-green swirls of the foamy surf. On land, the beach is silvery brown, etched with wisps of darker, charcoal-color sand and flecked with fool's gold.

San Diego's beaches have a different vibe from their northern counterparts in neighboring Orange County and glitzy Los Angeles farther up the coast. San Diego is more laid-back and less of a scene. Cyclists on cruiser bikes whiz by as surfers saunter toward the waves and sunbathers bronze under the sun, be it July or November.

Whether you're seeking a safe place to take the kids or a hot spot to work on your tan, you'll find a beach that's just right for you. La Jolla Shores and Mission Bay both have gentle waves and shallow waters that provide safer swimming for kids; whereas the high swells at Black's and Tourmaline attract surfers worldwide. If you're looking for dramatic ocean views, Torrey Pines State Beach and Sunset Cliffs provide a desertlike chaparral backdrop, with craggy cliffs overlooking the ocean below. Beaches farther south in Coronado and Silver Strand have longer stretches of sand that are perfect for a contemplative stroll or a brisk jog. Then there are those secluded, sandy enclaves that you may happen upon on a scenic drive down Highway 101.

⇨ *Beach reviews are listed geographically from south to north.*

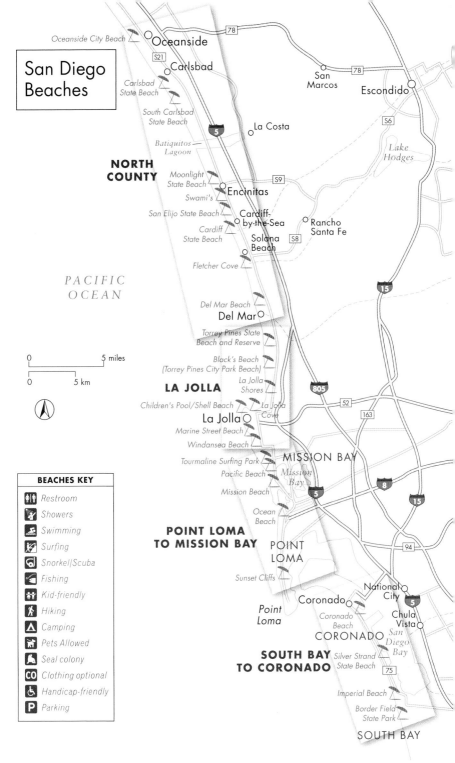

San Diego Beaches

Oceanside City Beach — Oceanside
78
S21
Carlsbad
Carlsbad State Beach
South Carlsbad State Beach
5
La Costa
San Marcos
Escondido
78
S6
Lake Hodges
Batiquitos Lagoon

NORTH COUNTY

Moonlight State Beach
S9
Encinitas
Swami's
San Elijo State Beach
Cardiff-by-the-Sea
Cardiff State Beach
Solana Beach
S8
Rancho Santa Fe

Fletcher Cove

PACIFIC OCEAN

Del Mar Beach — Del Mar

15

Torrey Pines State Beach and Reserve

Black's Beach (Torrey Pines City Park Beach)

LA JOLLA
La Jolla Shores
805
52
163

Children's Pool/Shell Beach
La Jolla Cove
La Jolla
Marine Street Beach
Windansea Beach
Tourmaline Surfing Park
MISSION BAY
Pacific Beach
Mission Bay
Mission Beach
8
15

Ocean Beach

POINT LOMA TO MISSION BAY
5
POINT LOMA
94

Sunset Cliffs

National City
5
Coronado
Chula Vista

Point Loma
Coronado Beach
CORONADO
San Diego Bay

SOUTH BAY TO CORONADO
Silver Strand State Beach
75

Imperial Beach

Border Field State Park

SOUTH BAY

0   5 miles
0   5 km

BEACHES KEY

- Restroom
- Showers
- Swimming
- Surfing
- Snorkel/Scuba
- Fishing
- Kid-friendly
- Hiking
- Camping
- Pets Allowed
- Seal colony
- **CO** Clothing optional
- Handicap-friendly
- **P** Parking

BEACH PLANNER

WATER TEMPERATURE

Even at summer's hottest peak, San Diego's beaches are cool and breezy. Ocean waves are large, and the water will be colder than what you experience at tropical beaches—temperatures range from 55°F to 65°F from October through June, and 65°F to 73°F from July through September.

SURF FORECAST

For a surf and weather report, call San Diego's Lifeguard Services at ☎ 619/221–8824. These websites also provide live webcams on surf conditions and water temperature forecasts: ⊕ *www.surfingsandiego, com* ⊕ *www.surfline.com.*

THE GREEN FLASH

Some people think it's a phony phenomenon, but the fleeting "green flash" is real, if rare. On a clear day and under certain atmospheric conditions, higher-frequency green light causes a brief green flash at the moment when the sun sinks into the sea.

WHAT TO BRING

In addition to beach essentials like sunscreen, many beachgoers bring boogie boards to ride the waves, blankets to lie on, buckets for the kids to make sand castles, and a beach umbrella for shade. Many beaches do not have shoreline concessions, so bring your own bottles of water and snacks. Surfers and bodysurfers often wear wet suits, which are available for purchase or rental in the shops in beach towns.

Despite Southern California's famous balminess, fog and a marine layer may creep in unexpectedly at various parts of the day. This happens particularly often in early summer, when the effect is called "June Gloom." Bring a light sweater in case the fine mist rolls in, or if you plan on staying at the beach until dark, when temperatures get cooler.

GETTING TO THE BEACH

San Diego Transit buses (⊕ *www.sdcommute.com*) stop a short walk from the beaches, but it's better to rent a car to explore on your own. Driving the scenic coastal routes is fun in itself. County Highway S21 runs along the coast between Torrey Pines State Beach and Reserve and Oceanside, although its local names (Old Highway 101 or Coast Highway 101, for example) vary by community.

PARKING

Parking is usually near the beaches but some in a few cases, such as Black's Beach, you'll have to hike a bit. Finding a parking spot near the ocean can be hard in summer, but for the time being, unmetered parking is available at all San Diego city beaches. Del Mar has a pay lot and metered street parking around the 15th Street Beach. La Jolla Shores, Mission Beach, and other large beaches have visitor parking lots, but space can be limited. Your best bet is to arrive early.

BEACH RULES

Pay attention to signs listing illegal activities; undercover police often patrol the beaches. Smoking and alcoholic beverages are completely banned on city beaches. Drinking in beach parking lots, on boardwalks,

12

and in landscaped areas is also illegal. Glass containers are not permitted on beaches, cliffs, and walkways, or in park areas and adjacent parking lots. Littering is not tolerated, and skateboarding is prohibited at some beaches. Fires are allowed only in fire rings or elevated barbecue grills. Although it may be tempting to take a sea creature from a tide pool as a souvenir, it may upset the delicate ecological balance, and it's illegal, too.

SAFETY

Lifeguards are stationed at city beaches from Sunset Cliffs up to Black's Beach in the summertime, but coverage in winter is provided by roving patrols only. When swimming in the ocean be aware of rip currents, which are common in California shores. If you are caught in one, don't panic. Swim parallel to the shore until you can reach land without resistance. To be safe, go swimming near lifeguard posts where you will be visible. Few beaches have lockers to keep your belongings secure. If you're going to the beach solo and plan on going in the water, leave your wallet out of sight in your car.

POLLUTION

San Diego's beaches are well maintained and very clean during summertime, when rainfall is infrequent. Beaches along San Diego County's northern cities are typically cleaner than ones farther south. Pollution is generally worse near river mouths and storm-drain outlets, especially after heavy rainfall. Call San Diego's Lifeguard Services at ☎ *619/221–8824* for a recorded message that includes pollution reports along with surfing and diving conditions. The Heal the Bay organization (⊕ *www.healthebay.org*) monitors and grades California coastal water conditions yearly.

BEACH CAMPING

Overnight camping is not allowed on any San Diego city beach, but there are campgrounds at some state beaches (☎ *800/444–7275 for reservations* ⊕ *www.reserveamerica.com*) throughout the county.

DOG BEACHES

Leashed dogs are permitted on most San Diego beaches and adjacent parks from 6 pm to 9 am; they can run unleashed anytime at Dog Beach at the north end of Ocean Beach and, from the day after Labor Day through June 14, at Rivermouth in Del Mar. It's rarely a problem, however, to take your pet to isolated beaches in winter.

RED TIDE

When sporadic algae blooms turn coastal waters a reddish-brown hue, San Diegans know the "red tide" has arrived. Environmentalists may see it as a bane to healthy ocean life, but the phenomenon is welcomed as a chance to witness ocean phosphorescence. The phytoplankton that causes the discoloration is unsightly only until nightfall. After dark, the algae-rich waters crash against the sand, inciting bioluminescent plankton to emit a bluish-green neon light. The result is a marvelous display of glow-in-the-dark waves.

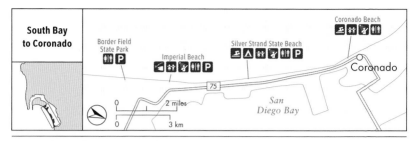

BEACHES BY NEIGHBORHOOD

SOUTH BAY TO CORONADO

SOUTH BAY

Border Field State Park. This southernmost San Diego beach is different from most California beaches—the fence at the parking lot's southern end marks the U.S.–Mexican border. The beach lies within Border Field State Park, an area with sand dunes and salt marshes favored by horseback riders and hikers. The Tijuana River Estuary, designated as a Wetland of National Importance, is a haven for endangered birds. Newly renovated picnic sites at Monument Mesa offer scenic ocean views and have barbecue grills and a shaded group area. Flooding in winter often restricts access, but normally the park is open to pedestrians, hikers, and equestrians on weekdays. Because of state budget cuts, motorized vehicles are permitted only on weekends and holidays. △ Beware: Swimming and wading are discouraged due to inshore holes and rip currents, and because no lifeguards are on duty. **Amenities:** parking (fee), toilets. **Best for:** solitude, walking. ⊠ *Exit I–5 at Dairy Mart Rd. and head west along Monument Rd., South Bay* ⊕ *www.parks.ca.gov/?page_id=664* ⊠ *$5 per vehicle.*

☺ **Imperial Beach.** In July or early August this classic Southern California beach is the site of the U.S. Open Sandcastle Competition (⊕ *www. usopensandcastle.com*). The rest of the year, the laid-back beach is a great place for long walks and bird-watching—more than 370 species can be spotted here. The beach break is often excellent, but sewage contamination can be a problem after heavy rains. There are year-round lifeguards, a park with picnic areas, a playground, and volleyball and basketball courts. Among the many restaurants nearby are the one at Pier South, a new luxury hotel by Marriott. The fishing pier, popular for surf fishing, has views of Mexico to the south and Point Loma to the north. A walk on the beach south toward Border Field State Park or north toward Coronado is a great way to experience a quiet, uncrowded shore. **Amenities:** lifeguards, food and drink, parking (fee), showers, toilets. **Best for:** surfing, swimming, walking, solitude. ⊠ *Take Palm Ave. west from I–5 until it hits water, South Bay* ⊠ *Parking $2 a day.*

The grassy palm-lined park above La Jolla Cove is great for picnics.

CORONADO

Silver Strand State Beach. This quiet Coronado beach is ideal for families. The water is relatively calm, lifeguards and rangers are on duty year-round, and there are places for boating, water sports, biking, volleyball, and fishing. Picnic tables, grills, and fire pits are available, and the Silver Stand Beach Cafe is open during the summer. The beach sits across the street from Loews Coronado Bay Resort and the Coronado Cays, an exclusive community popular with yacht owners and celebrities. You can reserve RV sites ($50 beach; $35 inland) at ⊕ *www.reserveamerica. com.* Four day-use parking lots provide room for more than 1,000 cars. Foot tunnels under Route 75 lead to a bayside beach with great views of the San Diego skyline. **Amenities:** food and drink, lifeguards, parking (fee), showers, toilets. **Best for:** walking, swimming, surfing. ⊠ *From San Diego–Coronado Bridge, turn left onto Orange Ave., which becomes Rte. 75, and follow signs, Coronado* ☎ *619/435–5184* ⊕ *www.parks. ca.gov/silverstrand* ☞ *Parking $10; $15 peak weekends and holidays.*

Coronado Beach. With the famous Hotel Del Coronado as a backdrop, this sandy white beach is one of San Diego County's largest and most picturesque strands. It's perfect for sunbathing, people-watching, and Frisbee tossing. Exercisers might include Navy SEAL teams or other military units that conduct training runs on beaches in and around Coronado. There are picnic tables, grills and fire rings, a playground, and (on the northern end) a dog run. Free parking is available along Ocean Boulevard, though it's often hard to snag a space. **Amenities:** food and drink, lifeguards, showers, toilets. **Best for:** walking, swimming. ⊠ *From San Diego–Coronado bridge, turn left on Orange Ave. and follow signs, Coronado.*

Fodor's Choice
★

POINT LOMA, MISSION BAY, AND LA JOLLA

POINT LOMA

Sunset Cliffs. Semi-secluded Sunset Cliffs is popular with surfers and locals but offers little in the way of amenities. A few miles long, it lies beneath jagged cliffs on the Point Loma peninsula's western side. Low tide at the southern end, near Cabrillo Point, reveals tide pools teeming with small sea creatures. Farther north the waves lure surfers, and the lonely coves attract sunbathers. Stairs at the foot of Pescadero and Bermuda avenues provide beach access, as do some cliff trails, which are treacherous at points. Osprey Point offers good fishing off the rocks. A visit here is more enjoyable at low tide or at sunset when the views are sensational. Check WaveCast (⊕ *wavecast.com/tides*) for tide schedules. **Amenities:** parking (no fee). **Best for:** solitude, sunset. ⊠ *Take I–8 west to Sunset Cliffs Blvd. and head west, Point Loma.*

Ocean Beach. Much of this mile-long beach south of Mission Bay's channel entrance is a haven for volleyball players, sunbathers, and swimmers. The area around the municipal pier at the southern end is a hangout for surfers and transients. The pier stays open 24 hours a day for fishing and walking. There's a restaurant about halfway out, and more places to grab a snack can be found on the streets near the beach. Swimmers should beware of strong rip currents around the main lifeguard tower. There's a dog beach at the northern end; during summer there can be as many as 100 dogs running in the sand. For picnic areas (with fire rings) and a paved path, check out Ocean Beach Park, across from Dog Beach. **Amenities:** lifeguards, parking (no fee), showers, toilets. **Best for:** surfing, swimming, walking. ⊠ *Take I–8 west to Sunset Cliffs Blvd. and head west; a right turn off Sunset Cliffs Blvd. takes you to water, Point Loma.*

MISSION BAY

☺ ★ **Mission Beach.** San Diego's most popular beach draws huge crowds on hot summer days, but it's lively year-round. The 2-mile-long stretch extends from the northern entrance of Mission Bay to Pacific Beach. A wide boardwalk paralleling the beach is popular with walkers, joggers, roller skaters, rollerbladers, and bicyclists. Surfers, swimmers, and volleyball players congregate at the southern end. Scantily clad volleyball players practice on Cohasset Court. Toward its northern end, near the Belmont Park roller coaster, the beach narrows and the water becomes rougher. The crowds grow thicker and somewhat rougher as well. For parking, you can try for a spot on the street, but your best bets are the two big lots at Belmont Park. **Amenities:** lifeguards, parking (no fee), showers, toilets. **Best for:** swimming, surfing, walking. ⊠ *Exit I–5 at Grand Ave. and head west to Mission Blvd.; turn south and look for parking near roller coaster at West Mission Bay Dr., Mission Bay.*

Pacific Beach/North Pacific Beach. The boardwalk of Mission Beach turns into a sidewalk here, but there are still bike paths and picnic tables along the beach. Pacific Beach runs from the northern end of Mission Beach to Crystal Pier. The scene here is lively on weekends, with nearby restaurants, beach bars, and nightclubs providing a party atmosphere. North Pacific Beach, extending north from the pier, attracts families. There are designated swimming and surfing areas, and fire rings are available, as are places to eat. Parking can be a challenge. **Amenities:** food and drink, lifeguards, parking (no fee), showers, toilets. **Best for:** partiers, swimming, surfing. ⊠ *Exit I–5 at Grand Ave. and head west to Mission Blvd. Turn north and look for parking, Mission Bay.*

Tourmaline Surfing Park. Offering slow waves and frequent winds, this is one of the most popular beaches for beginning surfers, longboarders, windsurfers, and kiteboarders. Separate areas designated for swimmers and surfers are strictly enforced. The 175-space parking lot at the foot of Tourmaline Street normally fills to capacity by midday. **Amenities:** lifeguards, parking (no fee), showers, toilets. **Best for:** windsurfing, surfing. ⊠ *Take Mission Blvd. north (it turns into La Jolla Blvd.) and turn west on Tourmaline St., 600 Tourmaline St., Mission Bay.*

LA JOLLA

Windansea Beach. Named for a hotel that burned down in the late 1940s, Windansea Beach has become famous for the unusual A-frame waves the reef break here creates—and for the eclectic group of surfers those waves attract. This is one of San Diego County's most popular surf spots, and with its incredible views and secluded sunbathing spots set among sandstone rocks, Windansea is also one of the most romantic of West Coast beaches, especially at sunset. You can usually find nearby street parking. **Amenities:** lifeguards. **Best for:** sunset, surfing, solitude. ⊠ *Take Mission Blvd. north (it turns into La Jolla Blvd.) and turn west on Nautilus St., La Jolla.*

Marine Street Beach. A wide expanse of white sand, this beach often teems with sunbathers, swimmers, walkers, joggers, and folks just out for the incredible views. This is a great spot for bodysurfing, but be aware that the waves break in extremely shallow water. You'll also need to watch out for riptides. Picnic tables, showers, and toilets are available at the nearby cove. **Amenities:** lifeguards. **Best for:** solitude, swimming, walking. ⊠ *Accessible from Marine St., off La Jolla Blvd., La Jolla.*

🐚 **Children's Pool.** This shallow cove, protected by a seawall, has small waves
★ and no riptide—because of its location at the tip of the La Jolla peninsula, you can actually look east to get unmatched panoramic views of the
coastline and ocean. The area just outside the pool is popular with scuba
divers, who explore the offshore reef when the surf is calm. Groups of
harbor seals hang out along the beach, claiming it as their own during
the winter pupping season. While kids love to watch the seals and sea
lions, swimming is not advised. **Amenities:** lifeguards, showers, toilets.
Best for: solitude, walking. ⊠ *Follow La Jolla Blvd. north, when it forks,
stay to left, then turn right onto Coast Blvd., La Jolla.*

Shell Beach. North of Children's Pool is a small cove, accessible by stairs,
with a relatively secluded beach. The exposed rocks off the coast have
been designated a protected habitat for sea lions; you can watch them
sun themselves and frolic in the water. Picnic tables, showers, and toilets are available near the cove. **Amenities:** lifeguard. **Best for:** solitude.
⊠ *Continue along Coast Blvd. north from Children's Pool, La Jolla.*

🐚 **La Jolla Cove.** This shimmering blue inlet is what first attracted everyone
Fodor'sChoice to La Jolla, from Native Americans to the glitterati; it's the secret to
★ the village's enduring cachet. You'll find "the Cove"—as locals refer to
it, as though it were the only one in San Diego—beyond where Girard
Avenue dead-ends into Coast Boulevard, marked by towering palms
that line a promenade where people strolling in designer clothes are
as common as Frisbee throwers. Ellen Browning Scripps Park sits atop
cliffs formed by the incessant pounding of the waves and offers a great
spot for picnics with a view. At low tide the pools and cliff caves are a
destination for explorers. Divers, snorkelers, and kayakers can check
out the underwater delights of the **San Diego–La Jolla Underwater
Park Ecological Reserve.** The cove is also a favorite of rough-water
swimmers. **Amenities:** lifeguards, showers, toilets. **Best for:** snorkeling,
swimming, walking. ⊠ *Follow Coast Blvd. north to signs, or take La
Jolla Village Dr. exit from I–5, head west to Torrey Pines Rd., turn left,
and drive downhill to Girard Ave.; turn right and follow signs, La Jolla.*

🐚 **La Jolla Shores.** This is one of San Diego's most popular beaches, so
★ get here early on summer weekends. The lures are an incredible view
of La Jolla peninsula, a wide sandy beach, a grassy park that's adjacent to **San Diego La Jolla Underwater Park Ecological Reserve,** and
the gentlest waves in San Diego. Several surf and scuba schools teach
here, and kayak rentals are nearby. A concrete boardwalk parallels the
beach, and a boat launch for small vessels lies 300 yards south of the
lifeguard station at Avenida de Playa. Arrive early to get a parking spot

in the lot at the foot of Calle Frescota. **Amenities:** lifeguards, parking (no fee), showers, toilets. **Best for:** surfing, swimming, walking. ⊠ *8200 Camino del Oro from I–5 take La Jolla Village Dr. west and turn left onto La Jolla Shores Dr.; head west to Camino del Oro or Vallecitos St., turn right, La Jolla.*

★ **Black's Beach.** The powerful waves at this beach, officially known as Torrey Pines City Park beach, attract world-class surfers, and the strand's relative isolation appeals to nudist nature lovers (although by law nudity is prohibited) as well as gays and lesbians. Backed by cliffs whose colors change with the sun's angle, Black's can be accessed from Torrey Pines State Beach to the north, or by a narrow path descending the cliffs from Torrey Pines Glider Port. Access to parts of the shore coincides with low tide. Lifeguards patrol the area only between spring break and mid-October. Strong rip currents are common—only experienced swimmers should take the plunge. Storms have weakened the cliffs in the past few years; they're dangerous to climb and should be avoided. Part of the fun here is watching hang gliders and paragliders ascend from atop the cliffs. Parking is available at the Torrey Pines Glider Port and La Jolla Farms. **Amenities:** None. **Best for:** solitude, nudists, surfing. ⊠ *Take Genesee Ave. west from I–5 and follow signs to Torrey Pines Glider Port; easier access, via a paved path, available on La Jolla Farms Rd., but parking is limited to 2 hrs, La Jolla.*

★ **Torrey Pines State Beach and Reserve.** One of San Diego's best beaches encompasses 2,000 acres of bluffs and bird-filled marshes. A network of meandering trails leads to the wide, sandy shoreline below. Along the way enjoy the rare Torrey pine trees, found only here and on Santa Rosa Island, offshore. Guides conduct tours of the nature preserve on weekends. Torrey Pines tends to get crowded in summer, but you'll find more isolated spots heading south under the cliffs leading to Black's Beach. **Amenities:** lifeguards, parking (fee), showers, toilets. **Best for:** swimming, surfing, walking. ⊠ *Take Carmel Valley Rd. exit west from I–5, turn left on Rte. S21, 12600 N. Torrey Pines Rd.* ☎ *858/755–2063* ⊕ *www.torreypine.org* ⌨ *Parking $12–$15 per vehicle depending on day and season.*

NORTH COUNTY BEACHES

DEL MAR

Del Mar Beach. The numbered streets of Del Mar, from 15th north to 29th, end at a wide beach popular with volleyball players, surfers, and sunbathers. The portion of Del Mar south of 15th Street is lined with cliffs and rarely crowded. Leashed dogs are permitted on most sections of the beach, except Main Beach, where they are prohibited from June 15th through Labor Day. For the rest of the year, dogs may run under voice control at North Beach, also known as Dog Beach. Food, hotels, and shopping are all within an easy walk of Del Mar beach. Parking costs from $1.50 to $3 per hour at meters and pay lots on Coast Boulevard and along Camino Del Mar. **Amenities:** food and drink, lifeguards, parking (fee), showers, toilets. **Best for:** swimming, walking. ⊠ *Take Via de la Valle exit from I–5 west to Rte. S21 (also known as Camino del Mar in Del Mar) and turn left, Del Mar.*

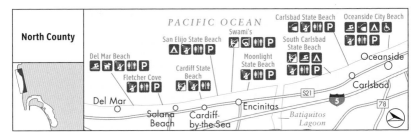

SOLANA BEACH

Fletcher Cove. Most of the beaches in the little city of Solana Beach are nestled under cliffs, and access is limited to private stairways. However, at the west end of Lomas Santa Fe Drive you'll find an entrance to a small beach, known locally as Fletcher Cove. Also here are a parking lot and restrooms. During low tide it's an easy walk under the cliffs to nearby beaches, but high tide can make some of the beach impassable. At the northern end of town there are also restrooms, a pay lot, and easy beach access. Tides and surf conditions are posted at a kiosk by this parking lot. **Amenities:** lifeguards, parking (no fee), showers, toilets. **Best for:** surfing, solitude, swimming, walking. ⊠ *From I–5 take Lomas Santa Fe Dr. west, Solana Beach.*

CARDIFF-BY-THE-SEA

Cardiff State Beach. This beach, popularly known as George's, begins at the parking lot immediately north of the cliffs at Solana Beach. A reef break draws surfers, although this stony beach is not particularly appealing otherwise. A walk south, however, provides access to some of Solana Beach's secluded coves. Pay attention to the incoming tide, though, or you may have to wade or swim back to the parking lot. **Amenities:** lifeguards, parking (fee), showers, toilets. **Best for:** surfing, swimming. ⊠ *From I–5 turn west on Lomas Santa Fe Dr. to Rte. S21 (Old Hwy. 101) and turn right, Cardiff-by-the-Sea* ☎ *760/753–5091* ⊕ *www.parks.ca.gov* ⊑ *$10 per vehicle; $15 peak weekends/holidays.*

San Elijo State Beach. Campsites sit atop a scenic bluff at this park, which also has a store and shower facilities, plus beach access for swimmers and surfers. Ocean sites cost $55, inland ones $35 (☎ *800/444–7275* ⊕ *www.parks.ca.gov for reservations*). Park for a fee in nearby lots or for free off U.S. 101. **Amenities:** lifeguards, parking (fee), showers, toilets. **Best for:** surfing, snorkeling, swimming. ⊠ *From I–5 exit at Encinitas Blvd. head west. Turn left (south) on S. Coast Hwy. for about 2 mi, Cardiff-by-the-Sea* ☎ *760/753–5091* ⊑ *Parking $10 per vehicle; $15 peak weekends/holidays.*

ENCINITAS

★ **Swami's.** The palms and the golden lotus-flower domes of the nearby Self-Realization Center temple and ashram earned this picturesque beach, also a top surfing spot, its name. Extreme low tides expose tide pools that harbor anemones, starfish, and other sea life. The only access is by a long stairway leading down from the cliff-top Seaside Roadside Park, where there's free parking. On big winter swells, the bluffs are lined with

Check out the scene along Carlsbad State Beach's pedestrian walkway.

gawkers watching the area's best surfers take on—and be taken down by—some of the county's best big waves. Offshore, divers do their thing at North County's underwater park, Encinitas Marine Life Refuge. **Amenities:** lifeguards, parking (no fee), showers, toilets. **Best for:** snorkeling, surfing, swimming. ⊠ *Follow Rte. S21 north from Cardiff, or Exit I–5 at Encinitas Blvd., go west to Rte. S21, and turn left, Encinitas.*

Moonlight State Beach. Its large parking areas and many facilities make this beach tucked into a break in the cliffs an easy getaway. The volleyball courts on the northern end attract many competent players, including a few professionals who live in the area. Moonlight is easily accessible from the Encinitas Coaster train station. **Amenities:** food and drink, lifeguards, parking (no fee), showers, toilets. **Best for:** solitude, surfing, swimming. ⊠ *Take Encinitas Blvd. exit from I–5, head west to 3rd St., and turn left; parking lot is on your right at top of hill, Encinitas.*

CARLSBAD

South Carlsbad State Beach/Carlsbad State Beach. Erosion from winter storms has made the southern Carlsbad beaches rockier than most beaches in Southern California. This is particularly true of South Carlsbad, a stretch of which is named in honor of Robert C. Frazee, a local politician and civic booster. Still, it's a good swimming spot, there are fine street- and beach-level promenades, and for self-contained RVs there's overnight camping (☎ 800/444–7275). Farther north at Carlsbad State Beach, you can't camp, but you can fish, and there's a parking lot. The beach here has separate swimming and surfing sections. In summer, the south swell creates good surf when other San Diego beaches are bereft. The cement walkway that borders the beach continues into downtown Carlsbad. **Amenities:** lifeguards, parking (fee), showers, toilets. **Best for:** walking, swimming, surfing. ⊠ *Exit I–5 at La Costa Ave. and head west to Rte. S21, turn north and follow coastline, Carlsbad* ☎ *760/438–3143* ⊕ *www.parks.ca.gov* ⌸ *$10 per vehicle.*

OCEANSIDE

Oceanside City Beach. Swimmers, surfers, and U.S. Marines from nearby Camp Pendleton often come to play here. The surf is good around the Oceanside Pier, one of the longest wooden piers on the West Coast. Free concerts take place at the Pier Plaza Amphitheater in spring and summer. Self-serve RV camping is permitted in the parking lot at the northernmost end of Harbor Beach, but there's no tent camping. Pay lots and meters are located around the pier and also in the Oceanside Harbor area. A free two-hour lot can be found east of the pay lots on Harbor Drive South. **Amenities:** food and drink, parking (fee), toilets, showers. **Best for:** surfing, swimming, walking. ⊠ *Take Vista Way west from I–5 to Rte. S21 (Coast Hwy.) and turn right; best access points are from Cassidy St., Oceanside Pier, and Oceanside Harbor area, Oceanside* ⌸ *$5 parking.*

Sports and the Outdoors

WORD OF MOUTH

"If you are adventuresome, my two favorite recommendations are [first,] kayaking in La Jolla Cove. You are likely to see and maybe even be surrounded by leopard sharks, which are completely harmless. It is a stunning experience. [Second,] hiking at the Torrey Pines State Park. My favorite is the beach hike."

—ncounty

SURFING SAN DIEGO

Head to a San Diego beach on any given day and chances are you'll see a group of surfers in the water, patiently waiting to ride a memorable break. Spectators as well as enthusiasts agree that catching a perfect wave is an unforgettable experience.

(above) La Jolla Shores is a good beach for beginner surfers. (lower right) Surfer at the end of a good ride. (upper right) Instructors at Surf Diva Surf School cater to women.

Surfing may have originated in Hawaii, but modern surfing culture is inextricably linked to the Southern California lifestyle. From the Malibu setting of *Gidget* to the surf-city sounds of Jan and Dean and the Beach Boys, and TV's *Laguna Beach* and *The OC*, the entertainment industry brought a California version of surfing to the landlocked, and in the process created an enduring mystique.

San Diego surfing in particular is unique. Underwater kelp beds help keep waves intact, preventing the choppiness that surfers bemoan. Santa Ana winds that begin to arrive in fall and throughout early winter bring coveted offshore winds that contribute to morning and evening "glass" (the stillness of the water that encourages smooth waves).

BEST TIME TO GO

In San Diego the biggest swells usually occur in winter, although good-size waves can form year-round. Generally, swells come from a northerly direction in winter and from the south in summer. Certain surf spots are better on different swells. In winter, try beaches like Swami's or Black's Beach. Summer spots are La Jolla's Windansea and nearby Tourmaline Surfing Park.

TYPES OF BREAKS

Beach break: Waves that break over sandbars and the sea-floor and are usually tamer and consistently long, thus typically the best type for beginners, with the exception of Black's Beach, which is legendary for its uniquely large beach breaks. **La Jolla Shores**, **Mission Beach**, and **Pacific Beach** are destinations for gentler, more forgiving waves.

Point break: Created as waves hit a point jutting into the ocean. Surfers then peel down the swell it creates. With the right conditions, this can create very consistent waves. **Swami's** has an excellent point break.

Reef break: Waves break as they hit reef. It can create great (but dangerous) surf. There's a good chance of getting smashed and scraped over extremely sharp coral or rocks. Many of San Diego's best breaks occur thanks to underwater reefs, as at **San Elijo**, **La Jolla Cove**, and **Windansea**.

SAN DIEGO SURF FINDER

Get a closer view of surfers doing their thing from any municipal pier, such as at **Oceanside**, **Pacific**, and **Mission beaches**. The high bluffs of **Black's Beach** are also excellent points to watch surfers.

Swami's: Famous for its point break and beautiful waters.

Black's Beach: This is where to go for beach breaks. Serious surfers carry their boards and take a hike to reach the beach.

Windansea Beach: A dual beach for surf and romance. Known for its reef breaks.

Tourmaline Surfing Park: Windsurfers and surfers share Tourmaline's smooth waves.

La Jolla Shores: First-timers head here for more modest waves.

13

SURF SLANG

Barrel: The area created when a wave breaks onto itself in a curl.

Close out: When a wave breaks all at once, rather than breaking steadily in one direction.

Cutback: The most basic turn in surfing; executed to maintain position close to the barrel.

Dropping in: A severe breach of etiquette wherein a second surfer joins the wave later and cuts off the original rider.

Goofy foot: Having a right-foot-forward stance on the surfboard. The opposite is known as natural.

Grom: An affectionate term for those sun-bleached kids with tiny surfboards.

Hollow: Not all barrels create hollows, which are barrels big enough to create a tube that a surfer can ride within—also called the green room.

Lineup: A group of surfers waiting beyond the breakers for waves to come in.

Turtle roll: A maneuver in which the surfer rolls over on the surfboard, going underwater and holding the board upside down.

Updated by
Claire Deeks
van der Lee

Evidence of San Diego's outdoorsy spirit is apparent everywhere; you'll find an occasional hot-air balloon floating into the sunset like a piece of candy in the sky, groups of surfers bobbing in the water at dawn, hang gliders swooping off sandstone cliffs, and white sails gliding gracefully along the shore. They are as much a part of San Diego's landscape as the sea, sand, and hills.

As you'd expect, the ocean is one of San Diego's most popular natural attractions. Surfers, swimmers, kayakers, divers, snorkelers, and sailboarders have 70 miles of shorefront to explore. You can rent equipment and take lessons in these sports, or head out on a fishing or whale-watching excursion aboard a charter boat. Even if you're inclined to do no more than sightsee, you can take a low-impact sunset stroll on a wide, sandy beach or explore secluded coves at low tide. At the end of the day at any beach in the county, you'll see a local ritual, as everyone stops what they're doing to watch the sun's orange orb slip silently into the blue-gray Pacific.

SPORTS AND THE OUTDOORS PLANNER

SAN DIEGO BY THE SEASONS

San Diego has miles of beaches and bays, numerous lakes, mountains, and deserts to explore. With balmy average temperatures and less than a foot of rain per year, the lure to go play outside is hard to resist. That said, Southern California isn't as seasonless as some claim. While the weather is generally mild and sunny year-round, the seasons do bring different outdoor activities.

Summer is the best time to plan your trip from an outdoor activities point of view (this is peak tourist season for a reason). San Diego's proximity to the ocean offers an almost endless selection of water activities. Rent kayaks at La Jolla Cove, take a charter boat off Point Loma for deep-sea tuna fishing, or simply hit the beach and go for a swim. The

TOP OUTDOOR EXPERIENCES

Kayak La Jolla's caves: Join a tour to explore the seven caves off La Jolla Cove; you'll see lots of wildlife, including seals, sea lions, and maybe leopard sharks and dolphins.

Bike the boardwalk: Rent a beach cruiser and pedal along the Mission Bay boardwalk. You'll be in good company among the scene-making muscle men and babes in bikinis.

Catch a wave: Surf La Jolla Cove's famous reef breaks or watch the surfers at Swami's beach from the Self-Realization Foundation's meditation gardens on the cliffs above.

Try Frisbee golf: Check out this local sport at Balboa Park's Morley Field. It's like golf, but with Frisbees.

Hit the links: With so many courses in San Diego, there's sure to be something for every golfer. Add to that the perfect weather and sweeping views of the ocean and it's tee time.

Bahia Resort at Mission Bay offers Jet Ski and sailboat rentals to help you enjoy the shimmering bay. Visitors planning a trip in early summer should be aware of the phenomenon known as "May Gray and June Gloom," when fog often blankets the coast in the morning. Things usually clear up by the afternoon, but occasionally the fog lasts all day, making a trip to the beach a damp and chilly affair.

The temperature begins to cool down for winter, but before it does, Santa Ana winds usher a warm dry spell throughout Southern California through the **fall.** It's the perfect time to shoot 18 holes at the Park Hyatt Aviara in Carlsbad, or take a hike at the Bayside Trail at Cabrillo National Monument—fall's cloudless skies allow for a crisp, clear vision of the Pacific. And although the foliage in San Diego doesn't turn into burnished reds and golds, you can appreciate the rare species of evergreen at Torrey Pines State Reserve.

Winter in California is hardly bitter or harsh, but the weather certainly gets too cold for water sports. Serious surfers love the breaks best in winter, when the swells are high. Black's Beach continues to be one of the most challenging surfing beaches in San Diego. Winter is also when gray whales migrate to warmer waters. Charter boats offer whale-watching trips between December and March. View the whales with San Diego Harbor Excursion or with one of the more intimate sailboat charters offered around town.

In **spring,** wildflowers begin to appear at Anza-Borrego Desert Park. At peak months, the desert terrain blooms with vibrant colors.

If you're interested in something sportier, Escondido's lakes are filled with bass, bluegill, and catfish waiting to be hooked.

PARTICIPATION SPORTS

BALLOONING

Enjoy views of the Pacific Ocean, the mountains, and the coastline south to Mexico and north to San Clemente from a hot-air balloon at sunrise or sunset; most excursions include beverages and snacks, too. The conditions are perfect: wide-open spaces and just enough wind to breeze you through them.

California Dreamin'. Head here for hot-air balloon rides, specializing in Temecula wine country flights and Del Mar sunset coastal excursions. ⊠ *33133 Vista del Monte Rd., Temecula* ☎ *800/373–3359* ⊕ *www. californiadreamin.com.*

Skysurfer Balloon Company. Lift off for a one-hour champagne and sunset flight in Del Mar. ⊠ *Del Mar* ☎ *858/481–6800* ⊕ *www. sandiegohotairballoons.com.*

BICYCLING

BIKE PATHS

Lomas Santa Fe Drive. Experienced cyclists follow this route in Solana Beach east into Rancho Santa Fe, perhaps even continuing east on Del Dios Highway, past Lake Hodges, to Escondido. These roads can be narrow and winding in spots.

Mission Beach Boardwalk. A ride here is a great way to take in a classic California scene. Just don't expect a cardio workout, as the gawkers and crowds often slow foot and bike traffic to a crawl.

Route S21. On many summer days, Route S21, aka Old Highway 101, from La Jolla to Oceanside looks like a freeway for cyclists. About 24 miles long, it's easily the most popular and scenic bike route around, never straying far from the beach. Although the terrain is fairly easy, the long, steep Torrey Pines grade is famous for weeding out the weak. Another Darwinian challenge is dodging slow-moving pedestrians and cars pulling over to park in towns like Encinitas and Del Mar.

BIKE TOURS AND RENTALS

★ **The Bike Revolution.** Rent any type of bike and join biking tours in the downtown waterfront and Gaslamp areas, to and around Coronado Island, up to Cabrillo National Monument, and elsewhere in the city. ⊠ *522 6th Ave., Downtown* ☎ *619/238–2444* ⊕ *www. thebikerevolution.com.*

Cheap Rentals Mission Beach. Right by the boardwalk, this place has good daily and weekly prices for bike rentals, which include beach cruisers, tandems, hybrids, and two-wheeled baby carriers. ⊠ *3689 Mission Blvd., Mission Beach* ☎ *858/488–9070 or 800/941–7761* ⊕ *www. cheap-rentals.com.*

Hike Bike Kayak San Diego. This outfitter offers a wide range of guided bike tours, from easy excursions around Mission Bay and Coronado Island to slightly more rigorous trips through coastal La Jolla.

Coast Highway 101 is a haven for bicyclists from Oceanside down to La Jolla.

Mountain-biking tours are also available, and the company also rents bikes of all types (and can deliver them to your hotel). ⊠ *2246 Ave. de la Playa, La Jolla* ☎ *858/551–9510* ⊕ *www.hikebikekayak.com.*

Holland's Bicycles. This great bike rental source on Coronado Island has another store (**Bikes and Beyond** ☎ *619/435–7180)* located at the ferry landing, so you can jump on your bike as soon as you cross the harbor from downtown San Diego. ⊠ *977 Orange Ave., Coronado* ☎ *619/435–3153* ⊕ *www.hollandsbicycles.com.*

Wheel Fun Rentals. Surreys, cruisers, mountain bikes, tandems, and electric bicycles, among other two-, three-, and four-wheeled contraptions, are available at the downtown Holiday Inn and a number of other locations around San Diego; call or visit the website for details. ⊠ *1355 N. Harbor Dr., Downtown* ☎ *619/239–3347* ⊕ *www.wheelfunrentals.com.*

DIVING AND SNORKELING

San Diego City Lifeguard Service. Call the San Diego City Lifeguard Service hotline for prerecorded, up-to-date diving information and conditions. ☎ *619/221–8824* ⊕ *www.sandiego.gov/lifeguards.*

DIVE SITES

Mission Beach. The HMCS *Yukon,* a decommissioned Canadian warship, was intentionally sunk off Mission Beach to create the main diving destination in San Diego. A mishap caused the ship to settle on its side, creating a surreal, M.C. Escher–esque diving environment. This is a technical dive and should be attempted only by experienced divers; even diving instructors have become disoriented inside the wreck.

San Diego–La Jolla Underwater Park Ecological Preserve. Diving enthusiasts the world over come to San Diego to snorkel and scuba dive off La Jolla at the underwater preserve. Because all sea life is protected here, this 533-acre preserve (all of La Jolla Cove to La Jolla Shores) is the best place to see large lobster, sea bass, and sculpin (scorpion fish), as well as numerous golden garibaldi damselfish, the state marine fish. It's common to see hundreds of beautiful (and harmless) leopard sharks schooling at the north end of the cove, near La Jolla Shores, especially in summer.

> **THE GREAT WIDE OPEN**
>
> An $8.50 round-trip ferry ride transports you and your bike from downtown San Diego to hyper-flat, super-cruisable Coronado, with a wide, flat beach, the historic Hotel Del Coronado (an unbeatable background for photos), and the beautifully manicured gardens of its many residential streets.

Scripps Canyon. Off the south end of Black's Beach, the rim of Scripps Canyon lies in about 60 feet of water and comprises the Marine Life Refuge. The canyon plummets more than 900 feet in some sections.

DIVE TOURS AND OUTFITTERS

Ocean Enterprises Scuba Diving. Stop in for everything you need to plan a diving adventure, including equipment, advice, and instruction. ✉ *7710 Balboa Ave., Suite 101, Clairemont Mesa* ☎ *858/565–6054* ⊕ *www.oceanenterprises.com.*

Scuba San Diego. This center is well regarded for its top-notch instruction and certification programs, as well as for guided dive tours. Trips include dives to kelp reefs in La Jolla Cove, night diving at La Jolla Canyon, and unguided charter boat trips to Mission Bay's Wreck Alley or to the Coronado Islands (in Mexico, just south of San Diego). ✉ *San Diego Hilton Hotel, 1775 E. Mission Bay Dr., Mission Bay* ☎ *619/260–1880* ⊕ *www.scubasandiego.com.*

FISHING

San Diego's waters are home to many game species; you never know what you'll hook. Depending on the season, a half- or full-day ocean charter trip could bring in a yellowfin, dorado, sea bass, or halibut. Longer trips to Mexican waters can net you bigger game like a marlin or a bigeye tuna. Pier fishing doesn't offer as much excitement, but it's the cheapest ocean fishing option available. No license is required to fish from a public pier, which includes those at Ocean Beach, Imperial Beach, and Oceanside.

Public lakes are frequently stocked with a variety of trout and largemouth bass, but also have resident populations of bluegill and catfish.

California Department of Fish and Game. A fishing license, available at most bait-and-tackle and sporting-goods stores, is required for fishing from the shoreline. Nonresidents can purchase an annual license or a 10-day, 2-day, or 1-day short-term license. Licenses can also be purchased online through the Department's website or at the San Diego headquarters. Children under 16 do not need a license.

Note that some city reservoirs no longer sell snacks, drinks, bait, or fishing licenses, nor do they rent pedal boats or electric motors. They also accept cash only for day-use fees. Make sure to check updated concession availability for your specific destination, or obtain a fishing license in advance. ⊠ *3883 Ruffin Rd.* ☎ *858/467–4201* ⊕ *www.dfg.ca.gov.*

FRESHWATER FISHING

Dixon, Hodges, and Wohlford. These three freshwater lakes surround the North County city of Escondido.

Lake Jennings. County-operated Lake Jennings is stocked with trout in winter and catfish during the summer; it's a popular fly-fishing spot. ⊠ *9535 Harritt Rd., Lakeside* ☎ *619/443–2510* ⊕ *www.lakejennings.org.*

Lake Morena. This spot is popular for fishing and camping. ⊠ *2550 Lake Morena Dr., Campo* ☎ *619/579–4101, 619/478–5473 recorded information.*

Sutherland. This city-operated reservoir, open March through September on weekends, is a good spot for catching bluegill and bass. ⊠ *22850 Sutherland Dam Rd., Ramona* ☎ *619/668–2050.*

SALTWATER FISHING

Fisherman's Landing. You can book space on a fleet of luxury vessels from 57 feet to 124 feet long and embark on multiday trips in search of yellowfin tuna, yellowtail, and other deep-water fish. Half-day fishing and whale-watching trips are also available. ⊠ *2838 Garrison St., Point Loma* ☎ *619/221–8500* ⊕ *www.fishermanslanding.com.*

H&M Landing. Join up for fishing trips, plus whale-watching excursions from December through March. ⊠ *2803 Emerson St., Point Loma* ☎ *619/222–1144* ⊕ *www.hmlanding.com.*

Helgren's Sportfishing. Your best bet in North County, Helgren's offers trips from Oceanside Harbor. ⊠ *315 Harbor Dr. S, Oceanside* ☎ *760/722–2133* ⊕ *www.helgrensportfishing.com.*

GO FISH

The California Department of Fish and Game (⊕ *www.dfg.ca.gov*) issues "Fishing Passports" showing 150 different species of fresh and saltwater fish and shellfish found throughout the state. In San Diego County fishing aficionados can catch (and, hopefully, release) many of the species listed, receiving a stamp for each species caught.

13

FRISBEE GOLF

Morley Field Disc Golf Course. Disc golf is a popular local sport that's like golf, except it's played with Frisbees. The Morley Field course, in Balboa Park, is open daily from dawn to dusk. Frisbees are available to rent for a small fee, and there's also a small fee for using the course (it's first come, first served). Rules are posted for those new to the sport. ⊕ *www.morleyfield.com.*

Torrey Pines Golf Course has fantastic views to go along with its challenging holes.

GOLF

San Diego's climate—generally sunny, without a lot of wind—is perfect for golf, and there are some 90 courses in the area, appealing to every level of expertise. Experienced golfers can play the same greens as PGA-tournament participants, and beginners or rusty players can book a week at a golf resort and benefit from expert instruction. You'd also be hard-pressed to find a locale that has more scenic courses—everything from sweeping views of the ocean to verdant hills inland.

During busy vacation seasons it can be difficult to get a good tee time. Call in advance to see if it's possible to make a reservation. You don't necessarily have to stay at a resort to play its course; check if the one you're interested in is open to nonguests. Most public courses in the area provide a list of fees for all San Diego courses.

COURSES

Below are some of the best courses in the area. The adult public's green fees for an 18-hole game are included for each course, as well as the courses' championship (blue) yardage; carts (in some cases mandatory), instruction, and other costs are additional. Rates go down during twilight hours, and San Diego residents may be able to get a better deal. Prices change regularly, so check with courses for up-to-date green fees and deals.

★ **Arrowood Golf Course.** Sited next to a nature preserve, this peaceful coastal course in Oceanside is quite scenic. ⊠ *5201 Village Dr., Oceanside* ☎ *760/967–8400* ⊕ *www.arrowoodgolf.com* ⅄ *18 holes. 6721 yds. Par 71. Green Fee: $87/$110* ☞ *Facilities: Driving range, putting* *green, pitching area, golf carts, rental clubs, pro shop, golf academy/ lessons, restaurant, bar.*

Balboa Park Municipal Golf Course. In the heart of Balboa Park, this course is convenient for downtown visitors. ✉ *2600 Golf Course Dr., Balboa Park* ☎ *619/235–1184* ⛳ *18 holes. 6281 yds. Par 72. Green Fee: $40/$50* ☞ *Facilities: Driving range, putting green, pitching area, golf carts, pull carts, rental clubs, pro shop, golf academy/lessons, restaurant, bar.*

★ **Coronado Municipal Golf Course.** Views of San Diego Bay and the Coronado Bridge from the front 9 make this course popular—it's difficult to get on unless you reserve a tee time, 3 to 14 days in advance, for an additional $60. ✉ *2000 Visalia Row, Coronado* ☎ *619/435–3121* ⊕ *www.golfcoronado.com* ⛳ *18 holes. 6590 yds. Par 72. Green Fee: $30/$35. Reservations essential* ☞ *Facilities: Driving range, putting green, pitching area, golf carts, pull carts, rental clubs, pro shop, golf academy/lessons, restaurant, bar.*

Encinitas Ranch. Tucked away in the former flower fields of coastal North County, Encinitas is a hilly course that provides beautiful views of the Pacific as you play its championship holes. ✉ *1275 Quail Gardens Dr., Encinitas* ☎ *760/944–1936* ⊕ *www.jcgolf.com* ⛳ *18 holes. 6587 yds. Par 72. Green Fee: $67/$89. Reservations essential* ☞ *Facilities: Driving range, putting green, golf carts, pull carts, rental clubs, pro shop, golf academy/lessons, restaurant, bar.*

Mission Bay Golf Course. A not-very-challenging executive course with par 3 and 4 holes, Mission Bay is lighted for night play (the final tee time is at 7:45 pm for 9 holes). ✉ *2702 N. Mission Bay Dr., Mission Bay* ☎ *858/581–7880* ⛳ *18 holes. 2719 yds. Par 58. Green Fee: $29/$36* ☞ *Facilities: Driving range, putting green, pitching area, golf carts, pull carts, rental clubs, lessons.*

Riverwalk Golf Clubs. Near the Fashion Valley shopping center, this course has a combination of three different 9-hole courses, which means less waiting. ✉ *1150 Fashion Valley Rd., Fashion Valley* ☎ *619/296–4653* ⊕ *www.riverwalkgc.com* ⛳ *27 holes. Presidio: 3397 yds. Mission: 3153 yds. Friars: 3230 yds. Par 72. Green Fee: $89/$99* ☞ *Facilities: Driving range, putting green, golf carts, rental clubs, pro shop, golf academy/ lessons, restaurant, bar.*

Fodor's Choice
★ **Torrey Pines Golf Course.** One of the best public golf courses in the United States, Torrey Pines was the site of the 2008 U.S. Open and has been the home of the Buick Invitational (now the Farmers Insurance Open) since 1968. The par-72 South Course receives rave reviews from the touring pros. Redesigned by Rees Jones in 2001, it's longer, more challenging, and more expensive than the North Course. Tee times may be booked from 8 to 90 days in advance at ☎ *877/581–7171* and are subject to an advance booking fee ($43). A full-day or half-day instructional package includes cart, green fee, and a golf-pro escort for the first 9 holes. ✉ *11480 N. Torrey Pines Rd., La Jolla* ☎ *858/452–3226 or 800/985–4653* ⊕ *www. torreypinesgolfcourse.com* ⛳ *36 holes. South: 7227 yds., North: 6874 yds. North and South: Par 72. Green Fee: South: $183/$229, North: $100/$125* ☞ *Facilities: Driving range, putting green, pitching area,*

golf carts, pull carts, caddies upon request in advance, rental clubs, pro shop, golf academy/lessons, restaurant, bar.

RESORTS

Barona Creek. Hilly terrain and regular winds add to the challenge at this East County resort course. Fast greens will test your finesse. If your game is on, you can always see if your luck holds in the adjacent casino. ⊠ *1932 Wildcat Canyon Rd., Lakeside* ☎ *619/387–7018* ⊕ *www.barona.com* ⌗ *18 holes. Approx. 7000 yds. Par 72. Green Fee: $120/$160. Reservations essential* ☞ *Facilities: Driving range, putting green, pitching area, golf carts, rental clubs, pro shop, lessons, snack bar.*

★ **Carlton Oaks Lodge and Country Club.** Lots of local qualifying tournaments are held at this difficult course, designed by Pete Dye to include many trees and water hazards. ⊠ *9200 Inwood Dr., Santee* ☎ *619/448–4242* ⊕ *www.carltonoaksgolf.com* ⌗ *18 holes. 6700 yds. Par 72. Green Fee: $55/$85. Reservations essential* ☞ *Facilities: Driving range, putting green, pitching area, golf carts, rental clubs, pro shop, lessons, restaurant, bar.*

★ **La Costa Resort and Spa.** One of the premier golf resorts in Southern California, La Costa is home to the PGA Tour Golf Academy, whose instructors include past and present touring pros and coaches. The resort recently remodeled its Champions Course, host to more than three dozen PGA events. After a day on the links you can wind down with a massage, steam bath, and dinner at the resort. ⊠ *2100 Costa del Mar Rd., Carlsbad* ☎ *800/854–5000* ⊕ *www.lacosta.com* ⌗ *Champions: 18 holes. 6608 yds. Par 72. Green Fee: $225/$250. South: 18 holes. 6524 yds. Par 72. Green Fee: $175/$185. Reservations essential* ☞ *Facilities: Driving range, putting green, pitching area, golf carts, caddies, rental clubs, pro shop, golf academy/lessons, restaurant, bar.*

Fodor's Choice **Park Hyatt Aviara Golf Club.** Designed by Arnold Palmer, this top-quality ★ course includes views of the protected adjacent Batiquitos Lagoon and the Pacific Ocean. The carts, which are fitted with GPS systems that tell you the distance to the pin, are included in the cost. ⊠ *7447 Batiquitos Dr., Carlsbad* ☎ *760/603–6900* ⊕ *www.golfaviara.com* ⌗ *18 holes. 7007 yds. Par 72. Green Fee: $215/$235* ☞ *Facilities: Driving range, putting green, pitching area, golf carts, rental clubs, pro shop, golf academy/lessons, restaurant, bar.*

★ **Rancho Bernardo Inn and Country Club.** The management at this recently renovated course is JC Golf, which operates several other respected courses throughout Southern California. ⊠ *17550 Bernardo Oaks Dr., Rancho Bernardo* ☎ *858/385–8733* ⊕ *www.ranchobernardoinn.com* ⌗ *18 holes. 6631 yds. Par 72. Green Fee: $100/$135* ☞ *Facilities: Driving range, putting green, golf carts, rental clubs, pro shop, golf academy/lessons, restaurant, bar.*

Redhawk. This challenging course is good enough to have earned a four-star rating from *Golf Digest* and a top 10 ranking from *California Golf* magazine. ⊠ *45100 Redhawk Pkwy., Temecula* ☎ *951/302–3850* ⊕ *www.redhawkgolfcourse.com* ⌗ *18 holes. 7110 yds. Par 72. Green Fee: $70/$90* ☞ *Facilities: Driving range, putting green, pitching area,* *golf carts, pull carts, rental clubs, pro shop, golf academy/lessons, restaurant, bar.*

★ **Sycuan Resort & Casino.** A *Golf Digest* favorite, this course also comes highly recommended by anyone who's played here. Hackers will love the executive par-3 course; seasoned golfers can play the championship courses. ⊠ *3007 Dehesa Rd., El Cajon* ☎ *619/219–6028 or 800/457–5568* ⊕ *www.sycuanresort. com* ✓ *54 holes. Willow: 6687 yds., Oak: 6682 yds., Pine: 2508 yds. Willow and Oak: Par 72, Pine: Par 54. Green Fee: Willow and Oak $90/$110, Pine $19/$26* ✏ *Facilities: Driving range, putting green, pitching area, golf carts, pull carts, rental clubs, pro shop, golf academy/lessons, restaurant, bar.*

HANG GLIDING AND PARAGLIDING

Torrey Pines Gliderport. Perched on the cliffs overlooking the ocean north of La Jolla, this is one of the most spectacular spots to hang glide in the world. It's for experienced pilots only, but hang gliding and paragliding lessons and tandem rides for inexperienced gliders are available. Those who'd rather just watch can grab a bite at the snack shop after parking in the large dirt lot, but barriers keep them from looking right over the cliff, which would give better views of their airborne fellows. ⊠ *2800 Torrey Pines Scenic Dr., La Jolla* ☎ *858/452–9858* ⊕ *www. sandiegofreeflight.com.*

HIKING AND NATURE TRAILS

From beachside bluffs and waterfront estuaries to the foothills and trails of the nearby Laguna Mountains and the desert beyond, San Diego County has several vegetation and climate zones—and plenty of open space for hiking. Even if you lack the time to explore the outskirts, a day hike through the canyons and gardens of Balboa Park or the canyons and hills of Mission Trails Park is a great way to escape to nature without leaving the city. A list of scheduled walks appears in the *Reader* (⊕ *www.sandiegoreader.com*).

Guided hikes are conducted regularly through Los Peñasquitos Canyon Preserve and the Torrey Pines State Beach and Reserve.

HIKING

Fodor's Choice
★ **Bayside Trail at Cabrillo National Monument.** Driving here is a treat in itself, as a vast view of the Pacific unfolds before you. The view is equally enjoyable on Bayside Trail (2 miles round-trip), which is home to the same coastal sagebrush that Juan Rodriguez Cabrillo saw when he first discovered the California coast in the 16th century. After the hike, you can explore nearby tide pools, the monument statue, and the Old

Point Loma Lighthouse. ✉ *1800 Cabrillo Memorial Dr., from I–5, take Rosecrans exit and turn right on Canon St. then left on Catalina Blvd.; continue following signs to park, Point Loma* ☎ *619/557–5450* ⊕ *www.nps.gov/cabr.*

Hike Bike Kayak San Diego. Join guided treks through Torrey Pines State Beach and Reserve, and Mission Trails Regional Park, the latter including Cowles Mountain and Fortuna Mountain. ✉ *2246 Ave. de la Playa, La Jolla* ☎ *858/551–9510* ⊕ *www.hikebikekayak.com.*

Los Peñasquitos Canyon Preserve. Trails at this inland park north of Mira Mesa accommodate equestrians, runners, walkers, and cyclists as well as leashed dogs. Look at maps for trails specific to bikes and horses. A small waterfall among large volcanic rock boulders is one of the park's most popular sites—it's an unexpected oasis amid the arid valley landscape. ✉ *12020 Black Mountain Rd., from I–15, exit Mercy Rd,. and head west to Black Mountain Rd.; turn right then left at first light; follow road to Ranch House parking lot, Rancho Peñasquitos* ☎ *858/484–7504* ⊕ *www.sandiego.gov.*

Mission Trails Regional Park. This park 8 miles northeast of downtown encompasses nearly 5,800 acres of wooded hillsides, grasslands, chaparral, and streams. Trails range from easy to difficult; they include one with an impressive view of the city from Cowles Mountain and another along a historic missionary path. Lake Murray is at the southern edge of the park, off Highway 8. ✉ *1 Father Junípero Serra Trail, Mission Valley* ☎ *619/668–3281* ⊕ *www.mtrp.org.*

★ **Torrey Pines State Reserve.** Hiking aficionados will appreciate this park's many winning features: a number of modest trails that descend to the sea, an unparalleled view of the Pacific, and a chance to see the Torrey pine tree, one of the rarest pine breeds in the United States. The reserve hosts guided nature walks as well. All food is prohibited at the reserve so save the picnic until you reach the beach below. Parking is $12. ✉ *12600 N. Torrey Pines Rd., exit I–5 at Carmel Valley Rd. and head west toward Coast Hwy. 101 until you reach Torrey Pines State Beach; turn left, La Jolla* ☎ *858/755–2063* ⊕ *www.torreypine.org.*

NATURE TRAILS

Anza-Borrego Desert State Park. At more than 600,000 acres, this is the largest state park in California. There are 500 miles of dirt roads and countless trails for hiking. Visits here are especially popular during the two-week desert wildflower bloom, which happens between early

---

OVER-THE-LINE

A giant beach party as much as a sport, Over-the-Line is a form of beach softball played with two teams of just three people each. Every July, over two weekends that include wild beer drinking and partying, the world championships are held on Fiesta Island. (The district's councilman pulled some strings to exempt OTL tournament from the city's beach booze ban.) Admission is free, but parking is impossible, and traffic around Mission Bay can become unbearable (shuttle buses are available). Check the Old Mission Beach Athletic Club's website (⊕ www.ombac.org) for more information.

February and late April. The exact timing depends on winter rains, so it's best to call the park ahead for advice. The park is about a two-hour drive east of downtown San Diego, at the far eastern end of San Diego County. ✉ *200 Palm Canyon Dr., Borrego Springs* ☏ *760/767–4205* ⊕ *www.parks.ca.gov.*

San Dieguito River Park. This 55-mile corridor begins at the mouth of the San Dieguito River in Del Mar and heads from the riparian lagoon area through coastal sage scrub and mountain terrain to end in the desert, which is east of Volcan Mountain near Julian. It's open to hikers, bikers, and horses. This expansive park has several entrances, so consult a trail map before setting out. ✉ *18372 Sycamore Creek Rd., Escondido* ☏ *858/674–2270* ⊕ *www.sdrp.org.*

Tijuana Estuary. Mostly contained within Border Field State Park, this estuary is one of the last riparian environments in Southern California. The freshwater and saltwater marshes shelter migrant and resident waterfowl. Horse-riding trails fringe the south end of the Tijuana Estuary in Border Field State Park. The visitor center is open Wednesday through Sunday, but the trails are open daily. ✉ *301 Caspian Way, exit I–5 at Coronado Ave., head west to 3rd St., turn left onto Caspian, which leads into estuary parking lot, Imperial Beach* ☏ *619/575–3613* ⊕ *www.tijuanaestuary.com.*

HORSEBACK RIDING

Bright Valley Farms. Take riding lessons or join a trail ride on the winding paths of the Sweetwater River valley. ✉ *12310 Campo Rd., Spring Valley* ☏ *619/670–1861* ⊕ *www.brightvalleyfarms.com.*

Sweetwater Farms. Join the farm's guides for trail rides through the stunning nature trails of inland San Diego County's Bonita area. ✉ *3051 Equitation La., Bonita* ☏ *619/475–3134* ⊕ *www.sweetwaterhorses.com.*

JET SKIING

Jet Skis can be launched from most ocean beaches, although you must ride beyond surf lines, and some beaches have special regulations governing their use.

California Watersports. Waveless Mission Bay and the smaller Carlsbad Lagoon, east of the intersection of Tamarack Avenue and I–5, are easy to reach from this water recreation center, with a beach and landing ramp. ✉ *4215 Harrison St., Carlsbad* ☏ *760/434–3089* ⊕ *www.carlsbadlagoon.com.*

El Capitan Reservoir. The only freshwater lake that allows Jet Skis is 30 miles northeast of the city near Lake Jennings. Take I–8 north to Lake Jennings Park Road, head east on El Monte Road, and follow signs; there's a day-use fee of $10 per person.

San Diego Jet Ski Rentals. The shop is open daily in spring, summer, and fall; in winter, call ahead for a reservation. ✉ *4275 Mission Bay Dr., Pacific Beach* ☏ *858/272–6161* ⊕ *www.sdjetski.com.*

Seaforth Boat Rentals. You can rent Yamaha WaveRunners and explore San Diego Bay or Mission Bay. Alternatively, from Friday to Sunday, join a waverunner tour of La Jolla coast. ✉ *1715 Strand Way, Coronado* ☎ *619/437–1514 or 888/834–2628* ⊕ *www.seaforthboatrental.com.*

JOGGING

Balboa Park. There are uncongested sidewalks all through the area, but the alternative in the downtown area is to head east to Balboa Park, where trails snake through the canyons. Joggers can start out from any parking lot, but it's probably easiest to start anywhere along the 6th Avenue side. Entry to the numerous lots is best where Laurel Street connects with 6th Avenue. There's also a fitness circuit course in the park's **Morley Field** area.

Del Mar. Park your car near 15th Street and run south along the cliffs for a gorgeous view of the ocean.

Embarcadero. The most popular run downtown is along the Embarcadero, which stretches for 2 miles around the bay.

Mission Bay. This area is popular with joggers for its wide sidewalks and basically flat landscape. Trails head west around Fiesta Island, providing distance as well as a scenic route.

Mission Beach boardwalk. This is a great place to run while soaking up the scenery and beach culture.

Roadrunner Sports. Stop in at Roadrunner for all the supplies and information you'll need for running in San Diego. ✉ *5553 Copley Dr.* ☎ *858/974–4475* ⊕ *www.roadrunnersports.com.*

KAYAKING

There are several places to kayak throughout San Diego. You can spend an especially memorable afternoon exploring the seven caves off La Jolla Cove, where you can often see seals, sea lions, and even dolphin.

Hike Bike Kayak San Diego. This shop offers several kayak tours, from easy excursions in Mission Bay that are well suited to families and beginners on to more advanced jaunts. Tours include kayaking the caves off La Jolla coast, whale-watching (from a safe distance) December through March, moonlight and sunset trips, and a cruise into the bay to see SeaWorld's impressive fireworks shows over the water in the summer. Tours last two to three hours and cost between $50 and $70 per person; cost includes kayak, paddle, life vest, and guide. ✉ *2246 Ave. de la Playa, La Jolla* ☎ *858/551–9510* ⊕ *www.hikebikekayak.com.*

SAILING AND BOATING

★ The city's history is full of seafarers, from the ships of the 1542 Cabrillo expedition to the America's Cup that once had a home here. Winds in San Diego are fairly consistent, especially in winter. You can rent a slip at one of several marinas if you're bringing your own boat. If not, you can rent vessels of various sizes and shapes—from small paddleboats and kayaks to Hobie Cats—from various vendors. In addition, most

A kayak trip is the best way to experience the sea caves off La Jolla Cove.

bayside resorts rent equipment for on-the-water adventures. Kayaks are one of the most popular boat rentals, especially in La Jolla, where people kayak around the Underwater Park and Ecological Reserve at the cove. Most of what's available from these outlets is not intended for the open ocean—a dangerous place for the inexperienced.

For information, including tips on overnight anchoring, contact the **Port of San Diego Mooring Office** (☎ 619/686–6227 ⊕ *www.portofsandiego.org*).

For additional information contact the **San Diego Harbor Police** (☎ 619/686–6272).

BOAT RENTALS

Bahia Resort Hotel. This facility and its sister location, the **Catamaran Resort Hotel** (✉ *3999 Mission Blvd., Mission Beach* ☎ 858/488–2582), rent paddleboats, kayaks, powerboats, and sailboats from 14 to 22 feet. Both are also great places for beginners to try their hand at paddleboarding, thanks to their location on the calm waters of Mission Bay. ✉ *998 W. Mission Bay Dr., Mission Bay* ☎ 858/488–2582 ⊕ *www.bahiahotel.com*.

Carlsbad Paddle Sports. This shop handles kayak sales, rentals, and instruction for coastal North County. ✉ *2002 S. Coast Hwy., Oceanside* ☎ 760/434–8686.

Seaforth Boat Rentals. You can book charter tours and rent kayaks, Jet Skis, fishing skiffs, powerboats and sailboats at Seaforth's five locations around town. They also can hook you up with a skipper for a deep-sea fishing trip. Seaforth also rents paddleboards at their Mission Bay location, and surf boards at the Coronado location. ✉ *1715 Strand Way, Coronado* ☎ 619/437–1514 or 888/834–2628 ⊕ *www.seaforthboatrentals.com*.

BOAT CHARTERS

California Cruisin'. Contact California Cruisin' for yachting charter excursions and dinner cruises. ⊠ *1450 Harbor Island Dr., Downtown* ☎ *619/296–8000* ⊕ *www.californiacruisin.com.*

Harbor Sailboats. You can rent sailboats from 22 to 41 feet long here for open-ocean adventures. The company also offers skippered charter boats for whale-watching, sunset sails, and bay tours. ⊠ *2040 Harbor Island Dr., Harbor Island* ☎ *619/291–9568 or 800/854–6625* ⊕ *www. harborsailboats.com.*

Hornblower Cruises and Events. This outfit operates harbor cruises, sunset cocktail and dining cruises, whale-watching excursions, and yacht charters. ⊠ *1066 N. Harbor Dr., Embarcadero* ☎ *619/686–8700 or 888/467–6256* ⊕ *www.hornblower.com.*

San Diego Harbor Excursion. Get on board here for harbor tours, two-hour dinner and brunch cruises, and a ferry to Coronado. ⊠ *1050 N. Harbor Dr., Embarcadero* ☎ *619/234–4111 or 800/442–7847* ⊕ *www.sdhe.com.*

SURFING

If you're a beginner, consider paddling in the waves off Mission Beach, Pacific Beach, Tourmaline Surfing Park, La Jolla Shores, Del Mar, or Oceanside. More experienced surfers usually head for Sunset Cliffs, La Jolla reef breaks, Black's Beach, or Swami's in Encinitas. All necessary equipment is included in the cost of all surfing schools. Beach-area Y's offer surf lessons and surf camp in the summer months and during spring break.

★ **Hike Bike Kayak San Diego.** Sign up for group and private lessons in La Jolla, year-round. If you know what you're doing but didn't bring your stick, they rent boards, too. ⊠ *2246 Ave. de la Playa, La Jolla* ☎ *858/551–9510* ⊕ *www.hikebikekayak.com.*

Kahuna Bob's Surf School. This surf school conducts two-hour lessons in coastal North County seven days a week; in summer there's surf camp for kids. ☎ *760/721–7700 or 800/524–8627* ⊕ *www.kahunabob.com.*

San Diego Surfing Academy. Choose from private and group lessons and customizable surf camps for teens, kids, and adults. Instructional videos are also available online. The academy, which has been running since 1995, is based near South Carlsbad State Beach and meets for lessons at Seapointe Resort in Carlsbad. ☎ *760/230–1474 or 800/447–7873* ⊕ *www.surfingacademy.com.*

★ **Surf Diva Surf School.** Check out clinics, surf camps, surf trips, and private lessons especially formulated for girls and women. Most clinics and trips are for women only, but there are some co-ed options. Guys can also book private lessons from the nationally recognized staff. ⊠ *2160 Ave. de la Playa, La Jolla* ☎ *858/454–8273* ⊕ *www.surfdiva.com.*

SURF SHOPS

Cheap Rentals Mission Beach. Many local surf shops rent both surf and bodyboards. Cheap Rentals Mission Beach is right off the boardwalk, just steps from the waves. They rent wet suits, bodyboards, and skimboards in addition to soft surfboards and long and short fiberglass

Longboarding vs. Shortboarding

Longboarders tend to ride boards more than 8 feet long with rounded noses. Shortboarders ride lightweight, high-performance boards from 5 to 7 feet long with pointed noses. (Funboards are a little longer than shortboards, with broad, round noses and tails that make them good for beginners who want something more maneuverable than a longboard.) A great longboarder will have a smooth, fluid style and will shuffle up and down the board, maybe even riding on the nose with the toes of both feet on the very edge ("hanging 10"). Shortboarders tend to surf faster and more aggressively. The best shortboarders surf perpendicular to the wave face and may even break free of the wave—known as "aerials" or "catching air." Nonsurfers are often most impressed and amused by the mistakes. "Wipeouts," the sometimes spectacular falls, inevitably happen to all surfers.

rides. They also have good hourly to weekly pricing on paddleboards and accessories. ✉ *3689 Mission Blvd., Mission Beach* ☎ *858/488–9070 or 800/941–7761* ⊕ *www.cheap-rentals.com.*

Hansen's. A short walk from Swami's beach, Hansen's is one of San Diego's oldest and most popular surf shops. It has an extensive selection of boards, wet suits, and clothing for sale, and a rental department as well. ✉ *1105 S. Coast Hwy. 101, Encinitas* ☎ *760/753–6595 or 800/480–4754* ⊕ *www.hansensurf.com.*

TENNIS

Most of the more than 1,300 courts around the county are in private clubs, but a few are public.

Balboa Tennis Club at Morley Field. Practice your backhand at one of the 25 courts, 19 of them lighted. The adjacent Babycakes café serves snacks, salads, sandwiches, and a selection of their famous cupcakes. Courts are available on a first-come, first-served basis for a daily $6-per-person fee. Heaviest use is 9–11 and after 5; at other times you can usually arrive and begin playing. Pros offer clinics and classes. ✉ *2221 Morley Field Dr., Balboa Park* ☎ *619/295–9278* ⊕ *www.balboatennis.com.*

La Costa Resort and Spa. This tennis complex has 17 hard and clay courts, 7 of them lighted, plus professional instruction, clinics, and workouts. ✉ *2100 Costa Del Mar Rd., Carlsbad* ☎ *760/931–7501* ⊕ *www.lacosta.com.*

La Jolla Tennis Club. This club has nine public courts near downtown; five are lighted; the daily fee is $10. The club has a reservations system (call one to three days ahead to reserve a court) for members only. ✉ *7632 Draper Ave., La Jolla* ☎ *858/454–4434* ⊕ *www.ljtc.org.*

Several San Diego resorts have top-notch tennis programs staffed by big-name professional instructors.

A kiteboarder joins the surfers waiting for a wave at Pacific Beach.

Rancho Valencia Resort. One of the top tennis resorts in the nation has 18 hard courts and several instruction programs. Tennis shoes and tennis attire (no T-shirts) are required. ⊠ *5921 Valencia Circle, Rancho Santa Fe* ☎ *858/759–6224* ⊕ *www.ranchovalencia.com.*

VOLLEYBALL

Ocean Beach, South Mission Beach, Del Mar Beach, Moonlight Beach, and the western edge of Balboa Park are major congregating points for volleyball enthusiasts. These are also the best places to find a pickup game.

WATERSKIING

Mission Bay is popular for waterskiing, although the bay is often polluted, especially after a heavy rain. As a general rule, it's best to get out early, when the water is smooth and the crowds are thin.

Seaforth Boat Rentals. Boats and equipment can be rented at the Mission Bay or Coronado locations. ⊠ *1715 Strand Way, Coronado* ☎ *619/437–1514 or 888/834–2628 reservations* ⊕ *www.seaforthboatrental.com.*

WHALE-WATCHING CRUISES

Whale-watching season peaks in January and February, when thousands of gray whales migrate south to the warm weather, where they give birth to their calves. Head to Cabrillo National Monument's Whale Overlook to see the whales pass through Point Loma. If you want a closer look, charter boats and cruises host whale-watching excursions.

Hornblower Cruises and Events. Yachts take passengers to catch a glimpse of gray whales and perhaps an occasional school of dolphins. Rates are $37 on weekdays and $42 on weekends. ✉ *1066 N. Harbor Dr., Embarcadero* ☎ *619/686–8700 or 888/467–6256* ⊕ *www.hornblower.com.*

San Diego Harbor Excursion. Join one of the twice-daily whale-watching trips during the season. Rates are from $37 during weekdays and $42 on weekends. ✉ *1050 N. Harbor Dr., Embarcadero* ☎ *619/234–4111 or 800/442–7847* ⊕ *www.flagshipsd.com.*

> **PETCO PARK TOURS**
>
> Most San Diegans love the PETCO baseball park, but it wasn't always so. After voters narrowly approved the project, more than a dozen lawsuits stalled construction for years. Issues were traffic, downtown congestion, and the fact that San Diego already had a perfectly serviceable baseball stadium. Take a tour before any home game and see whether the $450-million-plus price tag was worth it.

13

WINDSURFING

Also known as sailboarding, windsurfing is a sport best practiced on smooth waters, such as Mission Bay. More experienced windsurfers will enjoy taking a board out on the ocean. Wave jumping is especially popular at the Tourmaline Surfing Park in La Jolla and in the Del Mar area, where you can also occasionally see kiteboarders practice their variation on the theme.

Mission Bay Aquatic Center. The world's largest instructional waterfront facility offers lessons in wakeboarding, sailing, surfing, waterskiing, rowing, kayaking, and windsurfing. Equipment rental is also available, but the emphasis is on instruction, and most rentals require a minimum two-hour orientation lesson before you can set out on your own. Reservations are recommended, particularly during the summer. Skippered keelboats and boats for waterskiing or wakeboarding are also available for hire with reservations. Free parking is also available. ✉ *1001 Santa Clara Pl., Mission Beach* ☎ *858/488–1000* ⊕ *www.mbaquaticcenter.com* ☉ *Sept.–May, Tues.–Sun. 8–5; June–Aug., daily 8–7.*

SPECTATOR SPORTS

BASEBALL

Fodor's Choice ★ Long a favorite spectator sport in San Diego, where games are rarely rained out, baseball gained even more popularity in 2004 with the opening of PETCO Park, a stunning 42,000-seat facility in the heart of downtown. In March 2006, the semifinals and the final game of the first-ever World Baseball Classic, scheduled to be a quadrennial event fielding teams from around the world, took place here.

San Diego Padres. The Padres slug it out for bragging rights in the National League West from April into October. Tickets are usually available on game day, but games with such rivals as the Los Angeles Dodgers and the San Francisco Giants often sell out quickly. For an inexpensive day at the ballpark, go for the park pass ($5–$12, depending on demand, available for purchase at the park only) and have a picnic on the grass, while watching the game on one of several giant-screen TVs. ✉ *100 Park Blvd., East Village* ☎ *619/795–5000 or 877/374–2784* ⊕ *sandiego.padres.mlb.com.*

FOOTBALL

Holiday Bowl. One of college football's most-watched playoff games takes place in Qualcomm Stadium around the end of December. ☎ *619/283–5808* ⊕ *www.holidaybowl.com.*

San Diego Chargers. The Chargers play their NFL home games at Qualcomm Stadium. Games with AFC West rivals the Oakland Raiders are particularly intense. ✉ *9449 Friars Rd., Mission Valley* ☎ *858/874–4500 Charger Park, 877/242–7437 season tickets* ⊕ *www.chargers.com.*

GOLF

★ **Farmers Insurance Open.** This tournament brings the pros to the Torrey Pines Golf Course in late January or early February. ☎ *858/ 886–4653 year-round, 858/535–4500 during tournament* ⊕ *www. farmersinsuranceopen.com.*

HORSE RACING

★ **Del Mar Thoroughbred Club.** For seven short weeks in summer, during the annual meeting of the Del Mar Thoroughbred Club on the Del Mar Fairgrounds, racing forms and racing fans can be seen all over Del Mar. The track attracts the best horses and jockeys in the country. Racing begins in mid-July and continues through early September. The track hosts lots of events such as the summer concert series and the well-loved hat contest that's long been a festive part of opening day celebrations. ✉ *2260 Jimmy Durante Blvd., Del Mar* ✛ *Take I–5 north to Via de la Valle exit* ☎ *858/755–1141* ⊕ *www.dmtc.com.*

Shopping

WORD OF MOUTH

"Coronado is a must! Check out the Hotel Del for high tea. Walk behind the hotel along the amazing beach. A few blocks away are a bunch of shops and restaurants on the ocean side of the city."

—TMP

SEAPORT VILLAGE AND CORONADO

Seaport Village along the Embarcadero's waterfront has more than 50 stores. Coronado, across San Diego Bay, is a charming beach community perfect for strolling and window-shopping. Whether you have two hours or a whole day to browse, there's plenty of bounty on both sides of the bay.

(above) Four miles of cobblestone pathways wind through the 54 shops of Seaport Village. (right) A 15-minute ferry ride will take you from Downtown to Coronado Ferry Landing.

Begin your shopping tour at the 14-acre Seaport Village, where you'll find stores stocking seashells and collectibles, trendy surf wear and jewelry. Then head down to the Broadway Pier, and take the 15-minute ferry ride to Coronado; you can also drive or take the Old Town Trolley Tour over the San Diego–Coronado Bridge. The postcard view of the skyline and the magnificent bridge is well worth the trip. Coronado Ferry Landing has a dozen browse-worthy shops, plus good food options, including some with amazing views. The Coronado Shuttle takes passengers from Ferry Landing to Orange Avenue, the city's main drag for shopping, dining, and people-watching.

BEST TIME TO GO

Both Seaport Village and Coronado attract hordes of visitors on weekends, so opt for a weekday visit or arrive before noon. Ferries ($4.25 each way) from Seaport Village's Broadway Pier depart hourly on weekdays from 9 to 9, and until 10 on weekends.

BEST BOOKS

Upstart Crow and **Bay Books** offer independent bookstore charm.

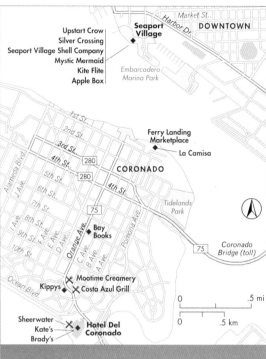

REFUELING IN CORONADO

Stop in at **Mootime Creamery** for a handcrafted ice-cream creation. Mandy Moore, Jason Alexander, and Cuba Gooding Jr. have all been spotted enjoying a Mootime treat.

Relax with a cocktail or fruit smoothie on the patio of the breezy **Sheerwater** restaurant at the Hotel Del Coronado. You can also drink in the view of the spectacular beach.

For a tasty lunch alfresco, the **Costa Azul Grill** serves great nachos and fish tacos.

WHAT YOU'LL WANT

CLOTHES

Brady's. European-designed menswear and sexy leather jackets.

Kate's. The flirty frocks here will dazzle dinner mates.

Kippys. For the rock-star look, check out the fabulous beaded belts.

JEWELRY

Mystic Mermaid. This store sells bracelets made from typewriter keys and handmade beaded, silver, and ceramic earrings.

Silver Crossing. The rings, earrings, charms, and pendants at this standout shop in Seaport Village won't blow your budget.

KIDS' STUFF

Apple Box. Pick up a personalized wooden toy from a collection of more than 1,500 battery-free playthings.

Kite Flite. You can try out the amazing collection of high-flying toys before you buy just outside their door.

UNIQUE SOUVENIRS

La Camisa. You'll find everything here from San Diego Chargers hoodies to Coronado Bridge snow globes.

Seaport Village Shell Company. Shop for seashell jewelry, ornaments, and carved wooden fish.

OLD TOWN

Within Old Town, you'll find gifts, art, crafts, and clothes that are hard to find in other parts of the city, and many of the retail shops also brim over with San Diego souvenirs—key chains, snow globes, T-shirts, and banners supporting the Chargers and Padres.

(above) Don't miss Old Town Saturday Market every Saturday from 9 to 4. (right) Old Town Trolley Tours stop at Old Town San Diego State Historic Park.

Old Town Historic State Park has more than a dozen sites that pay homage to San Diego's early California past (from 1821 to 1872). For those who don't have the time to venture south of the border, the shops are a chance to browse through handcrafted wares made by local and regional Mexican artists, while also soaking up the festive atmosphere. Bazaar del Mundo, Old Town Market, and Fiesta de Reyes are the major shopping areas, but you'll also find unique shops along San Diego Avenue amid the numerous Mexican restaurants there. Old Town is easily reachable by car or via the San Diego Trolley and bus system.

BEST TIME TO GO

Plan to visit any day but Sunday, when crowds are at their peak. Many of the shops close early weekdays, so try to wrap up your shopping before 5 pm. If you're here on Saturday, be sure to check out Old Town Saturday Market.

BEST FOR KIDS

For an old-fashioned sugar rush, head to **Cousin's Candy Shop**.

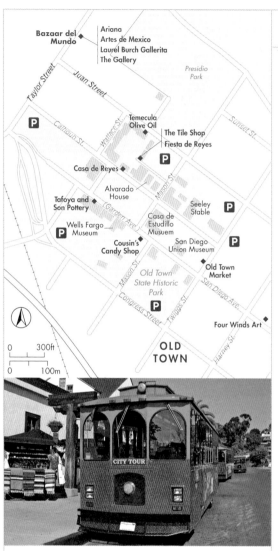

OLD
TOWN

0   300ft
0   100m

REFUELING

A midafternoon margarita and savory plate of nachos at the festive **Casa de Reyes,** inside Old Town State Historic Park, will lift your spirits. For lunch or dinner, try the homemade tamales, sizzling fajitas, or one of the massive combination plates. Blazing fire pits, strolling live musicians, and waitresses in colorful Mexican dresses add to the party feel.

WHAT YOU'LL WANT

CLOTHING AND ACCESSORIES

Ariana. You'll find fiesta skirts, peasant blouses, woven shawls, and unique jewelry at this local favorite.

HOME DECOR

Tafoya & Son Pottery. Drop in here for colorful pottery, baskets, jewelry, and crafts from around the world.

Four Winds Art. Casual buyers and serious collectors come here for Native American art, gourds, beadwork, weavings, and other folk art.

The Tile Shop. Spiff up your home with hand-painted tile house numbers in wrought-iron frames.

MEXICAN WARES

Artes de Mexico. The best stop for Mexican folk art, with hand-carved boxes, ceramic masks, and silver jewelry.

Fiesta de Reyes. You'll find mini sombreros, piñatas, and Day of the Dead figurines.

Old Town Market. Free music performances plus 18 carts and specialty shops with wares from Mexico and South America.

14

Updated
by Amanda
Knoles

San Diego's retail venues are as diverse as the city's vibrant neighborhoods. From La Jolla's tony boutiques to the outlet malls at San Ysidro, you'll find stores that appeal to every taste and budget. Enjoy near-perfect weather year-round as you explore shops along the scenic waterfront. Whether you're on a mission to find the perfect souvenir, or browsing for a sharp outfit to wear out on the town, you'll find much to offer in every area of the city.

Into kitschy gifts and souvenirs? Downtown's Seaport Village has an abundance of quirky shops that won't disappoint, plus you'll be able to enjoy the coastal breezes while you shop for that Coronado Bridge snow globe.

The Gaslamp Quarter, downtown's trendy hot spot, is where you'll find independent shops selling urban apparel, unique home decor items, and vintage treasures. If you can't find it in the boutiques, head for Westfield Horton Plaza, the downtown mall with more than 130 stores and 26 eateries. Nearby, Little Italy is the place to find contemporary art, clothing from local designers, and home decor items.

Old Town is a must for pottery, ceramics, jewelry, and handcrafted baskets. Uptown is known for its mélange of funky bookstores, offbeat gift shops, and nostalgic collectibles, and the beach towns have the best swimwear and sandals. La Jolla's chic boutiques offer a more intimate shopping experience along with some of the classiest clothes, jewelry, and shoes in the county.

Trendsetters will have no trouble finding must-have handbags and designer apparel at the world-class Fashion Valley mall in Mission Valley, a haven for luxury brands such as Hermès, Jimmy Choo, and Carolina Herrera.

Most malls have free parking in a lot or garage, and parking is not usually a problem. Westfield Horton Plaza and some of the shops in the Gaslamp Quarter offer validated parking or valet parking.

SHOPPING PLANNER

OPENING HOURS

Shops near tourist attractions and the major shopping malls tend to open early and close late. Standard hours are typically 10–9 on weekdays and 10–10 on weekends. Smaller shops may close as early as 5 on weekdays and Sunday. It's best to call ahead if you have your heart set on visiting a particular shop.

FINDING UNIQUE GIFTS

The city's major attractions have gift shops with more than just stuffed animals and T-shirts. The museum shops at Balboa Park (☎ 619/239–0512) brim with affordable treasures. The ZooStore and Ituri Forest Outpost (☎ 619/231–1515) at the San Diego Zoo carry international crafts, world music, and hats, while the Bazaar (☎ 760/747–8702) at the San Diego Wild Animal Park sells authentic African artifacts, books, home-decor items, and apparel. The Big Shop (☎ 760/918–5346) at LEGOLAND is great for collectors and collectors-in-training, with the largest selection of LEGO sets in the nation.

SNAG A BARGAIN AT OUTLET MALLS

Some hotels offer free shuttles to shopping centers, outlet malls, and nearby casinos. Check with the concierge for schedules.

Carlsbad Premium Outlets. A 40-minute drive north of downtown San Diego, this complex contains 90 outlet stores, including Banana Republic, DKNY, BabyGap, Michael Kors, Oakley, and Juicy Couture. ■ TIP➡ On Tuesday many stores offer shoppers fifty and over a 10% discount. ✉ *5620 Paseo del Norte, Suite 100, Carlsbad* ☎ *760/804–9000* ⊕ *www.premiumoutlets.com.*

Las Americas Premium Outlets. Near the international border in San Ysidro, this outlet mall has about 120 shops, including two duty-free outlets, and a clutch of fast-food and sit-down restaurants. The usual brand names are here, including **Adidas, Ed Hardy, J. Crew,** and **Polo/ Ralph Lauren,** and there's a huge **Nike Factory Store.** ■ TIP➡ Shuttle service to Las Americas is available from many San Diego area hotels, and the San Diego Trolley's San Ysidro stop is a five-minute walk from the mall. ✉ *4211 Camino de la Plaza, off I–5, San Ysidro* ☎ *619/934–8400* ⊕ *www.premiumoutlets.com.*

♻ **Viejas Outlet Center.** Head east 30 miles from Mission Valley to reach this mall across the street from Viejas Casino. Major brands represented here include Coach, Brooks Brothers, Chico's, Levi's, Osh Kosh, and Eddie Bauer. ■ TIP➡ Free entertainment is offered year-round at the ShowCourt. Kids enjoy the FunZone arcade, bowling, and minigolf. ✉ *5000 Willow Rd., off I–8, Exit 33, Alpine* ☎ *619/659–2070* ⊕ *www. viejasoutletcenter.com.*

14

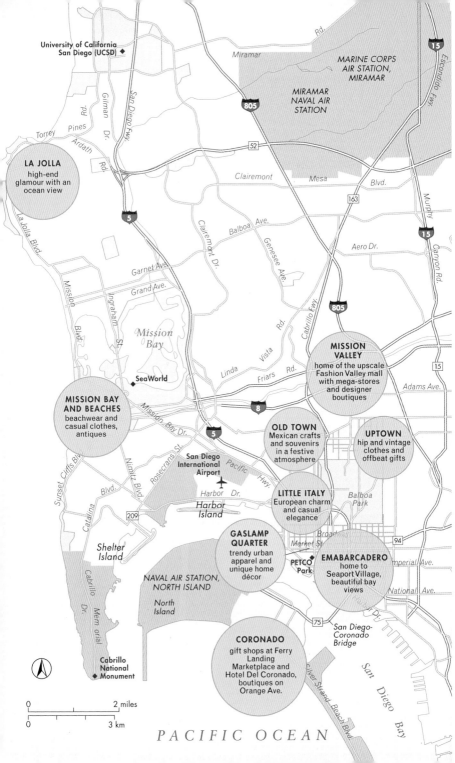

University of California
San Diego (UCSD) ◆

Miramar Rd.

MARINE CORPS
AIR STATION,
MIRAMAR

MIRAMAR
NAVAL AIR
STATION

15

805

52

Clairemont Mesa Blvd.

163

15

Balboa Ave.

Aero Dr.

Torrey Pines Rd.

Ardath Rd.

La Jolla Blvd.

LA JOLLA
high-end
glamour with an
ocean view

5

Gilman Dr.

San Diego Fwy.

Clairemont Dr.

Genesee Ave.

Cabrillo Fwy.

Murphy Canyon Rd.

Escondido Fwy.

Garnet Ave.

Grand Ave.

Mission Bay

◆ SeaWorld

Mission Blvd.

Ingraham St.

Linda Vista Rd.

Friars Rd.

MISSION
VALLEY
home of the upscale
Fashion Valley mall
with mega-stores
and designer
boutiques

15

Adams Ave.

8

MISSION BAY
AND BEACHES
beachwear and
casual clothes,
antiques

Mission Bay Dr.

5

OLD TOWN
Mexican crafts
and souvenirs
in a festive
atmosphere

UPTOWN
hip and vintage
clothes and
offbeat gifts

San Diego
International
Airport

Pacific Hwy.

Balboa
Park

LITTLE ITALY
European charm
and casual
elegance

Sunset Cliffs Blvd.

Nimitz Blvd.

Rosecrans St.

Catalina Blvd.

Harbor
Island

Harbor Dr.

209

Shelter
Island

GASLAMP
QUARTER
trendy urban
apparel and
unique home
décor

Broadway

Market St.

PETCO
Park ◆

94

Imperial Ave.

EMBARCADERO
home to
Seaport Village,
beautiful bay
views

National Ave.

NAVAL AIR STATION,
NORTH ISLAND

North
Island

Cabrillo Mem'rial Dr.

Cabrillo
National
Monument ◆

CORONADO
gift shops at Ferry
Landing
Marketplace and
Hotel Del Coronado,
boutiques on
Orange Ave.

75

San Diego-
Coronado
Bridge

Silver Strand Beach Blvd.

San Diego Bay

⊕

0 ————— 2 miles
0 ————— 3 km

PACIFIC OCEAN

TOP SHOPPING EXPERIENCES

Fashion Valley: Bloomingdale's, Nordstrom, Saks, Neiman Marcus, and haute boutiques are all under one roof.

Gaslamp Quarter: Transform yourself from tourist into hipster in no time with finds from the Gaslamp's trendy boutiques.

La Jolla: At the ocean-side enclave of the rich and famous, prices might leave your credit card reeling . . . but browsing is free.

Old Town: No need for a passport. Mexico's finest crafts, artwork, and jewelry are all here north of the border.

Seaport Village: Souvenir central offers something for all ages.

14

SHOPPING BY NEIGHBORHOOD

DOWNTOWN

The city's ever-changing downtown offers a variety of shopping venues including the open-air Westfield Horton Plaza, a traditional mall; the eclectic-to-edgy shops of the Gaslamp Quarter; and touristy Seaport Village. Within easy walking distance of the Convention Center and downtown hotels, the area is a shopper's delight.

GASLAMP QUARTER

You'll find the usual mall stores as well as hip fashion boutiques and gift shops in the Gaslamp Quarter. The historic heart of San Diego has recently seen an explosion of specialty shops, art galleries, and boutiques; you'll find them in the Victorian buildings and renovated warehouses along 4th and 5th avenues. Some stores close early, starting as early as 5 pm, and many are closed Sunday.

SHOPPING CENTERS

★ **Westfield Horton Plaza.** Macy's and Nordstrom anchor this multilevel complex that has 130 smaller stores, plus fast-food and upscale dining, cinemas, and a game arcade. Park in the plaza garage and use validation machines to get three free hours parking (no purchase necessary). ■TIP➔ Horton Plaza sets aside parking spaces for expectant moms and families with small children; ask the attendant to direct you. ⊠ *Bordered by Broadway, 1st Ave., G St., and 4th Ave., Gaslamp Quarter* ☎ *619/239–8180* ⊕ *www.westfield.com/hortonplaza.*

SPECIALTY STORES

CLOTHING AND ACCESSORIES **Blends.** Minimalist decor provides a perfect backdrop for the wild colors and patterns featured on limited-edition sneakers from Nike, Reebok, Vans, and other in-demand brands. Prices are steep, but many of the styles are unique. ⊠ *726 Market St., Gaslamp Quarter* ☎ *619/233–6126.*

Bloom. Sample the hottest new styles by local designers along with the fashions of international brands, such as Tory Burch, Marc Jacobs,

Chaudry, and Mia Brazilia at this boutique. ⊠ *660 9th Ave., Gaslamp Quarter* 🕾 *619/202–7544* ⊕ *www.bloomsd.com.*

Cariloha. Eco-friendly Cariloha sells bamboo-based products only—men's and women's clothing, athletic apparel, super-comfy bedsheets, and phone cases and other gift items. ⊠ *435 J St., Gaslamp Quarter* 🕾 *619/550–1414* ⊕ *www.cariloha.com.*

Hat Works. Hat Works has been selling fedoras, Stetsons, and just about every other every kind of hat since 1922. ⊠ *433 E St., Gaslamp Quarter* 🕾 *619/234–0457.*

Industry 453. A contemporary shop catering to women seeking avant-garde styles not found in department stores, Industry 453 show-cases fashions by local designers. ⊠ *449 5th Ave., Gaslamp Quarter* 🕾 *619/696–3459* ⊕ *www.industry453.com.*

Puma. The knowledgeable sales associates at this sporty store will help you find stylish athletic shoes or a colorful hoodie with the trade-mark feline logo. ⊠ *410 5th Ave., Gaslamp Quarter* 🕾 *619/338–9601* ⊕ *www.puma.com.*

Quiksilver Boardriders Club. The shop carries Quiksilver's full line of surf clothing, accessories, and famous surfboards. ⊠ *402 5th Ave., Gaslamp Quarter* 🕾 *619/234–3125* ⊕ *www.quiksilver.com.*

Ron Stuart. Sharp-dressed men flock to this men's shop for Joseph Abboud suits, Tommy Bahama shirts, and expert on-site tailoring. ⊠ *225 A St., Gaslamp Quarter* 🕾 *619/232–8850* ⊕ *www.ronstuartmensclothing. com* ⊘ *Closed Sun.*

Urban Outfitters. You'll find street-vibe fashions, accessories, and shoes for men and women, plus home decor and whimsical gift items here. ⊠ *665 5th Ave., Gaslamp Quarter* 🕾 *619/231–0102* ⊕ *www. urbanoutfitters.com.*

HOME
ACCESSORIES
AND GIFTS
Bubbles Boutique. The creations of more than a dozen local designers grab the spotlight at this shop beloved by fashion mavens for its one-of-a-kind clothing, shoes, accessories, and jewelry. You'll also find fun gifts, including message bracelets, scarves, and travel items. ⊠ *226 5th Ave., Gaslamp Quarter* 🕾 *619/236–9003* ⊕ *www.bubblesboutique.com.*

Cuban Cigar Factory. San Diego Padres fans and other aficionados flock to this store and lounge that provides a comfy spot to savor a fine cigar—crafted from tobacco grown from Cuban seed—with a beer or a glass of wine. ⊠ *551 5th Ave., Gaslamp Quarter* 🕾 *619/238–2496* ⊕ *www.cubancigarfactory.net.*

Gaslamp Garage. Crammed floor to ceiling with merchandise and deco-rated to look like a 1950s auto repair shop, the city's largest gift shop is the place to head for a Coronado Bridge snow globe souvenir or San Diego Chargers back scratcher. Among the key chains and logo bean-ies, you'll also find cool T-shirts from Quiksilver and Roxy. ⊠ *301 5th Ave., Gaslamp Quarter* 🕾 *619/241–4240.*

Le Travel Store. Among the travel accessories sold here are luggage, totes, guidebooks, and maps. ▮ **TIP→ The friendly staffers are happy to share tips they've picked up on their worldwide adventures.** ⊠ *745 4th Ave., Gaslamp Quarter* 🕾 *619/544–0005* ⊕ *www.letravelstore.com.*

Vitreum. The Japanese artist Takao owns this gallery-like shop that sells beautifully handcrafted home-decor items—tableware, vases, and decorative gifts. ⊠ *619 W. Fir St., Little Italy* ☎ *619/237–9810* ⊕ *www. vitreum-us.com* ⊗ *Closed Sun.*

EAST VILLAGE

Just a hop, skip, and a jump from the Gaslamp Quarter, the 130-block East Village neighborhood contains shops catering to local hipsters and visitors looking for edgy street wear, novelty T-shirts, and offbeat accessories. Some of the best shopping can be found from 8th to 10th avenues between Broadway and J Street. During the convivial "Evenings in the East Village" events (⊕ *www.sdeastvillage.com*), residents and visitors stroll the area and enjoy art, music, and food.

SPECIALTY STORES

CLOTHING AND ACCESSORIES

5&A Dime. This popular hangout features labels like Rich & Rude, Brixton, Dekline, Motor Union, and Herschel. Choose from a fun selection of hats, shoes, sweaters, and tees for guys and gals, and don't miss the sunglasses and jewelry. ⊠ *701 8th Ave., East Village* ☎ *619/236–0364* ⊕ *www.5andadime.com.*

Rubber Soul. Fashionable men's and women's vintage clothing fills the racks at this shop oozing with a 1960s ambience. Treasures from the 1920s through the 1970s include dresses, hats, jewelry, skinny ties, and jackets. ▉ TIP→ On Friday all the merchandise is 10% off. ⊠ *625 8th Ave., East Village* ☎ *619/544–9222* ⊕ *www.rubbersoulvintage.com.*

Tease Boutique. Casual and dressy fashions, vintage finds and edgy accessories, and sexy swimwear make a play for your dollars at this upscale boutique. ⊠ *435 Island Ave.* ☎ *619/795–2690* ⊕ *www.teaseboutique.com.*

LITTLE ITALY

With more than 33,500 square feet of retail, Little Italy is an especially fun place to visit during holiday celebrations and special events like ArtWalk in April and Chalk la Strada in June. Many shops have a strong European ambience, and shoppers will find enticing wares that include colorful ceramics, handblown glassware, modern home accents, and designer shoes. Kettner Boulevard and India Street from Laurel to Date Street are the heart of the Art and Design District. The website Little Italy San Diego (⊕ *www.littleitalysd.com*) has detailed info about neighborhood shops and events.

SPECIALTY STORES

CLOTHING AND ACCESSORIES

Carol Gardyne Boutique. Shop here for hand-painted silk scarves, accessories, wall hangings, and stylish women's clothing. ⊠ *1840 Columbia St., Little Italy* ☎ *619/233–8066* ⊕ *www.carolgardyne.com.*

Kapreeza. Owner Renata Carlseen stocks her elegant boutique with upscale lingerie and sexy swimwear from European designers. ⊠ *2400 Kettner Blvd., #253, Little Italy* ☎ *619/702–6355* ⊕ *www.kapreeza. com* ⊗ *Closed Sun. and Mon.*

Rosamariposa. This charming jewelry shop specializes in necklaces, earrings, and bracelets crafted by Indonesian artists using natural fibers, wood, seeds, and recycled glass. ⊠ *611 W. Fir St., Little Italy* ☎ *619/ 237–8064* ⊕ *www.rosamariposasd.com.*

14

Vocabulary Boutique. A local favorite for its friendly vibe and stylish inventory, this cozy boutique often stars in regional fashion shoots. It's known for unique, affordable outfits for women, men, and kids. ☒ *414 W. Cedar St., Little Italy* ☎ *619/544–1100* ⊕ *www.vocabularyboutique.com.*

HOME
ACCESSORIES
AND GIFTS

Bella Stanza. The elegant Italian handmade gifts for the home sold here include colorful ceramics, glass, and art pieces. ☒ *1501 India St., Suite 120, Little Italy* ☎ *619/239–2929* ⊕ *www.bellastanzagifts.com* ⊘ *Closed Sun. and Mon.*

Blick Art Materials. Besides supplying local artists with their tools, Blick also carries art books, fine stationery, and beautiful leather-bound journals. ☒ *1844 India St., Little Italy* ☎ *619/687–0050* ⊕ *www.dickblick.com.*

Boomerang for Modern. Discover now-classic furniture and accessories produced by Charles and Ray Eames and George Nelson at this celebration of mid-20th-century modern design. Small exhibitions showcase vintage and recent works in the modernist spirit. ☒ *2475 Kettner Blvd., Little Italy* ☎ *619/239–2040* ⊕ *www.boomerangformodern.com* ⊘ *Closed Sun.*

French Garden Shoppe. Specializing in European home furnishings, this inviting store also offers great gift items like pottery, cookware, candles, and imported gourmet foods. ☒ *2307 India St., Little Italy* ☎ *619/238–4700* ⊕ *www.frenchgardenshoppe.com* ⊘ *Closed Mon.*

Masquerade Art of Living. Masquerade's collections include fine art and wearable art, as well as gifts and mirrors, lamps, and other home accessories. ☒ *1608 India St., Little Italy* ☎ *619/235–6564* ⊘ *Closed Mon.*

Mixture. Housed in a 1940s brick warehouse, Mixture blends art and high design for the home. You'll find stylish bedding, rugs, glassware, and bath and body products here, along with original art and sculpture. ☒ *2210 Kettner Blvd., Little Italy* ☎ *619/239–4788* ⊕ *www.mixturehome.com* ⊘ *Closed Mon.*

EMBARCADERO

Spanning 14 acres and offering more than 50 shops and 18 restaurants, Seaport Village is by far the most popular destination in waterfront Embarcadero neighborhood.

SHOPPING CENTERS

★ **Seaport Village.** Quintessentially San Diego, this complex of shops and restaurants has sweeping bay views, fresh breezes, and great strolling paths. An 1895 Looff carousel and frequent public entertainment are among the side attractions. In the East Plaza, keep an eye out for **Silver Crossing**, for rings, charms, chains, and jewelry; and **Seaport Village Shell Company**, for shells, coral, jewelry, and craft items. **Mystic Mermaid** is good for gifts like silk scarves and unique jewelry. The **Indian Trails** gallery is also good for gifts. At **Kite Flite**, you can try out the goods before you buy. Other shops throughout the complex sell toys, art, clothes for the whole family, and nostalgic collectibles. The **Apple Box** has all sorts of battery-free toys. If you get tired, stop at the waterfront **Upstart Crow Bookstore & Coffeehouse** for people-watching

and a snack. The Seaport is within walking distance of hotels, the San Diego Convention Center, and the San Diego Trolley. ∎ TIP→ Park for two hours for a dollar with purchase validation. ⊠ *849 W. Harbor Dr., at Pacific Hwy., Downtown* ☏ *619/235–4014* ⊕ *www.seaportvillage. com/shopping.*

Upstart Crow Bookstore & Coffeehouse. Contemporary fiction and general history are among the many strengths of this pleasant waterfront bookstore with a fine selection of journals, gifts, and greeting cards. ∎ TIP→ The outdoor coffee bar is great for people-watching while you grab a snack. ⊠ *Seaport Village, 835C W. Harbor Dr., Embarcadero* ☏ *619/232–4855* ⊕ *upstartcrowtrading.com.*

BALBOA PARK

SPECIALTY STORES

HOME ACCESSORIES AND GIFTS
★

Mingei International Museum Store. The shop at the Mingei showcases an international collection of textiles, jewelry, apparel, and home decor items. Artworks are displayed on a rotating basis in the store's gallery and there's a nice selection of books on crafts and folk art. ⊠ *1439 El Prado, Balboa Park* ☏ *619/239–0003* ⊕ *www.mingei.org/store* ☉ *Closed Mon.*

OLD TOWN AND UPTOWN

OLD TOWN

Tourist-focused Old Town, north of downtown off I–5 has festival-like ambience that also makes it a popular destination for locals. At Old Town Historic Park, you'll feel like a time traveler as you visit shops housed in restored adobe buildings. Farther down the street you'll find stores selling Mexican blankets, piñatas, and glassware. Old Town Market offers live entertainment, local artists selling their wares from carts, and a market crammed with unique apparel, home-decor items, toys, jewelry, and food. Dozens of stores sell San Diego logo merchandise and T-shirts at discounted prices, and you'll find great deals on handcrafted jewelry, art, and leather accessories. When you've tired of shopping, there are plenty of Mexican restaurants where you can dine, down a margarita, or both.

SHOPPING CENTERS

Fodor's Choice
★

Bazaar del Mundo Shops. An arcade with a Mexican villa theme, the Bazaar hosts riotously colorful gift shops such as **Ariana,** for ethnic and artsy women's fashions; **Artes de Mexico,** which sells handmade Latin American crafts and Guatemalan weavings; and **The Gallery,** which carries handmade jewelry, Native American crafts, collectible glass, and original serigraphs by John August Swanson. The **Laurel Burch Gallerita** carries the complete collection of the northern California artist's signature jewelry, accessories, and totes. ⊠ *4133 Taylor St., at Juan St., Old Town* ☏ *619/296–3161* ⊕ *www.bazaardelmundo.com.*

Fiesta de Reyes. Within the Old Town San Diego State Historic Park, Fiesta de Reyes exudes the easy feel of Old California. Friendly shopkeepers dressed in period attire host a collection of boutiques and eateries around a flower-filled square whose design reflects Old Town circa the 1850s. Many of the shops stock items reminiscent of that era. Visit **Fiesta Cocina** for festive kitchenware, **Temecula Olive Oil** for local olive oils and artisan foods, **Hot Licks** for gourmet hot sauces, and **Hacienda de Las Rosas** for wines and tastings. The **Tile Shop** carries hand-painted Mexican tiles, **Geppetto's** specializes in classic wooden toys, and **La Panaderia** sells baked goods made using early Mexican cooking methods. Two restaurants, **Casa de Reyes** and the **Barra Barra Saloon,** serve Mexican food. Shops are open daily from June to November. ⊠ *2754 Calhoun St., Old Town* ☎ *866/378–2943* ⊕ *fiestadereyes.com.*

Old Town Market. The atmosphere is colorful, upbeat, and Latin-centric at this eclectic market. Local artisans create some of the wares for sale, everything from dolls and silver jewelry to gourmet foods, home-decor items, and apparel. ⊠ *4010 Twiggs St., Old Town* ☎ *619/278–0955* ⊕ *www.oldtownmarketsandiego.com.*

★ **Old Town Saturday Market.** San Diego's largest artisan market presents live music and local artists selling jewelry, paintings, photography, hand-blown glass, apparel, pottery, and decorative items. The San Diego Trolley's Old Town stop is two blocks north of the market. ⊠ *3950– 3999 Harney St., west of San Diego Ave., Old Town* ☎ *858/272–7054* ⊕ *www.oldtownsaturdaymarket.com* ⊡ *Free* ⊙ *Sat. 9–4.*

OFF THE BEATEN PATH

Kobey's Swap Meet. Not far from Old Town, San Diego's premier flea market seems to expand every week. Sellers display everything from futons to fresh strawberries at the open-air event. The back section, with secondhand goods, is great for bargain hunters. ⊠ *Valley View Casino Center parking lot, 3500 Sports Arena Blvd., Sports Arena* ☎ *619/226– 0650* ⊕ *www.kobeyswap.com* ⊡ *$2 weekends, $1 Fri.* ⊙ *Fri.–Sun. 7–3.*

SPECIALTY STORES

HOME ACCESSORIES AND GIFTS

Cousin's Candy Shop. Sample homemade fudge made in 16 flavors and taffy that's been cooked, stretched, and wrapped right on-site. The old-time candies in nostalgic tins make thoughtful gifts. ⊠ *2711 San Diego Ave., Old Town* ☎ *619/297–2000.*

The Diamond Source. Specializing in fashionable diamond and precious gemstone jewelry, this shop showcases the creations of master jeweler Marco Levy. ⊠ *2474 San Diego Ave., Old Town* ☎ *619/299–6900* ⊕ *www.thediamondsource.com* ⊙ *Closed Mon.*

Four Winds Art. The excellent arts and crafts sold here include paintings, pottery, dolls, jewelry, and rugs created by Native Americans. ⊠ *2448 San Diego Ave., Old Town* ☎ *619/692–0466* ⊕ *www.4windsart.com.*

Tafoya & Son Pottery. This shop in a historic adobe building specializes in talavera and early American-style pottery. Hulchol beaded art, Oaxacan art, and handmade silver jewelry are also for sale. ⊠ *2769 San Diego Ave., Old Town* ☎ *619/574–0989* ⊕ *www.tafoyaandson.com.*

Tienda de Reyes. Festive Tienda de Reyes stocks Old Town's largest selection of Day of the Dead art and carries sculpture, handbags, and barware from Mexico and Peru. ⊠ *2754 Calhoun St., Old Town* ☎ *619/491–0611* ⊕ *www.tiendadereyes.com.*

Old Town is the place to go for colorful Mexican wares.

Variations Imports. Shop here for wall art, clocks, candleholders, Asian figurines, and unusual imports from around the world. ⊠ *3975 Twiggs St., Old Town* ☎ *619/260–1008* ⊕ *www.variationsimports.com.*

Ye Olde Soap Shoppe. The mere scent of Ye Olde's hand-fashioned soaps conjures up a relaxing bath. If you want to craft your own soaps, you'll find a full line of supplies. ⊠ *2497 San Diego Ave., Old Town* ☎ *800/390–9969* ⊕ *www.soapmaking.com.*

HILLCREST

The Uptown neighborhood of Hillcrest has many avant-garde apparel shops alongside gift, book, and music stores.

SPECIALTY STORES

BOOKS **Adams Avenue Bookstore.** Literature, history, and philosophy and theology are the specialties of this popular bookstore that carries used, rare, and out-of-print titles. ⊠ *3502 Adams Ave., Hillcrest* ☎ *619/281–3330* ⊕ *www.adamsavebooks.com.*

CLOTHING AND ACCESSORIES **Mint.** Affordably priced ballet flats and wild stilettos share space here with urban sneakers, retro boots, and colorful espadrilles. ⊠ *525 University Ave., Hillcrest* ☎ *619/291–6468* ⊕ *www.mintshoes.com.*

HOME ACCESSORIES AND GIFTS **Babette Schwartz.** This zany pop-culture store sells toys, books, T-shirts, and magnets. ⊠ *421 University Ave., Hillcrest* ☎ *619/220–7048* ⊕ *www.babette.com.*

Cathedral. Voted the "Best Place to Smell" in a local poll, this store is definitely worth a sniff around. It specializes in candles, fragrant oils, home decor items, and bath goods. ⊠ *435 University Ave., Hillcrest* ☎ *619/296–4046* ⊕ *www.shopcathedral.com.*

Ink by Kymberli Parker. Ink sells high-quality paper items, pens, cards, and unique gifts. Custom invitations and personalized stationery are also available. ⊠ *127 W. University Ave., Hillcrest* 🕾 *619/233–4203* ⊕ *www.inkbykp.com* ☽ *Closed Sun. and Mon.*

MISSION HILLS

The shops and art galleries in Mission Hills, west of Hillcrest, have a modern and sophisticated ambience that suits the well-heeled residents.

SPECIALTY STORES

CLOTHING AND ACCESSORIES
Le Bel Age Boutique. Owner Valeri designs some of the jewelry sold at this charming contemporary clothing boutique, in business since the '80s. ⊠ *1607 W. Lewis St., Mission Hills* 🕾 *619/297–7080* ☽ *Closed Sun. and Mon.*

HOME ACCESSORIES AND GIFTS
Maison en Provence. The French proprietors Pascal and Marielle Giai stock sunny fabrics and pottery from Provence. There are also fine soaps, antique postcards, and Laguiole cutlery. ⊠ *820 Ft. Stockton Dr., Mission Hills* 🕾 *619/298–5318* ⊕ *www.everythingprovence.com* ☽ *Closed Mon.*

Taboo Studio. This upscale gallery displays and sells the handcrafted jewelry of an international group of artists. The stars here are the limited-edition pieces that incorporate precious metals and gemstones. ⊠ *1615½ W. Lewis St., Mission Hills* 🕾 *619/692–0099* ⊕ *www.taboostudio.com* ☽ *Closed Sun. and Mon.*

MISSION VALLEY

Northeast of downtown near I–8 and Route 163, Mission Valley holds two major shopping centers and a few smaller strip malls. Fashion Valley hosts an impressive roster of high-end department stores—among them Neiman Marcus, Saks Fifth Avenue, Nordstrom, and Bloomingdale's—and a passel of luxury boutiques. Westfield Mission Valley is home to mainstays like Macy's and Old Navy, plus bargain-hunter favorites like Marshall's and Nordstrom Rack. The San Diego Trolley and city buses stop at both centers.

SHOPPING CENTERS

Fodor's Choice ★
Fashion Valley. San Diego's best and most upscale mall has a contemporary Mission theme, lush landscaping, and more than 200 shops and restaurants. Acclaimed retailers like Bloomingdale's, Neiman Marcus, and Tiffany are here, along with boutiques from fashion darlings like Michael Kors, Jimmy Choo, Tory Burch, and James Perse. H&M is a favorite of fashionistas in search of edgy and affordable styles. ▌▌TIP➜ Free wireless Internet service is available throughout the mall. Select "Simon WiFi" from any Wi-Fi–enabled device to log onto the network. ⊠ *7007 Friars Rd., Mission Valley* 🕾 *619/688–9113* ⊕ *www.simon. com/mall/fashion-valley.*

Park in the Valley. This U-shape mall is across the street from Westfield Mission Valley. At **Off 5th** (🕾 *619/296–4896*), you can score bargain-price fashions by Ralph Lauren, Armani, and Burberry seen at Saks the previous season. ⊠ *1750 Camino de la Reina, Mission Valley.*

☾ **Westfield Mission Valley.** The discount stores at San Diego's largest outdoor mall sometimes reward shoppers with the same merchandise as that sold in Fashion Valley, the mall up the road, but at lower prices. Shops include Macy's, American Eagle Outfitters, DSW Shoe Warehouse, and Victoria's Secret. ■ TIP➔ Car- and truck-theme Smarte Carte strollers provide a fun and safe shopping experience for kids while offering plenty of room for parents to stow purchases. Find them near Nordstrom Rack and Target. ✉ *1640 Camino del Rio, Mission Valley* ☎ *619/296–6375* ⊕ *www.westfield.com/missionvalley.*

UNIVERSITY HEIGHTS

University Avenue is good for furniture, gift, and specialty stores appealing to college students, singles, and young families.

NORTH PARK

North Park, east of Hillcrest, is a retro buff's paradise, with resale shops, trendy boutiques, and stores that sell a mix of old and new.

SPECIALTY STORES

CLOTHING AND ACCESSORIES **Mimi & Red Boutique.** Laid-back ambience, friendly service, and racks full of moderate to high-end women's fashions have made this shop a favorite with cool San Diegans. Nixon and Everly are here along with RVCA, BB Dakota, and affordably priced bath and body products. ✉ *3032 University Ave., North Park* ☎ *619/298–7933* ⊕ *www.mimiandred.com.*

RUFSKIN. The flagship boutique for the namesake denim line sells sexy jeans, casual and dress shirts for men, swimwear, bold accessories, and custom leather items. ✉ *3944 30th St., North Park* ☎ *619/564–7880* ⊕ *www.rufskin.com* ⏱ *Closed Sun.*

FOOD **Original Paw Pleasers.** At this bakery for dogs and cats you'll find oatmeal "dogolate" chip cookies, carob brownies, and "itty bitty kitty treats." ✉ *2818 University Ave., North Park* ☎ *619/293–7297* ⊕ *www.pawpleasers.com.*

Sprouts Farmers Market. Head to this farmers market–style grocery for fresh produce, bulk grains, nuts, snacks, dried fruits, and health foods. ✉ *4175 Park Blvd., North Park* ☎ *619/291–8287* ⊕ *www.sprouts.com.*

HOME ACCESSORIES AND GIFTS **Pigment.** Eco-friendly goods are the specialty of this sleekly modern shop that sells fashion accessories, bath and beauty products, books, cards, journals, and totes. ✉ *3827 30th St., North Park* ☎ *619/501–6318* ⊕ *www.shoppigment.com.*

SOUTH PARK

South Park's 30th, Juniper, and Fern streets have everything from the hottest new denim lines to baby gear and craft supplies.

SPECIALTY STORES

CLOTHING AND ACCESSORIES **Graffiti Beach.** Hip up the whole family at this fun and eco-friendly shop that promotes up-and-coming designers. The fashions include jeans, swimwear, accessories, organic T-shirts, and jewelry made from recycled materials. ✉ *2220 Fern St., South Park* ☎ *858/433–0950* ⏱ *Closed Mon.*

HOME ACCESSORIES AND GIFTS **The Grove.** Crafters stock up on beads, fabric trims, pattern books, and knitting and crochet supplies at this popular shop, which also offers instruction classes. You'll also find paintings by local artists, organic clothing, children's apparel, books, toys, and home decor items. ✉ *3010 Juniper St., South Park* ☎ *619/284–7684* ⊕ *www.thegrovesandiego.com* ⏱ *Closed Mon.*

MISSION BAY AND THE BEACHES

Mission, Grand, and Garnet are the big shopping avenues in the beach towns. Souvenir shops are scattered up and down the boardwalk, and along Mission Boulevard you'll find surf, skate, and bike shops, bikini boutiques, and stores selling hip T-shirts, jeans, sandals, and casual apparel. Garnet Avenue is the hot spot for resale boutiques, thrift stores, and pawn shops. The Ocean Beach Antique District in the 4800 block of Newport Avenue invites browsing with several buildings housing multiple dealers under one roof. Independent stores showcase everything from vintage watches and pottery to linens and retro posters.

MISSION BAY

SPECIALTY STORES

HOME
ACCESSORIES
AND GIFTS

Ocean Gifts & Shells. This huge beach-theme store is filled with seashells of every size and shape, nautical-decor items, wind chimes, swimwear, toys, and souvenirs. ⊠ *4934 Newport Ave., Mission Bay* ☎ *619/980–2651* ⊕ *www.oceangiftsandshells.com.*

MISSION BEACH

SPECIALTY STORES

CLOTHING AND
ACCESSORIES

Pilar's Beach Wear. Browse a large selection of major-label swimsuits, including styles and sizes for all ages and body types. The friendly staff will help you find the perfect fit. ⊠ *3790 Mission Blvd., Mission Beach* ☎ *858/488–3056* ⊕ *www.pilarsbeachwear.com.*

PACIFIC BEACH

SPECIALTY STORES

FOOD

Trader Joe's. Snacks on the beach are as necessary as sunscreen, so stop here for dried fruits and nuts, or wine and cheese for the evening. ⊠ *1211 Garnet Ave., Pacific Beach* ☎ *858/272–7235* ⊕ *www.traderjoes.com.*

HOME
ACCESSORIES
AND GIFTS

Great News! Cookware and Cooking School. Cooks drool over the bakeware, cutlery, tools, cookbooks, and gadgets sold here. There's an on-site cooking school, and the shop's customer service is excellent. ⊠ *1788 Garnet Ave., Pacific Beach* ☎ *858/270–1582* ⊕ *www.great-news.com.*

LA JOLLA

San Diego's answer to Rodeo Drive in Beverly Hills, La Jolla has chic boutiques, art galleries, and gift shops lining narrow, twisty streets that attract well-heeled shoppers and celebrities and their gawkers. Prospect Street and Girard Avenue are the primary shopping stretches, and North Prospect is packed with art galleries *(➾ see Chapter 11: The Arts, for information on art galleries).* The Upper Girard Design District stocks home decor accessories and luxury furnishings. Store hours vary widely, so it's wise to call in advance. Most shops on Prospect Street stay open until 10 pm on weeknights to accommodate evening strollers.

A note about parking: The locals seem to have a monopoly on downtown free parking spots, so do yourself a favor and head to one of the Prospect Street garages, between Wall and Silverado streets, or along Herschel, Girard, and Fay avenues. Rates range from $1.50 for 20 minutes to a maximum of $15 per day. After 4 pm, there is a flat rate of $10.

14

Stores on Prospect Street in La Jolla buzz with activity until late in the evening.

SHOPPING CENTERS

Westfield UTC. This popular outdoor mall on the east side of I–5 has more than 150 shops and 28 eateries, plus an ArcLight Cinemas and an ice-skating rink. **Nordstrom, Macy's,** and **Sears** anchor the center, and specialty stores of note include **Charles David** (☎ 858/625–0275), for high-fashion women's shoes; **Naartjie** for children's clothing and accessories; **Chuao Chocolatier,** for artisanal chocolates; and **Toys, Etc.** for dolls, train sets, games, and educational toys. **Papyrus** has interesting San Diego postcards and gifts. One of the country's greenest shopping centers, UTC has lush gardens, open-air plazas, and pedestrian-friendly walkways. Additional eco-friendly cred: Tesla, maker of electric automobiles, shows off its models here. ✉ *4545 La Jolla Village Dr., between I–5 and I–805, La Jolla* ☎ *858/546–8858* ⊕ *www.westfield.com/utc.*

SPECIALTY STORES

BOOKS **Warwick's.** An upscale bookstore and a La Jolla fixture since 1896, Warwick's often hosts big-name author signings. ✉ *7812 Girard Ave., La Jolla* ☎ *858/454–0347* ⊕ *warwicks.indiebound.com.*

CLOTHING AND ACCESSORIES **Ascot Shop.** The classic Ivy League look is king in this traditional haberdashery that sells menswear by Hugo Boss, Robert Talbott, and Robert Graham. In-house same-day tailoring is available. ✉ *7750 Girard Ave., La Jolla* ☎ *858/454–4222* ⊕ *www.ascotshop.com* ☉ *Closed Sun.*

Blended Industries. Summer Albertsen and *Bachelorette* star Jesse Kovacs run this posh boutique known for its trendy men's and women's apparel and elegant wine bar. ✉ *1025 Prospect Pl., Suite 220, La Jolla* ☎ *858/255–8205.*

Cinderella Shoe Clinic. Whether they're repairing pricey Louboutins or mending the straps on well-worn Louis Vuitton handbags, the staffers at this trusted shoe-repair shop work miracles. ⊠ *929 Silverado St., La Jolla* ☎ *858/454–0806.*

Fresh Produce. Sunny and spirited Fresh Produce sells beach-inspired clothing made from comfy fabrics. The boutique's easy-to-wear pieces are perfect for vacations and weekends away. ⊠ *1147 Prospect St., La Jolla* ☎ *858/456–8134* ⊕ *freshproduceclothes.com.*

Kerut. Featured in magazines such as *Elle* and *In Style*, this beach-theme boutique carries a mix of Bohemian and classic designs from Missoni, Rag & Bone, Yarnz, Leigh & Lucca, and other designers. ⊠ *7944 Girard Ave., La Jolla* ☎ *858/456–0800* ⊕ *www.kerut.com.*

La Jolla Surf Systems. One block from La Jolla Shores Beach, this local institution stocks hip beach and resort wear plus top-brand surfboards, boogie boards, and wetsuits. The shop also rents boards, bikes, beach chairs, kayaks, and snorkel gear. ⊠ *2132 Ave. de la Playa, La Jolla* ☎ *858/456–2777.*

Lulu Lemon Athletica. High-quality yoga and fitness wear and running gear for men and women are Lulu's specialties. ■**TIP**➜ The shop frequently hosts special events, complimentary yoga classes, and guest speakers. ⊠ *7835 Girard Ave., La Jolla* ☎ *858/459–4407* ⊕ *shop.lululemon.com.*

Rangoni of Florence. The boutique carries its own house brand as well as other, mostly Italian men's and women's footwear brands including Amalfi, Icon, and Pele Moda. ⊠ *7870 Girard Ave., La Jolla* ☎ *858/459–4469* ⊕ *www.rangonistore.com.*

Sauvage. Luxurious Sauvage sells sexy and sophisticated swimsuits, beachwear, jewelry, and accessories for women, and swim trunks, surf shorts, and workout wear for men. ⊠ *1025 Prospect St., La Jolla* ☎ *858/729–0015* ⊕ *www.sauvagewear.com.*

Sigi's Boutique. Women seeking high-end European designer fashions and accessories love this shop's fine cashmere from Scotland, stylish classics from Italy and France, and sportswear from Max Mara. ⊠ *7888 Girard Ave., La Jolla* ☎ *858/454–7244* ⊕ *sigislajolla.com* ☽ *Closed Sun.*

HOME ACCESSORIES AND GIFTS

Africa and Beyond. This gallery carries Shona stone sculpture, textiles, crafts, masks, and jewelry. ⊠ *1250 Prospect St., La Jolla* ☎ *858/454–9983* ⊕ *www.africaandbeyond.com.*

Burns Drugs. You almost expect to see the *Happy Days* gang at this '50s-era store. It's a great place to buy inexpensive postcards, souvenirs, and sunscreen, and the gift section features everything from whimsical figurines and novelty socks to trendy purses and kitchen-decor items. ⊠ *7824 Girard Ave., between Silverado and Wall Sts., La Jolla* ☎ *858/459–4285.*

Everett Stunz. Add a little luxury to your life with the lotions, linens, robes, and sleepwear in cashmere, silk, and Swiss cotton sold here. ⊠ *7616 Girard Ave., La Jolla* ☎ *800/883–3305* ⊕ *www.everettstunz.com.*

La Jolla Cove Gifts. At the ocean end of Girard and one block from La Jolla Cove, this gift shop sells T-shirts, souvenirs, seashells, jewelry, and nautical items. ⊠ *8008 Girard Ave., #120, La Jolla* ☎ *858/454–2297* ⊕ *www.lajollacovegifts.com.*

14

★ **La Mano.** Save yourself a trip to Venice and explore the wide selection of delightful papier-mâché and ceramic Carnival masks, many handmade. You'll also find the traditional Carnival costumes, including black hooded capes, for rent. ⊠ *1298 Prospect St., La Jolla* ☎ *858/454–7732* ⊕ *www.lamanomasks.com* ⊗ *Closed Sun. and Mon.*

Muttropolis. Dogs will love the chic chew toys (a Chewy Vuitton purse, a Cosmo-paw-litan) sold here. They'll also love the accessories, such as high-fashion coats and hoodies for strutting La Jolla's sun-splashed streets. There's haute cat-ture for felines here as well, and lots of catnip toys. ⊠ *7755 Girard Ave., La Jolla* ☎ *858/459–9663* ⊕ *www.muttropolis.com.*

Seaside Home. The coastal lifestyle receives a proper celebration at this upscale shop that sells bedding, crystal, porcelain, and home accessories. ⊠ *1055 Wall St., La Jolla* ☎ *858/454–0866* ⊕ *www.seaside-home.com.*

JEWELRY **CJ Charles.** An exquisitely appointed shop selling designer and estate jewelry, CJ Charles specializes in Omega, Cartier, and Bulgari watches, along with stunning fine jewelry, Baccarat crystal, and gift items. ⊠ *1135 Prospect St., La Jolla* ☎ *858/454–5390* ⊕ *cjcharles.com.*

Pomegranate. Contemporary and antique jewelry is paired here with fashions by American, European, and Asian designers. ⊠ *1152 Prospect St., La Jolla* ☎ *858/459–0629* ⊕ *www.pomegranatelajolla.com.*

Swiss Watch Gallery. One of the largest watch dealers on the West Coast, this family-owned shop carries all the top brands including Omega, Charriol, Cartier, and Tag Heuer. ⊠ *8867 Villa La Jolla Dr., #600B, La Jolla* ☎ *858/622–9000* ⊕ *swisswatchgallery.com.*

POINT LOMA AND CORONADO

POINT LOMA

SPECIALTY STORES

CLOTHING AND **Men's Fashion Depot.** San Diego insiders head to this warehouse-style
ACCESSORIES men's store for discounted suits and affordable tuxedos. Speedy alterations are available. ⊠ *3730 Sports Arena Blvd., Point Loma* ☎ *619/222–9570* ⊕ *www.mensfashiondepot.net.*

CORONADO

Coronado's resort hotels attract tourists in droves, but somehow the town has managed to avoid being overtaken by chain stores. Instead, shoppers can browse through family-owned shops, dine at sidewalk cafés along Orange Avenue, stroll through the arcade at the historic Hotel Del Coronado, and take in the specialty shops at Coronado Ferry Landing. Friendly shopkeepers make the boutiques lining Orange Avenue, Coronado's main drag, a good place to browse for clothes, home-decor and gift items, and gourmet foods.

SHOPPING CENTERS

Fodor's Choice **Coronado Ferry Landing.** A staggering view of San Diego's downtown
★ skyline across the bay and a dozen boutiques make this a delightful place to shop while waiting for a ferry. **La Camisa** (☎ *619/435–8009*) is a fun place to pick up kitschy souvenirs, T-shirts, fleece jackets, and postcards. **The French Room** (☎ *619/889–9004*) specializes in comfy women's shoes and affordable casual wear. **Men's Island Sportswear**

You can rent bikes at Coronado Ferry Landing to tour around Coronado.

(☎ 619/437–4696) sells hats, tropical sportswear, and accessories to complete your seaside getaway outfit. Get in touch with your Celtic roots at **Scottish Treasures** (☎ 619/435–1880), purveyor of apparel, gifts, tableware, and jewelry from Ireland, Scotland, England, and Wales. ✉ *1201 1st St., Coronado* ☎ *619/435–8895* ⊕ *www. coronadoferrylandingshops.com* ⊙ *Shops daily 10–7* ☞ *Farmers' market Tues. 2:30–6; some restaurants daily late-afternoon happy hr.*

Fodor's Choice
★ **Hotel Del Coronado.** At the dozen gift shops within the peninsula's main historic attraction, you can purchase sportswear, designer handbags, jewelry, and antiques. **Babcock & Story Emporium** carries an amazing selection of home decor items, garden accessories, and classy gifts. **Blue Octopus** is a children's store featuring creative toys, gifts and apparel. **Spreckels Sweets & Treats** offers old-time candies, freshly made fudge, and decadent truffles. Women will appreciate the stylish fashions and accessories at **Kate's** and **Isabel B**, while well-dressed men can't go wrong with a shirt or jacket from **Brady's**. For those celebrating a special occasion, **Del Coronado Jewels** features vintage, traditional, and modern jewelry. ✉ *1500 Orange Ave., Coronado* ☎ *619/435–6611 plus extension* ⊕ *www.hoteldel.com/shopping.*

SPECIALTY STORES

BOOKS
★ **Bay Books.** This old-fashioned bookstore is the spot to sit, read, and sip coffee on an overcast day by the sea. International travelers will find a large selection of foreign-language magazines and newspapers, and there's a section in the back devoted to children's books and games. There are plenty of secluded reading nooks and a sidewalk reading area

with a coffee bar. ⊠ *1029 Orange Ave., Coronado* ☎ *619/435–0070* ⊕ *www.baybookscoronado.com.*

CLOTHING AND
ACCESSORIES

Dale's Swim Shop. All things beachy catch your eye in this shop crammed with swimsuits, hats, sunglasses, and sunscreen. ⊠ *1150 Orange Ave., Coronado* ☎ *619/435–1757.*

Island Birkenstock. Do your feet a favor and check out the comfy sandals and walking shoes sold here. All the latest Birkenstock styles are available in sizes to fit men, women, and children. ⊠ *1350 Orange Ave., Coronado* ☎ *619/435–1071.*

Kippys. If you've ever envied the studded and bejeweled belts worn by celebs like Beyonce and Steven Tyler, Kippys will help you custom-design your very own. Choose from a rainbow of Swarovski crystals to adorn your choice of belt styles and patterns. Prices range from $200 to $800 and up, and belts are ready in two to three weeks. ⊠ *1114 Orange Ave., Coronado* ☎ *619/435–6218* ⊕ *www.kippys.com.*

HOME
ACCESSORIES
AND GIFTS

The Attic. Modern and vintage home-decor items and accessories are the Attic's specialties; the shop also sells jewelry and affordable gifts. ⊠ *1112 10th St., Coronado* ☎ *619/435–5614.*

Seaside Papery. This sister store of Seaside Home in La Jolla carries high-end wedding invitations, greeting cards, wrapping papers, and luxury personal stationery. ⊠ *1162 Orange Ave., Coronado* ☎ *619/435–5565* ⊕ *www.seasidepapery.com.*

Shorelines Gallery. The gallery sells reasonably priced wall art and glass, jewelry, metal, and mixed-media pieces created by dozens of American artists. ⊠ *919 Orange Ave., Coronado* ☎ *619/727–4080* ⊕ *www.slsdgallery.com.*

Wine Styles. Part store and part wine bar, the popular Wine Styles carries hundreds of boutique wines, along with craft beers and decadent desserts. Cigars, gifts, and wine-related accessories are for sale as well. ⊠ *928 Orange Ave., Coronado* ☎ *619/365–4953* ⊕ *www.winestyles.net/coronado.*

JEWELRY

D Forsythe Jewelry. Stepping into D Forsythe is like taking a quick spin around the world. The one-of-a-kind pieces sold here come from Denmark, Cambodia, Turkey, Bali, India, England, Thailand, and many other places. ⊠ *1136 Loma Ave., Coronado* ☎ *619/435–9211* ⊕ *dforsythe.com* ☉ *Closed Sun.*

North County and Environs

WORD OF MOUTH

"We took our son to San Diego when he was 12 years old. We visited the Zoo and the Wild Animal Park and he loved them both. We also went to LEGOLAND because our son was always a huge LEGO fan. While he might have been a little old for LEGOLAND, we still had a fun day. The LEGO structures were impressive."

—mikesmom

WELCOME TO NORTH COUNTY AND ENVIRONS

TOP REASONS TO GO

★ **Talk to the animals:** Get almost nose to nose with giraffes, lions, antelope, and gazelle at the San Diego Zoo Safari Park in Escondido.

★ **Build a dream at LEGOLAND California Resort:** Explore model cities including New Orleans, Washington, D.C., and New York City built with LEGO bricks.

★ **Be a beach bum:** Surf Swami's for towering blue-water break, tiptoe through the sand at Moonlight Beach, cruise the coast in a sailboat, or spot a whale spouting.

★ **Tour SoCal-style wineries:** There's more than a drop to drink while winery touring in Temecula, home to more than 35 wineries producing red and white wines, boutique lodging, and classy restaurants.

★ **Discover the desert wilderness:** Anza-Borrego Desert State Park encompasses more than 600,000 acres, most of it wilderness. Springtime, when the wildflowers are in full bloom, is glorious.

1 **North Coast.** From Del Mar to Oceanside are the quintessential beach towns marching north along I-5. These coastal cities have grown up recently and offer sophisticated shopping, art galleries, dining, and accommodations, but you'll still find great beaches where you can watch surfers testing the breaks in winter. LEGOLAND California Resort and other attractions are just east of I-5.

2 **Inland North County and Temecula.** Historically this is the citrus- and avocado-growing belt of San Diego County. Since the opening of the San Diego Zoo Safari Park in Escondido and expansion of the wine-making industry in Temecula Valley more than 20 years ago, visitors have added inland North County to their must-see lists.

3 **The Backcountry and Julian.** The backcountry consists of the mountain ranges that separate metropolitan San Diego and the North Coast from the desert. It's where San Diegans go to hike, commune with nature, share a picnic, and study the night sky. Julian, the only real community within these mountains, is famous for its apple pies.

4 **The Desert.** The Anza-Borrego Desert is desert at its best: vast mostly untracked wilderness where you can wander and camp where you wish; a huge repository of prehistoric beasts, illustrated by a large collection of life-size sculptures along desert roadsides; and the best wildflower display in Southern California in the springtime.

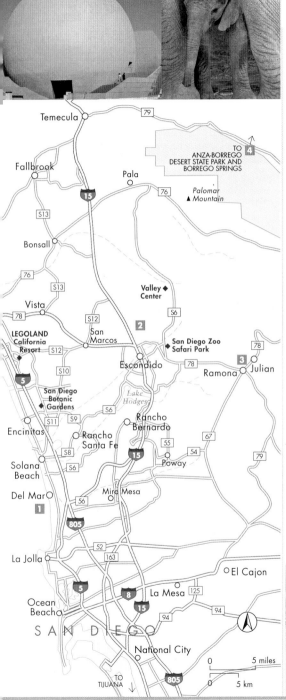

Temecula

79

TO
ANZA-BORREGO
DESERT STATE PARK AND
BORREGO SPRINGS

4

Fallbrook

Pala

76

Palomar
▲ Mountain

15

S13

Bonsall

76

S13

Valley ◆
Center

S6

Vista

78

S12

San
Marcos

2

LEGOLAND
California
Resort

S12

San Diego Zoo ◆
Safari Park

78

Escondido

78

3

Ramona ○ Julian

S10

5

San Diego
Botanic
Gardens ◆

Lake
Hodges

S6

S11

S9

Rancho
Bernardo

Encinitas

Rancho
Santa Fe

55

67

Solana
Beach

S8

15

54

79

S6

Poway

Del Mar○

1

Mira Mesa

56

805

52

La Jolla ○

163

○ El Cajon

5

La Mesa

125

Ocean
Beach

8

15

94

94

SAN DIEGO

National City

0   5 miles

0   5 km

TO
TIJUANA ↓

805

GETTING
ORIENTED

San Diego's North County, encompassing the portion of San Diego County that lies north of the metro area from the ocean to the desert, has some of the same attractions of the city to the south: perpetual sunshine, great beaches, and entertainment, including the ever-growing LEGOLAND Resort complex and the San Diego Zoo's Safari Park. A visit to North County offers a chance to escape the metro area and find a little quiet in the backcountry, serious wine tasting and good eating in Temecula, several luxury resorts and golf courses, some world-class destination spas, art and historic centers, a bit of gold-rush era history, and a more laid-back lifestyle.

15

LEGOLAND CALIFORNIA RESORT

This 128-acre theme park based on the popular LEGO bricks has evolved into LEGOLAND California Resort that includes the original LEGOLAND containing 15,000 LEGO models crafted from 35 million brightly colored bricks, the shark-infested Sea Life Aquarium, and the splash-around LEGOLAND Water Park.

(above) A builder puts finishing touches on Miniland's San Francisco. (lower right) The model of New York City includes the new Freedom Tower, which has yet to be built. (upper right) LEGOLAND entrance.

The LEGO-building-block theme prevails throughout the three venues. However, Sea Life is located outside the main gates, and both Sea Life and the LEGOLAND Water Park have separate entrance fees. You can spend a day visiting all three or spend the whole time at LEGO-LAND. The attractions at LEGOLAND are wrapped around a lagoon with toddler-size rides and attractions to the left as you enter and rides for bigger kids to the right. Kids of any age love the water features. The official LEGOLAND Hotel is scheduled to open in spring 2013.

SERVICE INFORMATION

✉ 1 LEGOLAND Dr. Exit I–5 at Cannon Rd. and follow signs east ¼ mile ☎ 760/918–5346 ⊕ california.legoland. com ⌨ $76 adults, $68 kids; Sea Life $20 adults, $13 kids; Water Park $12; 1-day Hopper (3 venues) $95 adults, $86 kids; 2-day Hopper $110 adults, $100 kids; additional fees for some rides, parking $12, $15 for campers/RVs ☉ Closed Tues. and Wed., call for information.

THE BEST OF LEGOLAND RESORT

Most LEGOLAND attractions appeal to specific age groups so organize your visit around the attractions that will most appeal to your children. If you have very small kids, expect to spend a lot of time in **Fun Town** and exploring **Castle Hill,** where they can drive miniature cars and joust astride mechanical horses. Water features at **Pirate Shores** and rides in the **Land of Adventure** appeal to all ages; kids need to meet height requirements (generally 34"–36") in both areas.

LEGOLAND'S centerpiece, **Miniland USA** may amaze adults more than the kids with its animated depictions of New York, Washington, D.C., New Orleans, the California coastline, built with 24 million LEGO blocks.

Sea Life Aquarium (requires a separate ticket) offers a quiet educational diversion from the theme park. You can spend a couple of hours walking through the displays that include an underwater acrylic tunnel through a 200,000-gallon tank with sharks, stingrays, and tropical fish. You'll also get eyeball to eyeball with rays, eels, a giant Pacific octopus, and seahorses. The animals are most active during feeding time; the website has a feeding schedule.

LEGOLAND Water Park (requires a separate ticket) is perfect on a hot day to splash down waterslides, build a LEGO raft, cruise down a lazy river, get soaked under a splash tower, and even go wading at a sandy beach. There are a restaurant, cabanas, and changing rooms.

LEGOLAND Hotel, set to open in mid-2013, is filled with Lego-style decor and has interactive play areas, a restaurant, a bar, and a swimming pool. Best of all, guests get early admission to the park. For more information check
⊕ *www.legolandtravel.com.*

TIPS

■ Bring swimsuits—you'll get wet at **Pirate Shores,** riding the **Bionicle** or **Aquazone,** and at the **Water Works.** Lockers are at the entrance and at Pirate Shores.

15

■ Little kids up to 10 or 12 years love LEGOLAND, but your older children will probably find it a bit juvenile or may want to spend the whole time in the Water Park.

■ The best ticket value is one of the **Hoppertickets** that give you one admission to LEGOLAND plus Sea Life and the Water Park.

■ Crowds are much lighter midweek.

■ The **Model Mom Care Center** is a comfortable nook to feed and change your baby. It holds a rocking chair, refrigerator, and changing station.

■ Be sure to try Granny's Apple Fries, Castle Burgers, and Pizza Mania for pizzas and salads. The Market near the entrance has excellent coffee, fresh fruit, and yogurt.

SAN DIEGO ZOO SAFARI PARK

The San Diego Zoo Safari Park, an 1,800-acre preserve set in the hills outside Escondido, offers a fabulous peek into the lives of wild animals largely unconfined and free to move about as they would in their native habitat.

(above) An African rhinoceros greets a guest at the Safari Park. (lower right) A giraffe is on view for the Journey Into Africa tour. (upper right) Campers at the Roar and Snore Sleepover.

Originally created to protect and breed endangered animals in the 1970s, the Safari Park has become a living laboratory of species protection and recovery. A visit to the preserve will show you how the animals live in natural surroundings, interact with other species, give birth, and raise their young. More than 3,500 animals of more than 400 species roam or fly above the expansive grounds. The park is a part of the San Diego Zoo, but quite apart from it in many ways. Located in the San Pasqual Valley 35 miles north of the zoo, it has expansive enclosures where animals can roam and a large collection of botanical gardens. The park is dedicated to conservation and has operated a very successful breeding program that is bringing back many endangered species.

SERVICE INFORMATION

✉ *15500 San Pasqual Valley Rd. Take I-15 north to Via Rancho Pkwy. and follow signs, 6 miles*
☎ *760/747-8702*
🌐 *www.sdzsafaripark.org*
💳 *$44 1-day basic pass; there are many multiday and multipark options; special safaris are extra; parking $10* ⏱ *Daily 9–dusk, later in summer.*

THE BEST OF SAN DIEGO ZOO SAFARI PARK

The best way to see these preserves is to take the 25-minute, **Africa Tram Safari** tour. As you pass in front of the large, naturally landscaped enclosures, you can see animals bounding across prairies and mesas as they would in the wild. Predators are separated from prey by deep moats, but only the elephants, tigers, lions, and cheetahs are kept in isolation. Photographers with zoom lenses can get spectacular shots of zebras, gazelles, and rhinos. In summer, when the park stays open late, the trip is especially enjoyable in the early evening, when the heat has subsided and the animals are active and feeding. When the tram travels through the park after dark, sodium-vapor lamps illuminate the active animals.

At the heart of the park, **Nairobi Village** holds things to see and do. Animals in the **Petting Kraal** here affectionately tolerate tugs and pats and are quite adept at posing for pictures with toddlers. At the **Congo River Village** 10,000 gallons of water pour each minute over a huge waterfall into a large lagoon.

Hidden Jungle, an 8,800-square-foot greenhouse, is a habitat for creatures that creep, flutter, or just hang out in the tropics. Gigantic cockroaches and bird-eating spiders share the turf with colorful butterflies and hummingbirds and oh-so-slow-moving two-toed sloths.

Lorikeet Landing, simulating the Australian rain forest, holds 75 of the loud and colorful small parrots—you can buy a cup of nectar at the aviary entrance to induce them to land on your hand.

The **Lion Camp** gives you a close-up view of the king of beasts in a slice of African wilderness. As you walk through this exhibit, you can watch the giant cats lounging around through a 40-foot-long window. The last stop is a research station where you can see them all around you through glass panels.

TIPS

■ Kids can feed animals at the **Petting Kraal,** check out baby animals at the **Animal Care Center,** and ride the **Conservation Carousel** ($3 one ride, $6 all day).

■ You can soar above it all on the **Flightline** zip line ($70), scoot around on a **Segway Safari** ($80), or get an inside view on a Behind the Scenes Safari ($70). Serious shutterbugs might consider joining one of the special two- to three-hour **Caravan Safari** tours ($137–$192). All safari prices are in addition to park admission (reserve in advance).

■ The 2-mile **Kilimanjaro Safari Walk** winds past lowland gorillas, the Lion Camp, cheetahs, and the elephant overlook.

■ Find the best views at Baja Garden, Elephant Overlook, Great Rift Lift Deck, and Kilmia Point.

■ Rental strollers and wheelchairs are available.

■ You can stay overnight on a **Roar and Snore Sleepover** (adults $182–$262, kids 8–11 $152–$192).

15

SPAS SAN DIEGO STYLE

Personal pampering rules at San Diego area spas. San Diego can claim one of the largest concentrations of destination spas in the United States as well as many elegant resort spas.

(above) La Costa Resort's Spanish colonial style is chic yet inviting. (lower right) The beautiful Mediterranean garden pool at La Costa Resort. (upper right) Couples' massage room at Devine spa.

At destination spas, a treatment program including meals, exercise classes, and recreation is developed especially for you based on your needs. Prices are steep, but the stay is all-inclusive except for tax and tips. Check spa websites for reduced rate weeks. Before you visit a destination spa, you'll fill out a form about your health and fitness levels and goals. Meals are healthy and delicious and cater to your weight goals. You also receive a spa wardrobe to wear during your stay.

Resort spas are adjunct to other resort facilities. Many resorts have special treatment facilities for couples; they also typically offer elegant lounges, fitness facilities, and locker rooms. Resort spas are open to nonguests, but reservations are essential. Spa customers can sometimes use other facilities such as the restaurant, pool, or gym. Each spa has its own personality and signature treatments, so look for the one that best suits your needs and budget.

SPA KNOW-HOW

Tipping: If you're unsure of the spa's policy on gratuities, ask. The total of your tips should add up to between 15% and 20% of the total cost of your treatment.

Chilling: You can have a glass of your favorite wine or a cocktail while being rubbed and scrubbed at most resorts.

Modesty: Some resort spas have coed lounges, so be sure to don your robe.

DESTINATION SPAS

Cal-a-Vie Health Spa. Celebrities like Julia Roberts and Oprah Winfrey have stayed at Cal-a-Vie, and so can you. Signature experience: The yin/yang of romping through the hillsides and then cooling off in your antiques-filled villa and being rubbed and wrapped. Services are wide-ranging: fitness, beauty treatments, health and wellness guidance, and nutrition counseling, plus golf and tennis. All inclusive except spa treatments price: $8,095 to $8,595 per week, $5,595 for four days, and $4,195 for three days. Upgrade to one of seven recently added suites for an additional fee. ✉ *29402 Spa Havens Way, Vista* ☎ *760/945–2055 or 866/772–4283* ⊕ *www.cal-a-vie.com.*

Golden Door. Considered by many to be the world's best destination spa, the venerable Golden Door occupies a serene canyon. Signature experience: The serenity of your surroundings will awaken your soul. Explore it from your zen-like Honjin inn–inspired room where you have a traditional private shrine, secluded garden, and deck. Set on 377 wooded acres, the spa offers massages, beauty treatments, fitness work with a personal trainer, and healthy cuisines. Price: $6,000–$7,750 per week, $4,725 for four days, and $3,625 for three days. Check the website for specialty weeks. ✉ *777 Deer Springs Rd., San Marcos* ☎ *760/744–5777 or 800/424–0777* ⊕ *www.goldendoor.com.*

RESORT SPAS

La Costa Resort and Spa. Bring your swimsuit to one of the top spas in the country and join friends in the picture-perfect Mediterranean garden, where you can swim, sun, and shower. Signature experience: The Reflexology Path, where you meander barefoot on smooth stones to improve balance and reduce stress. Price: Body treatments $155–$295; ayurvedic treatment at the Chopra Center $205–$395; day spa $275–$425. ✉ *2100 Costa Del Mar Rd., Carlsbad* ☎ *800/854–5000* ⊕ *www.lacosta.com.*

SPA GLOSSARY

Ayurveda: Refers to Indian techniques including massage, oils, herbs, and diet to encourage perfect body balance.
Hot stone massage: A massage that employs hot smooth stones either rested on the body on applied to the skin with pressure.
Reflexology: Massage on the pressure points of feet, hands, and ears.
Shiatsu: Japanese massage applied with fingers, elbows, feet, and hands.
Swedish massage: A technique that relaxes muscles through stroking, kneading, and tapping.
Swiss shower: A multijet bath that alternates hot and cold water, frequently used after body treatments and mud wraps.
Vichy shower: A body treatment in which a person lies on a cushioned waterproof mat and is showered by overhead jets.
Watsu: A treatment conducted in a warm pool involving gentle massage and stretches.

15

Updated by
Bobbi Zane

A whole world of scenic grandeur, fascinating history, and scientific wonder lies just beyond San Diego's city limits. If you travel north along the coast, you'll encounter the great beaches for which the region is famous, along with some sophisticated towns holding fine restaurants, great galleries, and museums.

Learn about sea creatures and the history of music in Carlsbad, home of LEGOLAND, LEGOLAND Water Park, and Sea Life Aquarium. If you travel east, you'll find fresh art hubs in Escondido, home of the San Diego Zoo Safari Park, a pair of world-class destination spas, a selection of challenging golf courses, and nightlife in bucolic settings. Inspiring mountain scenery plus beautiful places to picnic and hike can be found in the Cuyamaca Mountains, the historic gold-rush-era town of Julian (now known far and wide for its apple pies), and Palomar Mountain, home of the world-famous telescope. The vast wilderness of the Anza-Borrego Desert holds a repository of ancient fossils like no other, and is also home to one of the most colorful displays of native spring flowers. Just beyond the county limits in Temecula you can savor Southern California's only developed wine country, where more than three dozen wineries offer tastings and tours.

NORTH COUNTY AND ENVIRONS PLANNER

GETTING HERE AND AROUND

BUS AND TRAIN TRAVEL

The Metropolitan Transit System covers the city of San Diego up to Del Mar.

Buses and trains operated by North County Transit District serve all coastal communities in San Diego County, going as far east as Escondido. Routes are coordinated with other transit agencies serving San Diego County. Amtrak stops in Solana Beach and Oceanside.

Coaster operates commuter rail service between San Diego and Oceanside, stopping in Old Town, Sorrento Valley, Solana Beach, Encinitas, and Carlsbad en route. The last Coaster train leaves San Diego at about 7 each night. The North County Transit District Sprinter runs a commuter service between Oceanside and Escondido.

Bus and Train Contacts Metropolitan Transit System ☎ *619/233-3004* ⊕ *Transit.sd511.com.* **Amtrak** ☎ *760/722-4622 in Oceanside, 800/872-7245* ⊕ *www.amtrakcalifornia.com.* **Coaster** ☎ *800/262-7837* ⊕ *Transit.511sd.com.*

CAR TRAVEL

Interstate 5 is the main freeway artery connecting San Diego to Los Angeles, passing just east of the beach cities from Oceanside south to Del Mar. Running parallel west of I–5 is Route S21, also known and sometimes indicated as historic Highway 101, Old Highway 101, or Coast Highway 101, which never strays too far from the ocean. An alternate, especially from Orange and Riverside counties, is I–15, the inland route through Temecula, Escondido, and eastern San Diego.

A loop drive beginning and ending in San Diego is a good way to explore the backcountry and Julian area. You can take the S1, the Sunrise National Scenic Byway (sometimes icy in winter) from I–8 to Route 79 and return through Cuyamaca Rancho State Park (also icy in winter). If you're only going to Julian (a 75-minute trip from San Diego in light traffic), take either the Sunrise Byway or Route 79, and return to San Diego via Route 78 past Santa Ysabel to Ramona and Route 67; from here I–8 heads west to downtown.

Escondido sits at the intersection of Route 78, which heads east from Oceanside, and I–15, the inland freeway connecting San Diego to Riverside, which is 30 minutes north of Escondido. Route 76, which connects with I–15 north of Escondido, veers east to Palomar Mountain. Interstate 15 continues north to Fallbrook and Temecula.

To reach the desert from downtown San Diego, take I–8 east to Highway 79 north, to Highway 78 east, to routes S2 and S22 east.

RESTAURANTS

Dining in the North County tends to reflect the land where the restaurant is located. Along the coast, for example, you'll find one luxury fine-dining spot after another. Most have dramatic water views and offer platters of exquisite fare created by graduates of the best culinary schools. Right next door you can wander into a typical beach shack or diner for the best hamburger you've ever tasted. You'll find locally sourced food at restaurants throughout the area, although a few chefs have adopted molecular gastronomy techniques. Backcountry cuisine is generally served in huge portions and tends toward home cooking, steak and potatoes, burgers, and anything fried.

Prices in the reviews are the average cost of a main course at dinner or, if dinner is not served, at lunch.

HOTELS

Like the restaurants, hotels in the North County reflect the geography and attractions where they are set. There are a number of luxury resorts that offer golf, tennis, entertainment, and classy service. For those who want the ultimate pampered vacation, the North County holds two world-class spas: Cal-a-Vie and the Golden Door. Along the beach,

15

there are quite a few stand-alone lodgings that attract the beach crowd; they may lack in appeal and service but charge a big price in summer. Lodgings in the Carlsbad area are family-friendly, some with their own water parks. In Temecula, some of the best and most delightful lodgings are tied to wineries; they offer a whole experience: accommodations, spa, dining, and wine. One-of-a-kind bed-and-breakfasts are the rule in the Julian area.

Prices in the reviews are the lowest cost of a standard double room in high season. For expanded hotel reviews, facilities, and current deals, visit Fodors.com.

VISITOR INFORMATION
San Diego Convention and Visitors Bureau ☎ 619/232–3101
⊕ www.sandiego.org.

NORTH COAST: DEL MAR TO OCEANSIDE

Once upon a time, to say that the North Coast of San Diego County was different from the city of San Diego would have been an understatement. From the northern tip of La Jolla up to Oceanside, a half dozen small communities developed separately from urban San Diego—and from one another. Del Mar, because of its 2 miles of wide beaches, splendid views, and Thoroughbred horse-racing complex, was the playground of the rich and famous. Up the road, agriculture played a major role in the development of Solana Beach and Encinitas.

Carlsbad, too, rooted in the old Mexican rancheros, has agriculture in its past, as well as the entrepreneurial instinct of a late-19th-century resident, John Frazier, who promoted the area's water as a cure for common ailments and constructed a replica of a European mineral-springs resort. Oceanside was a beachside getaway for inland families in the 19th century; its economic fortunes changed considerably with the construction of Camp Pendleton as a Marine Corps training base during World War II. Marines still train at the huge base today.

What these towns shared was at least a half-century's worth of Southern California beach culture—think Woodies (wood-bodied cars), surfing, the Beach Boys, alternate lifestyles—and the road that connected them. That was U.S. Highway 101, which nearly passed into oblivion when I–5 was extended from Los Angeles to the Mexican border.

Then began an explosion of development in the 1980s, and the coast north of San Diego has come to resemble a suburban extension of the city itself. Once-lovely hillsides and canyons have been bulldozed and leveled to make room for bedroom communities in Oceanside, Carlsbad, and even such high-price areas as Rancho Santa Fe and La Jolla.

If you venture off the freeway and head for the ocean, you'll discover remnants of the old beach culture surviving in the sophisticated towns of Del Mar, Solana Beach, Cardiff-by-the-Sea, Encinitas, Leucadia, Carlsbad, and Oceanside, where the arts, fine dining, and elegant lodgings also now rule. As suburbanization continues, the towns are reinventing themselves—Carlsbad, for instance, is morphing from a farming

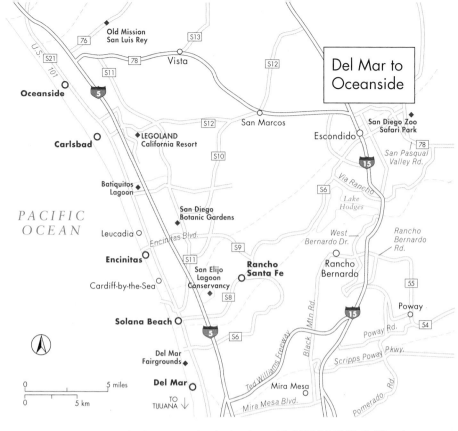

community into a tourist destination with LEGOLAND California, several museums, and an upscale outlet shopping complex. Oceanside, home of one of the longest wooden piers on the West Coast (its first pier was built in the 1880s), promotes its beach culture with a yacht harbor, and beachside resort hotel construction is underway.

DEL MAR

23 miles north of downtown San Diego on I–5, 9 miles north of La Jolla on Rte. S21.

Del Mar comprises two sections: the small historic village adjacent to the beach west of I–5 and a growing business center surrounded by multimillion-dollar tract housing east of the freeway. Tiny Del Mar village, the smallest incorporated city in San Diego County, holds a population of 4,500 tucked into a 2.1-square-mile beachfront. It's known for its quaint half-timbered Tudor-style architecture, 2 miles of accessible beaches, and the Del Mar racetrack and San Diego County Fairgrounds complex. The village attracted rich and famous visitors from the beginning; they still come for seclusion and to watch the horses run. Its new face is the Del Mar Gateway business complex with high-rise hotels and fast-food outlets east of the interstate at the entrance to Carmel Valley. Both Del Mars, old and new, hold expensive homes belonging to staff and scientists who work in the biotech industry and at UC San Diego in adjacent La Jolla. Access to Del Mar's beaches is from the streets that run east–west off Coast Boulevard; access to the business complex is via Highway 56.

TOUR OPTIONS

Civic Helicopters gives whirlybird tours of the area along the beaches. The cost varies according to the model of helicopter and the number of passengers, so call for pricing. Barnstorming Adventures conducts excursions aboard restored 1920s-vintage open-cockpit biplanes and military-style *Top Dog* air combat flights on prop-driven Varga VG-21s. Flights are from Montgomery Field and start at $219 per couple for 20 minutes.

Tour Contacts Barnstorming Adventures ☎ *760/930–0903 or 800/759–5667* ⊕ *www.barnstorming.com.* **Civic Helicopters** ☎ *760/438–8424* ⊕ *www.civichelicopters.com.*

EXPLORING

Del Mar Fairgrounds. The Spanish Mission–style fairground is the home of the **Del Mar Thoroughbred Club** (☎ *858/755–1141* ⊕ *www.dmtc.com*). Crooner Bing Crosby and his Hollywood buddies—Pat O'Brien, Gary Cooper, and Oliver Hardy, among others—organized the club in the 1930s, and the racing here (usually July–September, Wednesday–Monday, post time 2 pm) remains a fashionable affair. Del Mar Fairgrounds hosts more than 100 different events each year, including the San Diego County Fair, which draws more than a million visitors annually. ⊠ *2260 Jimmy Durante Blvd.* ☎ *858/793–5555* ⊕ *www.delmarfairgrounds.com.*

Del Mar Plaza. Along with its collection of shops, the plaza contains outstanding restaurants and landscaped plazas and gardens with Pacific views. The shops and restaurants are pricey, but the view—best enjoyed from the upper-level benches and chairs—is free. ⊠ *1555 Camino del Mar* ⊕ *www.delmarplaza.com.*

Freeflight. This small exotic-bird training aviary adjacent to the Del Mar Fairgrounds houses a collection of parrots and other exotic birds—a guaranteed child pleaser. ⊠ *2132 Jimmy Durante Blvd.* ☎ *858/481–3148* ⌑ *$5* ⊘ *Thurs.–Tues. 10–4, Wed. 10–3.*

Seagrove Park. Free summer evening concerts take place monthly at the west end of this small stretch of grass overlooking the ocean. ⊠ *15th St.* ☎ *858/755–1536.*

WHERE TO EAT

$$$$
FRENCH
Fodor's Choice
★

✕ **Addison.** The sophisticated and stylish dining room and adjacent bar feel Italian and clubby, with intricately carved dark-wood motifs, and the tables, by contrast, are pure white, adorned with a single flower. Acclaimed chef William Bradley serves up explosive flavors in his four-course prix-fixe dinners, such as Prince Edward Island mussels with champagne sabayon and lemon verbena jus or foie gras de canard with Le Puy lentils, port wine, and smoked bacon mousse. Entrées might

The San Diego County Fair comes to Del Mar Fairgrounds every June to July.

include spring lamb *persille* (parsely and garlic topping) with pistachio pâté brisée and caramelized garlic puree or wild Scottish salmon with sauce *vin jaune* (white wine from France's Jura region). Addison challenges wine lovers with 160 pages of choices. $ *Average main: $158* ✉ *5200 Grand Del Mar Way* ☎ *858/314–1900* ⊕ *www.addisondelmar. com* 🍴 *Reservations essential* ☾ *Closed Sun. and Mon. No lunch.*

$$
VIETNAMESE
✗ **Le Bambou.** Small, carefully decorated, and more elegant than any Vietnamese restaurant in San Diego proper, Le Bambou snuggles into the corner of a neighborhood shopping center and is easy to overlook. Those in the know, however, seek it out for authoritative versions of such classics as ground shrimp grilled on sugarcane; Imperial rolls generously stuffed with shrimp and noodles; and make-your-own meat wraps at the table. $ *Average main: $19* ✉ *2634 Del Mar Heights Rd.* ☎ *858/259–8138* ⊕ *www.lebamboudelmar.com* ☾ *Closed Mon. No lunch weekends.*

$$$
AMERICAN
Fodor's Choice
★
✗ **Market Restaurant + Bar.** Carl Schroeder, one of California's hottest young chefs, draws well-heeled foodies to sample his creative and fun California fare, much of it with an Asian flare. The menu changes regularly depending upon what's fresh. Schroeder's seasonally inspired dishes have a playful spirit, whether it's a blue cheese soufflé with seasonal fruit, a Maine lobster salad with mango, or a local black cod with soba noodles. A well-edited wine list offers food-friendly wines by the best and brightest young winemakers around the world. Desserts are exquisite, such as the lemon soufflé tart with buttermilk ice cream or the milk chocolate panna cotta with espresso caramel. $ *Average main: $30* ✉ *3702 Via de la Valle* ☎ *858/523–0007* ⊕ *www.marketdelmar. com* 🍴 *Reservations essential* ☾ *No lunch.*

$$$ ✕ **Pacifica Del Mar.** The view of the shimmering Pacific from this lovely
SEAFOOD restaurant perched atop Del Mar Plaza is one of the best along the
★ coast, and complements the simply prepared, beautifully presented sea-
food. The highly innovative menu is frequently rewritten to show off
such creations as barbecue sugar-spice salmon with mustard sauce and
mustard catfish with Yukon Gold potato–corn succotash. The crowd
ranges from young hipsters at the bar to well-dressed businesspeople
on the outdoor terrace overlooking the surf, where glass screens block
any hint of a chilly breeze. $ *Average main: $30 ⊠ Del Mar Plaza,*
1555 Camino del Mar ☎ 858/792–0476 ⊕ www.pacificadelmar.com
⚐ Reservations essential.

WHERE TO STAY
For expanded hotel reviews, visit Fodors.com.

$$$$ 🏨 **The Grand Del Mar.** Mind-blowing indulgence in serene surround-
☾ ings, from drop-dead beautiful guest accommodations to outdoor
Fodor's Choice adventures, sets the opulent Mediterranean-style Grand Del Mar
★ apart from any other luxury hotel in San Diego. **Pros:** ultimate luxury;
secluded, on-site golf course. **Cons:** service can be slow; hotel is not
on the beach. $ *Rooms from: $425 ⊠ 5200 Grand Del Mar Ct., San*
Diego ☎ 858/314–2000 or 888/314–2030 ⊕ www.thegranddelmar.com
⤶ 218 rooms, 31 suites.

$$$$ 🏨 **L'Auberge Del Mar Resort and Spa.** A sophisticated beach estate is bright
HOTEL and airy with an outdoor feel, even when you're indoors, and most guest
★ rooms, accented by sea grass–color walls and carpeting, have balco-
nies or patios. **Pros:** sunset views from the Waterfall Terrace; excellent
service; walk to the beach. **Cons:** even with good soundproofing the
Amtrak train can be heard as it roars through town; adult atmosphere;
ground-level rooms surrounding the terrace are very public. $ *Rooms*
from: $375 ⊠ 1540 Camino del Mar ☎ 858/259–1515 or 800/245–
9757 ⊕ www.laubergedelmar.com ⤶ 112 rooms, 8 suites.

$$ 🏨 **San Diego Marriott Del Mar.** Guest rooms are quiet and warmly decorated; public areas are homey, with comfortable sofas and fireplaces;
and the location is convenient for business travelers. The pool area
holds a collection of private cabanas with flat-screen TVs and some
outdoor fireplaces, and the Arterra restaurant is popular with locals.
Pros: friendly ambience in public areas; lots of wonderful art; within
walking distance of companies in the Carmel Valley Corporate Center.
Cons: freeway noise in outside public areas; rooms are on the small
side. $ *Rooms from: $199 ⊠ 11966 El Camino Real ☎ 858/523–1700*
⊕ www.marriott.com ⤶ 281 rooms, 3 suites.

SHOPPING
Del Mar Plaza. The tiered, Mediterranean-style Del Mar Plaza has flower-
filled courtyards with fountains surrounding high-end shops, and a
spectacular view of the Pacific. Among several fine restaurants is Flavor
Del Mar, an intimate wine bar. Some businesses validate parking, which
is underground. ⊠ *1555 Camino Del Mar ⊕ www.delmarplaza.com.*

SOLANA BEACH

1 mile north of Del Mar on Rte. S21, 25 miles north of downtown San Diego on I–5 to Lomas Santa Fe Dr. west.

Once-quiet Solana Beach is *the* place to look for antiques, collectibles, and contemporary fashions and artwork. The Cedros Design District, occupying four blocks south of the Amtrak station, contains shops, galleries, designers' studios, restaurants, and a popular jazz and contemporary music venue, the Belly Up Tavern. The town is known for its excellent restaurants, but most area lodging (excluding a Holiday Inn) is in adjacent Del Mar and Encinitas. Solana Beach was the first city in California to ban smoking on its beaches. Now most cities in San Diego have followed suit.

WHERE TO EAT

$ ✕ **Don Chuy.** Family-run and utterly charming, Don Chuy serves authen-
MEXICAN tic Mexican cuisine to patrons who, before dining here, may have tasted only a pale version of the real thing. The flavors are savory and convincing, and the portions sufficient to banish hunger until the following day. For something straight from the soul of Mexican home cooking, try the *nopales con chorizo y huevos,* a scramble of tender cactus leaves, crumbled spicy sausage, and eggs; this is served with piles of rice and beans as well as a warm tortilla and the palate-warming house salsa. $ *Average main: $12* ⊠ *650 Valley Ave.* ☎ *858/794–0535* ⊕ *www.donchuymexicanrestaurant.com* ☯ *No lunch Mon.–Thurs., breakfast on Sun. only.*

$$ ✕ **The Fish Market.** There's no ocean view at the North County branch
SEAFOOD of downtown's waterfront restaurant, but this eatery remains popular
☯ with residents and tourists for its simple preparations of very fresh fish
★ and shellfish from a menu that changes daily. The oyster bar here is popular. The scene is lively, crowded, and noisy—a great place to bring the kids. $ *Average main: $27* ⊠ *640 Via de la Valle* ☎ *858/755–2277* ⊕ *www.thefishmarket.com.*

$$$$ ✕ **Pacific Coast Grill.** This casual beachy-style eatery offers a sweeping
SEAFOOD ocean view and seasonal Pacific Coast fare that reflects California's Mexican and Asian influences. Lunch in the spacious dining room or on the dog-friendly sunny patio brings excellent crispy popcorn shrimp, a Brie-stuffed burger with port wine sauce, or perfect fried-fish tacos washed down with a margarita that sings with fresh lime and lemon juice. Evenings are a scene, as attractive beachy types sip microbrews and well-priced wines along with morsels from the sushi bar. $ *Average main: $37* ⊠ *2526 S. Hwy. 1010, Cardiff-by-the-Sea* ☎ *760/479–0721* ⊕ *www.pacificcoastgrill.com.*

$$$$ ✕ **Pamplemousse Grille.** One of North County's best restaurants, across
FRENCH the street from the racetrack, offers casual French-country dining Cali-
★ fornia style. Chef-proprietor Jeffrey Strauss brings a caterer's sensibilities to the details, like a mix-or-match selection of sauces—such as wild mushroom, grain mustard, or peppercorn—to complement the simple but absolutely top-quality grilled meats and seafood. Appetizers can be very clever, like the Kim Chee seafood martini. Whatever you do, save room for dessert; you can watch the pastry chef build it for you at the

15

demonstration area in the dining room. Popular sweet endings include pear tart tatin, roasted pineapple cake, and chocolate peanut-butter bombe. The comfortable rooms are painted with murals of bucolic country scenes, and the service is quiet and professional. [$] *Average main: $45* ✉ *514 Via de la Valle* ☎ *858/792–9090* 🌐 *www.pgrille.com* ✍ *Reservations essential* 🕑 *No lunch Sat.–Thurs.*

$ PIZZA 🍴 **Pizza Port.** Local families flock here for great pizza and handcrafted brews. Pick a spot at one of the long picnic-type tables, choose traditional or whole-grain beer crust for your pie and any original topping—such as the Monterey, with pepperoni, onions, mushrooms, and artichoke hearts—and tip back a brew from one of the longest boutique lists in San Diego. Even dessert reeks of hops: stout floats with homemade ice cream for the over-21 set, or made with root beer for everyone else. [$] *Average main: $15* ✉ *135 N. Hwy. 101* ☎ *858/481–7332* 🌐 *www.pizzaport.com* ✍ *Reservations not accepted.*

$$$$ STEAKHOUSE 🍴 **Red Tracton's.** Across the street from the Del Mar racetrack, this deluxe old-fashioned steak and seafood house is a high-roller's heaven. Everyone from the bar pianist to the exceptional waitresses is well aware that smiles and prompt service can result in tips as generously sized as the gigantic Australian lobster tails that the menu demurely lists at "market price." The food is simple but good, and the menu highlights roasted prime rib in addition to prime New York sirloin, top-grade pork back ribs, panfried scallops, and such starters as lobster bisque and "jumbo" shrimp on ice. [$] *Average main: $39* ✉ *550 Via de la Valle* ☎ *858/755–6600* 🌐 *www.redtractonssteakhouse.com* ✍ *Reservations essential* 🕑 *Sun. lunch late summer only.*

NIGHTLIFE

Belly Up Tavern. A fixture on local papers' "best of" lists, but has been drawing crowds since it opened in the mid-1970s. Its longevity attests to the quality of the eclectic entertainment on its stage. Within converted Quonset huts, critically acclaimed artists play everything from reggae and folk to—well, you name it. ✉ *143 S. Cedros Ave., Solana Beach* ☎ *858/481–8140* 🌐 *www.bellyup.com.*

SHOPPING

Amba Gallery. Handwoven scarves, shawls, clothing, and textiles are on offer at this gallery that reinvests profits to develop the skills of its India-based artisans so they'll become self-sustaining. ✉ *353 N. Hwy. 101, Solana Beach* ☎ *858/259–2622* 🌐 *www.ambagallery.com* 🕑 *Open Fri. and Sat. 11–4:30, other days by appt.*

★ **Antique Warehouse.** Antique Warehouse holds more than 100 booths that carry American and European antiquities, art, books, glass, dolls, and jewelry. ✉ *212 S. Cedros Ave.* ☎ *858/755–5156* 🕑 *Closed Thurs.*

Cedros Design District. The Cedros Design District is a collection of more than 85 shops that specialize in interior design, apparel, jewelry, and gifts. Local chefs shop the Sunday Farmers Market 1–5. ✉ *444 S. Cedros Ave.* 🌐 *www.cedrosavenue.com.*

Curve Couture. "Runway styles for real sizes" describes the mission of this upscale boutique that stocks designer fashions size 12 and above, including casual, office, and evening wear. ✉ *415 S. Cedros Ave., Solana Beach* ☎ *858/847–9100* 🌐 *www.curve-couture.com.*

Muttropolis. Cool accessories, such as designer beds, toys, apparel, and totes for haute dogs, are at Muttropolis. ✉ *227 S. Cedros Ave.* ☎ *858/755–3647* 🌐 *www.muttropolis.com.*

RANCHO SANTA FE

4 miles east of Solana Beach on Rte. S8, Lomas Santa Fe Dr., 29 miles north of downtown San Diego on I–5 to Rte. S8 east.

Groves of huge, drooping eucalyptus trees cover the hills and valleys of this affluent and exclusive town east of I–5. Rancho Santa Fe and the areas surrounding it are primarily residential, where you'll see mansions at every turn in the road. It's also common to see entire families riding horses on the many trails that crisscross the hillsides.

15

Modeled after a Spanish village, the town was designed by Lilian Rice, one of the first women to graduate with a degree in architecture from the University of California. Her first structure, a 12-room house built in 1922, evolved into the Inn at Rancho Santa Fe, which became a gathering spot for celebrities such as Bette Davis, Errol Flynn, and Bing Crosby in the 1930s and 1940s. The challenging Rancho Santa Fe Golf Course, the original site of the Bing Crosby Pro-Am, is considered one of the best courses in Southern California.

WHERE TO EAT AND STAY

For expanded hotel reviews, visit Fodors.com.

$$$ FRENCH 🍴 **Mille Fleurs.** From its location in the heart of wealthy, horsey Rancho Santa Fe to the warm Gallic welcome extended by proprietor Bertrand Hug and the talents of chef Martin Woesle, Mille Fleurs is a winner. The quiet dining rooms are decorated like a French villa. Menus are written daily to reflect the market and Woesle's mood, so you'll find some interesting seasonal choices, such as antelope with peppercorn-cacao sauce, hazelnut spätzle, and roasted pear. Other selections include a duck salad done three ways (confit, prosciutto, and foie gras) or Maine lobster risotto with saffron with a light sorrel–champagne sauce. Finish the evening with a decadent dessert. [$] *Average main: $35* ✉ *Country Squire Courtyard, 6009 Paseo Delicias* ☎ *858/756–3085* ✍ *Reservations essential* 🕒 *No lunch Sat.–Mon.*

$$$$ RESORT Fodor's Choice ★ 🏨 **Rancho Valencia Resort and Spa.** Luxurious, two-level, Spanish-style casitas, appointed with corner fireplaces, luxurious carpeting, and shuttered French doors leading to private patios, are tucked into 40 acres in one of Southern California's most affluent neighborhoods. **Pros:** splendid surroundings; impeccable service; large rooms. **Cons:** secluded; expensive. [$] *Rooms from: $659* ✉ *5921 Valencia Circle* ☎ *858/756–1123 or 866/233–6708* 🌐 *www.ranchovalencia.com* 🛏 *49 suites.*

SHOPPING

The Country Friends. The Country Friends, operated by a nonprofit foundation, is a great place for unusual gifts and carries collectibles, silver, and antiques donated or consigned by community residents. ✉ *6030 El Tordo* ☎ *858/756–1192* 🌐 *www.thecountryfriends.org.*

Vegetable Shop. The Vegetable Shop is the place to buy the same premium (and very expensive) fruits and rare baby vegetables that the Chino Family Farm grows for many of San Diego's upscale restaurants, and for such famed California eateries as Chez Panisse in Berkeley and Spago in Los Angeles. ⊠ *6123 Calzada del Bosque* ☏ *858/756–3184.*

ENCINITAS

6 miles north of Solana Beach on Rte. S21, 7 miles west of Rancho Santa Fe on Rte. S9, 28 miles north of downtown San Diego on I–5.

Flower breeding and growing has been the major industry in Encinitas since the early part of the 20th century; the town now calls itself the Flower Capital of the World, thanks to the large number of nurseries operating here. The city, which encompasses the coastal towns of Cardiff-by-the-Sea and Leucadia as well as inland Olivenhain, is home to Paul Ecke Poinsettias (open only to the trade), which tamed the wild poinsettia in the 1920s and today is the largest producer and breeder of the Christmas blossom in the world. During the spring blooming season some commercial nurseries east of I–5 are open to the public. The palms and the golden domes of the Self-Realization Fellowship Retreat mark the southern entrance to downtown Encinitas.

U.S. 101—now Route S21—was the main route connecting all the beach towns between southern Orange County and San Diego before the I–5 freeway was constructed to the east of Encinitas. Local civic efforts are bringing back the historic California–U.S. 101 signs and restoring the boulevard's historic character.

GETTING HERE AND AROUND

From San Diego, head north on I–5. If you're already on the coast, drive along Route S21. You'll find lodgings, restaurants, and the beach along Route S21 (Old Highway 101) west of the freeway. The San Diego Botanic Gardens and commercial plant nurseries lie to the east of the freeway.

EXPLORING

San Diego Botanic Gardens. More than 4,000 rare, exotic, and endangered plants are on display on 35 landscaped acres. Displays include plants from Central America, Africa, Australia, the Middle East, the Mediterranean, the Himalayas, Madagascar, and more; the most diverse collection of bamboo in North America; California native plants; and subtropical fruits. The park contains the largest interactive children's garden on the West Coast, where kids can roll around in the Seeds of Wonder garden, explore a baby dinosaur forest, discover a secret garden, or play in a playhouse. An Under the Sea Garden displays rocks and succulents that uncannily mimic an underwater environment. ⊠ *230 Quail Gardens Dr.* ☏ *760/436–3036* ⊕ *www.sdbgarden. org* ⊑ *$12* ⊗ *Daily 9–5.*

San Elijo Lagoon Conservancy. Between Solana Beach and Encinitas, this is the most complex of the estuary systems in San Diego North County. A 7-mile network of trails surrounds the 1,000-acre park, where more than 700 species of plants, fish, and birds (many of them migratory) live. Be sure to stop by the LEED-certified gold New San Elijo Lagoon Nature Centre. The center, open 9 to 5 daily, offers museum-quality exhibits about the region and a viewing deck overlooking the estuary. Docents offer free public walks every Saturday from 10 to 11:30 am. ✉ *2710 Manchester Ave., Cardiff-by-the-Sea* ☎ *760/436–3944* 🌐 *www.sanelijo.org* 🎟 *Free* 🕒 *Daily dawn–dusk.*

Self-Realization Fellowship Retreat. Founded in 1936 as a retreat and place of worship, the retreat center also offers one of the best views along the Pacific Coast, a sweeping seascape extending north and south as far as the eye can see. Paramahansa Yogananda, author of the classic *Autobiography of a Yogi,* created two beautiful meditation gardens that are open to the public. The gardens are planted with flowering shrubs and trees and contain a series of ponds connected by miniature waterfalls populated by tropical fish. Swami's Point at the south end of the gardens is a popular surfer's break. ✉ *215 K St.* ☎ *760/753–1811* 🌐 *www.encinitastemple.org* 🎟 *Free* 🕒 *Tues.–Sun. 10–5.*

15

WHERE TO EAT

$ CAFÉ 🍴 **Bubby's Gelato.** A hardworking French couple makes the region's best gelato and sorbets in this unassuming little shop tucked away in the Lumberyard Shopping Center. Each flavor is clear and intense, with a dense creaminess. Sit on the sunny patio whiling away the afternoon as flavors of honey-lavender, green tea, or roasted banana wash over you. The rainbow of flavors ranges from chocolate-hazelnut to vanilla tinged with rose. On the lighter side, try the sunset-color apricot sorbet or the deep-red raspberry. Bubby's also serves an assortment of tasty sandwiches. [$] *Average main: $5* ✉ *937 S. Coast Hwy. 101* ☎ *760/436–3563* 💳 *No credit cards.*

$$ VEGETARIAN 🍴 **Ki's Restaurant.** Veggies with a view could be the subtitle for this venerable Cardiff-by-the-Sea restaurant that grew from a simple juice shack. Ki's is well known for heart-healthy, locally sourced, ovo-lacto, vegetarian-friendly dishes like huevos rancheros, filling tofu scrambles, egg salad wraps, chopped salads with feta and nuts, watermelon juice, and carrot ice-ream smoothies. The menu also includes turkey wraps piled on wheat bread and dinner entrées such as pork chops with apple amaretto glaze and spicy seafood stew, all prepared with minimal fat. Get a table up top for incomparable ocean views, but be prepared for a wait, as service is rather poor. [$] *Average main: $20* ✉ *2591 S. Coast Hwy. 101, Cardiff-by-the-Sea* ☎ *760/436–5236.*

$ MEXICAN 🍴 **La Especial Norte.** Casual to the point of funkiness, this Mexican café is a great hit with locals who flock here to slurp up large bowls of delicious homemade soups. Try the chicken, beans, and rice, or the Seven Seas fish soup accompanied by tortillas and a dish of cabbage salad. You can also order renditions of the standard burrito, enchilada, and taco, washed down with premium margaritas. [$] *Average main: $13* ✉ *644 N. Coast Hwy. 101* ☎ *760/942–1040* 🌐 *www.laespecial101.com.*

WHERE TO STAY

For expanded hotel reviews, visit Fodors.com.

$ **Moonlight Beach Motel.** This folksy, laid-back motel just steps from the surf looks better on the outside than inside. **Pros:** within walking distance of the beach; great ocean views; public barbecues. **Cons:** plain motel; small rooms. [$] *Rooms from: $145* ✉ *233 2nd St.* ☎ *760/753–0623 or 800/323–1259* 🌐 *www.moonlightbeachmotel.com* 🛏 *24 rooms.*

$ **Ocean Inn Hotel.** Across from the train tracks on the main drag through the north end of Leucadia, this basic motel is apt to be somewhat noisy. **Pros:** basic motel; close to beach. **Cons:** on busy highway. [$] *Rooms from: $89* ✉ *1444 N. Coast Hwy. 101* ☎ *760/436–1988 or 800/546–1598* 🌐 *www.oceaninnhotel.com* 🛏 *50 rooms* 🍴 *Breakfast.*

SHOPPING

Souvenir items are sold at shops along U.S. 101 and in the Lumberyard Shopping Center. Encinitas also abounds in commercial plant nurseries where you can pick up a bit of San Diego to take home.

Anderson's La Costa Nursery. Anderson's La Costa Nursery offers rare and hard-to-find orchids, bromeliads, cactus, and succulents. ✉ *400 La Costa Ave.* ☎ *760/753–3153* 🌐 *www.andersonslacostanursery.com.*

Hansen's. Hansen's, one of San Diego's oldest surfboard manufacturers, is owned by Don Hansen, surfboard shaper extraordinaire, who came here from Hawaii in 1962. The store also stocks a full line of surf apparel, wet suits, surf cams, and casual wear. ✉ *1105 S. Coast Hwy. 101* ☎ *800/480–4754* 🌐 *www.hansensurf.com.*

Weideners' Gardens. Weideners' Gardens carries begonias, fuchsias, and other flowers. It's closed sporadically in fall and winter; call for hours. ✉ *695 Normandy Rd.* ☎ *760/436–2194* 🌐 *www.weidners.com.*

CARLSBAD

6 miles from Encinitas on Rte. S21, 36 miles north of downtown San Diego on I–5.

Once-sleepy, Carlsbad, lying astride I–5 at the north end of a string of beach towns extending from San Diego to Oceanside, has long been popular with beachgoers and sunseekers. On a clear day in this village you can take in sweeping ocean views that stretch from La Jolla to Oceanside by walking the 2-mile-long sea walk running between the Encina power plant and Pine Street. En route, you'll find several stairways leading to the beach and quite a few benches. More recently, however, much of the attention of visitors to the area has shifted inland, east of I–5, to LEGOLAND California and other attractions in its vicinity—two of the San Diego area's most luxurious resort hotels, one of the last remaining wetlands along the Southern California coast, a discount shopping mall, golf courses, the cattle ranch built by movie star Leo Carrillo, and colorful spring-blooming Flower Fields at Carlsbad Ranch. Until the mid-20th century, when suburban development began to sprout on the hillsides, farming was the main industry in Carlsbad, with truckloads of vegetables shipped out year-round. Some agriculture remains. Area farmers develop and grow new varieties of flowers, including the ranunculus that transform a hillside into a rainbow each spring, and Carlsbad strawberries are among the sweetest you'll find in Southern California; in spring you can pick them yourself in fields on both sides of I–5.

GETTING HERE AND AROUND

LEGOLAND California Resort, off Cannon Road east of I–5, is surrounded by the Flower Fields, hotels, and the Museum of Making Music. On the west side of the freeway you'll find beach access at several points and quaint Carlsbad village shops.

ESSENTIALS

Visitor Information **Carlsbad Convention and Visitors Bureau** ⊠ *400 Carlsbad Village Dr.* ☎ *760/434–6093 or 800/227–5722* ⊕ *visitcarlsbad.com.*

15

EXPLORING

Batiquitos Lagoon. Development has destroyed many of the lagoons and saltwater marsh wildlife habitats that used to punctuate the North County coastline, but the 610-acre lagoon has been restored to support fish and bird populations. A stroll along the 2-mile trail from the Batiquitos Lagoon Foundation Nature Center along the north shore of the lagoon reveals nesting sites of the red-winged blackbird; lagoon birds such as the great blue heron, the great egret, and the snowy egret; and life in the mud flats. This is a quiet spot for contemplation or a picnic. Free docent tours are offered on weekends. Take the Poinsettia Lane exit off I–5, go east, and turn right onto Batiquitos Drive, then right again onto Gabbiano Lane. ⊠ *7380 Gabbiano La.* ☎ *760/931–0800* ⊕ *www.batiquitosfoundation.org* ⊙ *Weekdays 9–12:30, weekends 9–3.*

Carlsbad Mineral Water Spa. Remnants from late 1800s, including the original well dug by John Frazier and a monument to him, are found here. The elaborately decorated stone building houses a small day spa and the Carlsbad Water Company, a 21st-century version of Frazier's waterworks, where the Carlsbad water is still sold. ⊠ *2802 Carlsbad Blvd.* ☎ *760/434–1887* ⊕ *www.carlsbadmineralspa.com.*

Fodor's Choice ★ **Flower Fields at Carlsbad Ranch.** In spring the hillsides are abloom on this, the largest bulb production farm in Southern California, when thousands of Giant Tecolote ranunculus produce a stunning 50-acre display of color against the backdrop of the blue Pacific Ocean. Other knockouts include the rose gardens—with examples of every All-American Rose Selection award-winner since 1940—and a historical display of Paul Ecke poinsettias. Family activities include a LEGO Flower Garden and a kids' playground. ⊠ *5704 Paseo del Norte, east of I–5* ☎ *760/431–0352* ⊕ *www.theflowerfields.com* 🎟 *$11* ⊙ *Mar.–May, daily 9–6.*

LEGOLAND California Resort.
Fodor's Choice ★
⇨ *See the highlighted listing in this chapter.*

Leo Carrillo Ranch Historic Park. This was a real working ranch with 600 head of cattle owned by actor Leo Carrillo, who played Pancho in the *Cisco Kid* television series in the 1950s. Before Carrillo bought the spread, known as Rancho de Los Kiotes, in 1937, the rancho was the home of a band of Luiseno Indians. Carrillo's hacienda and other buildings have been restored to reflect the life of the star when he hosted his Hollywood friends for long weekends in the country. Four miles of trails take visitors through colorful native gardens to the cantina, washhouse, pool and cabana, barn, and stable that Carrillo used. You can see the insides of these buildings on weekends when guided tours are offered. After Carrillo's death in 1961, the ranch remained in the family until 1979, when part of the acreage was acquired by the city for a park. ✉ *6200 Flying Leo Carrillo La.* ☎ *760/476–1042* 🌐 *www.leocarrilloranch.org* 🎟 *Free* 🕒 *Tues.–Sat. 9–5, Sun. 11–5.*

Museum of Making Music. Take an interactive journey through 100 years of popular music that displays more than 500 vintage instruments and samples of memorable tunes from the past century. Hands-on activities include playing a digital piano, drums, guitar, and electric violin. ✉ *5790 Armada Dr., east of I–5* ☎ *760/438–5996* 🌐 *www.museumofmakingmusic.org* 🎟 *$8* 🕒 *Tues.–Sun. 10–5.*

WHERE TO EAT

$$$$ AMERICAN
🍴 **Argyle Steakhouse.** Even if you don't play golf, the Argyle, occupying the Aviara Golf clubhouse, is a good choice for breakfast or lunch on a sunny day. The 18th green, Batiquitos Lagoon, and the Pacific create beautiful vistas from nearly every table, whether you are inside at the clubby bar or outside on the deck. The breakfast menu lists classics like smoked salmon, omelets, and breakfast burrito. Soups, salads, sandwiches, and "lite" entrées fill the bill at lunch. By dinnertime the Argyle becomes a steak house purveying dry-aged prime Wagyu beef. [$] *Average main: $46* ✉ *7100 Aviara Resort Dr.* ☎ *760/603–6800* 🌐 *www.parkhyattaviara.com* ✍ *Reservations essential* 🕒 *Closed Mon.*

$$ AMERICAN
🍴 **Bistro West.** This busy spot, part of the West Inn complex, might be called the boisterous bistro, especially if you get there during happy hour when it appears that all of Carlsbad is tipping back a few. The bistro specializes in comfort food; a huge chicken potpie tops the list that also includes meat loaf, several burger variations, pastas, and pizza. You can select from a long wine list of mostly California products at fair prices; many are available by the glass. [$] *Average main: $23* ✉ *4960 Av. Encinas* ☎ *760/930–8008* 🌐 *www.bistrowest.com* ✍ *Reservations essential* 👔 *Jacket required.*

$$$ MEDITERRANEAN
Fodor's Choice ★
🍴 **BlueFire Grill.** Fire and water drama defines this signature restaurant that's part of La Costa resort complex. The centerpiece of the resort's entrance plaza, the grill holds an outdoor patio with fire pits, fountains, and a year-round floral display. Inside is a contemporary Mission-style room surrounding a green bottle glass fountain that extends the length of the main dining room. The menu features local seafood and vegetables combined in exciting ways. As a starter, try the Carlsbad

The spring blooms at the Flower Fields at Carlsbad Ranch are not to be missed.

mussels and Manila clams in a Riesling broth, followed by a prime flatiron steak with white truffle and lobster mac and cheese. Tantalizing desserts include luscious Carlsbad strawberries marinated in balsamic and lemon herb crème brûlée. $ *Average main: $27* ✉ *2100 Costa Del Mar Rd.* ☎ *760/929–6306* ⊕ *www.dinebluefire.com* ⌖ *Reservations essential* ☾ *Closed Sun.–Tues. No lunch.*

WHERE TO STAY
For expanded hotel reviews, visit Fodors.com.

$$$ 🍴 **Carlsbad Inn Beach Resort.** At this sprawling inn and time-share condominium complex with direct access to the beach, rooms range from cramped to large and are furnished Queen Anne style, with pencil-post beds and wall sconces; many have ocean views, balconies, and kitchenettes, and some also have fireplaces and hot tubs. **Pros:** walk to the beach; warm ambience. **Cons:** lots of kids; on the main drag. $ *Rooms from: $259* ✉ *3075 Carlsbad Blvd.* ☎ *760/434–7020 or 800/235–3939* ⊕ *www.carlsbadinn.com* ⤳ *54 rooms, 7 suites.*

$$$ 🍴 **Grand Pacific Palisades Resort & Hotel.** One-, two-, and three-bedroom time-shares, surrounding a swimming pool, are the best choice for families at the Grand Pacific, with its LEGO-decorated lobby and direct access to LEGOLAND. **Pros:** close walk to LEGOLAND; gorgeous adult pool with Pacific view; kid area and pool; nice views of the Flower Fields at Carlsbad Ranch. **Cons:** some rooms are small; a lot of kids and tour groups. $ *Rooms from: $259* ✉ *5805 Armada Dr.* ☎ *800/725–4723* ⊕ *www.grandpacificpalisades.com* ⤳ *90 rooms, 162 time-share villas.*

$$$ 👶 🏨 **Hilton Carlsbad Oceanfront Resort & Spa.** Sea and sand loom large: rooms (complete with sitting areas) are filled with sea views and sea breezes, colors schemes are sand and blue, and surfing photos adorn the walls. **Pros:** South Carlsbad State Park across the highway; ocean view from fitness center; afternoon coastal breezes. **Cons:** on main highway. [$] *Rooms from: $279* ✉ *1 Ponto Dr., Carlsbad* ☎ *760/602–0800* 🌐 *www.hiltoncarlsbadoceanfront.com* 🛏 *215 rooms.*

WORD OF MOUTH

"The Grand Pacific Palisades and Grand Pacific MarBrisa resorts have large two-bedroom units that would be perfect for your family especially since they have full kitchens. All are walking distance to LEGOLAND, Sea Life Aquarium, and LEGOLAND Water Park. Since these are timeshares, your best choice for renting by the night is Grand Pacific's partner company ResorTime.com."

—unomos

$$$ RESORT 👶 Fodor's Choice ★ 🏨 **La Costa Resort and Spa.** A legendary '50s-style resort is a chic Spanish colonial oasis, where ample guest rooms, in shades of brown and sand with oversize chairs and sofas, are spread among a collection of handsome two-story buildings. **Pros:** huge glamorous spa; excellent kids' facilities; popular restaurant. **Cons:** very spread out, making long walks necessary; lots of kids, so if you're not in the market for a family-friendly stay, look elsewhere. [$] *Rooms from: $259* ✉ *2100 Costa del Mar Rd.* ☎ *760/438–9111 or 800/854–5000* 🌐 *www.lacosta.com* 🛏 *610 rooms, 120 villas.*

$$$ RESORT 👶 Fodor's Choice ★ 🏨 **Park Hyatt Aviara Resort.** The quietly elegant hilltop retreat is one of the most luxurious hotels in the San Diego area, where rooms have every possible amenity (including private terraces and deep soaking tubs) and one of the most sublime views in Southern California, overlooking Batiquitos Lagoon and the Pacific. **Pros:** unbeatable location; many nature trails; beach butler service. **Cons:** a little stiff; some complaints about service; $25 resort fee. [$] *Rooms from: $285* ✉ *7100 Four Seasons Point* ☎ *800/233–1234 or 760/448–1234* 🌐 *www.parkhyattaviara.com* 🛏 *329 rooms, 44 suites.*

$$ HOTEL 🏨 **Sheraton Carlsbad Resort & Spa.** Spacious modern-looking rooms are done in tones of beige, brown, and white and overlook colorful gardens that rim the complex through floor-to-ceiling windows. **Pros:** private entrance to LEGOLAND; lovely views from many rooms; expansive bathrooms with soaking tubs; social hour. **Cons:** high noise level in public areas. [$] *Rooms from: $159* ✉ *5480 Grand Pacific Dr.* ☎ *760/827–2400 or 800/444–3515* 🌐 *www.sheratoncarlsbadresort.com* 🛏 *250 rooms.*

$$ B&B/INN 👶 ★ 🏨 **West Inn and Suites.** Everything here exudes a warm and friendly atmosphere, with large, well-appointed guest rooms furnished with streamlined Arts and Crafts decor and an inviting lobby/sitting room where a stone fireplace takes the chill off a cool day. **Pros:** family- and pet-friendly; full buffet breakfast; organized activities; shuttle services for guests within the Carlsbad area; near beaches. **Cons:** adjacent to railroad tracks and freeway. [$] *Rooms from: $169* ✉ *4970 Av. Encinas* ☎ *760/448–4500 or 866/431–9378* 🌐 *www.westinnandsuites.com* 🛏 *86 rooms, 36 suites* 🍴 *Breakfast.*

SHOPPING

★ **Carlsbad Premium Outlets.** Carlsbad Premium Outlets, part of the growing LEGOLAND complex, is one of two designer factory outlets in the San Diego area. Within this attractively landscaped complex you can find Barney's New York, Crate and Barrel, Dooney & Bourke, Salvatore Ferragamo, Le Creuset, and Polo Ralph Lauren. ✉ *5620 Paseo Del Norte* ☎ *760/804–9000 or 888/790–7467* ⊕ *www. premiumoutlets.com/carlsbad.*

Saratoga Saddlery. Sidle on up to the Saddlery for a peek at the store's handsome lines of riding and hiking boots, belts, accessories, and clothing from Emu Australia, Lucchese, Joules, and DuBarry. You could drop a bundle here, but the quality is impeccable. ✉ *1555 Camino Del Mar, Suite 117, Del Mar* ☎ *858/755–7752* ⊕ *www.saratogasaddlery.com.*

OCEANSIDE

15

8 miles north of Carlsbad on Rte. S21, 37 miles north of downtown San Diego on I–5.

The beach culture is alive and well in Oceanside, despite redevelopment activities that are changing the face of the waterfront. Mixed-use hotels and residences are under construction to enhance the beach culture and make it more accessible. Visitors to this part of downtown Oceanside can stay within walking distance of the city's best swimming and surfing beaches: Harbor Beach, brimming with beach activities and fun, and Buccaneer Beach, where you'll find some of the best surfing in North County. Many who have been in the military link Oceanside with Camp Pendleton, the sprawling U.S. Marine base that lies at the north end of the city. Until recently the military was Oceanside's main industry, now being eclipsed by tourism; proximity to the base still has its benefits, as most businesspeople offer discounts to active military personnel and their families. Also home to the largest and one of the best-preserved California missions, Mission San Luis Rey, Oceanside's history extends back to the 1700s, when the Spanish friars walked along the California coast founding missions as they went. Today Oceanside celebrates its historic culture with the regionally exciting Oceanside Museum of Art, displaying the works of San Diego area artists. Residents and visitors gather weekly at the farmers' market and Sunset Market, where shopping for fresh-picked produce is a pleasant pastime.

GETTING HERE AND AROUND

The northernmost of the beach towns, Oceanside, lies 8 miles north of Carlsbad via I–5; exit the freeway on Mission Avenue. If you go west, you'll come to the redeveloped downtown and harbor where you'll find most of the restaurants, lodgings, and attractions. Downtown Oceanside is quite walkable from the Transportation Center, where Amtrak, the Coaster, and Sprinter stop. Buses and taxis are also available at the Transportation Center.

ESSENTIALS

Visitor Information Oceanside Welcome Center ✉ *928 N. Coast Hwy.* ☎ *760/721–1101 or 800/350–7873* ⊕ *www.californiawelcomecenter.org* ⊙ *Daily 9–5.*

EXPLORING

TOP ATTRACTIONS

California Surf Museum. A large collection of surfing memorabilia, photos, vintage boards, apparel, and accessories are on display here. ⊠ *312 Pier View Way* ☎ *760/721–6876* ⊕ *www.surfmuseum.org* ⊒ *$5; free on Tues.* ⊗ *Daily 10–4, until 8 Thurs.*

Camp Pendleton. The nation's largest amphibious military training complex encompasses 17 miles of Pacific shoreline. It's not unusual to see herds of tanks and flocks of helicopters maneuvering through the dunes and brush alongside I–5. You may also see herds of sheep keeping the bushland down and fertile fields growing next to the Pacific coastline. You can make advance arrangements to tour historic sites on the base by contacting the community relations office. ☎ *760/725–5799* ⊕ *www. mccscamppendleton.com.*

   ♺   **Old Mission San Luis Rey.** Known as the King of the Missions, the 18th
Fodor'sChoice   and largest and most prosperous of California's missions was built in
   ★   1798 by Franciscan friars under the direction of Father Fermin Lasuen to help educate and convert local Native Americans. The *sala* (parlor), the kitchen, a friar's bedroom, a weaving room, and a collection of religious art and old Spanish vestments convey much about early mission life. A location for filming Disney's 1950's *Zorro* TV series, the well-preserved mission is still owned by the Franciscans. ⊠ *4050 Mission Ave.* ☎ *760/757–3651* ⊕ *www.sanluisrey.org* ⊒ *$5* ⊗ *Weekdays 9:30–5, weekends 10–5.*

Oceanside Pier. At 1,600 feet, this is one of the longest piers on the West Coast. The water surrounding it is known for its surf breaks and good fishing. A restaurant, Ruby's Diner, stands at the end of the wooden pier's long promenade. ⊠ *Pier View Way.*

WORTH NOTING

Oceanside Harbor. With 1,000 slips, this is North County's fishing, sailing, and water-sports center. There's a small dining and retail area at the north end of the harbor where you can linger and watch the boats coming and going. ⊠ *1540 Harbor Dr. N* ☎ *760/435–4000* ⊕ *www. ci.oceanside.ca.us.*

Oceanside Museum of Art. Housed in side-by-side buildings designed by two Southern California modernist architects—the old City Hall designed by Irving Gill and the Central Pavilion designed by Frederick Fisher—the museum showcases works by San Diego area artists, including paintings and photography. ⊠ *704 Pier View Way* ☎ *760/435–3720* ⊕ *www.oma-online.org* ⊒ *$8* ⊗ *Tues.–Sat. 10–4, Sun. 1–4.*

Wave Waterpark. A 3-acre water park run by the city of Vista is one of the few places in the country with a flow-rider, a type of standing wave that allows riders on bodyboards to turn, carve, and slash almost as though they were surfing on a real wave. If you haven't learned how to do that, you can tube down the park's own river or slip down the 35-foot waterslide. ⊠ *101 Wave Dr., Vista* ☎ *760/940–9283* ⊕ *www. thewavewaterpark.com* ⊒ *$17* ⊗ *Memorial Day–Labor Day, weekdays 10–4, weekends noon–5:30; Labor Day–Sept., weekends noon–5.*

WHERE TO EAT

$ AMERICAN ✕ **101 Cafe.** A diner dating back to 1928 is both a local hangout and the headquarters of the historic Highway 101 movement. You'll find all kinds of Highway 101 memorabilia here along with breakfast and lunch. The bountiful breakfast menu lists omelets, eggs any way you want, pancakes, and French toast. Burgers, sandwiches, and salads are on offer at lunch. $ *Average main: $6* ✉ *631 S. Coast Hwy.* ☎ *760/722–5220* ⊕ *www.101cafe.net* ⚶ *Reservations not accepted* ▭ *No credit cards.*

$ SEAFOOD ✕ **Harbor Fish & Chips.** Pick up a basket of fresh-cooked fish-and-chips at this dive and you're in for a treat. The shop has been serving the combo—and clam chowder, shrimp cocktail, and fish sandwiches—to boaters and visitors for more than 40 years. It looks like it, too, with fish trophies hung on walls and from the ceiling. Outdoor tables offer terrific views of the Oceanside Marina. $ *Average main: $10* ✉ *276 S. Harbor Dr.* ⊕ *www.harborfishandchips.net.*

WHERE TO STAY

For expanded hotel reviews, visit Fodors.com.

$ ★ ⊞ **Oceanside Marina Suites.** These unusually large rooms and one- and two-bedroom suites, with fireplaces and expansive balconies in many, are on a spit of land, surrounded by water and cool ocean breezes on all sides. **Pros:** best sunsets; spacious rooms; free parking. **Cons:** marina location apt to be busy on weekends. $ *Rooms from: $109* ✉ *2008 Harbor Dr. N* ☎ *760/722–1561 or 800/252-2033* ⊕ *www.omihotel. com* ⤳ *6 rooms, 51 suites* ⎮○⎮ *Breakfast.*

$ ⊞ **Wyndham Oceanside Pier Resort.** Just steps from the beach and Oceanside Pier, these spacious two-bedroom suites are ideal for families and have fully equipped kitchens, balconies, and whirlpool tubs; hotel rooms are smaller but have the same views and amenities. **Pros:** beachfront location; family-friendly. **Cons:** no spa; limited hotel rooms, two-night minimum stay. $ *Rooms from: $129* ✉ *333 N. Myers* ☎ *760/901–1200 or 800/210–0948* ⊕ *www.wyndhamoceansidepier.com* ⤳ *24 rooms, 132 suites* ⎮○⎮ *No meals.*

SHOPPING

Oceanside Photo & Telescope. Oceanside Photo & Telescope is the place to pick up a telescope or binoculars for viewing San Diego County's dazzling night sky. Call for information about stargazing parties the store holds regularly in the San Diego area. ✉ *918 Mission Ave.* ☎ *800/483–6287* ⊕ *www.optcorp.com.*

INLAND NORTH COUNTY AND TEMECULA

Long regarded as San Diego's beautiful backyard, replete with green hills, quiet lakes, and citrus and avocado groves, inland San Diego County and the Temecula wine country are among the fastest-growing areas in Southern California. Subdivisions, many containing palatial homes, now fill the hills and canyons around Escondido and Rancho Bernardo. At the northern edge of this region, Fallbrook (longtime self-proclaimed Avocado Capital of the World) has morphed into an emerging arts community. Beyond Fallbrook is Temecula, the premium

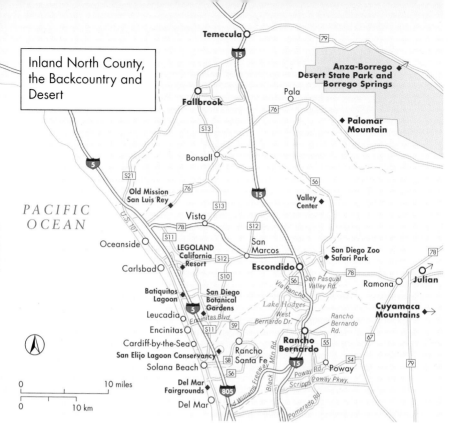

Inland North County,
the Backcountry and
Desert

Temecula

Anza-Borrego
Desert State Park and
Borrego Springs

Pala

Fallbrook

Palomar
Mountain

Bonsall

Old Mission
San Luis Rey

Vista

Valley
Center

PACIFIC
OCEAN

Oceanside

LEGOLAND
California
Resort

San
Marcos

Carlsbad

Escondido

San Diego Zoo
Safari Park

Ramona

Julian

Batiquitos
Lagoon

San Diego
Botanical
Gardens

San Pasqual
Valley Rd.

Via Rancho

Lake Hodges

Cuyamaca
Mountains

Leucadia

Encinitas Blvd.

West
Bernardo Dr.

Rancho
Bernardo
Rd.

Encinitas

Cardiff-by-the-Sea

San Elijo Lagoon Conservancy

Rancho
Santa Fe

Rancho
Bernardo

Poway

Solana Beach

Scripps Poway Pkwy.

Black Mtn. Rd.

0   10 miles

Del Mar
Fairgrounds

Del Mar

Ted Williams Freeway

Pomerado Rd.

0   10 km

wine-making area of southern Riverside County. Growth notwithstanding, inland San Diego County still has such natural settings as the San Diego Zoo Safari Park, Rancho Bernardo, and the Welk Resort. The region is also home to a number of San Diego County's Indian casino resorts, among them Pala, Harrah's Rincon, Valley View, and Pauma. Pachenga lies just over the county line near Temecula.

RANCHO BERNARDO

23 miles northeast of downtown San Diego on I–15.

Rancho Bernardo straddles a stretch of I–15 between San Diego and Escondido and is technically a neighborhood of San Diego. Originally sheep- and cattle-grazing land, it was transformed in the early 1960s into a planned suburban community, one of the first, and a place where many wealthy retirees settled down. It's now home to a number of high-tech companies, the most notable of which is Sony. If you want to spend some time at the nearby San Diego Zoo Safari Park, this community, home of the world-class Rancho Bernardo resort, makes a convenient and comfortable headquarters for a multiday visit.

WHERE TO EAT

$$ FRENCH — 🍴 **Bernard'O.** Intimate despite its shopping-center location, Bernard'O is the choice for a romantic dinner. Sit fireside in the small dining room, dine by candlelight, and savor contemporary versions of California bouillabaisse or grilled Scottish salmon with asparagus. Many items also appear on the reduced price Happy Hour menu, served from 4:30 to 7. An extensive wine list includes rare old vintages from California and France along with well-priced newer bottles. [$] *Average main: $22* ✉ *12457 Rancho Bernardo Rd.* ☎ *858/487–7171* ✍ *Reservations essential* ⏲ *Closed Sun. No lunch Sat.–Mon.*

$ SICHUAN 👶 — 🍴 **Chin's Szechwan Cuisine.** Locals pick Chin's for special occasions. It feels rich, with dark-red walls, blooming orchids everywhere, and heavy wooden furnishings. The extensive menu lists popular items such as Kung Pao chicken, sizzling beef and scallops, and tangerine crispy beef. [$] *Average main: $17* ✉ *15721 Bernardo Heights Pkwy.* ☎ *858/676–0166* 🌐 *www.govisitchins.com.*

$$$ FRENCH — 🍴 **El Bizcocho.** Locals rate this candlelit dinng room at the Rancho Bernardo Inn tops for style and cuisine. Plush banquettes and quiet, live piano music make for a tranquil setting. The ever-changing menu might feature locally caught sea bass, Brandt Farms shortribs, or Berkshire pork belly. The chef regularly offers four- and six-course tasting menus starting at $75 per person. The wine list has more than 1,500 entries, including rare vintages, although the by-the-glass selection is limited. [$] *Average main: $35* ✉ *Rancho Bernardo Inn, 17550 Bernardo Oaks Pkwy.* ☎ *858/675–8550* 🌐 *www.ranchobernardoinn.com/bizcocho* ✍ *Reservations essential* 👔 *Jacket required* ⏲ *Closed Mon. No lunch Tues.–Sat.*

$$ FRENCH — 🍴 **French Market Grille.** The flower-decked dark-wood dining room and patio with twinkling lights will help you forget that you're eating in a shopping center. The French fare changes with the seasons; typical entrées include rack of lamb, oven-roasted swordfish and lobster with vermouth, or Pacific Coast bouillabaisse. If you love desserts, save room for one of the French classics offered here, apple tarte tatin, crèpes suzette, and crème brûlée. Sorry to say, there have been recent complaints about slow service. [$] *Average main: $25* ✉ *15717 Bernardo Heights Pkwy.* ☎ *858/485–8055* 🌐 *www.frenchmarketgrille.com* ✍ *Reservations essential.*

WHERE TO STAY

For expanded hotel reviews, visit Fodors.com.

$$$ RESORT 👶 ★ — 🏨 **Rancho Bernardo Inn Resort and Spa.** Public areas throughout this two-story, red-roof adobe resort are a collection of small sitting rooms where Spanish Mission–style sofas and fireplaces invite you to linger with a good book and ample guest rooms hold platform beds tucked into corner upholstered banquettes. **Pros:** gorgeous flower-decked 265-acre grounds; excellent service; popular golf course; good value in off-season. **Cons:** walking required in spacious grounds; distance from most visitor attractions. [$] *Rooms from: $199* ✉ *17550 Bernardo Oaks Dr.* ☎ *858/675–8500 or 877/517–9340* 🌐 *www.ranchobernardoinn.com* 🛏 *287 rooms, 15 suites.*

15

SHOPPING

Bernardo Winery. A trip to the oldest operating winery in Southern California, founded in 1889 and run by the Rizzo family since 1928, feels like traveling back to early California days; some of the vines on the former Spanish land-grant property have been producing grapes for more than a hundred years. Most of the grapes now come from other wine-growing regions. Cafe Merlot serves lunch daily except Monday, and shops sell cold-pressed olive oil and other gourmet goodies, as well as apparel, home-decor items, and arts and crafts. A glassblowing artist is often working at the outdoor furnace. ⊠ *13330 Paseo Del Verano Norte* ☎ *858/487–1866* ⊕ *www.bernardowinery.com* ✉ *Winery free, tastings $10* ⊙ *Weekdays 9–5, weekends 9–6, shop hrs vary.*

ESCONDIDO

8 miles north of Rancho Bernardo on I–15, 31 miles northeast of downtown San Diego on I–15.

Escondido and the lovely rolling hills around it were originally a land grant bestowed by the governor of Mexico on Juan Bautista Alvarado in 1843. The Battle of San Pasqual, a bloody milestone in California's march to statehood, took place just east of the city. For a century and a half, these hills supported citrus and avocado trees, plus large vineyards. The rural character of the area began to change when the San Diego Zoo established its Safari Park in the San Pasqual Valley east of town in the 1970s. By the late 1990s suburban development had begun to transform the hills into housing tracts. The California Center for the Arts, opened in 1993, now stands as the downtown centerpiece of a burgeoning arts community that includes a collection of art galleries along Grand Avenue. Despite its urbanization, Escondido still supports several pristine open-space preserves that attract nature lovers, hikers, and mountain bikers.

ESSENTIALS

Visitor Information Escondido Visitors Bureau ⊠ *720 N. Broadway* ☎ *760/745–2125* ⊕ *visitescondido.com.*

EXPLORING
TOP ATTRACTIONS

☺ **California Center for the Arts.** An entertainment complex with two theaters, an art museum, and a conference center, the center presents operas, musicals, plays, dance performances, and symphony and chamber-music concerts. Performers conduct free workshops for children; check the website for dates. The museum, which focuses on 20th-century art, occasionally presents blockbuster exhibits such as the glass art of Dale Chihuly or photos by Ansel Adams, making a side trip here worthwhile. ⊠ *340 N. Escondido Blvd.* ☎ *800/988–4253 box office, 760/839–4138 museum* ⊕ *www.artcenter.org* ⊙ *Hrs vary, call ahead.*

☺ **Daley Ranch.** A 3,058-acre conservation area and historic ranch site is laced with more than 20 miles of multipurpose trails for hikers, mountain bikers, and equestrians. The 2.4-mile Boulder Loop affords sweeping views of Escondido, and the 2.5-mile Ranch House Loop passes two small ponds, the 1928 Daley family ranch house, and the site of

Enjoying the wine at Orfila Vineyards in Escondido

the original log cabin. Private cars are prohibited on the ranch, but a Sunday shuttle service is provided from the parking area to the entrance. Free naturalist-guided hikes are offered on a regular basis; call for schedule. Leashed dogs permitted. ⊠ *3024 La Honda Dr.* ☎ *760/839–4680* ⊕ *www.ci.escondido.ca.us* ✉ *Free* ⊙ *Daily dawn–dusk.*

ⓒ **San Diego Zoo Safari Park.**

Fodor's Choice ⇨ *See the highlighted listing in this chapter.*
★

WORTH NOTING

Escondido Arts Partnership Municipal Gallery. Showcasing works by local artists, the gallery has regular exhibitions and year-round special events. ⊠ *262 E. Grand Ave.* ☎ *760/480–4101* ⊕ *www.escondidoarts.org* ⊙ *Tues.–Sat. 11–4.*

Escondido History Center. This outdoor museum adjacent to the California Center for the Arts in Grape Day Park consists of several historic buildings moved here to illustrate local development from the late 1800s, when grape growing and gold mining supported the economy. Exhibits include the 1888 Santa Fe Depot, Escondido's first library, the Bandy Blacksmith shop, a furnished 1890 Victorian house, and other 19th-century buildings. ⊠ *321 N. Broadway* ☎ *760/743–8207* ⊕ *www.escondidohistory.org* ✉ *$3 suggested donation* ⊙ *Tues.–Sat. 1–4.*

Orfila Vineyards. Visitors here can taste award-winning Syrah, Sangiovese, and Viognier produced from grapes harvested from the 10,000-acre vineyard. The Rose Arbor has a picnic area, and there's a gift shop with wine-related merchandise. ⊠ *13455 San Pasqual Rd.* ☎ *760/738–6500* ⊕ *www.orfila.com* ✉ *Tastings $10* ⊙ *Daily 10–6, free guided tours at noon.*

Queen Califia's Magical Circle. The last work by sculptor Niki de Saint Phalle (1930–2002), this sculpture garden consists of nine totemic figures up to 21 feet tall. Adorned with stylized monsters, animals, protective deities, geometric symbols, and crests, they evoke ancient tales and legends. Saint Phalle designed the garden for the entertainment of children, who can climb on the giant fanciful figures. ✉ *Kit Carson Park, Bear Valley Pkwy. and Mary La.* ☎ *760/839–4691* 🌐 *www.queencalifia.org* 🎫 *Free* 🕒 *Tues.–Sun., daily 8–dusk except when raining.*

San Dieguito River Park. The park maintains several hiking and walking trails in the Escondido area. These are part of an intended 55-mile-long Coast to Crest Trail that will eventually link the San Dieguito Lagoon near Del Mar with the river's source on Volcan Mountain, north of Julian. Among the existing trails are three that circle Lake Hodges: the **North Shore Lake Hodges Trail;** the **Piedras Pintadas Trail,** which informs about native American Kumeyaay lifestyles and uses for native plants; and the **Highland Valley Trail,** the first mile of which is the Ruth Merrill Children's Walk. Three trails in **Clevenger Canyon** lead to sweeping views of the San Pasqual Valley. Visit the website for a list of upcoming guided hikes. ✉ *18372 Sycamore Creek Rd.* ☎ *858/674–2270* 🌐 *www.sdrp.org* 🎫 *Free* 🕒 *Daily dawn–dusk.*

OFF THE BEATEN PATH

Keys Creek Lavender Farm. In spring a visit to this organic lavender farm is worth a detour. A self-guided walk takes you through 6 acres planted with 28 varieties of lavender and to an area where plants are distilled into essential oils. A gift shop sells lavender products and plants. The farm serves a three-course English High Tea at 2 on Sunday. ✉ *12460 Keys Creek Rd., Valley Center* ☎ *760/742–0523* 🌐 *www.keyscreeklavenderfarm.com* 🎫 *Free* 🕒 *Daily 10–3.*

WHERE TO EAT AND STAY

For expanded hotel reviews, visit Fodors.com.

With the exception of the Welk Resort, which is now primarily a timeshare property, Escondido has little to offer in the way of accommodations.

$$ FRENCH

🍴 **Vincent's on Grand.** Here's an excellent choice for lunch or dinner before an event at the nearby California Center for the Arts. Original paintings decorate the walls, and crisp white tablecloths cover the tables, adorned with fresh flowers. The menu changes frequently; offerings might include tournedos Merlot, sweet potato ravioli, beef Wellington, or duck à l'orange. The wine list is serious, as are the desserts. The service is friendly and attentive. [$] *Average main: $26* ✉ *113 W. Grand Ave.* ☎ *760/745–3835* ✍ *Reservations essential* 🕒 *Closed Sun. and Mon. No lunch weekends.*

$$ RESORT

🏨 **Welk Resort.** At this time-share property built by bandleader Lawrence Welk in the 1960s, nicely furnished and appointed one- and two-bedroom villas include fireplaces, hot tubs, original art, and balconies or patios. **Pros:** excellent theater; popular golf course; near the Safari Park. **Cons:** located outside the city; very spread out; rooms may not always be available due to time-sharing. [$] *Rooms from: $169* ✉ *8860 Lawrence Welk Dr.* ☎ *760/749–3000 or 800/932–9355* 🌐 *www.welkresorts.com* 🛏 *574 suites* 🍽 *No meals.*

SHOPPING

Although farmland began to give way to suburbs in the 1990s, and the area's fruit, nut, and vegetable bounty has diminished, you can still find overflowing farm stands in the San Pasqual Valley and in Valley Center, just east of the city.

Bates Nut Farm. Bates Nut Farm is the home of San Diego's largest pumpkin patch in fall, where you might find 200-pound squash. The 100-acre farm, in the Bates family for five generations, sells locally grown pecans, macadamia nuts, and almonds. There's a petting zoo, a picnic area, and a gift shop. ✉ *15954 Woods Valley Rd., Valley Center* ☎ *800/642–0348* ⊕ *www.batesnutfarm.biz* ⏱ *Daily 9–5.*

Canterbury Gardens. Canterbury Gardens, occupying an old winery, specializes in giftware and seasonal decorative accessories for the home, plus a year-round selection of Christmas ornaments and collectibles by Christopher Radko, Mark Robert's Fairies, and Department 56. ✉ *2402 S. Escondido Blvd.* ☎ *760/746–1400* ⊕ *www. canterburygardens.com.*

15

FALLBROOK

19 miles northwest of Escondido on I–15 to Mission Rd., Rte. S13, to Mission Dr.

A quick 5-mile detour off I–15 between Temecula and San Diego, Fallbrook bills itself as the Avocado Capital of the World. Avocado orchards fill the surrounding hillsides, and guacamole is served in just about every eatery. You can even pig out on avocado ice cream at the annual Avocado Festival in April. But this small agricultural town is also morphing into an interesting arts center. The art and cultural center showcases the work of local and regional painters, sculptors, and fiber artists. The National Gourd and Fiber Show in June draws lovers of this art from all over Southern California. You'll find several intriguing galleries displaying antiques, jewelry, watercolors, and photography on Main Avenue. Innovative restaurants now supplement the staple fast-food joints, and the Fallbrook Winery is making a name for itself in the South Coast wine region.

EXPLORING

Brandon Gallery. This Fallbrook art institution that has been showing works of regional emerging and professional artists for more than 30 years is the place to find excellent quality watercolors, ceramics, jewelry, and baskets. It's a cooperative in which all work shown is judged and artists showing are members. ✉ *105 N. Main Ave.* ☎ *760/723–1330* ⊕ *www.fallbrookbrandongallery.org.*

Fallbrook Art Center. Housed in a typical midcentury modern building that served as the Rexall Pharmacy for 30 years, the spacious center mounts 10–12 local and regional art shows yearly, including the annual Galaxy of Glass, World of Watercolor, and Reflections of Nature. The center also hosts a number of national touring art shows, among them the National Watercolor Society Show. The Café des Artistes, tucked into a back corner of the center, serves salads and sandwiches. ✉ *103*

S. Main St. ☎ *760/728–1414* 🌐 *www.fallbrookartcenter.org* 🎟 *$6* 🕒 *Mon.–Sat. 10–4, Sun. noon–3; occasionally closed between shows. Café: Closed Sun. No dinner.*

Fallbrook Winery. It's worth visiting this winery, perched on a lovely hillside outside Fallbrook, where winemakers Duncan Williams and Vernon Kindred produce bottles that bring back medals from state and national competitions. They make wine from grapes grown on 36 hilly acres surrounding the winery and from other areas in California. Try the estate-bottled Rosato Sangiovese rosé, fruity sauvignon blanc reserve, or the big Syrah special selection. ✉ *2554 Via Rancheros* ☎ *760/728–0156* 🌐 *www.fallbrookwinery.com* 🎟 *$7 tours* 🕒 *Open by appointment only.*

WHERE TO EAT AND STAY

For expanded hotel reviews, visit Fodors.com.

$$ SEAFOOD 🍴 **AquaTerra.** This pleasant room in the Pala Mesa Golf Resort is locally popular. Most come for the seafood selections on the wide-ranging menu that lists St. Louis barbecued ribs, pan roasted local sea bass, and Parmesan halibut, or the expertly made items on the sushi bar menu. Tables here offer good golf-course views, and in warm weather you can dine outside on the patio. [$] *Average main: $23* ✉ *2001 Old Hwy. 395* ☎ *760/728–5881* 🌐 *www.palamesa.com.*

$$ MEDITERRANEAN 🍴 **Brothers Bistro.** Everything from sauces to breads is made in-house at this cozy bistro that's tucked into a back corner of the Major Market Shopping Center. Owner/chef Ron Nusser has a New York touch with Italian specialties such as Alla Diana Pasta, an antipasto-like Monterey seafood salad, and roasted halibut. But the most popular item on the menu is homemade lasagna, nearly a pound per serving with house-made marinara and three cheeses. Eat in the small dining room, where huge paintings adorn every wall, or on the tree-shaded patio outdoors. There's an extensive list of California wines, many available by the glass. [$] *Average main: $21* ✉ *835 S. Main St., Suite A* ☎ *760/731–9761* 🌐 *www.brothersbistro.net* ✍ *Reservations essential* 🕒 *No lunch weekends.*

$ MEXICAN 🍴 **La Caseta.** The "little cottage" serves up small surprises. Chef Delos Eyer brings traditional Mexican fare up to date with options including grilled chicken wrap with achiote sauce and savory black beans, San Filipe fish tacos, charbroiled shrimp diablo, and meatless black bean quesadillas. Don't miss the fabulous Xango, a banana caramel cheesecake chimichanga with vanilla ice cream, and Death by Chocolate, a tower of chocolate ice cream perched on a huge chocolate walnut cookie. The casual cottage with wraparound windows and colorful murals is bright and cheerful, and in good weather you can dine outside on the patio. [$] *Average main: $12* ✉ *111 N. Vine St.* ☎ *760/728–9737* 🌐 *www.lacasetafinemexicanfood.com* 🕒 *Closed Sun.*

$$ RESORT 🏨 **Pala Casino Resort Spa.** Lovely spacious rooms and suites, a big selection of dining options, a tranquil spa, and an enticing entertainment schedule are all designed to pamper guests. **Pros:** classy ambience; cabanas at pool; all rooms with mountain or pool views. **Cons:** remote location; challenging drive from I–15. [$] *Rooms from: $189* ✉ *11154 Hwy. 76* ☎ *877/946–7275* 🌐 *www.palacasino.com* 🛏 *425 rooms, 82 suites.*

$$ ⛳ **Pala Mesa Golf Resort.** A vague Hawaiian feel prevails at this friendly
HOTEL two-story resort, where large, simply furnished rooms have floor-to-
★ ceiling windows and most have balconies, some with great fairway,
garden, or mountain views. **Pros:** attractive grounds; spacious rooms;
dog-friendly; popular with golfers. **Cons:** adjacent to freeway; popular
with convention groups; resort's age is showing. $ *Rooms from: $149*
✉ *2001 Old Hwy. 395* ☎ *760/728–5881 or 800/722–4700* ⊕ *www.*
palamesa.com ⤴ *133 rooms* ⦿ *Some meals.*

TEMECULA

29 miles from Escondido, 60 miles from San Diego on I–15 north to
Rancho California Rd. east.

Once an important stop on the Butterfield Overland Stagecoach route
and a market town for the huge cattle ranches surrounding it, Temecula
(pronounced teh-*mec*-yoo-la) is now a developed wine region, desig-
nated the South Coast region, which also includes some wineries in San
Diego County. Known for its gently rolling hills, the region is studded
with ancient oak trees and vernal pools. Until recently the offering
at many of the wineries were just okay, but things have changed in
the last decade when winemakers discovered that French and Italian
grapes would thrive in the valley's hot climate. Vines were replanted
with the European varieties and now winemakers are creating lus-
cious blended reds and whites that resemble rich Rhones and Tuscan
vintages. Because most of the wineries sell their bottles only at the
wineries, it pays to stock up if you find something you especially enjoy.
Most of the wineries that line both sides of Rancho California Road as
it snakes east from downtown offer tours and tastings (for a fee) daily
and have creatively stocked boutiques, picnic facilities, and restaurants
on the premises. Lately, visitors will also find that some wineries have
opened luxury boutique lodgings and fine dining restaurants. Several
with sprawling elegant facilities host weekend weddings. Meanwhile,
local developers have created an Old Town along historic Front Street
on the west side of I–15. This section is home to boutique shops, good
restaurants, a children's museum, and a theater. In addition to its visitor
appeal, Temecula is also a suburban bedroom community for many
who work in San Diego North County.

TOUR OPTIONS

Several companies offer individual and group tours of the Temecula
wine country with departures from San Diego and Temecula. Some
include lunch or refreshments as part of the package.

Limousine Tours Destination Temecula. Let someone else do the driving
and enjoy this tour service that takes groups of 1 to 15 in luxury vans for
tasting and touring Temecula wineries. ☎ *951/695–1232 or 800/584–8162*
⊕ *www.destem.com.* **Grapeline Wine Country Shuttle.** Daily tours include four
wineries, picnic lunches, and behind the scenes vintner tours. ✉ *43500 Ridge*
Park Dr., Suite 204 ☎ *951/693–5755* ⊕ *www.gogrape.com* ⤴ *Tours $88–$118.*

15

Temecula Carriage Company. Temecula Carriage runs horse-drawn shuttles between Ponte, Wiens, and South Coast wineries. Shuttle trips, drawn by handsome Percheron horses, are $99 per person including a picnic, or $40 per person for transportation only. Couples special occasion winery tours, by reservation, include tastings at each winery and picnic lunch ($250 per couple). ⊠ *40001 Berenda Rd., Temecula* 🕾 *858/205–9161* ⊕ *www.temeculacarriageco.com.*

ESSENTIALS

Visitor Information Temecula Valley Visitor Center ⊠ *28690 Mercedes St., Suite A* 🕾 *951/506–0056* ⊕ *www.visittemecula.org.*

Temecula Valley Winegrowers Association. The Temecula Valley Winegrowers Association, which distributes brochures and sells tickets to special wine events, is a good resource for information on Temecula's 35-some wineries. ⊠ *34567 Rancho California Rd.* 🕾 *951/699–6586 or 800/801–9463* ⊕ *www.temeculawines.org* ◷ *Weekdays 9–5.*

EXPLORING

Pennypickle's Workshop: Temecula Children's Museum. This is the imaginary home of Professor Phineas Pennypickle, where kids accompanied by parents enter a time machine that carries them through six rooms of interactive exhibits demonstrating perception and illusion, music making, flight and aviation, chemistry and physics, plus power and electricity. The shop stocks an array of educational toys, games, and books. ⊠ *42081 Main St.* 🕾 *951/308–6370* 🖅 *$4.50* ◷ *2-hr sessions Tues.–Sat. at 10, 12:30, and 3; Fri., also at 5:30, Sun. at 12:30 and 3.*

Old Town Temecula. Once a hangout for cowboys, Old Town has been updated and expanded while retaining its Old West appearance. A walking tour put together by the **Temecula Valley Historical Society,** starting at the Temecula Valley Museum, covers some of the old buildings; most are identified with bronze plaques.

Santa Rosa Plateau Ecological Reserve. This 9,000-acre wooded preserve provides a glimpse of what this countryside was like before the developers took over. Trails wind through ancient oak forests and past vernal pools and rolling grassland. A visitor and operations center has interpretive displays and maps; some of the reserve's hiking trails begin here. There are designated trails for leashed dogs, horses, and mountain bikers. Take I–15 south to Clinton Keith Road exit and head west 5 miles. ⊠ *39400 Clinton Keith Rd., Murietta* 🕾 *951/677–6951* ⊕ *www.santarosaplateau.org* 🖅 *$3* ◷ *Daily dawn–dusk; visitor center Tues.–Sun. 9–5.*

Temecula Valley Museum. Adjacent to Sam Hicks Monument Park, this museum focuses on Temecula Valley history, including early Native American life, Butterfield stage routes, and the ranchero period. A hands-on interactive area for children holds a general store, photographer's studio, and ride-a-pony station. Outside there's a playground and picnic area. ⊠ *28314 Mercedes St.* 🕾 *951/694–6450* ⊕ *www.temeculavalleymuseum.org* 🖅 *$2 suggested donation* ◷ *Tues.–Sat. 10–4, Sun. 1–4.*

WINERIES

Europa Village. The tasting room offers Tempranillo, En Vie Rhone style blend, and Rousanne, among others, and the owners here have big plans to open three additional wineries, each specializing in a different European-style wine. The Inn at Europa Villiage, perched on an adjacent hilltop, offers 10 guest rooms. ⊠ *3347 La Serena Way* ☎ *951/216–3380* ⊕ *www.europavillage.com* 🍷 *Tastings $15* ☉ *Daily 10–7.*

Fodor's Choice ★ **Hart Family Winery.** The Mediterranean varietals grown on these 11 acres are considered to be some of the best red wines in Temecula Valley. Joe Hart, one of the area's pioneer winemakers, creates small lots of big-flavored Zinfandel, Cabernet Sauvignon, and Sangiovese wines. The winery's purple tasting room is decked out with ribbons, medals, and awards. ⊠ *41300 Av. Biona* ☎ *951/676–6300* ⊕ *www.hartfamilywinery.com* 🍷 *Winery free, tastings $10* ☉ *Daily 9–4:30.*

Leoness Cellars. Owner Mike Rennie and his staff create Italian and French blended wines at their mountaintop facility, where you can select from about 16 varieties of red and white blends. You can dine outdoors Tuscan style on weekends, and the winery hosts private tours (reservations required) that include rides and walks through the vineyards, tastings, wine and cheese pairings, and a bit of chocolate with dessert wines. ⊠ *38311 DePortola Rd.* ☎ *951/302–7601* ⊕ *www.leonesscellars.com* 🍷 *Winery free, tastings $16, tours $14–$75* ☉ *Daily 11–5.*

Miramonte Winery. At Temecula's hippest winery, perched on a hilltop, listen to Spanish-guitar recordings while sampling the Opulente Meritage, a supple Sauvignon Blanc, or the sultry Syrah. Owner Cane Vanderhoof's wines have earned dozens of awards. While you're enjoying your wine on the deck, order an artisan cheese plate. On Friday and Saturday nights from 7 to 10, the winery turns into a local hot spot with tastings of signature wines ($6 to $10) and beer, live music, and dancing that spills out into the vineyards. ⊠ *33410 Rancho California Rd.* ☎ *951/506–5500* ⊕ *www.miramontewinery.com* 🍷 *Winery free, tastings $15, tours $20–$25 (reservations required)* ☉ *Tastings Sun.–Thurs. 11–6, Fri. and Sat. 11–10.*

Mount Palomar Winery. One of the original Temecula Valley wineries, opened in 1969, introduced Sangiovese grapes, a varietal that has proven perfectly suited to the region's soil and climate. New owners have transformed the homey winery into a grand Mediterranean villa with acres of gardens and trees. The wine menu lists vintages made from grapes brought from Italy nearly 50 years ago. Try the dry Sangiovese or Bordeaux-style Meritage. Shorty's Bistro, open for lunch daily and for dinner on Friday and weekends, presents live entertainment on Friday nights. ⊠ *33820 Rancho California Rd.* ☎ *951/676–5047* ⊕ *www.mountpalomar.com* 🍷 *Winery free, tastings $12 Mon.–Thurs., $15 Fri.– Sun.* ☉ *Mon.–Thurs. 10:30–6, Fri.–Sun. 10:30–7.*

Wilson Creek Winery & Vineyard. One of the busiest tasting rooms in the Temecula Wine Country offers a warm welcome and inviting parklike grounds. In addition to the sparkling wine now also available in Peach Bellini and Orange Mimosa styles, Wilson Creek produces some appealing table wines, such as a medal-winning Reserve Syrah. The

15

Creekside Grill Restaurant serves sandwiches, salads, and such entrées as gluten-free vegetable potpie and Mexican white sea bass. You can select a picnic spot on the expansive property and the servers will deliver your lunch to you. ⊠ *35960 Rancho California Rd.* ☎ *951/699–9463* ⊕ *www.wilsoncreekwinery.com* 🖾 *Winery free, tastings $12 weekdays, $15 weekends* ⊙ *Daily 10–5, restaurant daily 11–5.*

WHERE TO EAT

$$ ✕ **Baily's Fine Dining and Front Street Bar & Grill.** Locals swoon over chef
AMERICAN   Neftali Torres's well-executed cuisine upstairs (dinner only) at Baily's Fine Dining. The menu varies according to his creative whims and might include chicken schnitzel drizzled in lemon-caper-wine sauce or salmon Wellington. Temecula Valley wines are well represented on the extensive list here. The fare is more casual—burgers, barbecue, soups, and salads—downstairs at Front Street, which often has live entertainment. 🟊 *Average main: $26* ⊠ *28699 Old Town Front St.* ☎ *951/676–9567* ⊕ *www.oldtowndining.com.*

$$$ ✕ **Café Champagne.** The spacious patio, with its bubbling fountain, flow-
ECLECTIC   ering trellises, and views of Thornton Winery's vineyards, is the perfect
Fodor's Choice   place to lunch on a sunny day. Inside, the dining room is decked out
★   in French country style, and the open kitchen turns out such dishes as braised boneless beef short ribs and bouillabaisse. The reasonably priced wines served here include the signature Thornton sparklers. 🟊 *Average main: $28* ⊠ *32575 Rancho California Rd.* ☎ *951/699–0088* ⊕ *www.thorntonwine.com/cafe.html* 🖾 *Reservations essential.*

$ ✕ **Front Street Bar & Grill.** Having fun is the rule here, where you can
SOUTHERN   dine in a big indoor room or outside on a quiet patio. The easy-on-the-budget menu lists eight gourmet burgers, chipotle-braised barbecued ribs, chili-stuffed chicken, and jambalaya. You can also nosh on Irish nachos and jalapeno calamari tempura. This can be a noisy place as there's entertainment weekend nights. 🟊 *Average main: $28* ⊠ *28699 Old Town Front St.* ☎ *951/676–9567* ⊕ *www.oldtowndining.com* 🖾 *Reservations not accepted.*

$$$ ✕ **Vineyard Rose.** Big and barnlike, the Vineyard Rose is a good choice
EUROPEAN   for Mediterranean-style family dining, one that will give the kids a
☾   chance to sample some excellent cooking. Consider seared sea bass and sea scallops with risotto or Shelton Farms chicken. The restaurant, part of the South Coast Winery complex, serves three meals daily. 🟊 *Average main: $28* ⊠ *34843 Rancho California Rd.* ☎ *951/587–9463 or 866/994–6379* ⊕ *www.wineresort.com* 🖾 *Reservations essential.*

WHERE TO STAY

For expanded hotel reviews, visit Fodors.com.

$$ 🏨 **Inn at Europa Village.** Most of the attractive, spacious rooms at this
B&B/INN   10-room bed-and-breakfast open to step out balconies where you can take in a sweeping view of surounding vineyards and orchards. 🟊 *Rooms from: $180* ⊠ *33350 La Serena Way, Temecula* ☎ *877/676–7047* ⊕ *www.europavillage.com/inn* ⮧ *10 rooms* ⫪⃝ *Breakfast.*

$$ 🏨 **Ponte Vineyard Inn.** Comfortable and relaxed digs offer vineyard and
HOTEL   garden views and have an Old California feel, with lots of dark wood, leather furnishings, and open spaces. **Pros:** fire pits in garden; excellent

service; live music weekends. **Cons:** many weddings on weekends. $ *Rooms from: $199* ✉ *35051 Rancho California Rd.* ☎ *951/587–6688* ⊕ *www.pontevineyardinn.com* ⤳ *60 rooms* ⊗ *No meals.*

$$ 🛏 **South Coast Winery Resort & Spa.** The Temecula wine country's most luxurious resort offers richly appointed rooms surrounded by 38 acres of vineyards. **Pros:** elegantly appointed rooms; full-service resort; good value. **Cons:** spread out property requires lots of walking; $15 resort fee. $ *Rooms from: $169* ✉ *34843 Rancho California Rd.* ☎ *951/587–9463 or 866/994–6379* ⊕ *www.wineresort.com* ⤳ *76 rooms, 2 suites* ⊗ *Breakfast.*

$$ 🛏 **Temecula Creek Inn.** Each room has a private patio or balcony over-**RESORT** looking the championship golf course and is decorated in soothing earth tones with a Southwestern theme. **Pros:** beautiful grounds; top golf course; spacious, comfortable rooms. **Cons:** location away from Old Town and wineries. $ *Rooms from: $169* ✉ *44501 Rainbow Canyon Rd.* ☎ *951/694–1000 or 877/517–1823* ⊕ *www.temeculacreekinn.com* ⤳ *130 rooms, 1 guesthouse* ⊗ *No meals.*

SPORTS AND THE OUTDOORS

A Grape Escape Balloon Adventure. A Grape Escape Balloon Adventure has morning hot-air balloon lift-offs from Europa Village Winery. ✉ *40335 Winchester Rd., Suite E* ☎ *951/699–9987 or 800/965–2122* ⊕ *www.hotairtours.com* 🖂 *$155.*

Balloon and Wine Festival. Temecula draws thousands of people to its Balloon and Wine Festival at Lake Skinner Recreation Area in late spring. Festivities include concerts with headliner entertainment and wine tasting. ✉ *41755 Rider Way, Unit 1* ☎ *951/676–6713* ⊕ *www.tvbwf.com.*

California Dreamin'. California Dreamin' schedules hot-air balloon rides from a private Temecula vineyard. ✉ *33133 Vista Del Monte Rd.* ☎ *800/373–3359* ⊕ *www.californiadreamin.com.*

SHOPPING

Temecula Lavender Co. Owner Jan Schneider offers an inspiring collection of the herb that fosters peace, purification, sleep, and longevity. Bath salts, hand soaps, essential oil—she's got it all, even dryer bags to freshen up the laundry. ✉ *28561 Old Town Front St.* ☎ *951/676–1931* ⊕ *www.temeculalavenderco.com* ⊗ *Weekdays 11–5, weekends 10–6.*

Temecula Olive Oil Company. Tastings of locally pressed olive oil are offered at the Temecula Olive Oil Company, where you can find a selection of oils seasoned with garlic, herbs, and citrus. This Old Town shop has dipping and cooking oils, locally crafted oil-based soaps and bath products, and a selection of preserved and stuffed olives. ✉ *28653 Old Town Front St.* ☎ *951/693–0607* ⊕ *www.temeculaoliveoil.com.*

15

THE BACKCOUNTRY AND JULIAN

The Cuyamaca and Laguna mountains to the east of Escondido—sometimes referred to as the backcountry by county residents—are favorite weekend destinations for hikers, nature lovers, stargazers, and apple-pie fanatics. Most of the latter group head to Julian, a historic mining town now better known for apple pie than for the gold once extracted from its hills. Much of nearby Cuyamaca Rancho State Park, once a luscious ancient oak and pine forest, burned in a 2003 fire, but many of the park's ancient oak trees have come back to life.

CUYAMACA MOUNTAINS

The Cuyamaca and Laguna mountains separate coastal and inland San Diego from the desert. Abundant winter rainfall produces thick oak and pine forests, year-round streams, and sparkling waterfalls here. The mountains were also home to a small gold rush in the 1870s, remnants of which can be seen throughout the region. Wildlife including deer, coyotes, and mountain lions is abundant.

Cuyamaca Rancho State Park. Spread over more than 25,000 acres of open meadows, oak woodlands, pine forests and mountains and rising to 6,512 feet at Cuyamaca Peak, much of the park, including its infrastructure, burned during a wildfire in 2003. Many of the camps, picnic areas, and trails are open again, and abundant seasonal wildflowers and other native plants emerge from the earth in a breathtaking display. For an inspirational desert view, stop at the lookout about 2 miles south of Julian on Route 79; on a clear day you can see several mountain ranges in hues ranging from pink to amber stepped back behind the Salton Sea. ⊠ *13652 Hwy. 79* ☎ *760/765–3020* ⊕ *www.parks.ca.gov.*

☮ **Lake Cuyamaca.** Behind a dam constructed in 1888 (the second oldest in California) this 110-acre lake offers fishing, boating, picnicking, nature hikes, and wildlife-watching. Anglers regularly catch trout, smallmouth bass, and sturgeon. A shaded picnic area occupies the lakeshore. Families can rent small motorboats, rowboats, and paddleboats by the hour. Free fishing classes for adults and kids are held Saturday at 10 am. Fishing licenses and advice are available at the tackle shop. Two rental condominiums, three sleeping cabins, 19 RV campsites with hookups, and 21 tent sites are available with reservations (call Monday through Thursday). ⊠ *15027 Hwy. 79* ☎ *760/765–0515 or 877/581–9904* ⊕ *www. lakecuyamaca.org* ⊒ *$6 per vehicle for picnic area* ☉ *Daily dawn–dusk.*

Sunrise National Scenic Byway. In the Cleveland National Forest, this is the most dramatic approach to Julian—its turns and curves reveal amazing views of the desert from the Salton Sea all the way to Mexico. You can spend an entire day roaming these mountains; an early-morning hike to the top of Garnet Peak (mile marker 27.8) is the best way to catch the view. Springtime wildflower displays are spectacular, particularly along Big Laguna Trail from Laguna Campground. There are picnic areas along the highway at Desert View and Pioneer Mail. The Visitor Center, located inside the Blue Jay Lodge, is open weekends. ⊠ *Hwy. 79, Descanso* ⊕ *www.byways.org.*

Ready for lift-off at the Temecula Valley Balloon and Wine Festival

WHERE TO EAT

$ 🍴 **Franz's Lake Cuyamaca Restaurant.** This tidy, lace-curtained lakefront café specializes in Austrian fare, highlights of which include a selection of schnitzels and wursts, plus several chicken and steak entrées. Austrian beers are on tap. The restaurant, as well as the adjacent food market, is popular with anglers and locals. [$] *Average main: $17* ✉ *15027 Hwy. 79* ☎ *760/765–0700* 🌐 *www.lakecuyamacarestaurant.com.*

AUSTRIAN

JULIAN

62 miles from San Diego to Julian, east on I–8 and north on Rte. 79.

Gold was discovered in the Julian area in 1869, and gold-bearing quartz a year later. More than $15 million worth of gold was taken from local mines in the 1870s. Many of the buildings along Julian's Main Street and the side streets today date back to the gold-rush period; others are reproductions.

When gold and quartz became scarce, the locals turned to growing apples and pears. During the fall harvest season you can buy fruit, sip apple cider (hard or soft), eat apple pie, and shop for local original art, antiques, and collectibles. But spring is equally enchanting (and less congested), as the hillsides explode with wildflowers—thousands of daffodils, lilacs, and peonies. More than 50 artists have studios tucked away in the hills surrounding Julian; they often show their work in local shops and galleries. The Julian area comprises three small crossroads communities: Santa Ysabel, Wynola, and historic Julian. You can find bits of history, shops, and dining options in each

Casino Country

San Diego County, along with the Temecula area, is the Indian gaming capital of California, with more than 13 tribes operating casinos in the region's backcountry. The casinos range from resorts with headliner entertainment and golf courses, to small rooms tucked away on rural crossroads with slot machines and cards. Although the gaming options may resemble what you might find in Las Vegas, the action is definitely different. The casinos stand alone on back roads, so it's not practical to travel from one to another. The big casinos—Viejas, Barona, Sycuan, Rincon, Pala, and Pachenga—are popular with local seniors and some Asian visitors. Many casinos offer bus transport, so call before visiting and save on gas. Gambling age is 18 years, 21 in some casinos.

Viejas Casino. Viejas Casino is a massive Native American–theme entertainment and shopping complex. Viejas has more than 2,500 slot machines, plus blackjack, poker, bingo, pai gow, and off-track wagering. There are six restaurants, a cocktail lounge, and a VIP lounge. The Viejas Outlet Center, a factory outlet mall across from the casino, has more than 50 shops, restaurants, an amphitheater, and the California Welcome Center. ⊠ *5000 Willows Rd., Alpine* ☎ *619/445–5400 or 800/847–6537* ⊕ *www.viejas.com.*

Barona Valley Ranch Resort and Casino. Barona Valley Ranch Resort and Casino is an all-in-one Western-style destination with gaming, hotel, restaurants, and golf course. In the casino you can find 2,000 slots, more than 80 gaming tables including blackjack, a poker room, and off-track betting. The 400-room Barona Valley

Ranch hotel has a fitness center, day spa, and pool. ⊠ *1932 Wildcat Canyon Rd., Lakeside* ☎ *619/443–2300 or 888/722–7662* ⊕ *www.barona.com.*

Sycuan Casino. More compact than other area casinos, Sycuan Casino has 2,000 slot machines; table games such as blackjack, poker, and pai gow; and a bingo parlor. Portions of the casino are smoke-free. The tribe also owns the nearby Sycuan Resort. ⊠ *5469 Casino Way, El Cajon* ☎ *619/320–6078 or 800/279–2826* ⊕ *www.sycuan.com.*

Harrah's Rincon Casino & Resort. Harrah's Rincon Casino & Resort lies in the shadow of Palomar Mountain. The resort has 662 rooms and five entertainment venues. The casino has 2,000 slot machines and 60 table games, and there are seven restaurants, plus a spa, pool, and gym. Two show rooms offer entertainment most nights. ⊠ *777 Harrah's Rincon Way, Valley Center* ☎ *760/751–3100* ⊕ *www.harrahs.com.*

Pechanga Resort & Casino. Pechanga Resort & Casino has some of the best accommodations. The resort hotel has 517 rooms, plus 45 sites in its RV park, seven restaurants and a food court, a gym, sauna, swimming pool, spa, and golf course. The casino has 3,400 slot machines, more than 132 table games, a high-limit gaming area with VIP lounge, and no-smoking poker room. Several night clubs offer live entertainment nightly. The casino presents championship boxing matches year-round. ⊠ *45000 Pechanga Pkwy., Temecula* ☎ *951/693–1819* ⊕ *www.pechanga.com.*

—Bobbi Zane

community. Most visitors come to spend a day in town, but the hillsides support small bed-and-breakfast establishments for those who want to linger longer.

ESSENTIALS

Visitor Information Julian Chamber of Commerce ⊠ *Town Hall, 2129 Main St.* ☏ *760/765–1857* ⊕ *www.julianca.com* ⊙ *Daily 8–4.*

Backcountry Visitor Center. A local landmark, the Santa Ysabel General Store has been updated and backdated to 1884, when it was an important stop on the road between the mountains and San Diego. You'll find good advice, maps and guides to backcountry trails, and info on cultural sites and recreational activities. The store side of the adobe structure sells heirloom seeds and bulbs, do-it-yourself cheese or craft beer making kits, and specialty honey, pickled vegetables, and preserves put up in micro batches by food artisans. ⊠ *30275 Hwy. 78, Santa Ysabel* ☏ *760/765–1270* ⊕ *sohosandiego.org* ⊙ *Fri.–Sun. 10–4.*

EXPLORING

TOP ATTRACTIONS

☺ **California Wolf Center.** This center, just outside Julian, is one of the few
★ places in North America where you can get an up-close view of the gray wolves that once roamed much of the continent. The center participates in breeding programs and houses several captive packs, including some rare Mexican grays, a subspecies of the North American gray wolf that came within seven individuals of extinction in the 1970s. The animals are kept secluded from public view in 3-acre pens, but some may be seen by visitors during weekly educational tours. Private tours are by appointment. ⊠ *Hwy. 79 at KQ Ranch Rd.* ☏ *619/234–9653* ⊕ *www. californiawolfcenter.org* ☝ *$20, reservations required* ⊙ *Tours: Sat. 2 and 4:30, Sun. 10 (call for additional seasonal tour times).*

☺ **Julian Pioneer Museum.** When the gold mines in Julian played out, the mobs of gold miners who had invaded it left, leaving behind discarded mining tools and empty houses. Today the Julian Pioneer Museum, a 19th-century brewery, displays remnants of that time, including pioneer clothing, a collection of old lace, mining tools, and original photographs of the town's historic buildings and mining structures. ⊠ *2811 Washington St.* ☏ *760/765–0227* ☝ *$3* ⊙ *Thurs.–Sun., 10–4.*

Observer's Inn. One of the best ways to see Julian's star-filled summer sky is by taking a sky-tour at Mike and Caroline Leigh's observatory, with research-grade telescopes. The hosts guide you through the star clusters and galaxies, pointing out planets and nebulae. They also offer solar tours at noontime, when you can get a good look at the sun using a telescope designed for this purpose. It's also an inn, if you wish to stay the night. Reservations are necessary for tours and lodging. ⊠ *3535 Hwy. 79* ☏ *760/765–0088* ⊕ *www.observersinn.com* ☝ *$25* ☝ *Reservations essential.*

Volcan Mountain Wilderness Preserve. The Volcan Mountain Foundation and San Diego Parks and Recreation manage the 3,000-acre preserve, where hikes challenge your stamina and views are stunning. A 1¼ -mile trail through the preserve passes through Engelmann oak forest, native manzanita, and rolling mountain meadows to a viewpoint

15

where the panorama extends north all the way to Palomar Mountain. On a clear day you can see Point Loma in San Diego. At the entrance you pass through gates designed by James Hubbell, a local artist known for his ironwork, wood carving, and stained glass. You can see splendid views from the 5-mile Volcan Summit Trail. Guided hikes on the Sky Island Trail and the Oak Walk Trail are offered regularly. ⊠ *From Julian take Farmer Rd. to Wynola Rd., go east a few yards, and then north on continuation of Farmer Rd.* ☎ *760/765–2300* ⊕ *www.volcanmt.org* ⊠ *Free* ☉ *Daily dawn–dusk.*

> ## JULIAN'S BLACK HISTORY
>
> According to local history and old photos, the Julian area had a large population of African-Americans in the years following the Civil War. Indeed, it was a black man, Fred Coleman, who discovered gold in Julian, and the Julian Hotel was founded and operated by Albert and Margaret Robinson, also black. Headstones recognizing the contributions of Julian's black pioneers continue to be placed in the old section of the Pioneer Cemetery.

WORTH NOTING

Banner Queen Trading Post Gallery. A step inside what was the mine superintendent's home in the run-down-looking remnant of an old gold mine dug into a hillside on Banner Grade, 5 miles east of Julian, reveals a wealth of contemporary art. Five rooms are filled with paintings, photos, sculpture, ceramics, stained glass, and woven pieces by Julian artists. Prices range from $30 or less for photos and pottery to hundreds for paintings. ⊠ *36766 Hwy. 78* ☎ *760/765–2168* ☉ *Fri.–Sun. 1–5.*

☉ **Eagle Mining Company.** Five blocks east of the center of Julian, you can take an hour-long tour of an authentic Julian gold mine. Displays include authentic tools and machinery, gold extraction process, and gold quartz bearing veins. A small rock shop and gold-mining museum are also on the premises. ⊠ *Box 624* ☎ *760/765–0036* ⊠ *$10* ☉ *Daily 10–3, weather permitting.*

Mission Santa Ysabel. West of Santa Ysabel, this tiny late-19th-century adobe mission continues to serve several local Native American communities. A small museum on the premises (*Daily 8–3*) houses memorabilia from local families, Native Americans, and the parish. ⊠ *23013 Hwy. 79* ☎ *760/765–0810.*

★ **Santa Ysabel Preserve.** Three Native American tribes live in this valley, which looks pretty much the way the backcountry appeared a century ago, with sweeping meadows surrounded by oak-studded hillsides. The tribes operate small farms and run cattle here. The San Dieguito River (Santa Ysabel Creek) emerges from Volcan Mountain here and winds its way 55 miles to Dog Beach at Del Mar. A hiking, biking, and equestrian trail system follows the river from Farmer Road in Julian to the West Entrance just west of Santa Ysabel. Legacy oak tree shade the trail, waterfalls provide a background sound, there are spectacular views along the way, and picnic tables abound. ⊕ *www.sdrvc.org.*

WHERE TO EAT

$ ✕ **Bailey Woodfired Barbecue & Julian Brewery.** Even though the restaurant
BARBECUE sports a rustic look with long picnic tables suitable for groups and
families and meals served in baskets, this is best place in the area to
dance the night away and get cold smoked barbecue, garlic fries, and
local brew. The menu features huge portions of barbecue plates and
ribs: pulled pork, beef brisket (gets raves), and baby back ribs. They
also offer sandwiches and salads. The micro brewery out back makes
Bailey Pale Ale, Dru's Dry Hopped Pale, 1870 IPA, and Ghost Tree
Stout, all on tap and sold only here. On weekends the place becomes a
nightclub with local music and dancing. $ *Average main: $17* ⊠ *2307
Main St.* ☎ *760/765–3757* ⊕ *www.BaileyBBQ.com* ⌂ *Reservations
not accepted* ⊘ *Closed Mon. and Tues.*

$$ ✕ **Jeremy's on the Hill.** Jeremy's is the place to go in Julian for a quiet
MODERN dinner, pleasant surroundings, and some of the best burgers around.
AMERICAN While the menu features grilled steak, rack of lamb, and locally caught
mussels, the stars are the San Diego burger stuffed with blue cheese
Fodor'sChoice cream and Dijon cream sauce and accompanied by onion rings and
★ garlic fries and the gloppy bacon-wrapped Bison burger made with
locally raised meat. Jeremy specializes in local produce, wine, and brews
such as Julian Hard Cider, Stone Brewing Levitation Ale, and Shadow
Mountain Viognier. There's entertainment weekend nights but note
that Jeremy's closes relatively early: at 8 pm Sun.–Thurs. and at 9 pm
on Fri.–Sat. $ *Average main: $27* ⊠ *4354 Hwy. 78* ☎ *760/765–1587*
⊕ *www.jeremysonthehill.com* ⌂ *Reservations essential.*

$ ✕ **Julian Pie Company.** The apple pies that made Julian famous come
AMERICAN from the Smothers family bakery in a one-story house on Main Street.
★ In pleasant weather you can sit on the front patio and watch the world
go by while savoring a slice of hot pie—from Dutch apple to apple
mountain berry crumb—topped with homemade cinnamon ice cream.
The Smothers family has been making pies in Julian since 1986; by 1989
they had bought their own orchard, and by 1992 they had built a larger
bakery in Santa Ysabel that makes and serves only pies. At lunchtime
the Julian location also serves soup and sandwiches ($8.95). $ *Average
main: $14* ⊠ *2225 Main St.* ☎ *760/765–2449* ⊕ *www.julianpie.com.*

$ ✕ **Julian Tea and Cottage Arts.** Sample finger sandwiches, scones topped
CAFÉ with whipped cream, and lavish sweets are served during afternoon tea
inside the Clarence King House, built by Will Bosnell in 1898. Regular
sandwiches, soups, salads, and a children's tea are also available. Victo-
rian teas are presented during the holiday season. $ *Average main: $17*
⊠ *2124 3rd St.* ☎ *760/765–0832 or 866/765–0832* ⊕ *www.juliantea.
com* ⊘ *Closed Tues. and Wed. No dinner.*

$ ✕ **Soups 'n Such Cafe.** It's worth the wait for breakfast or lunch at this
CAFÉ cozy café, where everything is fresh and made to order. The breakfast
standout is eggs Benedict, both classic and vegetarian, and for lunch you
can chose among several classic salads. $ *Average main: $10* ⊠ *2000
Main St.* ☎ *760/765–4761* ⊘ *Closed Tues. and Wed.*

$ ✕ **Wynola Pizza Express.** Locals and San Diegans come to this quaint and
ITALIAN casual indoor-outdoor restaurant for delicious, single-portion pies, such
as pesto pizza, Thai chicken pizza, vegan pizza, and tostada pizza. Other

15

items include chili, lasagna, seared Cajun salmon, and a killer fire-roasted artichoke dip served with homemade buffalo crackers. Entertainers usually perform on weekends in the adjacent Red Barn or, in good weather, outdoors. $ *Average main: $13* ✉ *4355 Hwy. 78, Santa Ysabel* ☎ *760/765–1004* ⊕ *www.wynolapizzaexpress.com.*

WHERE TO STAY

For expanded hotel reviews, visit Fodors.com.

$ 🔲 **Butterfield Bed and Breakfast.** This inn on a 3-acre hilltop is cordial
B&B/INN   and romantic, with knotty-pine ceilings, Laura Ashley accents, and rooms that have such nice touches as fireplaces or woodstoves and private entrances. **Pros:** great food; interesting hosts; secluded. **Cons:** very quiet; no room phones. $ *Rooms from: $135* ✉ *2284 Sunset Dr.* ☎ *760/765–2179 or 800/379–4262* ⊕ *www.butterfieldbandb.com* ➤ *5 rooms* ⫦ *Breakfast.*

$ 🔲 **Julian Gold Rush Hotel.** Built in 1897 by freed slave Albert Robin-
B&B/INN   son and his wife, Margaret, this old hotel is Julian's only designated national landmark and offers antiques-filled rooms and cottage accommodations with private entrances and fireplaces. **Pros:** genuine historic hotel; convivial atmosphere. **Cons:** small rooms; no TV. $ *Rooms from: $135* ✉ *2032 Main St.* ☎ *760/765–0201 or 800/734–5854* ⊕ *www.julianhotel.com* ➤ *14 rooms, 2 suites* ⫦ *Breakfast.*

$ 🔲 **Julian Lodge.** In this replica of a late-19th-century inn, rooms and
B&B/INN   public spaces are furnished with antiques and on chilly days you can warm yourself at the large stove in the small lobby. **Pros:** in-town location; free parking. **Cons:** limited facilities; simple appointments; busy surroundings. $ *Rooms from: $85* ✉ *2720 C St.* ☎ *760/765–1420 or 800/542–1420* ⊕ *www.julianlodge.com* ➤ *23 rooms* ⫦ *Breakfast.*

$$$ 🔲 **Orchard Hill Country Inn.** On a hill above town, this lodge and five
B&B/INN   Craftsman-style cottages have a sweeping view of the countryside and
★   offer luxurious accommodations decorated with antiques, original art, and handcrafted quilts. **Pros:** most luxurious digs in Julian; good food. **Cons:** limited amenities. $ *Rooms from: $300* ✉ *2502 Washington St.* ☎ *760/765–1700 or 800/716–7242* ⊕ *www.orchardhill.com* ➤ *10 rooms, 12 suites* ⫦ *Breakfast.*

$$ 🔲 **Wikiup Bed and Breakfast.** Best known for its herd of llamas, this
B&B/INN   contemporary cedar-and-brick inn is decorated with romantic furnishings and offers guest rooms with fireplaces and outdoor hot tubs for stargazing. **Pros:** private entrances; pleasant surroundings. **Cons:** limited facilities; decor may be a bit much for some; two-night minimum. $ *Rooms from: $185* ✉ *1645 Whispering Pines Dr.* ☎ *760/765–1890 or 800/694–5487* ⊕ *www.wikiupbnb.com* ➤ *5 rooms* ⫦ *Breakfast.*

SHOPPING

The Julian area has a number of unique shops that are open weekends, but midweek hours vary considerably. In autumn locally grown apples, pears, nuts, and cider are available in town and at a few roadside stands. The best apple variety produced here is a Jonagold, a hybrid of Jonathan and Golden Delicious.

Birdwatcher. The Birdwatcher offers items for wild-bird lovers, including birdhouses, birdseed, hummingbird feeders, plus bird-theme accessories such as jewelry, apparel, novelties, and guidebooks for serious birders. ✉ *2775 B St.* ☎ *760/765–1817.*

Falcon Gallery. The Falcon Gallery, in a replica of one of Julian's original hotels, has works by local artists, books about area history including Native American history, and limited edition print books. ✉ *2015 A Main St.* ☎ *760/765–1509.*

Mountain Gypsy. Mountain Gypsy is popular area-wide for an extensive collection of jewelry and trendy apparel and shoes in petite and plus sizes. ✉ *2007 Main St.* ☎ *760/765–0643.*

Santa Ysabel Art Gallery. Santa Ysabel Art Gallery shows fine art including watercolors, stained glass, sculptures, fiber, and other creations by local artists. ✉ *30352 Hwy. 78, Santa Ysabel* ☎ *760/765–1676.*

PALOMAR MOUNTAIN

15

35 miles northeast of Escondido on I–15 to Rte. 76 to Rte. S6, 66 miles northeast of downtown San Diego on Rte. 163 to I–15 to Rte. 76 to Rte. S6.

Palomar Mountain, at an altitude of 6,140 feet and with an average of 300 clear nights per year, has the distinction of being the home of one of the world's most significant astronomical observation sites, the Hale 200-inch telescope installed at the Palomar Observatory in 1947. Before that, the mountain played a role in San Diego County's rich African-American history and culture. One of many who migrated to the area in the mid-19th century was Nathan Harrison, a former slave who owned a large swath of property on the mountain where he farmed and raised cattle, the importance of which is just being revealed through archaeological excavations conducted by local university students. According to local historians, Harrison and other former slaves made up a major segment of the backcountry population until about 1900.

EXPLORING

☾ **Mission San Antonio de Pala.** A living remnant of the mission era, built in 1816, still ministers to the Native American community, making it the only original Spanish mission still serving its initial purpose. The old jail and cemetery are part of the original mission. The school, long operated by Sisters of the Blessed Sacrament and the Sisters of Precious Blood, is now a charter school operated by the Bonsall USD. You can take a self-guided tour of the mission and grounds. ✉ *Pala Mission Rd. off Rte. 76, 6 miles east of I–15, 3015 Pala Mission Rd., Pala* ☎ *760/742–3317* ⊕ *www.missionsanantonio.org* ▭ *$2* ◷ *Wed.–Sat. 9–4.*

☾ **Palomar Mountain State Park.** One of the few areas in Southern California with a Sierra-like atmosphere, the park is carpeted with a forest of pines, cedars, western dogwood, native azalea, and other plants. Wildflower viewing is good in spring. **Boucher Lookout,** on one of several nature/hiking trails, affords a sweeping view to the west. There's trout fishing in Doane Pond. The Doane Valley campground offers 31 sites with tables, fire pits, and flush toilets. From May to October, reservations are strongly recommended, and can be made seven months in advance. ✉ *Off Hwy. S6 at Hwy. S7, 19952 State Park Rd., Palomar Mountain* ☎ *760/742–3462 ranger station, 800/444–7275 campsite reservations* 🌐 *www.parks.ca.gov* 🎟 *Camping $30, $8 reservation fee.*

Palomar Observatory. Atop 6,000-foot Palomar Mountain, the observatory is owned and operated by the California Institute of Technology, whose astronomy faculty conducts research here. The observatory houses the Hale Telescope, as well as 60-inch, 48-inch, 24-inch, 18-inch, and Snoop telescopes. Some of the most important astronomical discoveries of the 20th century were made here, and already in this century scientists using the observatory's 48-inch telescope have detected a 10th planet. For the time being, this most distant known object in the solar system, a body larger than fellow dwarf-planet Pluto, has been named Eris. **TIP→** The observatory closes without advance notice during inclement weather. Call in advance during winter. The small museum contains photos of some of these discoveries, as well as photos taken by NASA's Hubble Space Telescope and from recent NASA–European Space Agency missions to Mars and Saturn. A park with picnic areas surrounds the observatory. ✉ *Rte. S6 north of Rte. 76, east of I–15, 35899 Canfield Rd., Palomar Mountain* ☎ *760/742–2119* 🌐 *www.astro.caltech.edu/palomar* 🎟 *Free, $5 guided tours* 🕒 *Daily 9–4 during daylight savings time; 9–3 during standard time; guided tours weekends Apr.–Oct. at 11 and 1:30.*

WHERE TO EAT

$ VEGETARIAN 🍴 **Mother's Kitchen.** This popular stop for motorcyclists (the road up there is the most popular biker route in Southern California) serves up huge portions of vegetarian fare, including salads, mountain chili, Boca tacos, macaroni and cheese, and lasagna. Sides include steaming-hot soup, nachos, and quesadillas. The atmosphere is mountain casual, with open-beam ceilings, knotty-pine tables, and fresh flowers everywhere. Waitresses are friendly, and local musicians entertain on weekends. [$] *Average main: $10* ✉ *Junction of Hwys. S6 and S7, Palomar Mountain* ☎ *760/742–4233* 🌐 *www.motherskitchenpalomar.com* 🕒 *Closed Mon.–Wed. Labor Day–Memorial Day. No dinner.*

THE DESERT

In most spring seasons the stark desert landscape east of the Cuyamaca Mountains explodes with colorful wildflowers. The beauty of this spectacle, as well as the natural quiet and blazing climate, lures many tourists and natives each year to Anza-Borrego Desert State Park, about a two-hour drive from central San Diego.

For hundreds of years the only humans to linger here were Native Americans of the Cahuilla and Kumeyaay tribes, who made their winter homes in the desert. It was not until 1774, when Mexican explorer Captain Juan Bautista de Anza first blazed a trail through the area seeking a shortcut from Sonora, Mexico, to San Francisco, that Europeans had their first glimpse of the oddly enchanting terrain.

The desert is best visited from October through May to avoid the extreme summer temperatures. Winter temperatures are comfortable, but nights (and sometimes days) are cold, so bring a warm jacket.

ANZA-BORREGO DESERT STATE PARK

88 miles from downtown San Diego (to park border due west of Borrego Springs).

GETTING HERE AND AROUND

You'll need a car to visit the Anza-Borrego Desert and Borrego Springs, which is totally surrounded by wilderness. The trip from San Diego is about 88 scenic miles, and it takes about two hours. Once there be prepared to drive on dusty roads as there is no public transportation. The best route to Borrego Springs is via I–8 east out of San Diego; exit east on Highway 79 and take the scenic drive through the Cuyamaca Mountains to Julian, where Highway 79 intersects with Highway 78 going east. Follow Highway 78 into the desert to Yaqui Pass Road, turn left and follow the signs to Borrego Springs Christmas Circle. Take Borrego Palm Canyon west to reach the Anza-Borrego Desert State Park headquarters.

TOUR OPTIONS

California Overland Excursions offers day tours and overnight excursions into hard-to-reach scenic desert destinations using open-air, military-transport vehicles. Typical destinations include Font's Point, the Badlands, and 17-Palm Oasis.

Tour Information **California Overland Excursions**
✉ *1233 Palm Canyon Dr., Borrego Springs* ☎ *760/767–1232 or 866/639–7567* ⊕ *www.californiaoverland.com.*

ESSENTIALS

Visitor Information **Anza-Borrego Desert State Park** ✉ *200 Palm Canyon Dr., Borrego Springs* ☎ *760/767–5311* ⊕ *www.parks.ca.gov.*
State Park Reservations ☎ *800/444–7275* ⊕ *www.reserveamerica.com.*
Wildflower Hotline ☎ *760/767–4684.*

EXPLORING

Anza-Borrego State Park. Today more than 1,000 square miles of desert and mountain country are included in the Anza-Borrego Desert State Park, one of the few parks in the country where you can follow a trail and pitch a tent wherever you like. Five hundred miles of paved and dirt roads traverse the park, and you are required to stay on them so as not to disturb its ecological balance. There are also 110 miles of hiking and riding trails that allow you to explore canyons, capture scenic vistas, and tiptoe through fields of wildflowers in spring. The park is also home to rare Peninsula bighorn sheep, mountain lions, coyotes, black-tailed jackrabbit, and roadrunners. State Highway 78, which runs north and south through the park, has been designated the Juan Bautista de Anza National Historic Trail, marking portions of the route of the Anza Colonizing Expedition of 1775–76 that went from northern Mexico to the San Francisco Bay area. In addition, 28,000 acres have been set aside in the eastern part of the desert near Ocotillo Wells

Spring Wildflowers

Southern California's famous warm, sunny climate has blessed this corner of the continent with an ever-changing, year-round palette of natural color. It's hard to find a spot anywhere around the globe that produces as spectacular a scene as San Diego does in spring—from the native plant gardens found tucked away in mountain canyons and streambeds to the carpets of wildflowers on the desert floor. You'll have to see it yourself to believe just how alive the deceptively barren desert really is.

WHEN TO GO
Spring debuts in **late February or early March.** Heavy winter rains always precede the best bloom seasons. And good blooms also bring even more beauty—a bounty of butterflies. A further boon: here in this generally temperate climate, the bloom season lasts nearly all year.

Some drought-tolerant plants rely on fire to germinate, and the years following wildfires generally produce a profusion of plant life not normally seen. Although wildfires in the Cuyamaca and Laguna mountains in 2002 and 2003 destroyed much of the ancient forest, subsequent years saw brilliant and unusual wildflower displays as a result.

WHAT TO SEE
Look for rare western redbud trees erupting into a profusion of crimson flowers, sometimes starting as early as February. Native California lilacs (ceanothus) blanket the hillsides throughout the backcountry with fragrant blue-and-white blossoms starting in May and showing until August.

Native varieties of familiar names show up in the mountain canyons and streambeds. A beautiful white western azalea would be the star in anyone's garden. A pink California rose blooms along streambeds in spring and summer. Throughout the year three varieties of native dogwood show off white blooms and beautiful crimson fall foliage. The **Cuyamaca Mountains** usually put on a display of fall color as the native oaks turn gold and red. By winter the rare toyon, known as the California Christmas tree, lights up the roadside with its red berries.

Farther east in the **Anza-Borrego Desert State Park,** the spring wildflower display can be spectacular: carpets of pink, purple, white, and yellow verbena and desert primrose as far as the eye can see. Rocky slopes yield clumps of beavertail cactus topped with showy pink blossoms, clumps of yellow brittlebush tucked among the rocks, and crimson-tip ocotillo trees. For a good introduction to desert vegetation, explore the visitor center demonstration garden, adjacent to the park's underground headquarters.

For a vivid view of both the mountain and desert spring flora, take I–8 east to Route 79, go north to Julian, and then east on Route 78 into Anza-Borrego park.

for off-road enthusiasts. General George S. Patton conducted field training in the Ocotillo area to prepare for the World War II invasion of North Africa.

Many of the park's sites can be seen from paved roads, but some require driving on dirt roads, where it's easy to sink up to your wheel covers in dry sand. Rangers recommend using four-wheel-drive vehicles on the dirt roads. Carry the appropriate supplies: shovel and other tools, flares, blankets, and plenty of water. Canyons are susceptible to flash flooding; inquire about weather conditions before entering.

Wildflowers, which typically begin to bloom in January and are at their peak in mid-March, attract thousands of visitors each spring. A variety of factors including rainfall and winds determine how extensive the bloom will be in a particular year. However, good displays of low-growing sand verbena and white evening primrose can usually be found along Airport Road and DiGeorgio Road. Following wet winters, spectacular displays fill the dry washes in Coyote Canyon and along Henderson Canyon Road. The best light for photography is in early morning or late afternoon.

Erosion Road, a self-guided, 18-mile auto tour along Route S22. The **Southern Emigrant Trail** follows the route of the Butterfield Stage Overland Mail, the route used by half of the argonauts heading for the gold fields in Northern California.

At **Borrego Palm Canyon,** a few minutes west of the visitor information center, a 1½-mile trail leads to a small oasis with a waterfall and palms. The Borrego Palm Canyon campground is the only developed campground with flush toilets and showers in the park. (Day use is $8 and camping is $25 in high season, $35 with hookup.)

Geology students from all over the world visit the Fish Creek area of Anza-Borrego to explore a famous canyon known as **Split Mountain** (*Split Mountain Rd. south from Rte. 78 at Ocotillo Wells*), a narrow gorge with 600-foot perpendicular walls that was formed by an ancestral stream. Fossils in this area indicate that a sea covered the desert floor at one time. A 2-mile nature trail west of Split Mountain rewards hikers with a good view of shallow caves created by erosion. ⊠ *200 Palm Canyon Dr., Borrego Springs* ☎ *760/765–5311* ⊕ *www.parks.ca.gov.*

Visitor Information Center. Rangers and displays at an excellent visitor information center can point you in the right direction. Most of the desert plants can also be seen in the demonstration desert garden at the visitor center. ⊠ *200 Palm Canyon Dr., Borrego Springs* ☎ *760/767–4205, 760/767–4684 wildflower hotline* ⊕ *www.parks.ca.gov* ☉ *Oct.–Apr. daily 9–5; May–Sept. weekends 9–5.*

BORREGO SPRINGS

31 miles from Julian, east on Rte. 78 and Yaqui Pass Rd., and north on Rte. S3.

A quiet town with a handful of year-round residents, Borrego Springs is set in the heart of the Anza-Borrego Desert State Park and is emerging as a destination for desert lovers. From September through June, temperatures hover in the 80s and 90s, and you can enjoy activities such as hiking, nature study, golf, tennis, horseback riding, and mountain-bike riding. Even during the busier winter season, Borrego Springs feels quiet. There are three golf resorts, two bed-and-breakfast inns, and a growing community of winter residents, but the laid-back vibe prevails. If winter rains cooperate, Borrego Springs puts on some of the best wildflower displays in the low desert.

ESSENTIALS

Visitor Information **Borrego Springs Chamber of Commerce** ✉ *786 Palm Canyon Dr.* ☎ *760/767–5555 or 800/559–5524* 🌐 *www.borregospringschamber.com.*

EXPLORING

Galleta Meadows. Flowers aren't the only things popping up from the earth in Borrego Springs. At Galleta Meadows camels, llamas, saber-toothed tigers, tortoises, and monumental gomphotherium (a sort of ancient elephant) appear to roam the earth again. These life-size bronze figures are of prehistoric animals whose fossils can be found in the Borrego Badlands. The collection, more than 50 sets of animals, is the project of a wealthy resident who has installed the works of art on property he owns for the entertainment of locals and visitors. Maps are available from Borrego Springs Chamber of Commerce. ✉ *Borrego Springs Rd. from Christmas Circle to Henderson Canyon* ☎ *760/767–5555* 🌐 *www.galletameadows.com* 🎟 *Free.*

WHERE TO EAT

$ AMERICAN 🍴 **The Arches.** Set right on the edge of the Borrego Springs Golf Course, this is one of the most pleasant dining rooms in the area. There's indoor and outdoor seating, and the offerings, mostly of the comfort food style, are surprisingly good: try the tortilla crusted chicken for dinner. Service can be super casual. [$] *Average main: $17* ✉ *1112 Tilting T Dr.* ☎ *760/767–5700* 🕒 *Summer hrs vary; call ahead.*

$$ AMERICAN 🍴 **Carlee's Bar & Grill.** This local watering hole seems to collect characters ranging from hippies to mountain men and is the place to go any night of the week. A large, dimly lighted room houses the bar and dining tables, and the menu lists pasta and pizza in addition to old-fashioned entrées such as liver and onions, ribs and steaks, and a mixed grill. Dinners come with soup or salad. [$] *Average main: $21* ✉ *660 Palm Canyon Dr.* ☎ *760/767–3262.*

$ MEXICAN 🍴 **Carmelita's Mexican Grill and Cantina.** A friendly family-run eatery tucked into a back corner of what is called "The Mall," Carmelita's draws locals and visitors all day whether it's for a hearty breakfast, a cooked-to-order enchilada or burrito, or a brew at the bar. The menu lists typical combination plates (enchiladas, burritos, tamales,

If you think the desert is just a sandy wasteland, the stark beauty of the Anza-Borrego Desert will shock you.

and tacos). Salsas have a bit of zing, and masas are tasty and tender. $\boxed{\$}$ *Average main: $14* ✉ *575 Palm Canyon Dr.* ☎ *760/767–5666.*

$$
AMERICAN
✕ **Krazy Coyote Bar & Grill/Red Ocotillo.** Two popular restaurants provide a nice choice at the Palms at Indianhead. The Krazy Coyote is a trendy mid-'50s-style café, with dark red walls adorned with movie posters and other memorabilia, and serves substantial fare that includes filet mignon and salmon. The Red Ocotillo serves inexpensive comfort food, including sandwiches, burgers, and chicken-fried steak. $\boxed{\$}$ *Average main: $20* ✉ *2220 Hoberg Rd.* ☎ *760/767–7788* ⊕ *www.thepalmsatindianhead. com* ⌕ *Reservations essential* ☽ *No lunch in Krazy Coyote; call for hrs in summer.*

WHERE TO STAY
For expanded hotel reviews, visit Fodors.com.

$
RESORT
⌂ **Borrego Springs Resort & Spa.** Large rooms fitted out with nice amenities and furnishings surround a swimming pool and all have shaded balconies or patios with pleasant desert views. **Pros:** golf and tennis on-site; most rooms have good desert views. **Cons:** limited amenities; average service. $\boxed{\$}$ *Rooms from: $149* ✉ *1112 Tilting T Dr.* ☎ *760/767–5700 or 888/826–7734* ⊕ *www.borregospringsresort.com* ⇆ *66 rooms, 34 suites* ⍥ *No meals.*

$$
B&B/INN
★
⌂ **Borrego Valley Inn.** Desert gardens of mesquite, ocotillo, and creosote surround adobe buildings housing spacious rooms with plenty of natural light, original art, pine beds, and double futons facing corner fireplaces. **Pros:** swim under the stars in the clothing-optional pool; exquisite desert gardens. **Cons:** potential street noise in season; not a good choice for families with young children or pets. $\boxed{\$}$ *Rooms from: $200* ✉ *405*

Palm Canyon Dr. ☎ *760/767–0311 or 800/333–5810* 🌐 *www.borregovalleyinn.com* 🛏 *15 rooms, 1 suite* 🍴 *Breakfast.*

$ B&B/INN 🏨 **The Palms at Indian Head.** Spectacular desert views can be had from this small hotel that displays an authentic midcentury look, with handcrafted, Southwest lodgepole furniture and original art by local artists. **Pros:** quiet, oasis-like atmosphere; star connection; great views. **Cons:** somewhat remote location; simple decor; no room phones. [$] *Rooms from: $149* ✉ *2220 Hoberg Rd.* ☎ *760/767–7788 or 800/519–2624* 🌐 *www.thepalmsatindianhead.com* 🛏 *12 rooms* 🍴 *Breakfast.*

UNBURIED TREASURE

The Anza-Borrego Desert is one of the most geologically active spots in North America and a repository of geologic and paleontological treasure. Beneath its surface are fossil-bearing sediments containing the record of 7 million years of climate change, tectonic activity, upthrust, and subsidence—the richest fossil deposits in North America. Reading the fossil record, scientists have revealed that the badlands were once a wonderland of green, the home of saber-toothed tigers, flamingos, zebras, camels, the largest known mammoths, and a flying bird with a 16-foot wingspan.

SPORTS AND THE OUTDOORS

Borrego Springs Resort and Country Club. The 27-hole course at Borrego Springs Resort and Country Club is open to the public. The green fees range from $40 to $65, including mandatory cart; discounts may be available to foursomes midweek. ✉ *1112 Tilting T Dr.* ☎ *760/767–3330* 🌐 *borregospringsresort.com.*

Roadrunner Club. This club has an 18-hole par 3 golf course. The greens fee is $35, including cart. ✉ *1010 Palm Canyon Dr.* ☎ *760/767–5373* 🌐 *www.roadrunnerclub.com.*

OFF THE BEATEN PATH

Ocotillo Wells State Vehicular Recreation Area. The sand dunes and rock formations at this 70,000-plus acre haven for off-road enthusiasts are fun and challenging. Camping is permitted throughout the area, but water is not available. The only facilities are in the small town (really no more than a corner) of Ocotillo Wells. ✉ *Rte. 78, 18 miles east from Borrego Springs Rd., 5780 Hwy. 78* ☎ *760/767–5391* 🌐 *www.parks.ca.gov.*

Travel Smart
San Diego

WORD OF MOUTH

"From almost anywhere downtown (Gaslamp, Seaport Village area, Embarcadero) you can walk to the ferry to Coronado. From the Gaslamp area you can take a bus to Balboa Park and its zoo, or go the 2–3 miles by cab at minimal cost. La Jolla is only 13 or so miles away but a long trip by bus."

—d_claude_bear

GETTING HERE AND AROUND

When traveling in the San Diego area, consider the big picture to avoid getting lost. Water lies to the west of the city. To the east and north, mountains separate the urban areas from the desert. If you keep going south, you'll end up in Mexico.

Downtown San Diego is made up of several smaller communities, including the Gaslamp Quarter and Balboa Park, that you can easily explore by walking, driving, riding the bus or trolley, or taking a taxi. In the heart of the city, numbered streets run west to east and lettered streets run north to south. The business district around the Civic Center, at 1st Avenue and C Street, is dedicated to local government and commerce.

▌ AIR TRAVEL

Flying time to San Diego is 5 hours from New York, 3½ hours from Chicago, 3½ hours from Dallas, and 45 minutes from Los Angeles.

Airline Security Issues Transportation Security Administration ⊕ www.tsa.gov.

AIRPORT

The major airport is San Diego International Airport (SAN), called Lindbergh Field locally. Major airlines depart and arrive at Terminal 1 and Terminal 2; commuter flights identified on your ticket with a 3000-sequence flight number depart from a third commuter terminal. A red shuttle bus provides free transportation between terminals. With only one runway serving two main terminals, San Diego's airport is too small to accommodate the heavy traffic of busy travel periods. Small problems including fog and rain can cause congested terminals and flight delays. Delays of 20–30 minutes in baggage claim aren't unusual.

Major construction started at the airport in 2010 and is scheduled for completion in summer 2013. The result will be improved traffic flow, better parking, expanded waiting areas, 10 additional gates at Terminal 2, more shopping and dining options, and a public art collection. The airport's Cultural Exhibits Program in Terminal 2 showcases a variety of stimulating and educational exhibits that highlight the city's culture and history. Exhibits change several times per year. Terminal 2 also features a performing arts series between 7 pm and 9:15 pm on the second and fourth Friday of each month. In addition, if you have a flight delay, consider catching a 10-minute cab ride downtown to go shopping or take one last stroll around the city.

If you need travel assistance at the airport, there are two Travelers Aid information booths, one in Terminal 1 and one in Terminal 2, open daily 6 am–11 pm.

Airlines and Airports Airline and Airport Links.com ⊕ www.airlineandairportlinks.com. **San Diego International Airport** ✉ 3225 N. Harbor Dr., off I–5 ☎ 619/400–2400 ⊕ www.san.org.

GROUND TRANSPORTATION

San Diego International Airport is 3 miles from downtown. Shuttle vans, buses, and taxis run from the Transportation Plaza, reached via the skybridges from terminals 1 and 2. The cheapest and sometimes most convenient shuttle is the Metropolitan Transit System's Flyer Route 992, red-and-blue-stripe buses that serve the terminals at 10- to 15-minute intervals between 5 am and 11 pm. These buses have luggage racks and make a loop from the airport to downtown along Broadway to 9th Avenue and back, stopping frequently within walking distance of many hotels; they also connect with the San Diego Trolley and Amtrak. The $2.25 fare includes transfer to local transit buses and the trolley, and you should have exact fare (in coins or bills) handy. Information about the Metropolitan Transit System's shuttles and buses, the San Diego Trolley, and Coaster commuter train can all be found on the joint transit website ⊕ *www.transit.511sd.com.*

If you're heading to North County, the Flyer can drop you off at the Santa Fe Depot, where you can take the Coaster commuter train as far north as Oceanside for $4–$5.50.

Of the various airport shuttles, only Cloud 9 Shuttle/SuperShuttle has tie-downs for wheelchairs.

Ground shuttle service is available between LAX and San Diego, but can be prohibitively expensive, with rates for the two-hour trip starting at $200, so a car rental may be a more economical option. All of the shuttles listed at the end of this section offer the service.

Taxis departing from the airport are subject to regulated fares—all companies charge the same rate ($2.80 initial fee, $3 per mile). Taxi fare is about $16 plus tip to most downtown hotels. The fare to Coronado runs about $30 plus tip. Limousine rates vary and are charged per hour, per mile, or both, with some minimums established.

Contacts Cloud 9 Shuttle/SuperShuttle
✉ *123 Caminio de la Riena* ☎ *800/974–8885*
⊕ *www.cloud9shuttle.com.* **San Diego Transit**
☎ *619/233-3004* ⊕ *transit.511sd.com.*

▌ BOAT TRAVEL

Many hotels, marinas, and yacht clubs rent slips short term. Call ahead, because available space is limited. The San Diego and Southwestern yacht clubs have reciprocal arrangements with other yacht clubs.

The San Diego Bay Ferry takes you between downtown and Coronado in a nostalgic, old-school ferry every hour from 9 am to 10 pm. The ride lasts about 15 minutes and costs $4.25 each way; bicycles and Segways are free. The Water Taxi is a great alternative for nighttime transit along San Diego Bay. It is on call daily from 3 to 10 and costs $7 each way.

SEAL Amphibious tours combine the best of land and sea, departing from Seaport Village daily. After exploring picturesque San Diego neighborhoods, the bus-boat hybrid rolls right into the water for a cruise around the bay. It's all narrated with fun fact, too.

Ferry Contacts San Diego Bay Ferry
✉ *1050 N. Harbor Dr.* ☎ *800/442-7847*
⊕ *www.sdhe.com.* **SEAL Amphibious tours**
⊕ *www.sealtours.com.* **Water Taxi** ✉ *1050 N. Harbor Dr.* ☎ *619/235-8294* ⊕ *www.sdhe.com.*

Marinas Best Western Island Palms Hotel & Marina ✉ *2051 Shelter Island Dr.* ☎ *619/223-0301.* **The Dana on Mission Bay** ✉ *1710 W. Mission Bay Dr.* ☎ *619/225-2141* ⊕ *www.thedana2-px.rtrk.com.* **Kona Kai Resort** ✉ *1551 Shelter Island Dr.* ☎ *619/224-7547* ⊕ *www.resortkonakai.com.* **San Diego Marriott Hotel and Marina** ✉ *3333 W. Harbor Dr.* ☎ *619/230-8955* ⊕ *www.marriott.com.* **San Diego Yacht Club** ✉ *1011 Anchorage La.* ☎ *619/221-8400* ⊕ *www.sdyc.org.* **Southwestern Yacht Club** ✉ *702 Qualtrough St.* ☎ *619/222-0438* ⊕ *www.southwesternyc.org.*

CRUISE TRAVEL

Cruise lines that make regular calls at San Diego include Holland American, Royal Caribbean, Princess, and Celebrity. Ships heading to and from Alaska, Mexico, and the Panama Canal arrive and depart from the Cruise Terminal, which is located on the B Street Pier (1140 N. Harbor Drive). This is a busy spot, where you can get advice at the International Visitor Center and catch the Coronado Ferry or Water Taxi. San Diego Harbor Excursion bay cruises also dock here. The San Diego Maritime Museum and the Midway Museum are just steps away, and the terminal is a short taxi ride from Balboa Park, Little Italy, and the Gaslamp Quarter. Fares from the cruise-ship terminal are $18 to Balboa Park, $15 to SeaWorld, and $14 to the Gaslamp Quarter.

Cruise Lines Celebrity ☎ *800/647–2251* ⊕ *www.celebrity.com.* **Holland America** ☎ *800/426–0327* ⊕ *www.hollandamerica.com.* **Princess Cruises** ☎ *800/774-6237* ⊕ *www.princess.com.* **Royal Caribbean International** ☎ *800/338-4962* ⊕ *www.royalcaribbean.com.*

BUS AND TROLLEY TRAVEL

Under the umbrella of the Metropolitan Transit System, there are two major transit agencies in the area: San Diego Transit and North County Transit District (NCTD). Day passes, available for 1 to 30 days and starting at $5, give unlimited rides on nonpremium regional buses and the San Diego Trolley. You can buy them from most trolley vending machines, at the downtown Transit Store, and at Albertsons markets. A $14 Regional Plus Day Pass adds Coaster service and premium bus routes.

The bright-red trolleys of the San Diego Trolley light-rail system operate on three lines that serve downtown San Diego, Mission Valley, Old Town, South Bay, the U.S. border, and East County. The trolleys operate seven days a week from about 5 am to midnight, depending on the station, at intervals of about 15 minutes. The trolley system connects with San Diego Transit bus routes—connections are posted at each trolley station. Bicycle lockers are available at most stations and bikes are allowed on buses and trolleys though space is limited. Trolleys can get crowded during morning and evening rush hours. Schedules are posted at each stop; on-time performance is excellent.

NCTD bus routes connect with Coaster commuter train routes between Oceanside and the Santa Fe Depot in San Diego. They serve points from Del Mar North to San Clemente, inland to Fallbrook, Pauma Valley, Valley Center, Ramona, and Escondido, with transfer points within the city of San Diego. NCTD also offers special express-bus service to Qualcomm Stadium for select major sporting events. The Sprinter light rail provides service between Oceanside and Escondido, with buses connecting to popular North County attractions.

San Diego Transit bus fares range from $2.25 to $5; North County Transit District bus fares are $1.75. You must have exact change in coins and/or bills. Pay upon boarding. Transfers are not included; the $5 day pass is the best option for most bus travel and can be purchased on board.

San Diego Trolley tickets cost $2.50 and are good for two hours, but for one-way travel only. Round-trip tickets are double the one-way fare.

Tickets are dispensed from self-service machines at each stop; exact fare in coins is recommended, although some machines accept bills in $1, $5, $10, and $20 denominations and credit cards. For trips on multiple buses and trolleys, buy a day pass good for unlimited use all day.

Bus and Trolley Information
North County Transit District ☎ 800/266–6883 ⊕ www.gonctd.com. **San Diego Transit** ☎ 619/233–3004 or 800/234–5005 ⊕ transit.511sd.com. **Transit Store** ⊠ 102 Broadway ☎ 619/234–1060 ⊕ www.sdmts.com.

CAR TRAVEL

A car is necessary for getting around greater San Diego on the sprawling freeway system and for visiting the North County beaches, mountains, and Anza Borrego Desert. Driving around San Diego County is pretty simple: most major attractions are within a few miles of the Pacific Ocean. Interstate 5, which stretches from Canada to the Mexican border, bisects San Diego. Interstate 8 provides access from Yuma, Arizona, and points east. Drivers coming from the Los Angeles area, Nevada, and the mountain regions beyond can reach San Diego on I–15. During rush hour there are jams on I–5 and on I–15 between I–805 and Escondido.

There are border inspection stations along major highways in San Diego County. Travel with your driver's license, and passport if you're an international traveler, in case you're asked to pull into one.

Gas is widely available in San Diego County, except in rural areas. Outlets are generally open 24 hours and accept major credit cards that can be processed at the pump. Full service is not generally available, but you will usually find window-washing tools next to a pump; water and air are available somewhere on the property. All fuel in California is unleaded and sold at three price levels. Pricing is per gallon pumped and varies widely by season, location, and oil company provider. In San Diego gas tends to cost about 15% more than it does in many other California cities.

■**TIP**➜ Many Costco outlets sell gas to members at prices up to 20% less than the going rate.

PARKING

Meters downtown usually cost 50¢ to $1.25 an hour; enforcement is 8–6 every day but Sunday. ■**TIP**➜ If you are headed to Horton Plaza, the mall validates for three hours with no purchase required. Be extra careful around rush hour, when certain on-street parking areas become tow-away zones. Violations in congested areas can cost you $25 or more. In the evening and during events downtown, parking spaces are hard to find. Most downtown hotels offer valet parking service. The Convention Center has nearly 2,000 spaces that go for $11 to $21 for event parking. On game day at PETCO Park, expect to pay $17 or more for a parking space a short walk from the stadium, less for a space farther away. Other downtown lots cost $5–$35 per day.

Balboa Park and Mission Bay have huge free parking lots, and it's rare not to find a space, though it may seem as if you've parked miles from your destination. Old Town has large lots surrounding the transit center, but parking spaces are still hard to find. Parking is more of a problem in La Jolla and Coronado, where you generally need to rely on hard-to-find metered street spots or expensive by-the-hour parking lots.

ROAD CONDITIONS

Highways are generally in good condition in the San Diego area. From 6 to 8:30 am and 3:30 to 6 pm, traffic is particularly heavy on I–5, I–8, I–805, and I–15. Before venturing into the mountains, check on road conditions; mountain driving can be dangerous. Listen to radio traffic reports for information on the length of lines waiting to cross the border from Mexico. For roadside assistance, dial 511 from a mobile phone.

RENTAL CARS

In California you must be 21 to rent a car, and rates may be higher if you're under 25. Some agencies will not rent to those under 25; check when you book. Children up to age six or 60 pounds must be placed in safety or booster seats. For non–U.S. residents an international license is recommended but not required.

Rates fluctuate with seasons and demand, but generally begin at $39 a day and $250 a week for an economy car with air-conditioning, automatic transmission, and unlimited mileage. This doesn't include an 8.75% tax.

▌TAXI TRAVEL

Fares vary among companies. If you are heading to the airport from a hotel, ask about the flat rate, which varies according to destination; otherwise you'll be charged by the mile (which works out to $15 or so from any downtown location). Taxi stands are at shopping centers and hotels; otherwise you must call and reserve a cab. The companies listed below don't serve all areas of San Diego County. If you're going somewhere other than downtown, ask if the company serves that area.

Taxi Companies **Orange Cab** ☎ 619/291–3333 ⊕ www.orangecabsandiego.com. **Silver Cabs** ☎ 619/280-5555 ⊕ www.sandiegosilvercab.com. **Yellow Cab** ☎ 619/444-4444 ⊕ www.driveu.com.

▌ TRAIN TRAVEL

Amtrak serves downtown San Diego's Santa Fe Depot with daily trains to and from Los Angeles, Santa Barbara, and San Luis Obispo. Connecting service to Oakland, Seattle, Chicago, Texas, Florida, and points beyond is available in Los Angeles. Amtrak trains stop in San Diego North County at Solana Beach and Oceanside. You can obtain Amtrak timetables at any Amtrak station, or by visiting the Amtrak website.

Coaster commuter trains, which run between Oceanside and San Diego Monday–Saturday, stop at the same stations as Amtrak as well as others. The frequency is about every half hour during the weekday rush hour, with four trains on Saturday (with additional Friday and Saturday night service in spring and summer). One-way fares are $4 to $5.50, depending on the distance traveled. The Oceanside, Carlsbad, and Solana Beach stations have beach access. The Sprinter runs between Oceanside and Escondido, with many stops along the way.

Metrolink operates high-speed rail service between the Oceanside Transit Center and Union Station in Los Angeles.

Amtrak and the Coaster vending machines accept all major credit cards. Metrolink requires cash. Many Amtrak trains require advance reservations, especially for long-distance routes. Reservations, which you can make online, are suggested for trains running on weekends between San Diego and Santa Barbara. For security reasons, Amtrak requires ticket holders to provide photo ID.

Information Amtrak ☎ 800/872–7245 ⊕ www.amtrak.com. **Coaster** ☎ 760/966–6683 ⊕ transit.511sd.com. **Metrolink** ☎ 800/371–5465 ⊕ www.metrolinktrains.com.

ESSENTIALS

▌ CUSTOMS AND DUTIES

Customs officers operate at the San Ysidro border crossing, at San Diego International Airport, and in the bay at Shelter Island.

You're always allowed to bring goods of a certain value back home without having to pay any duty or import tax. But there's a limit on the amount of tobacco and liquor you can bring back duty-free. If the total value of your goods is more than the duty-free limit, you'll have to pay a tax (most often a flat percentage) on the value of everything beyond that limit.

U.S. Information U.S. Customs and Border Protection ⊕ *www.cbp.gov.*

▌ MONEY

With the mild climate and proximity to the ocean and mountains, San Diego is popular with tourists and conventioneers and, accordingly, is a relatively expensive place to visit. Three-star rooms average between $200 and $280 per night in high season, but there is also a good variety of modest accommodations available. Meal prices compare to those in other large cities, and you can usually find excellent values by dining in smaller, family-run establishments. Admission to local attractions can cost anywhere from $10 to $70. Thankfully, relaxing on one of the public beaches or meandering through the parks and neighborhoods is free—and fun. ▌TIP→ To save money on restaurants, spas, and boutiques, scour the coupon section at ⊕ *www.sdreader.com.*

ITEM	AVERAGE COST
Cup of Coffee	$2
Glass of Wine	$9
Sandwich	$8
One-Mile Taxi Ride	$2.70
Museum Admission	$12

Prices throughout this guide are given for adults. Substantially reduced fees are almost always available for children, students, and senior citizens. Many museums offer free admission one day of the month.

▌ PACKING

San Diego's casual lifestyle and year-round mild climate set the parameters for what to pack. You can leave formal clothes and cold-weather gear behind.

Plan on warm weather at any time of the year. Cottons, walking shorts, jeans, and T-shirts are the norm. Pack bathing suits and shorts regardless of the season. Few restaurants require a jacket and tie for men. Women may want to also bring something a little dressier than their sightseeing garb.

Evenings are cool, even in summer, so be sure to bring a sweater or a light jacket. Rainfall in San Diego isn't usually heavy; you won't need a raincoat except in winter, and even then, an umbrella may suffice.

Be sure you have comfortable walking shoes. Even if you don't walk much at home, you will probably find yourself covering miles while sightseeing on your vacation. Also bring a pair of sandals or water shoes for the beach.

Sunglasses and sunscreen are a must in San Diego. Binoculars can also come in handy, especially if you're in town during whale-watching season, from December through March.

▌ RESTROOMS

Major attractions and parks have public restrooms. In the downtown San Diego area, you can usually use the restrooms at major hotels and fast-food restaurants. The Bathroom Diaries is a website that's flush with unsanitized information on restrooms the world over—each one located, reviewed, and rated.

Find a Loo The Bathroom Diaries ⊕ *www.thebathroomdiaries.com.*

SAFETY

San Diego is generally a safe place for travelers who observe all normal precautions. Dress inconspicuously (this means removing badges when leaving convention areas) and know the routes to your destination before you set out. At the beach, check with lifeguards about any unsafe conditions such as dangerous riptides or water pollution. The San Diego Tourism Authority offers a print and web version of Visitor Safety Tips, providing sensible precautions for many situations, *see Visitor Information.*

TIPPING

TIPPING GUIDELINES FOR SAN DIEGO	
Bartender	$1 to $5 per round of drinks, depending on the number of drinks
Bellhop	$1 to $5 per bag, depending on the level of the hotel
Hotel Concierge	$5 or more, if he or she performs a service for you
Hotel Doorman	$1–$2 if he helps you get a cab
Hotel Maid	$1 to $3 a day (either daily or at the end of your stay, in cash)
Hotel Room-Service Waiter	$1–$2 per delivery, even if a service charge has been added
Porter at Airport or Train Station	$1 per bag
Skycap at Airport	$1 to $3 per bag checked
Taxi Driver	15%–20%, but round up the fare to the next dollar amount
Tour Guide	10% of the cost of the tour
Valet Parking Attendant	$1–$2, but only when you get your car
Waiter	15%–20%, with 20% being the norm at high-end restaurants; nothing additional if a service charge is added to the bill

TOURS

BIKE TOURS

Biking is very popular in San Diego. You can find trails along the beach, in Mission Bay, and throughout the mountains. Pedal your way around San Diego with the Bike Revolution. Secret San Diego, by Where You Want To Be Tours, offers walking tours as well as tours on bike and Segway.

Contacts Bike Revolution ☎ 619/564–4843 ⊕ www.thebikerevolution.com. **Secret San Diego** ✉ 611 K St., #B224 ☎ 619/917–6037 ⊕ www.wheretours.com.

BOAT TOURS

Flagship Cruises and Events and Hornblower Cruises & Events both operate one- and two-hour harbor cruises departing from the Broadway Pier. No reservations are necessary for the tours, which cost $20–$25; both companies also do dinner cruises ($55–$70) and brunch cruises. These companies also operate during whale-watching season, from December to March. Other fishing boats that do whale watches in season include H&M Landing and Seaforth Boat Rentals.

Contacts Flagship Cruises and Events ☎ 855/955–9558 ⊕ www.flagshipsd.com. **H&M Landing** ✉ 2803 Emerson St. ☎ 619/222–1144 ⊕ www.hmlanding.com. **Hornblower Cruises & Events** ✉ 1066. N. Harbor Dr. ☎ 619/234–8687 or 800/668–4322 ⊕ www.hornblower.com. **San Diego Seal Tours** ⊕ www.sealtours.com. **Seaforth Boat Rentals** ☎ 888/834–2628 ⊕ www.seaforthboatrental.com.

BUS AND TROLLEY TOURS

Old Town Trolley Tours takes you to 11 sites, including Old Town, Seaport Village, Horton Plaza and the Gaslamp Quarter, Coronado, Little Italy, and El Prado in Balboa Park. The tour is narrated, and for the price of the ticket ($36 for adults, $18 for children 4–12; under 4, free) you can get on and off as you please at any stop. The trolley leaves every 30 minutes, operates daily, and takes two hours to make a full loop.

DayTripper, San Diego Scenic Tours, and Five Star Tours do one-day or multiple-day bus tours of attractions in Southern California.

Contacts DayTripper ☎ 619/299–5777 or 800/679–8747 ⊕ www.daytripper.com. **Five Star Tours** ✉ 1050 Kettner Blvd. ☎ 619/232–5040 ⊕ www.fivestartours.com. **Old Town Trolley Tours** ✉ 2115 Kurtz St. ☎ 619/298–8687 ⊕ www.trolleytours.com/san-diego. **San Diego Scenic Tours** ✉ 2255 Garnet Ave., #3 ☎ 858/273–8687 ⊕ www.sandiegoscenictours.com.

GO CAR TOURS

These miniature talking cars offer the benefits of a guided tour, but taken at your own pace. Tour the city in a bright yellow three-seater, equipped with GPS navigation and accompanying narration. Go Cars Tours offers two routes: choose from Downtown, Balboa Park, Uptown, and Old Town or Point Loma, Cabrillo National Monument, and Ocean Beach. The tours can be driven straight through, or visitors can park and explore any of the sights en-route. Rentals are $49 for the first hour, $39 for the second hour, and $29 for the third through fifth hours. There is a maximum daily charge of five hours if you want to keep the car for the entire day.

Contacts Go Car Tours ✉ 2100 Kettner Blvd. ☎ 800/914–6227 ⊕ www.gocartours.com.

WALKING TOURS

Several fine walking tours are available on weekdays or weekends; upcoming walks are usually listed in the *San Diego Reader*.

Coronado Walking Tours offers an easy 90-minute stroll ($12; Tuesday, Thursday, Saturday at 11 am) through Coronado's historic district, with departures from the Glorietta Bay Inn. Make reservations.

On Saturday at 10 am and 11:30 am, Offshoot Tours conducts free, hour-long walks starting at the Visitor Center through Balboa Park that focus on history, palm trees, and desert vegetation.

Urban Safaris, led by longtime San Diego resident Patty Fares, are two-hour-long

Saturday walks ($10) through interesting neighborhoods such as Hillcrest, Ocean Beach, and Point Loma. The tours, which always depart from a neighborhood coffeehouse, focus on art, history, and ethnic eateries. Reservations are required.

The Gaslamp Quarter Historical Foundation leads two-hour historical walking tours of the downtown historic district from the William Heath Davis House on Saturday at 11 am ($15).

Contacts Coronado Walking Tours ✉ 1630 Glorietta Blvd. ☎ 619/435–5993 ⊕ coronadowalkingtour.com. **Gaslamp Quarter Historical Foundation** ✉ 410 Island Ave. ☎ 619/233–4692 ⊕ www.gaslampquarter.org. **Offshoot Tours** ☎ 619/239–0512 ⊕ www.balboapark.org. **Urban Safaris** ☎ 619/944–9255 ⊕ www.walkingtoursofsandiego.com.

▮ VISITOR INFORMATION

For general information and brochures before you go, contact the San Diego Tourism Authority, which publishes the helpful *San Diego Visitors Planning Guide*. When you arrive, stop by one of the local visitor centers for general information.

Citywide Contacts San Diego Tourism Authority ☎ 619/232–3101 ⊕ www.sandiego.org. **San Diego Tourism Authority International Visitor Information Center** ✉ 1140 N. Harbor Dr., Downtown ☎ 619/243–1308 ⊕ www.sandiego.org.

San Diego County Contacts Borrego Springs Chamber of Commerce and Visitor Center ☎ 760/767–5555 ⊕ www.borregospringschamber.org. **The California Welcome Center Alpine** ☎ 619/445–0180 ⊕ www.visitcwc.com.

California Welcome Center Oceanside ⊠ 928 N. Coast Hwy., Oceanside ☎ 760/721–1101, 800/350-7873 ⊕ www.visitcwc.com/oceanside. **Carlsbad Convention & Visitors Bureau** ⊠ 400 Carlsbad Village Dr., Carlsbad ☎ 800/227-5722 ⊕ www.visitcarlsbad.com. **Coronado Visitor Center** ⊠ 1100 Orange Ave., Coronado ☎ 619/437-8788 ⊕ www.coronadovisitorcenter.com. **Encinitas Chamber of Commerce** ⊠ 527 Encinitas Blvd., Suite 106, Encinitas ☎ 760/753-6041 ⊕ www.encinitaschamber.com. **Julian Chamber of Commerce** ☎ 760/765-1857 ⊕ www.julianca.com. **La Jolla Information Center** ☎ 858/454-5718 ⊕ www.lajollabythesea.com.

Statewide Contacts California Travel and Tourism Commission ☎ 916/444-4429 or 877/225-4367 ⊕ www.visitcalifornia.com.

INSPIRATION

Check out these books for further San Diego reading. The novel *Drift* by Jim Miller explores San Diego's boom time through the eyes of a college professor in the year 2000. *Leave Only Paw Prints: Dog Hikes in San Diego* offers myriad walking spots that are dog-friendly, along with smart travel tips for your furry friend. *San Diego Legends: Events, People and Places That Made History* goes beyond the typical history-book material to reveal little-known stories about San Diego.

San Diego has a rich film history, thanks to the city's unique geography and proximity to Los Angeles. Some of the better-known films made here include *Top Gun*, *Traffic*, and *Almost Famous*. The bar scene in *Top Gun* was filmed at a local restaurant, Kansas City BBQ, on the corner of Kettner Boulevard and West Harbor Drive. And of course, don't forget to take *Anchorman* Ron Burgundy's advice, and "Stay classy, San Diego."

ONLINE RESOURCES

For a dining and entertainment guide to San Diego's most popular nightlife district, check out Gaslamp.org. Visit the HillQuest guide to Hillcrest, a historic neighborhood with a large number of gay and lesbian households. For insider tips from a local perspective, try Local Wally's San Diego Tourist Guide. For information on the birthplace of California, search the Old Town San Diego organization's site. Browse the website of San Diego's premier upscale lifestyle magazine, *Ranch and Coast*. *San Diego Magazine* also has a useful site. Search the site of Arts Tix for half-price show tickets. For a comprehensive listing of concerts, performances, and art exhibits, check out the local alternative paper *San Diego Reader*. For edgier arts and culture listings, pick up the *San Diego Citybeat* alt-weekly.

Websites Gaslamp Info ⊕ www.gaslamp.org. **Hillcrest** ⊕ www.hillquest.com. **Local Wally** ⊕ www.localwally.com. **Old Town San Diego** ⊕ www.oldtownsandiego.org. **Ranch and Coast Magazine** ⊕ www.ranchandcoast.com. **San Diego Citybeat Newspaper** ⊕ www.sdcitybeat.com. **San Diego Magazine** ⊕ www.sandiegomagazine.com. **Half Price Tickets** ⊕ sdartstix.com. **San Diego Reader Newspaper** ⊕ www.sdreader.com. **San Diego Union-Tribune** ⊕ www.signonsandiego.com.

INDEX

PHOTO CREDITS

1, Irene Chan/Alamy 3, Matthew Field/wikipedia.org. Chapter 1: Experience San Diego: 6-7, Brett Shoaf/Artistic Visuals. 8, Brett Shoaf/Artistic Visuals. 9 (left), San Diego CVB/Joanne DiBona. 9 (right), San Diego CVB. 10, Corbis. 11 (left), Doug Scott/age fotostock. 11 (right), Werner Bollmann/age fotostock. 12, Jeff Greenberg/age fotostock. 13 (left), Xiao Li/Shutterstock. 13 (right), John W. Warden/age fotostock. 16 (left), mlgb, Fodors.com member. 16 (top center), SuperStock/age fotostock. 16 (top and bottom right), San Diego CVB/Joanne DiBona. 17 (left and top center), San Diego CVB. 17 (bottom center), Epukas/wikipedia.org. 17 (right), SeaWorld San Diego. 18, Corbis. 19 (left), Paul M. Bowers. 19 (right), San Diego CVB. 20, Joelle Gould/iStockphoto. 21 (left), San Diego CVB. 21 (right) and 23, Corbis. 24, Steve Rabin/iStockphoto. 26, zoonabar/Flickr. 28, San Diego CVB. Chapter 2: Downtown: 29, Johnny Stockshooter/age fotostock. 31, Lowe Llaguna/Shutterstock. 32, Steve Snodgrass/Flickr. 34, Brett Shoaf/Artistic Visuals. 36, Robert Holmes. 39, Brett Shoaf/Artistic Visuals. Chapter 3: Balboa Park and San Diego Zoo: 41 and 43, Brett Shoaf/Artistic Visuals. 44 and 49, Brett Shoaf/Artistic Visuals. 53, Ambient Images/Alamy. 55 (top), Dreyer Peter/age fotostock. 55 (bottom), Epukas/wikipedia.org. 56, Robert Holmes. 57, Steve Snodgrass/Flickr. 58 (left and top center), fPat/Flickr. 58 (bottom center), Matthew Field/wikipedia.org. 58 (top right), Jim Epler/Flickr. 58 (bottom right), Philippe Renault/age fotostock. 59, lora_313/Flickr. 60 (left), Cburnett/wikipedia.org. 60 (right), Susann Parker/age fotostock. 61 (top), George Ostertag/age fotostock. 61 (bottom), Sally Brown/age fotostock. 62, John Elk III/Alamy. Chapter 4: Old Town and Uptown: 65, Brett Shoaf/Artistic Visuals. 67, dichohecho/Flickr. 68-77, Brett Shoaf/Artistic Visuals. Chapter 5: Mission Bay, Beaches, and SeaWorld: 79, Brett Shoaf/Artistic Visuals. 81, SD Dirk/Flickr. 82 and 83 (top), SeaWorld San Diego. 83 (bottom), Robert Holmes. 84, San Diego CVB. 87, Brett Shoaf/Artistic Visuals. Chapter 6: La Jolla: 89, Brett Shoaf/Artistic Visuals. 91, Roger Isaacson. 92, Jason Pratt/Flickr. 93, Philipp Scholz Rittermann. 94, Brett Shoaf/Artistic Visuals. Chapter 7: Point Loma and Coronado: 97 and 99, Brett Shoaf/Artistic Visuals. 100, San Diego CVB. 101 (top), jamesbenet/iStockphoto. 101 (bottom), Cass Greene/iStockphoto. 102, rkkwan, Fodors.com member. 104-05, Brett Shoaf/Artistic Visuals. Chapter 8: Where to Eat: 109, Lorena Whiteside. 110, Amy K. Fellows. 117, Brett Shoaf/Artistic Visuals. 125, Lorena Whiteside. 135, Tower 23 Hotel and JRDN. Chapter 9: Where to Stay: 161, Brett Shoaf/Artistic Visuals. 162, Hotel del Coronado. 167 (top), Hard Rock Hotel San Diego. 167 (bottom left), robjtak/Flickr. 167 (bottom right), Westgate Hotel. 170, Graham Blair. 174 (top), Courtyard San Diego Mission Valley/Hotel Circle. 174 (bottom left), Red Square, Inc. 174 (bottom right), Britt Scripps Inn. 177 (top), Lodge at Torrey Pines. 177 (bottom), Grande Colonial Hotel. 180 (top), San Diego CVB. 180 (bottom), Sue Gillingham. Chapter 10: Nightlife: 183, Tower 23 Hotel and JRDN. 184, Andaz San Diego. 188, Sandy Huffaker. 192, Brett Shoaf/Artistic Visuals. 199, Chris Woo. 203, Tower 23 Hotel and JRDN. Chapter 11: The Arts: 205, AlanHaynes.com/Alamy. 206, Lynn Susholtz. 209, Brett Shoaf/Artistic Visuals. 211, San Diego CVB. 213, J.T. MacMillan/Lamb's Players Theatre. Chapter 12: Beaches: 215 and 216, Brett Shoaf/Artistic Visuals. 217 (top), San Diego CVB. 217 (bottom), Dija/Shutterstock. 218, alysta/Shutterstock. 219 (top), Lowe Llaguno/Shutterstock. 219 (bottom), San Diego CVB. 220, Sebastien Burel/Shutterstock. 225 and 231, Brett Shoaf/Artistic Visuals. Chapter 13: Sports and the Outdoors: 233, Brett Shoaf/Artistic Visuals. 234, Sebastien Burel/Shutterstock. 235 (top), Janet Fullwood. 235 (bottom), Sebastien Burel/iStockphoto. 236, Stas Volik/Shutterstock. 239, Brett Shoaf/Artistic Visuals. 242, Sebastien Burel/Shutterstock. 246-47 and 251, Brett Shoaf/Artistic Visuals. 254, SD Dirk/Flickr. Chapter 14: Shopping: 257, Brett Shoaf/Artistic Visuals. 258, Paul M. Bowers. 259, Brett Shoaf/Artistic Visuals. 260, Old Town Trolleys of San Diego. 261, Lowe Llaguno/Shutterstock. 262, Paul M. Bowers. 269 and 272, Brett Shoaf/Artistic Visuals. 276, San Diego CVB/Joanne DiBona. 279, Richard Wong/ www.rwongphoto.com/Alamy. Chapter 15: North County and Environs: 281, Brett Shoaf/Artistic Visuals. 283 (top left), San Diego CVB. 283 (top right), Ken Bohn, San Diego Zoo. 283 (bottom), Alan Vernon/Flickr. 284, LEGOLAND California Resort. 285 (top), San Diego CVB/Joanne DiBona. 285 (bottom), San Diego CVB. 286, Robert Holmes. 287 (top and bottom), Ken Bohn, San Diego Zoo. 288, Brett Shoaf/Artistic Visuals. 289 (top), Rancho Valencia. 289 (bottom), La Costa Resort and Spa. 290, San Diego CVB. 295, Brett Shoaf/Artistic Visuals. 305, San Diego CVB/Joanne DiBona. 313, San Diego CVB. 323, Brett Shoaf/Artistic Visuals. 335, Brett Shoaf/Artistic Visuals.

NOTES

NOTES

NOTES

ABOUT OUR WRITERS

Seth Combs has spent some quality time obsessing over San Diego arts and nightlife. He's the former Arts & Culture editor at the alt-weekly *San Diego CityBeat* and was also an Associate Editor at *Riviera Magazine*. Now a freelance writer and editor, he contributes to publications including *Spin* and *The Hollywood Reporter*.

A veteran traveler, **Claire Deeks van der Lee** feels lucky to call San Diego home. An East Coast transplant, she never takes the near-perfect weather for granted. Claire loves playing tourist in her own city, exploring San Diego's cultural attractions as well as its myriad neighborhoods and Balboa Park—so it was a perfect fit for her to work on the neighborhood chapters of this book. She also updated the Sports chapter and the Experience chapter for this edition. Claire has traveled to more than 40 countries, and has contributed to *Everywhere* magazine. When not traveling, writing about travel, or planning future travel, she can often be found exploring Balboa Park or at the beach with her dog.

When **Maren Dougherty** moved to San Diego in 2005, she thought she'd stay for one year—maybe two. To her East Coast family's dismay, she fell in love with the year-round beach scene, perfectly mixed margaritas, and rooftop pool bars. Maren's freelance work has appeared in *San Diego Magazine* and *Alaska Airlines* magazine. She updated the Where to Eat and Where to Stay chapters for this edition of Fodor's San Diego.

Amanda Knoles has been a contributing writer for four editions of *Fodor's San Diego*. In this edition she shares her knowledge of the city's shopping venues and beaches. Amanda has been a travel writer for more than 15 years and lists San Diego as her favorite weekend getaway.

Longtime Southern Californian **Bobbi Zane** lives in the mountain hamlet of Julian, making her the perfect person to write for our North County chapter. Bobbi's byline has appeared in the *Los Angeles Times*, the *Los Angeles Daily News*, *Westways* magazine, and the *Orange County Register*. She has written about the Palm Springs area for Fodor's for more than 20 years and is a contributor to the Fodor's *National Parks of the West* guidebook.